The Microstructure Approach to Exchange Rates

The Microstructure Approach to Exchange Rates

Richard K. Lyons

The MIT Press
Cambridge, Massachusetts
London, England

This book was set in Palatino in 3B2 by Asco Typesetters, Hong Kong, and was printed and bound in the United States of America.

Library of Congress Cataloging-in-Publication Data

Lyons, Richard K.
    The microstructure approach to exchange rates / Richard K. Lyons.
        p.   cm.
    Includes bibliographical references and index.
    ISBN 0-262-12243-X (hc.)
    1. Foreign exchange rates—Mathematical models. I. Title.
HG3823 .L96   2001
332.4'5'015118—dc21   2001044337

I dedicate this book to my wonderful wife, Jen.

Contents

Preface

This book addresses a growing interaction between two fields—exchange rate economics and microstructure finance. Historically, these fields have progressed independently. More recently, however, they have begun to interact, and that interaction has stimulated new perspective within both. In exchange rate economics, that new perspective has given rise to a distinct approach—a microstructure approach.

A natural audience for this book includes people with expertise in only one of these two fields who are interested in learning more about the other. In the past this has not been easy—these areas have different intellectual traditions, so bridging them required a large investment of time. This book should facilitate that investment. To that end, I have tried to present material on both fields in an accessible way, so that readers lacking specialization in either one should find the material within reach. Practitioners, too, should find most of the material accessible (the empirical work in chapters 7 through 9 is most relevant to that audience).

A notable feature of this book is its treatment of both theoretical and empirical work (c.f. O'Hara's 1995 theory text). Indeed, the book is organized to highlight their interplay. Chapter 4 is dedicated to the canonical frameworks in microstructure theory. Some of these frameworks were originally developed to address the New York Stock Exchange, a market with a single dealer in each stock. The circumstances under which these frameworks are appropriate for foreign exchange markets (FX) is an important topic addressed in that chapter. Chapter 5 summarizes empirical microstructure frameworks, with emphasis on those employed in FX. These empirical frameworks draw heavily on chapter four's theory. The last four chapters, chapters 7–10, are applications of tools presented in the first six. They bring the theoretical/empirical interplay into sharp focus.

A second notable feature of this book is its emphasis on information economics rather than institutions. People unfamiliar with microstructure finance typically believe its focus is institutional (e.g., the consequences of different trading mechanisms). This is an important part of the field. But in terms of this book, it is not the most important part. The focus of this book is the economics of financial information and how microstructure tools clarify the types of information relevant to exchange rates. In keeping with this focus, I move immediately in chapter 2 to the economics of financial information, saving detailed institutional material on FX trading until chapter 3.

This book also has some notable features in terms of pedagogy. They are concentrated in chapters 4–6, the three survey chapters: microstructure theory, microstructure empirical frameworks, and exchange rate theory, respectively. In chapter 4, I begin the survey of microstructure models with the "rational expectations" model. The chapter proceeds from that model's implicit auctioneer to the explicit auctioneer of the Kyle model. Conceptually, I consider this a more natural progression than the typical sequencing in microstructure books. To maintain focus on essentials, chapter 4 also presents the microstructure models in a common format. I close chapter 4 with an appendix that collects several important technical tools for easy reference. On the empirical side, chapter 5 opens with a survey of available data sets and information on accessing them via the Internet (several are available from my web site: ⟨www.haas.berkeley. edu/~lyons⟩). Data quality has increased substantially in recent years (in large part due to the shift to electronic trading), and this survey provides an easy reference for familiarizing oneself. Chapter 6 is the transition from the earlier, more micro-oriented chapters, to the later, more macro-oriented chapters. That chapter begins its survey of exchange rate theory with a treatment of "valuation," which includes traditional definitions of exchange rate "fundamentals." This should help readers whose perspective on valuation comes primarily from the dividend-discount models used in equity markets. Chapter 6 also highlights the parallels between exchange rate models and microstructure models (such as the conceptual link between portfolio balance models and inventory models).

This book also contains new work. For example, some of the material in chapters 7 and 8 is new to the literature, and most of the material in chapter 9 is new. Many of the arguments and points made throughout other chapters are new as well (e.g., perspectives on the microstructure approach's potential applications). Much of the material in chapters 7 to 9 comes from work I have done jointly with three co-authors: Martin Evans, Mintao Fan, and Michael Moore.

For teaching, there are three types of courses for which this book would be appropriate. The first is a Ph.D. course in international macroeconomics. Of the ten chapters, the best ones for this type of course are chapters 1, 4, 6, 7, 8, and 9. A second course for which the book would be appropriate is a Ph.D. course in market microstructure. The best chapters for this type of course are 1, 2, 3, 4, 5, and 10. A third course for which the book would be appropriate is a Master's course in international finance. The best chapters for a course at this level include 1, 3, 6, 7, and 9.

Some caveats are in order. Like microstructure theory in general, my treatment of the microstructure approach emphasizes the role of order flow (signed transaction quantities) in price determination. This emphasis aligns closely with my own interests and my own work. Though much of the material I present is not my own, my work plays a more prominent role than it would in a balanced survey. To borrow the words of one reviewer, this book is more of a personal synthesis than a professional consensus. I apologize in advance to those whose work is underrepresented. (For those interested in a survey, let me recommend Sarno and Taylor 2000a.)

A second caveat is my use of the term "microstructure approach." Though there is no consensus definition of what constitutes a microstructure model, it is safe to say that the definition I adopt is rather broad. For me, the microstructure approach is not just a rich set of tools for addressing the issues, but also a way of framing those issues. Indeed, the framing *per se* is an important aspect of the approach's value. If I have done my job, the chapters that follow should make this point increasingly clear.

To these previous caveats I must add another. The tone of parts of this book may to some readers seem a bit missionary. This is particularly true of chapter 1, where I address the book's overarching themes. (Exchange rate economists will find these themes more provocative than will people in microstructure finance.) At the risk of appearing to over-sell, I felt it best to address these themes early. Most of the evidence that supports these themes appears in later chapters.

I owe thanks to many people. The support and encouragement of Victoria Richardson and Elizabeth Murry at MIT Press are much appreciated. I also want to thank several of my colleagues who, as anonymous reviewers of early drafts, provided valuable comments. I am indebted to them. I am also indebted to Alain Chaboud, Mike Dennis, Petra Geraats, Philipp Hartmann, Harold Hau, Jen Lyons, Michael Melvin, Michael Moore, Carol Osler, Richard Portes, Hélène Rey, Dagfinn Rime, Andrew Rose, Patrik Safvenblad, Sergio Schmukler, Mark Taranto, and Paolo Vitale for extensive comments and suggestions. A friend and colleague, Michael Klein, planted the seed for this book and also provided many insights along the way. I thank the University of Toulouse and Stockholm University for providing generous visiting opportunities while I was writing. Financial support from the National Science Foundation is gratefully acknowledged; this book (and much of the research underlying it) is in large part the product of their investment. Finally, I'd like to thank Jim McCarthy, a long-time buddy and FX trader who introduced me to the world of FX trading.

1   Overview of the Microstructure Approach

Ten years ago, a friend of mine who trades spot foreign exchange for a large bank invited me to spend a few days at his side. At the time, I considered myself an expert, having written my thesis on exchange rates. I thought I had a handle on how it worked. I thought wrong. As I sat there, my friend traded furiously, all day long, racking up over $1 billion in trades each day (USD). This was a world where the standard trade was $10 million, and a $1 million trade was a "skinny one." Despite my belief that exchange rates depend on macroeconomics, only rarely was news of this type his primary concern. Most of the time my friend was reading tea leaves that were, at least to me, not so clear. The pace was furious—a quote every five or ten seconds, a trade every minute or two, and continual decisions about what position to hold. Needless to say, there was little time for chat. It was clear my understanding was incomplete when he looked over in the midst of his fury and asked me, "What should I do?" I laughed. Nervously.

This book is an outgrowth of my subsequent interest in this area. It is principally concerned with the gap between what I knew before I sat down with my friend and what I saw when I got there. In effect, this gap is the space between two fields of scholarship: exchange rate economics on the one hand, and microstructure finance on the other. Exchange rate economists use models of exchange rate determination that are macroeconomic (i.e., rates are determined as a function of macro variables such as inflation, output, interest rates, etc.). These same exchange rate economists are largely unfamiliar with microstructure models. Most microstructure scholars, in contrast, view foreign exchange as the purview of international economists, and are unfamiliar with macroeconomic exchange rate models. Their traditional focus is the microeconomics of equity markets, particularly the New York Stock Exchange.

Though this book has several objectives, two deserve mention at the outset. The first is to lower entry barriers faced by scholars interested in this burgeoning area. Lowering barriers on both sides— exchange rate economics and microstructure finance—will help this research domain realize its potential. A second objective is to channel past work into a more unified approach—a microstructure approach. In the 1990s, many authors applied microstructure tools to foreign exchange (FX) markets, but existing work is still largely fragmented.

Does exchange rate economics need a new approach? Yes. It is in crisis. It is in crisis in the sense that current macroeconomic approaches to exchange rates are empirical failures. In their recent survey in the *Handbook of International Economics*, Jeffrey Frankel and Andrew Rose (1995, 1709) put it this way: "To repeat a central fact of life, there is remarkably little evidence that macroeconomic variables have consistent strong effects on floating exchange rates, except during extraordinary circumstances such as hyperinflations. Such negative findings have led the profession to a certain degree of pessimism vis-à-vis exchange rate research."

In the end, it is my hope that this book might rouse a little optimism.

1.1   Three Approaches to FX: Goods, Assets, and Microstructure

Before the 1970s, the dominant approach to exchange rate determination was the goods market approach. According to this approach, demand for currencies comes primarily from purchases and sales of goods. For example, an increase in exports increases foreign demand for domestic currency to pay for those exported goods. In this simple form, the implication is rather intuitive: countries with trade surpluses experience appreciation (which comes from the currency demand created by the surplus). Despite the approach's intuitive appeal, however, it fails miserably when one looks at the data: trade balances are virtually uncorrelated with exchange rate movements in major-currency FX markets. This negative result is perhaps not surprising given that trade in goods and services accounts for only a small fraction of currency trading—less than 5 percent of the average $1.5 trillion of FX traded daily.

In the 1970s, the asset market approach emerged. It built on the earlier approach by recognizing that currency demand comes not only from purchases and sales of goods, but also from purchases and sales of assets. For example, in order to purchase a Japanese government bond, a U.S. investor first purchases the necessary yen. In addition, the investor's dollar return will depend on movements in the yen, so his demand for the bond depends in part on his desire to speculate on those currency movements. This shift in perspective brought a shift in modeling strategy. Models began to conform to the notion of speculative "efficiency": exchange rates were modeled as efficient in that they incorporate all publicly available information, making public information useless for producing excess returns. This is a feature the goods market approach did not share.[1]

Disconcertingly, empirical work does not support the asset market approach either. The macroeconomic variables that underlie the approach do not move exchange rates as predicted. The classic reference is Meese and Rogoff 1983a; they show that asset approach models fail to explain major-currency exchange rates better than a simple "no change" model. Thus, asset approach models are not even consistently getting the direction right. In his later survey, Meese (1990) summarizes by writing that "the proportion of (monthly or quarterly) exchange rate changes that current models can explain is essentially zero." (The literature documenting this poor empirical performance is vast; for surveys see Frankel and Rose 1995; Isard 1995; and Taylor 1995.)

The FX market's enormous trading volume is also problematic for the asset approach. Explaining volume is difficult because actual transactions are awarded no role in mapping macroeconomic variables into exchange rate behavior. Rather, because all macroeconomic news is publicly available, when news occurs, the exchange rate is presumed to jump to the new consensus level; the change in expectations that causes the jump does not require any trading. Differing beliefs is not a driver of trading under this approach either, because the approach assumes homogeneous beliefs.

These negative observations do not imply that the asset market approach is "wrong"; indeed, most agree that it is, in broad terms, appropriate. Rather, it appears the approach is missing some key features—features that matter for how exchange rates are actually determined.

This book presents a new approach to exchange rates, the microstructure approach. Under this approach, like the asset market approach, the demand for currencies comes from purchases and sales of assets. In this sense these approaches are complementary, not competing. What distinguishes the microstructure approach is that it relaxes three of the asset approach's most uncomfortable assumptions:[2]

1. Information: microstructure models recognize that some information relevant to exchange rates is not publicly available.

2. Players: microstructure models recognize that market participants differ in ways that affect prices.

3. Institutions: microstructure models recognize that trading mechanisms differ in ways that affect prices.

People unfamiliar with microstructure believe its focus is on the third of these—the consequences of different trading mechanisms. *The focus of this book is resolutely on the first—the information economics.* (In keeping with this focus, the next chapter moves immediately to the economics of financial information; material on trader heterogeneity and trading mechanisms—points 2 and 3—is in chapter 3.)[3] Empirically, it is simply not true that all information used to determine market-clearing exchange rates is publicly available. We can analyze the consequences of this—theoretically and empirically—using tools within the microstructure approach. The resulting analysis shows that the public-information assumption is not a good one: it misses much of exchange rate determination.

Consider some examples that suggest that the microstructure approach is on target with respect to these three assumptions. Regarding non-public information, FX traders at banks regularly see trades that are not publicly observable. As I show in later chapters, this information forecasts subsequent exchange rates (e.g., seeing the demands of private participants or central banks before the rest of the market). Regarding differences across market participants, traders with common information regularly interpret it differently. Another example of differences across participants is motives for trade: some traders are primarily hedgers, whereas others are primarily speculators (and even among the latter, speculative horizons can differ dramatically). Regarding trading mechanisms that affect prices, consider a market where transparency is low (e.g., where individual transaction sizes and prices are not generally observable). Low transparency can slow the updating of beliefs about appropriate prices, thereby altering the path of realized prices.

From these examples one might describe the microstructure approach as taking an in-the-trenches, trading-room perspective. Given that exchange rates are actually determined in the trading room, this would seem a reasonable starting point. But can relaxing the three assumptions above help us understand exchange rates? Relaxing the corresponding assumptions for other asset classes has certainly deepened our understanding of these other markets. The final judgment, though, will be based on specific applications of microstructure tools. The latter half of this book presents a number of applications.

In advance of those applications, I urge the reader to bear in mind the overarching fact that traditional approaches are not consistent with the data. Indeed, this fact induces Flood and Taylor (1996, 286) to conclude that

Given the exhaustive interrogation of the macro fundamentals in this respect over the last twenty years, it would seem that our understanding of the short-run behavior of exchange rates is unlikely to be further enhanced by further examination of the macro fundamentals. And it is in this context that new work on the microstructure of the foreign exchange market seems both warranted and promising.

1.2 Hallmarks of the Microstructure Approach

The previous section introduces microstructure in the context of exchange rates but does not define the term as used in domestic finance. Maureen O'Hara (1995, 1) defines market microstructure as "the process and outcomes of exchanging assets under explicit trading rules." The definition I adopt here is consistent with hers. Because her definition is so broad, though, it may be helpful to clarify further.

When one moves from a macro approach to a micro approach, two variables that play no role in the macro approach take center stage. These variables are hallmarks of the micro approach, and as hallmarks, they help to define microstructure. These variables are

1. order flow, and
2. spreads (bid-ask).

If I labeled these "quantity" and "price," it would be clear that they are the old mainsprings of economics after all. These labels are a bit facile, though. Describing them as quantity and price viewed through a magnifying glass is nearer the truth. Let me clarify by touching on each.

Order Flow

Understanding order flow is essential for appreciating how the microstructure approach to exchange rates departs from earlier approaches. First, it is important to recognize that transaction volume and order flow are not the same. Order flow is transaction volume that is *signed*. For example, if you approach a dealer (marketmaker) and you decide to sell the dealer 10 units (shares, euros, etc.), then transaction volume is 10, but order flow is -10: You as the initiator of this transaction are on the sell side, so order flow takes on a negative sign. The quoting dealer is on the passive side of the trade. The trade is signed according to the active, or initiating side. Over time, order flow can then be measured as the sum of the signed buyer-initiated and seller-initiated orders. A negative sum means net selling pressure over the period. Thus, despite the immutable fact that all trades involve a buyer and a seller, microstructure theory provides a rigorous way of attaching a sign to individual transactions when measuring order flow.

This definition needs to be adjusted slightly for markets that do not have dealers. Some financial markets replace dealers with something known as a "limit order book."[4] Here is an example of a limit order: "Buy 10 units for me when the market reaches a price of 50." Limit orders are collected together in an electronic "book." The most competitive orders in the book define the best available bid and offer prices. For example, the limit order to buy with the highest buying price becomes the best bid in the market. If you entered the market and wanted to sell 10 units immediately, you could sell at this best bid price, but no higher. (Think of these best limit orders as analogous to dealer bid and offer quotes in markets that have dealers.) The limit orders are the passive side of any transaction, just as the quoting dealer is always on the passive side in the previous example. When orders arrive that require immediate execution (e.g., an order to "sell 10 units now at the best available price), these orders—called market orders—generate the signed order flow. In the example above, as in the earlier case, executing the market order to sell 10 units produces an order flow of -10.

Order flow, as used in microstructure finance, is a variant of a key term in economics, "excess demand." It is a variant of excess demand rather than a synonym for two reasons, the first relating to the excess part and the second relating to the demand part. For the former, note that excess demand equals zero in equilibrium by definition—there are two sides to every transaction. This is not true of order flow: in markets organized like foreign exchange, orders are initiated against a marketmaker, who if properly compensated, stands ready to absorb imbalances between buyers and sellers. These "uninitiated" trades of the marketmaker drive a wedge between the two concepts, excess demand and order flow. The second reason the concepts differ is that order flow is in fact distinct from demand itself. Order flow measures actual transactions, whereas demand shifts need not induce transactions. For example, the demand shifts that move price in traditional exchange rate models (e.g., the monetary models reviewed in chapter 6) are caused by the flow of public information, which moves exchange rates without transactions ever needing to occur.

A distinctive feature of microstructure models, across the board, is the central role order flow plays. This across the board property deserves emphasis because it expands the applicability of microstructure enormously. Recall that order flow plays no role in the asset approach; in the asset approach, order flow is not a variable that helps us understand exchange rates. That microstructure models of all types tell us this variable is important expands microstructure from the narrow concept of "institutional structures with price effects" to the broader concept of "a new lens for viewing markets." It instructs us that order flow deserves our attention. The question of order flow's importance in FX is distinct from—and in my judgment much larger than—the question of how specific FX institutions affect prices.

Consider a simple diagram that illustrates an important feature of microstructure models that relates directly to order flow. The diagram shows that information processing has two stages. The first stage is the analysis or observation of fundamentals by nondealer market participants (mutual funds, hedge funds, individuals with special information, etc.). The second stage is the dealer's—the price setter's—interpretation of the first-stage analysis. The dealer's interpretation comes from reading the order flow. Dealers set price on the basis of this interpretation.[5]

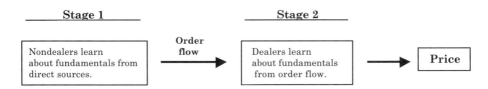

Figure 1.1
Two stages of information processing.

Order flow conveys information about fundamentals because it contains the trades of those who analyze fundamentals. In this sense, it is a transmission mechanism. Naturally, though, these informative trades may be mixed with uninformative trades, making the task of "vote counting" rather complex. In standard microstructure models, the dealer learns nothing about fundamentals that he or she does not learn from order flow. As a practical matter, this is clearly too strong. The dealer's dependence on learning from order flow arises in these models because the information being learned is not publicly known. When information is publicly known, dealers do not need to learn from order flow. In practice, though some information relevant to FX is publicly known, some is not, so learning from order flow can be important.

Spreads

Spreads—the second hallmark variable of the micro approach— receive a lot of attention within the field of microstructure. There are three reasons for this, one scientific, one practical, and one historical. The scientific reason relates to data: spread data are a core element of most data sets, and as such, are a ready target for testable hypotheses. This stands in contrast to other features of the trading environment that are important but not as readily measurable (such as information flow, belief dispersion, and liquidity-motivated order flow). The second reason spreads receive so much attention is practical. Practitioners are intensely concerned with managing trading costs. This concern, and the resources devoted to it, has naturally influenced the course of research within microstructure. The third reason spreads receive so much attention is historical. From the beginning, the field of microstructure sought to separate itself from the literature on trading under rational expectations. Rational expectations models abstract from trading mechanisms completely, the premise being that trading mechanisms have little effect on the relationship between underlying fundamentals and price. A natural means of distinguishing microstructure research was to orient it toward the following question: How does altering the trading mechanism alter price? This orientation led to a focus on the determination of real-world transaction prices—spreads.[6]

Though spreads receive a lot of attention, the subfield of spread determination is but one branch of the broader field of microstructure. Many microstructure models, for example, do not even include a spread (such as Kyle models, presented in chapter 4). I raise the issue early because for some people the association between spreads and microstructure is very tight. That many microstructure models have no spread should loosen this association.

Of the two hallmarks—order flow and spreads—this book focuses much more on order flow. In those instances where I do address spreads, my focus is on their information-theoretic implications, which can be substantial. For example, in chapter 2, I present evidence—gleaned from spread behavior alone—that implies that order flow forecasts price movements. This is important because it violates the premise of traditional models that all FX market participants are equally well informed: Some participants are better informed because they observe more order flow. Thus, on the basis of spread behavior alone, one reaches a rather profound conclusion: Contrary to the asset approach, exchange rate determination is not wholly a function of public news.[7]

1.3 Overarching Themes

Readers familiar with exchange rate economics are unlikely to be familiar with microstructure. For them, it may be helpful at the outset to address some of this book's overarching themes. Introducing them early provides valuable advance perspective on applications in later chapters. There are four themes in particular that exchange rate economists may find provocative.

Theme 1: Order Flow Matters for Exchange Rate Determination

Let me offer some perspective on this assertion, as it is one I will revisit. Consider an example, one that clarifies how economist and practitioner worldviews differ. The example is the timeworn reasoning used by practitioners to account for price movements. In the case of a price increase, practitioners will assert that "there were more buyers than sellers." Like other economists, I smile when I hear this. I smile because in my mind the expression is tantamount to "price had to rise to balance demand and supply." These phrases may not be equivalent, however. For economists, the phrase "price had to rise to balance demand and supply" calls to mind the Walrasian auctioneer, which is an abstract way to think about how price adjusts to a market-clearing level. The Walrasian auctioneer collects "preliminary" orders, which he uses to find the market-clearing price. All actual trades occur at this price—no trading occurs in the process of finding it. (Readers familiar with the rational expectations model of trading will recognize that in that model, this property is manifested by all orders being conditioned on a market-clearing price.[8])

Practitioners seem to have a different model in mind. In the practitioners' model there is a dealer instead of an abstract auctioneer. The dealer acts as a buffer between buyers and sellers. The orders the dealer collects are actual orders, rather than preliminary orders, so trading does occur in the transition to the new price.[9] Crucially, the dealer then determines new prices from information about demand and supply that is embedded in the order flow (as suggested in the "two-stage processing" diagram above).

Can the practitioner model be rationalized? Not at first blush, because it appears that trades are occurring at disequilibrium prices (prices at which the Walrasian auctioneer would not allow trading). This suggests irrational behavior. But this interpretation misses an important piece of the puzzle: Whether these trades are out of equilibrium depends on the information available to the dealer. If the dealer knows at the outset that there are more buyers than sellers, eventually pushing price up, then it is unclear why that dealer would sell at a low interim price. If the buyer/seller imbalance is not known, however, then rational trades can occur through the transition. (Put differently, in setting prices the dealer cannot condition on all the information available to the Walrasian auctioneer.) This is precisely the story developed in standard microstructure models. Trading that would be irrational if the dealer knew as much as the Walrasian auctioneer can be rationalized in models with more limited—and more realistic—conditioning information.

Theme 2: *Microstructure Implications Can Be Long-Lived*

It is common to associate "microstructure" with "high frequency." The association is natural, but deceptive. It is true that empirical work in microstructure is in general high frequency, but this does not imply that microstructure tools are irrelevant to lower frequency, resource relevant phenomena. Indeed, there are ample tools within the microstructure approach for addressing lower frequency phenomena, and new tools continue to emerge, thanks in part to recognition within the broader microstructure literature that resource allocation warrants greater attention. The later chapters of this book are dedicated to examples of lower frequency relevance, particularly chapter 7.

Regarding long-lived effects, the most important point to recognize is that when order flow conveys information, its effect on price *should* be long-lived. Indeed, a common empirical assumption for distinguishing information from pricing errors is that information's effects on price are permanent, whereas pricing errors are transitory (French and Roll 1986; Hasbrouck 1991a; chapter 2 provides details). The data in equity markets, bond markets, and FX markets bear out these long-lived effects. In FX, for example, Evans (1997), Evans and Lyons (1999), Payne (1999), and Rime (2000) show that order flow has significant, persisting effects on exchange rates. Indeed, statistically these effects appear to be permanent. Among microstructure's long-lived implications, this "information" channel is definitely the most fundamental.

Let me touch on another source of lower frequency relevance: multiple equilibria that depend on microstructure parameters. Certain parameters' values can determine whether multiple equilibria within a given model are possible, and if so, which equilibrium is more likely to be selected (e.g., Portes and Rey 1998; Hau 1998; Hartmann 1998a; Rey 2001). These different equilibria apply in some models to the exchange rate's level, and in other models to the exchange rate's volatility (multiple volatility states are the focus of Jeanne and Rose 1999 and Spiegel 1998). Either way, multiple equilibria that depend on microstructure parameters open another door through which price effects are long-lived (long-lived because a given equilibrium is by nature persistent).[10]

An analogy may be helpful. Microstructure can speak to longer horizon exchange rates in much the same way that microscopes speak to pathologies with macro impact. In medicine, microscopes provide resolution at the appropriate level—the level at which the phenomenon emerges. This is true irrespective of whether the phenomenon also has macro impact. Resolution at this level is the key to our understanding. Similarly, microstructure tools provide resolution at the level where its "phenomenon" emerges—the level where price is determined. What information do dealers have available to them, and what are the forces that influence their decisions? (Whether we like it or not, it is a stubborn fact that in the major currency markets, *there is no exchange rate other than the price these people set.*) Answering these questions does indeed help explain exchange rates over longer horizons. I provide evidence of this in section 7.1 and elsewhere.

Theme 3:   Microstructure Is Relevant to Macroeconomists

In 1987, stock markets crashed around the world, an event that most people consider macro relevant. What analytical tools did the profession use to address the crash? The tools were microstructure tools (see, e.g., Grossman 1988; Gennotte and Leland 1990; Jacklin, Kleidon, and Pfleiderer 1992; Romer 1993). These leading papers on the crash are explicit about relaxing all three of the asset approach assumptions noted above. In particular, the richness of these models comes from (1) information structure: which participants knew what; (2) heterogeneity: what types of participant were active and what were their motives for trading; and (3) institutions: what role did each participant play in the trading process and what trading information did each have available. The microstructure approach certainly bore fruit in this case.

Macroeconomists have also applied microstructure tools to understand exchange rate collapses during the 1990s financial crises in Asia. These papers also introduce information structures, heterogeneity, and institutional factors that are not in general present within the traditional macro approach (see Chen 1997; Calvo 1999; Corsetti, Morris, and Shin 1999; Carrera 1999).

Theme 4:   Exchange Rate Economics Merits an Information-Theoretic Perspective

In many ways, this theme follows from the first three. The information economics of traditional exchange rate models is rather simple.

Macroeconomic news is announced publicly, so everybody learns new information at the same time. This news can then be impounded directly in price. The aggregation of dispersed bits of information that are not publicly known is presumed to play no role. The question is, of course, whether this captures the essence of price determination, or whether it neglects something important. I address this question extensively in the next chapter.

1.4 Applying Microstructure Tools to Exchange Rate Puzzles

I turn now to puzzles within exchange rate economics and how microstructure helps to resolve them. Though later chapters address this in detail, let me offer some initial thoughts. Consider first the puzzle of the FX market's enormous trading volume ($1.5 trillion per day, by far the largest of any financial market). In fact, the microstructure approach has made considerable progress on this puzzle. I have in mind here recent findings on the volume-amplification effects of the so-called hot potato. Hot potato trading is the passing of unwanted positions from dealer to dealer following an initial customer trade. In the words of Burnham (1991, 135): "[When hit with an incoming order, a currency dealer] seeks to restore his own equilibrium by going to another marketmaker or the broker market for a two-way price. A game of 'hot potato' has begun. . . . It is this search process for a counterparty who is willing to accept a new currency position that accounts for a good deal of the volume in the foreign exchange market." Thus, the passing of unwanted positions is a consequence of dealer risk management. Under the asset approach, in contrast, volume is attributed to speculation.

Understanding the causes of high volume is not as important as understanding price determination, but it is still important. Three reasons come immediately to mind. First, misunderstanding the causes of high volume can lead to bad policy. Consider the issue of transaction taxes—an issue that has attracted much attention among exchange rate economists. Proponents of levying transaction taxes tend to associate high volume with excessive speculation. If instead much of this volume reflects dealer risk management, then a transaction tax would—unintentionally—impede that risk management. Second, high volume can impede order flow's information role. As suggested above and detailed in the next chapter, order flow conveys information. The precision of that information is a function of the underlying causes of order flow. It is important to understand whether those causes contribute to, or detract from, informational precision. Third, misunderstanding the causes of order flow can lead to bad theory. The mere existence of the volume puzzle is an indication that the asset approach is not addressing key features of the FX market. The features it is missing may not be important, but to be confident that they are unimportant requires a tremendous leap of faith.

What about the big puzzles in exchange rate economics? Chapter 7 addresses this question directly. The three biggest puzzles are[11]

1. the determination puzzle: Exchange rate movements are virtually unrelated to macroeconomic fundamentals (at least over periods of less than about two years);

2. the excess volatility puzzle: Exchange rates are excessively volatile relative to our best measures of fundamentals; and

3. the forward bias puzzle: Excess returns to speculating in foreign exchange are predictable and inexplicable.

The microstructure approach links these puzzles to one another through expectations formation—that is, how market participants form their expectations of future fundamentals. It makes this link without departing from the asset approach convention of rational expectations. Rather, the microstructure approach grounds expectations formation more directly in a richer, information-economic setting. The focus is on information *types* (such as public versus private) and *how* information maps into expectations (e.g., whether the aggregation of order flow "votes" is efficient).[12] The issues of information type and mapping to expectations are precisely where microstructure tools provide resolving power.

Chapter 7 addresses the three big puzzles and shows that the microstructure approach has already made empirical progress. Section 7.1 addresses the first puzzle; it reviews the work of Evans and Lyons (1999), who find that exchange rate movements can be explained—they are largely a function of order flow. Section 7.3 addresses the excess volatility puzzle by focusing on recent work on the sources of FX volatility (e.g., Killeen, Lyons, and Moore 2000a; Hau 1998; Jeanne and Rose 1999). Section 7.4 offers a microstructure-based explanation of the third puzzle—forward discount bias. It would be wrong for me to suggest that these three big puzzles have been put to rest by the above-mentioned work, but progress is being made.[13]

1.5   Spanning the Micro-Macro Divide

As noted above, a core distinction between the microstructure approach and the asset approach is the information role of trades. Under the asset approach, trades play no role (macroeconomic information is publicly announced), whereas in microstructure models trades are the driving force. It is instructive to frame this distinction with a bird's-eye view of structural models used by empiricists within these two approaches.

Structural Models: Asset Approach

Equations of exchange rate determination within the asset approach take the form:

$$\Delta P_t = f(i, m, z) + \varepsilon_t, \tag{1.1}$$

where ΔP_t is the change in the nominal exchange rate over the period, typically one month. The driving variables in the function $f(i, m, z)$ include current and past values of home and foreign nominal interest rates i, money supply m, and other macro determinants, denoted here by z.[14] Changes in these public-information variables are presumed to drive price without any role for order flow (though there is of course a role for demand; recall the distinction between order flow and demand in section 1.2). If any price effects from order flow should arise, they would be subsumed in the residual ε_t. Though logically coherent and intuitively appealing, a long literature documents that these macro determinants account for only a small portion (less than 10 percent) of the variation in floating exchange rates (see the surveys by Frankel and Rose 1995; Isard 1995; Taylor 1995).

Structural Models: Microstructure Approach

Within the microstructure approach, equations of exchange rate determination are derived from the optimization problem faced by the actual price setters (the dealers).[15] These models are variations on the following specification:

$$\Delta P_t = g(X, I, Z) + \varepsilon_t, \tag{1.2}$$

where now ΔP_t is the change in the nominal exchange rate between two transactions, versus the monthly frequency of the macro model in equation (1.1). The driving variables in the function $g(X, I, Z)$ include order flow X (signed so as to indicate direction), a measure of dealer net positions (or inventory) I, and other micro determinants, denoted by Z. It is interesting to note that the residual in this case is the mirror image of the residual in equation (1.1) in that it subsumes any price changes due to the public-information variables of the asset approach.

The key to spanning the micro-macro divide is the role of signed order flow X. Microstructure models predict a positive relation between signed order flow and price because order flow communicates nonpublic information, which can then be impounded in price. Empirical estimates of this relation between ΔP and X are uniformly positive and significant in securities markets generally (including stocks, bonds, and foreign exchange). It is noteworthy that these empirical estimates have been possible only a relatively short time: the switch to electronic trading means that we now have detailed records of order flows. What used to be a black box is no longer.

A Hybrid Approach

To establish the link between the micro and macro approaches, I investigate in chapter 7 equations with components from both approaches:

$$\Delta P_t = f(i, m, z) + g(X, I, Z) + \varepsilon_t. \tag{1.3}$$

These equations are estimable at frequencies corresponding to the asset approach through the use of time-aggregated measures of order flow X. The time-aggregated measures of X span much longer periods than those typically employed in empirical microstructure.

Estimates of this equation show that time-aggregated order flow has much more explanatory power than macro variables. In fact, chapter 7 shows that regressing daily changes in log DM/$ rates on daily order flow produces an R^2 statistic greater than 60 percent.[16] Figure 1.2 below provides a convenient summary of this explanatory power. The solid lines represent the spot rates of the DM and yen

DM/\$ **Yen\$**

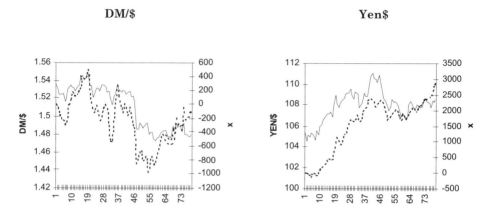

Figure 1.2
Four months of exchange rates (solid) and order flow (dashed). May 1–August 31, 1996.

against the dollar over the four-month sample of the Evans (1997) dataset (described in chapter 5). The dashed lines represent cumulative order flow for the respective currencies over the same period. Order flow, denoted by X, is the sum of signed trades over the sample period between foreign exchange dealers worldwide.[17] Cumulative order flow and nominal exchange rate levels are strongly positively correlated (price increases with buying pressure). This result is intriguing. Order flow appears to matter for exchange rate determination, and the effect appears to be persistent (otherwise the exchange rate's level would reflect only concurrent or very recent order flow and not *cumulative* order flow). This persistence is an important property, one that I examine more closely in later chapters. For order flow to be helpful in resolving big exchange rate puzzles, its effects have to persist over horizons that match those puzzles (monthly, at a minimum).[18]

That order flow matters for exchange rate determination does not imply that order flow is the underlying cause of exchange rate movements. Order flow is a proximate cause. The underlying cause is information. How, specifically, can one identify the information that determines order flow? The notion of order flow as an intermediate link between information and price suggests several strategies for answering this question, which I touch on now and address further in later chapters (particularly in chapters 7 and 9; readers may find a quick look at figure 7.1 helpful at this juncture).

One strategy for linking order flow to underlying determinants starts by decomposing order flow. (That it can be decomposed is one of its nice properties.) In chapter 9, I test whether all parts of the aggregate order flow have the same price impact. They do not: the price impact of FX orders from financial institutions (e.g., mutual funds and hedge funds) is significantly higher than the price impact of orders from nonfinancial corporations. This suggests that order flow is not just undifferentiated demand. Rather, the orders of some participants are more informative than the orders of others. Analyzing order flow's parts gives us a view of this market's underlying information structure.

A second strategy for linking order flow to underlying determinants is based on the idea that order flow measures individuals' changing expectations. As a measure of expectations, it reflects a willingness to back one's beliefs with money—the backed-by-money expectational votes, if you will. This strategy corresponds to the following variation on equation (1.3):

$$\Delta P_t = f(z_t, z_{t+1}^e) + \varepsilon_t, \tag{1.4}$$

where z_t denotes current macro fundamentals (interest rates, money supplies, etc.) and z_{t+1}^e denotes expected future macro fundamentals. These expected fundamentals are not well captured by macroeconometric techniques: estimates are slow moving and imprecise. If order flow is serving as an expectation proxy, then it should forecast surprises in important macroeconomic variables (like interest rates). New order flow data sets that cover up to six years of FX trading provide enough statistical power to test this.

2   The Economics of Order Flow Information

As noted in chapter 1, a focus of this book is the economics of order flow information. The objective of this chapter is to provide a foundation for that focus. How do we know order flow conveys information? What types of information does order flow convey? I answer both of these questions here.

In the section 2.1, I provide background on the information economics of traditional asset approach models. In section 2.2, I review recent empirical evidence on order flow information. The evidence supporting an information role for order flow comes from many sources, here documented using several different methodologies. In section 2.3, I provide a working definition of the term private information; if order flow is going to convey information that is not public, we need a clear sense of what that information is. The concluding section provides a more theoretical view of the types of information that order flow conveys. Specific examples that are grouped by type in that section include information about differential interpretation of macroeconomic announcements (inflation, money supply, real output, etc.), about changing institutional risk tolerance, about hedging demands and about portfolio rebalancing, among others. Although these types share certain characteristics, they also have important differences, which have implications for theory and empirical work.

This chapter does not extend to the mechanics of *how* order flow is impounded in price. I address that topic in chapter 4, which presents the key theoretical frameworks. It is only in the context of the theory that the details become meaningful. The goal of this chapter is more modest: to establish a comfort level with the idea that order flow is a transmission mechanism, a means of transmitting information to price.

2.1 Background

To many macroeconomists, the idea that order flow conveys incremental information relevant to exchange rates is controversial. In traditional models, macroeconomic news is announced publicly, and can therefore be impounded in price directly, without any role for order flow.[1] In light of this common belief, let me provide a bit more background before examining evidence that order flow does indeed play an information role.

As noted in chapter 1, models of exchange rate determination within the asset approach take the form:

$$\Delta P_t = f(i, m, z) + \varepsilon_t,$$

where ΔP_t is the change in the nominal exchange rate over the period, typically one month. The driving variables in the function $f(i, m, z)$ include current and past values of home and foreign nominal interest rates i, money supplies m, and other macro determinants (e.g., home and foreign real output), denoted here by z.

Now consider the possibility of private information. It is difficult to imagine circumstances in which agents would have private information about interest rates. Perhaps somebody had an enlightening conversation with the chairman of the Federal Reserve Board (Fed) that morning. Doubtful. Maybe somebody has inside information about the next Fed vote regarding monetary policy. Again, doubtful.[2] The natural presumption is that all agents have the same information about current—and future—interest rates. How about private information on money supplies, or real output? For these variables, too, it is natural to presume that agents are symmetrically informed. When money supply or real-output data are publicly announced, all agents learn new information at the same time. This is not a recipe for speculative activity based on information advantage.

With a slight shift in perspective, however, an information role for order flow emerges. This shift in perspective is perfectly consistent with the ideas of the last paragraph: even if exchange rate determination is based wholly on public information, this is not sufficient to rule out an information role for order flow. To understand why, recognize that there are in fact two crucial assumptions in these macro-asset models that disconnect order flow from price. These two assumptions are as follows:

1. all information relevant for exchange rates is publicly known; and

2. the mapping from that information to prices is also publicly known.

If either assumption is relaxed, then order flow can convey information that is relevant for prices. As an example of relaxing the second, suppose you and I are FX traders for large banks and we have both seen the same macro announcement. If I do not know how you will interpret the announcement's price implications, then I need to watch your trade to learn about your interpretation. Your trade—order flow—will both influence price and teach me something.

As an empirical matter, relaxing the assumption that everybody knows the mapping from public information to price should not be controversial. There is no existing consensus on the "right" macroeconomic model: extant macro-asset models fit the data poorly, as noted in chapter 1. In his book *Exchange Rate Economics*, Isard (1995, 182) puts it this way:

Thus, economists today still have very limited information about the relationship between equilibrium exchange rates and macroeconomic fundamentals. Accordingly, it is hardly conceivable that rational market participants with complete information about macroeconomic fundamentals could use that information to form precise expectations about the future market-clearing levels of exchange rates.

This fact has important implications for the role that order flow plays in mapping information to price.

Relaxing the all-agents-know-the-mapping assumption is not, however, the only way to restore a role for order flow. There are many types of information that do not conform to the first of the two macro-asset model assumptions—that all information relevant for exchange rates is publicly known. Section 2.3 reviews these types of information. In anticipation of that material, I offer a recent quotation from Rubinstein (2000, 17) that presages some of these information types: "Perhaps the most important missing generalization in almost all work on asset prices thus far has been uncertainty about the demand curves (via uncertainty about endowments or preferences) of other investors. This injects a form of endogenous uncertainty into the economy that may be on a par with exogenous uncertainty about fundamentals." Before reviewing these information types, let me first provide some empirical evidence on order flow's information role.

2.2   Empirical Evidence that Order Flow Is Informative

Four distinct empirical methodologies have been used to generate evidence of an information role for order flow; that these different methodologies produce similar results is an indicator of the evidence's robustness. The methodologies look in different places for indications of order flow's information effects: (1) persistent effects of order flow on price; (2) adverse selection components of bid-offer spreads; (3) volatility responses to trading halts; and (4) survey data from FX dealers. In this section, I briefly review some of the papers that fit in each of these four categories. I keep it brief here because it is too early to present these empirical methodologies in detail. The detailed material appears in chapter 5, which is dedicated to empirical frameworks.[3]

Methodology 1:   Persistent Order Flow Effects on Price

One methodology used to show that order flow is informative focuses on order flow's price effects and their persistence. It is common in the literature to distinguish between order flow that has transitory effects on price and order flow that has permanent effects on price. When order flow has transitory effects on price—sometimes called "indigestion" or "inventory" effects—these effects are often referred to as pricing errors. When order flow has permanent effects on price, however, these effects are taken to reflect underlying fundamental information. (French and Roll 1986 use this identification scheme, for example, in their celebrated paper on information arrival and stock return volatility.)

In empirical microstructure, the standard way to implement this idea is to estimate vector auto-regression models (VAR) and test whether innovations in order flow have long-run effects on price (Hasbrouck 1991a, b). When applied to data from major FX markets, one finds that order flow innovations do indeed have long-run effects on price, indicating that they convey bona fide information. Examples of findings along these lines include Evans 2001 and Payne 1999.

A second method for testing whether order flow effects are persistent uses time-aggregated order flow to explain price movements in FX markets. That is, rather than asking whether a single trade has an impact on price, this asks whether trades aggregated over time (say a day) have an impact on price. The idea is that if single trades have only fleeting effects on price, then order flow aggregated over the day will not be closely related to daily price movements. When applied to the FX market, one finds that daily order flow does remain strongly positively related to daily price changes. Examples of findings along these lines include Evans and Lyons 1999 and Rime 2000.[4]

Methodology 2:   Spreads and Informative Order Flow

Though not obvious to people new to microstructure, bid-offer spreads provide a means of testing whether order flow is informative. This is rather striking. It implies that on the basis of spread behavior alone, one can learn something quite important about the FX market's information structure. To wit, the information structure is not one of public information with a publicly known mapping of that information to price, but one where individual orders convey nonpublic information.

To understand why spreads provide a test, it is important to understand how spreads are determined. I show in chapter 5 that spreads exist because of three costs faced by dealers. One of these costs—typically referred to as an adverse selection cost—results from asymmetric information. Dealers know that when they trade with someone who is better informed, they can expect to lose money on the trade. If one could identify better-informed traders before trading, then this would not be a problem—dealers could choose not to trade, or could adjust price appropriately—but dealers typically cannot identify those who are better informed. Given this, one way to protect against losses is to increase the width of the quoted spread to all potential counterparties—informed and uninformed alike. That way, there is more room for prices to move against the dealer before he begins to lose money. When a dealer protects himself this way, we say that he has included an adverse selection effect (or component) in his spread. If we find this adverse selection component of the spread empirically, this indicates that dealers believe that some traders' orders reflect better information (despite the dealers' inability to identify exactly who those traders are).

Empirical findings show that an adverse selection effect is indeed present: dealers increase spreads to protect themselves against informative incoming order flow (Lyons 1995; Yao 1998b; Naranjo and Nimalendran 2000).[5] In Lyons 1995, for example, I find that the FX dealer I track protects himself from adverse selection by increasing the width of his spread by about one pip (or 0.0001 DM/\$) for every \$5 million increase in the size of the incoming order. (This estimate is a pure adverse selection effect on the spread; i.e., the model controls for other factors that affect spread width.) Yao (1998b) also finds an adverse selection effect on the spread. In addition, he finds that the dealer he tracks profits from trades executed after observing order flows. Unlike the Lyons and Yao papers, which look at market trading in general, Naranjo and Nimalendran (2000) focus on central bank trading—that is, intervention. They find that the adverse selection effect on the spread is positively related to the variance of unexpected intervention trades.

Methodology 3:   Volatility Responses to Trading Halts

The third methodology used to show that order flow is informative focuses on price volatility over periods that contain a subperiod during which trading is halted. (Think, for example, of the volatility of prices over weeks in which trading is halted on Wednesdays.) The trick in this case is to identify trading halts that are unrelated to the flow of public information. If the trading halt is related to the flow of public information—holidays, for example—then changes in volatility that occur because of the halt could easily be due to changes in that public information flow. If one is confident that the flow of public information has not changed, however, then changes in volatility that occur because trading is halted must be attributed to something else. In particular, a finding of *lower* volatility over periods that contain trading halts indicates that either (1) informative order flow is not reaching the market during the halt, (2) the lack of trading during the halt reduces pricing errors, or (3) some combination of both.

French and Roll (1986) were the first to use this methodology, which they applied to stock trading. They identified a set of days —mostly Wednesdays—on which the New York Stock Exchange (NYSE) was closed due to order processing backlogs. These were regular weekdays, not economy-wide holidays, so the closure had no impact on the underlying firms nor on the economy as a whole; the only difference was that the NYSE was not trading. Thus, there is no reason to believe the flow of public information changed (save, perhaps, firms' choosing not to release information due to the closure). French and Roll then measured the volatility of returns from Tuesday to Thursday in weeks when there was trading on Wednesdays, and compared this to the volatility of returns from Tuesday to Thursday in weeks with no trading on these special Wednesdays. They found that volatility was significantly lower in weeks with the Wednesday closures. This, together with other evidence they provide, leads them to conclude that the main source of the volatility reduction is possibility (1) above: informative order flow was not reaching the market during the Wednesday halts.

Ito, Lyons, and Melvin (1998) analyze an analogous experiment in the FX market. Their experiment was made possible by a change in the trading rules in the Tokyo FX market. Until December 1994, banks were restricted from trading in Tokyo over a lunch period (from 12:00 to 1:30 local time). In December 1994, the restriction was lifted. There were no other changes in policy or other shifts in the flow of macroeconomic information (e.g., announcement dates and times remained unchanged), so the flow of public information was not affected. Ito et al. find that after lifting the restriction, volatility in the $/yen market over the lunch period doubled.[6] Was this due to informative order flow or pricing errors? The increase in volatility does not, in itself, allow one to distinguish between them, but because it is unlikely that the increase is due *entirely* to pricing errors, this result also supports an information role for order flow.

Methodology 4: Surveys of Foreign Exchange Dealers

If we think dealers might believe order flow is informative, why not just ask them? This is the tack taken by Cheung and Yuk-Pang (1999, 2000), Cheung and Chinn (1999a, b) and Cheung, Chinn, and Marsh (1999). These papers survey foreign exchange dealers in major trading centers around the world (London, New York, and Tokyo). Fifty percent of the dealers surveyed by Cheung and Yuk-Pang believe that large players in the FX market have a competitive advantage that derives from "better information" and "a large customer base." The latter is often described as a source of advantage for dealers because it gives them privileged information about their customers' orders, and they can base their speculative trades on this information (see, e.g., Yao 1998b).

Other authors report results from discussions with dealers that are similar, though these results are less formal than the above-noted surveys. For example, Goodhart (1988, 456) writes, "A further source of informational advantage to the traders is their access to, and trained interpretation of, the information contained in the order flow." Similarly, based on interviews with nine FX dealers in London, Heere (1999) reports that the dealers emphasize the importance of asymmetric information. The dealers she interviews state that information asymmetry is based on both order flows and the identities of the institutions behind those order flows.

2.3 Defining Private Information

In this book, information is private information if it

1. is not known by all people; and

2. produces a better price forecast than public information alone.[7]

This is a natural definition. I should say, though, that it is a bit broader than some people have in mind. For example, under this definition, if a dealer has privileged order flow information and that information aids him or her in forecasting prices, then this constitutes private information. (The dealer could be expected to take speculative positions based on it.) For understanding motives for speculative trade, this definition is quite useful.

To add concreteness to the definition, let me identify two subcategories of private information and provide some examples from FX. Consider a simple two-period trading model in which trading occurs initially at a price P_0, again at $t = 1$ at a price P_1, and then a terminal payoff value V (e.g., an unknown final dividend) is realized at $t = 2$. The first type of private information that can arise in this setting is private information about the size of the terminal payoff V. Information that alters expectations of the payoff V will clearly be relevant for the prices P_0 and P_1. Let me offer two examples of private information in the FX market that are arguably of this type (the next section presents more examples). The first example is private information about central bank intervention: the dealer who receives a central bank's order has also received private information (Peiers

1997). The second example is dispersed private information about particular components of exchange rate fundamentals, for example, the trade balance: real trade in goods and services generates FX orders that provide information to dealers about trade balances long before published statistics are available (Lyons 1997a).

A second type of private information is unrelated to the payoff value V (in contrast to the first type), but is related to interim prices P_0 and P_1. P_0 and P_1 depend on many variables beyond expectations of the payoff V; in essence, this includes any variable that determines the risk premium in these prices. An example is traders' risk preferences. Other examples include traders' trading constraints, the supply/distribution of the risky asset, and other features of the trading environment. Insofar as these affect P_0 or P_1 without altering expectations of V, superior knowledge of them is private information of this second type.

Consider two examples from the FX markets of private non-payoff information. The first involves information about transitory risk premia, whereas the second involves information about persistent risk premia. In the first case, because the transparency of order flow in FX is low, dealers have better knowledge of their own inventory and that of other dealers than the general public. If inventory risk earns a risk premium, as many microstructure models predict, then superior knowledge of this kind allows a dealer to forecast interim price more accurately than the market at large.[8] As aggregate inventory across dealers becomes known, this induces a change in the risk premium and an attendant change in price, even though terminal payoff expectations remain unchanged.[9] (Discussions with FX dealers indicate that this type of private information is indeed relevant.) The second example of private non-payoff information, which involves persistent risk premia, is an extension of the first. Specifically, if the dealers' positions in aggregate are large enough that absorption by the rest of the market requires a sustained risk premium, then the dealers' superior information will forecast these price effects as well. (The following section provides more detail on this mechanism; see also Cao and Lyons 1998 and Saar 1999.)

This book tends to highlight the second of these two broad types of private information—information about interim prices. There are several reasons for this. First, in my judgment, this type of private information is especially relevant for the FX market. Second, people who believe that private information does not exist in the FX market typically have in mind only the first of the two types—private information about the payoff, V (which in the FX market translates to private information about future monetary fundamentals like interest differentials). Highlighting the second of the two information types broadens that perspective. Third, previous literature tends to neglect this category of private information. Information-theoretic models of trading are specified with private information about terminal payoffs. Empirical models follow suit. But this makes interpretation of empirical results difficult: should one interpret evidence of private information as reflecting the first type or the second type? The answer is not clear.

A Comment on the Term "Fundamentals"

The term fundamental means different things to different people. For example, one might be tempted to consider the second of my two private-information types as nonfundamental. The quote from Rubinstein (2000) that closed section 2.1 is suggestive of this narrower definition of fundamentals. In that quote, he distinguishes uncertainty about fundamentals (i.e., payoffs) from uncertainty about agents' preferences and endowments. But all of these factors are fundamental to asset pricing. My choice to put the two broad types of private information on equal footing recognizes the joint, complementary nature of these two categories of fundamentals. The issue is more than semantic; it affects the way we frame our thinking about price determination.

My use of the term "fundamental" to refer to information of both types is not so broad that it is no longer meaningful. The examples of private information above are all bona fide determinants of price in optimizing, well-specified models. None of the examples presented here require "bubbles," "greater fool" behavior, or irrationality.[10]

2.4   Extending the Taxonomy of Information Types

Let us shift to a more theoretical approach to identifying the types of information that order flow might convey. This section extends the last section by adding more granularity to the earlier two-category breakdown of private information. The danger in adding more granularity—and grounding it in theory—is that readers new to microstructure will find this section tougher going. Readers who do find this section more difficult should rest assured that the previous section is an ample introduction to the basic information-theoretic issues that arise later in the book.

Let us begin by recognizing an important connection within microstructure models between order flow and information. As we will see in chapter 4 (which reviews microstructure theory), order flow is the proximate determinant of price in all the standard models. This "all models" property is important: It ensures that the causal role played by order flow is not dependent on the specification of market structure.

To understand the specific types of information that order flow can convey, one needs to understand the specific channels through which order flow has price impact. At the broadest level, the information conveyed by order flow can be any information that currency markets need to aggregate (e.g., differential interpretation of macro announcements, changing institutional risk tolerance, shocks to hedging demands, etc.). Within this broad class, theory provides a taxonomy of different information types.

To set the stage for those different types, consider the following simplified view of asset pricing. Let us write the initial price of the risky asset in last section's two-period setting as

$$P_0 = \frac{E[V]}{1+d},\tag{2.1}$$

where P_0 is the price at $t = 0$, $E[V]$ is the expected value of the risky asset's payoff, and d is the market-clearing discount rate (two-period). In the case of a stock, where V is a dividend, this equation is the familiar dividend discount model. (The whole stream of discounted dividends would be included in a setting with multiple payoffs.) In the background of such a pricing equation is a market-clearing condition, which equates market demand with market supply (supply is typically assumed fixed). Any factor—other than the numerator $E[V]$—that affects market demand/supply will affect price through the market-clearing discount rate d.

Now we are ready to outline the types of information that order flow can convey. There are three key types that arise within microstructure theory:

1. Payoff information

2. Discount-rate information—inventory effects

3. Discount-rate information—portfolio balance effects

For a stock, payoff information refers to information about future dividends—the numerator $E[V]$ in our dividend discount model. For a bond, payoffs take the form of coupons and principal (which are publicly known as long as the bond is default free). For foreign exchange, payoffs include future short-term interest differentials (foreign minus domestic; see section 6.1 for more detail). These represent the net cash flows that accrue to holders of money market instruments denominated in foreign exchange—akin to the dividends that accrue to holders of a stock. (FX speculators who buy foreign exchange do not hold actual currency, which bears no interest, but instead invest their holdings in short-term, interest-bearing instruments.) We will see that private information about payoffs is the basis for a class of microstructure models known as information models (reviewed in chapter 4).

Let me provide examples of how order flow, per se, might convey private information about payoffs. The simplest example—though not so common in the major FX markets—is information about future interest rates conveyed in the orders of a central bank (intervention). A second example likely to operate on a more regular basis is information about people's *expectations* of future interest differentials (as noted in chapter 1).[11] To understand this example, recognize that in reality, people do not all share the same $E[V]$. Instead, each of us has our own expectation about the direction of future interest rates, based on the millions of bits of information we use to form this view. This can be described by expressing the numerator as $E[V \mid \Omega_i]$, where Ω_i denotes the information that market participant i uses to form expectations. Because participant i's orders depend on $E[V \mid \Omega_i]$, observing his or her orders conveys information about that expectation. Thus, order flow serves as a proxy for people's expectations about future payoffs, and the information embedded therein. These orders are the backed-by-money expectational votes that the market "counts" when determining price.[12]

Turning to discount-rate information, microstructure theory emphasizes two distinct causes of time variation in discount rates.[13] Both causes involve changing risk premia and rely on order flow to play the central role. The first of these causes is inventory effects. (These arise in the class of microstructure models known as inventory models; see chapters 4 and 5 for details.) The idea here is that risk-averse dealers will require compensation for absorbing transitory mismatches in supply and demand over time. The larger the mismatch, the greater the risk the dealer must assume and the greater the compensation the dealer requires. Suppose, for example, that the mismatch is such that the dealer needs to absorb market sell orders (i.e., the dealer needs to buy). The dealer may be willing to absorb a small amount at only a slightly lowered price, but he would require a significantly lowered price to absorb a large amount. Dealers thus earn a transitory risk premium for providing liquidity. These effects on price last only as long, on average, as the mismatches in market supply and demand. Once the supply-demand mismatch is remedied, the dealer no longer holds a position (inventory), so the effect on price dissipates—the risk is diversifiable. (In terms of equation 2.1, the inventory effect would alter the discount rate d that establishes p_0, but not the discount rate that later establishes p_1.) This type of order flow effect on price is what people have in mind when they assert that "microstructure effects fizzle quickly." To summarize, these effects arise because risk is not perfectly and instantaneously spread throughout the whole market; instead, dealers bear disproportionate risk in the short run, and this affects price in the short run.[14]

The second cause of time variation in discount rates—the third of our three information categories above—is what macroeconomists call portfolio balance effects. To distinguish these effects from inventory effects, the idea in this case is that even after risky positions are spread through the economy as a whole, order flow's effect on price will not disappear completely. (In terms of equation 2.1, the discount rates that establish both p_0 and p_1 are affected. With an infinite number of periods, all discount rates will in general be affected.) In other words, the risk that drives the portfolio balance effect is undiversifiable (unlike the risk that drives the inventory effect). Of course, to distinguish this from the first of our information types—information about payoffs—it must be shown that order flow is not conveying information about $E[V]$.

Let me offer two types of FX order flow that are unrelated to $E[V]$, but may be large enough to have persistent portfolio balance effects. These are orders—or the aggregation of orders—that arise from liquidity demand (e.g., importing and exporting) or from hedging demand. Consider a specific example. Suppose IBM sells equipment worth \$3 billion in Great Britain, is paid in pound sterling, and then dumps those pounds on the spot market to exchange them for dollars. (Suppose also that the transaction is unrelated to the future monetary fundamentals V.) Somebody must be willing to step up and hold those pounds for the indefinite future. (The word "indefinite" is important here: to keep the example simple I am assuming that IBM is not going to reverse its decision to sell the pounds sometime in the future—it is a permanent portfolio shift. Also, I am assuming that the equipment buyer makes no adjustment in its portfolio other than the pound payment.) If elasticity of market demand for those pounds is less than infinite—called imperfect substitutability in the macro literature—then the dollar price of a pound (the \$/£ rate) must fall to induce other market participants to purchase the pounds. Algebraically, for the market to clear we need

$$\bar{S} = D_1(E[V] - P) + D_2(\text{IBM}),$$

where I will assume that the aggregate supply of pounds, $\bar{S}$, is fixed by the bank of England, and the aggregate demand for pounds has two components: a speculative component D_1 and a nonspeculative component D_2 (here driven by IBM's liquidity demand for pounds). The speculative component depends negatively on the current spot rate, P (with less than infinite elasticity), and the nonspeculative component demands positively on the liquidity demand for pounds. Though quite simple, this example is in the same spirit as the portfolio balance effects from sterilized intervention by central banks—an example familiar to international economists. The only difference is that instead of the central bank forcing a (payoff-unrelated) position on the public, in my example it is a subset of the public forcing a (payoff-unrelated) position on the rest of the public. (See chapter 8 for more on central bank intervention, including the distinction between sterilized and unsterilized intervention.)

Let me relate the above discussion to the previous section's introduction of private information. In effect, the discussion above splits one of the earlier private information types into two parts. The previous section introduced a type of private information unrelated to

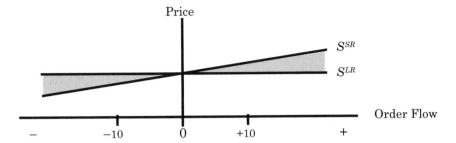

Figure 2.1
Supply curves with only transitory inventory effects. The dotted region represents the transitory inventory effects. The effective spread faced by a customer for a 10-unit order is the difference in price along the short-run net supply curve S^{SR} between -10 and $+10$. If a customer wants to buy 10 British pounds from the dealer—an order of $+10$—then he must pay the higher dollar price. If the customer wants to sell 10 pounds to the dealer—an order of -10—then he will receive the lower dollar price. Over the longer run, however, the dealer unloads his position on the rest of the market at a price that does not include the transitory inventory effects. The market's net supply is perfectly elastic, by assumption, which corresponds to a longer-run supply curve S^{LR} slope of zero. The linear relationship shown along S^{SR} is a special case, which I adopt for simplicity.

the payoff value V but relevant to interim prices P_0 and P_1—so-called nonpayoff information. This is what I am now calling private information about discount rates, of which I have established two distinct categories, inventory effects and portfolio balance effects. By splitting the earlier type in two, this section provides more granularity and links the earlier description more tightly to microstructure theory. It is helpful to distinguish between the two subcategories because their different properties allow us to isolate them empirically: inventory effects are transitory, but portfolio balance effects persist.

A Graphic View of These Information Types

To clarify these three types of order flow information further, I turn to a graphic interpretation. Consider, for example, the second type of information outlined above—information about transitory inventory effects. These effects are presumed to dissipate quickly because dealers are not holding these positions for long; the spreading of risky positions to nondealer participants occurs rapidly (within a day in foreign exchange). Figure 2.1 provides a qualitative illustration. The short-run market (net) supply curve, denoted S^{SR},

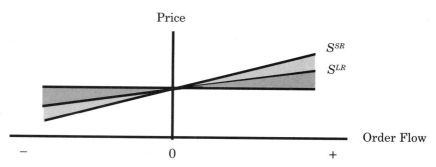

Figure 2.2
Supply curves with inventory and portfolio balance effects. The light-gray region represents the transitory inventory effects. The darker gray region represents persistent portfolio balance effects. Due to inventory effects, the short-run price impact of an incoming order is larger than the long-run impact. But the long-run impact is nonzero, due to imperfect substitutability; that is, the long-run net supply curve S^{LR} now slopes upward. The linear relationships shown are a special case, which I adopt for simplicity.

slopes up. (Think of this supply curve as the dealers' willingness to sell to accommodate incoming order flow, rather than as changes in the physical supply of foreign exchange.) If order flow is not conveying either of the other two information types whose effect on price persists beyond the short run, then longer run (net) supply curve S^{LR} is flat.[15]

Now let us add persistent portfolio balance effects.[16] Doing so implies that the market as a whole—being risk averse—needs to be compensated for holding a position it would not otherwise hold. This requires an enduring risk premium, which takes the form of a price-level adjustment (per the IBM example). This price adjustment is not temporary because the risk premium for holding this position must be sustained. Figure 2.2 illustrates this. The short-run market (net) supply curve still slopes up, but now it reflects both the transitory effect of inventory at the dealer level and the longer run effect from imperfect substitutability. It is, as a result, more steeply sloped than the short-run supply curve from inventory effects alone illustrated in figure 2.1. To understand why this short-run effect goes in the same direction as the longer run effect, think of the underlying dealer behavior. An individual dealer will buy pound sterling over the short run only at a relatively discounted dollar price. The market as a whole will take those pounds off the dealer's hands at a slightly discounted price, but not as discounted as was required by the dealer

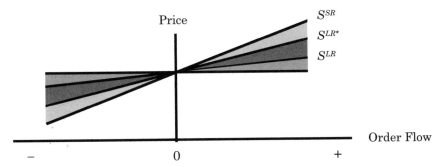

Figure 2.3
Supply curves when order flow conveys information about payoffs and discount rates. The light-gray region represents the transitory inventory effects. The dark-gray region represents persistent payoff-information effects. The medium-gray region represents persistent portfolio balance effects. The figure therefore reflects all three of the information types that arise in microstructure theory. The long-run supply curve S^{LR*} reflects the long-run effects from portfolio balance (S^{LR}), plus an additional long-run effect due to the payoff information conveyed by order flow. The linear relationships shown are a special case, which I adopt for simplicity.

in doing the trade initially with the customer. The dealer, knowing this cost of laying off his inventory has increased, will pass this on to the customer in his initial quotes.

Now I will allow order flow to convey information about expected future payoffs. Like in the case of portfolio balance effects, order flow effects on price from this channel will persist (see, e.g., French and Roll 1986; Hasbrouck 1991a, b). Mapped into the market supply curve, this channel adds additional slope to the long-run schedule shown in figure 2.2. Figure 2.3 provides an illustration of these long-run supply curves. Note that the short-run supply curve is more steeply sloped than either of the two long-run curves.

In figure 2.3 there is now a new long-run supply curve, S^{LR*}. This new long-run supply curve reflects both the long-run portfolio balance effects (S^{LR}), as in figure 2.2, plus an additional long-run effect due to the payoff information conveyed by order flow.

In later chapters, I address the slopes of these net supply curves empirically. At this stage, it is worth bearing one point in mind: order flows in the FX market are enormous relative to other asset markets. In the figures, this corresponds to being far to the left or far to the right of the order-flow-equals-zero point. Thus, even if the slopes of these supply curves are nearly zero, large order flow can still produce substantial price impact.

Concluding Thoughts

To conclude this chapter, it is worth stepping back to reflect on an important, overarching point. The microstructure tools applied in this chapter are useful for addressing a rather deep question:

What is the nature of the information this market is processing?

By focusing attention on order flow, these tools help to characterize which types of information are relevant, and how this information is aggregated.

In terms of financial markets' economic role, the aggregation of dispersed information is of profound conceptual importance. Nobel laureate Friedrich Hayek (1945, 519) provides an early and powerful articulation of this point. He writes:

The "data" from which the economic calculus starts are never for the whole society "given" to a single mind which could work out the implications, and can never be so given. The peculiar character of the problem of rational economic order is determined precisely by the fact that the knowledge of the circumstances of which we must make use never exists in concentrated or integrated form, but solely as dispersed bits of incomplete and frequently contradictory knowledge which all the separate individuals possess. The economic problem of society is thus ... a problem of the utilization of knowledge not given to anyone in its totality.

Relative to traditional exchange rate approaches, the information-theoretic perspective offered here is qualitatively different. As we shall see in chapter 6 (where I survey macro exchange rate models), exchange rate economics may warrant a richer information-theoretic perspective.

The Institutional Setting

Chapter 1 began with an overview of the microstructure approach, making the point that the approach relaxes three of the asset approach's most uncomfortable assumptions. Those assumptions are that (1) all FX-relevant information is publicly available, (2) all market participants are alike, and (3) trading mechanisms are inconsequential for prices. (To be fair, these are not assumptions that macroeconomists believe are literally true; they are employed as useful abstractions.) Chapter 2 addressed the first of these by providing frameworks for thinking about information that is both relevant and dispersed throughout the economy. This chapter addresses the other two assumptions: trader heterogeneity and the role of trading mechanisms.

In section 3.1, I provide an overview of the market participants and how they differ from one another. The first section also describes the trading mechanisms used in major FX markets and includes comparisons with other financial markets (see also Luca 2000 for a great deal of institutional information, including an historical account of FX market development). Section 3.2 introduces an important source of institutional information—the triennial central bank surveys summarized by the Bank for International Settlements (BIS 1999a, 2002). These survey data provide institutional perspective not available from any other source. Section 3.3 addresses market transparency, which is crucial to understanding how order flow information is conveyed. In markets that are highly transparent, order flow is observed by all participants, thereby affecting expectations rapidly and precisely. In opaque markets (the FX market is relatively opaque), order flow is not widely observed, so any information it conveys is impounded into prices more slowly. The concluding section, section 3.4, provides reflections on a common and powerful association— that between "institutions" and the field of microstructure.

One should be more careful than I have been thus far when referring to "the" FX market. Many people understand this term to mean spot markets in the major floating exchange rates, such as \$/euro and \$/yen, the two largest spot markets. In its broadest sense, though, the term includes markets other than spot and rates other than the major floaters. FX markets other than spot include the full array of derivative instruments (forwards, futures, options, and swaps). Rates other than the major floaters include those in smaller markets, such as emerging markets, and those in pegged regimes, such as Western Europe before the euro. When people quote the daily trading volume in FX at \$1.5 trillion, that statistic applies to the broadest definition of the market.[1]

Nevertheless, the essence of the FX market is the spot market. In 1998, the spot market accounted for 40 percent of total turnover across all FX instrument categories (\$600 billion out of \$1.5 trillion). Though this share has been trending downward—it was 59 percent in the BIS survey of 1989—the falling spot share is not due to lower spot turnover in absolute terms; rather, the derivatives markets have grown up around the spot market.

For the purposes of this book, however, a vital point must be understood about the previous paragraph's market share figures: Of the \$900 billion of daily volume that is not from the spot market, \$734 billion of this is FX swaps,[2] and *FX swaps have no order flow consequences in the FX market.* To understand why, one first needs to know what these swaps are. An FX swap bundles two FX transactions that go in opposing directions. For example, I agree to buy 100 million euros today for dollars (spot), and at the same time I agree to sell 100 million euros for dollars for settlement in one month (forward). This example is called a spot-forward swap. (One can also do forward-forward swaps, in which case the first of the two transactions is a nearer dated forward transaction than the other.) Note that the two orders in this example are of equal size, but opposite sign, so the net order flow impact is zero. Readers familiar with covered interest parity will recognize that this contract is a means of locking in an interest differential, and market participants use them for this purpose (whether hedging or speculating).[3] The net demand impact is therefore mainly on relative short-term interest rates, not on the FX market. This point is borne out in the behavior of banks: bankers tell me that when they design in-house models for forecasting exchange rates using order flow, they exclude FX-swap transactions from their order flow measures. The bottom line is that the spot market accounts for about $600 billion of $766 billion, or 78 percent, of the transaction activity that corresponds to the order flow models of this book.

Nevertheless, 78 percent is not 100 percent, so these statistics still highlight a tension in defining the scope of this book. On the one hand, defining the FX market broadly to include derivative instruments is consistent with official definitions like that of the BIS; moreover, arbitrage relationships link these submarkets tightly, suggestive of one market rather than many. On the other hand, these submarkets do not share the same market structure, particularly in the case of futures, which are often traded in physical pits using face-to-face open outcry.

To avoid these difficulties, henceforth I focus attention explicitly on the spot market, in particular the major floating-rate spot markets. (Fixed-rate spot markets are much smaller in terms of trading volume than floating-rate spot markets.) Unless otherwise noted, my use of the term "the FX market" corresponds to spot markets like $/euro and $/yen. Work thus far on FX microstructure is heavily concentrated on spot markets; broadening the scope to derivatives would bring us into uncharted terrain. I do not, however, completely exclude work on the derivatives segment—there are many notes and references to these related areas.[4]

3.1   Features of Spot FX Trading

Before digging deeper into institutional detail, it will be helpful to start by reviewing the basic institutional forms. Though in practice, most market structures are hybrids of these forms (or involve concurrent use of more than one form), appreciation of this fact requires familiarity with those forms. The three basic forms of market structure are

1. auction markets
2. single-dealer markets
3. multiple-dealer markets

Naturally, within each of these forms there are further refinements. Because this is not intended as a survey, I offer a few words about each and provide some examples.

In an auction market (in particular, a "two-sided" auction market), a participant can submit a buy order, a sell order, or both. These orders can be market orders (buy X units now at the best available price) or limit orders (buy X units when the market reaches a price of Y). In a pure auction market, there is no explicit dealer, so the most competitive limit orders define the best available bid and offer prices. Examples of auction markets include the Paris Bourse and the Hong Kong Stock Exchange, both of which operate electronically.[5]

In a single-dealer market, a lone dealer stands ready to buy at his bid quote and sell at his offer quote, thereby defining the best available price.[6] In this setting, incoming orders from customers are necessarily market orders—a customer either buys at the dealer's offer, sells at the dealer's bid, or chooses not to trade. Though some consider the "specialist system" of the New York Stock Exchange a single-dealer market, this is not accurate. In reality, the NYSE is a hybrid system, with both auction and single-dealer features. Each specialist (marketmaker) maintains a collection of customer limit orders—the limit order book. If a market order to buy arrives, the specialist can either match it with the best (i.e., lowest priced) sell limit order, or, if he offers an even lower price himself, then he can take the other side. (In the parlance, he can step in front of the limit order book.) Thus, the specialist must work within the parameters of the best buy and sell limit orders when trading for his or her own account. In this sense, the specialist is forced to compete against the limit order book. This constrains the specialist's ability to exercise monopoly power. Pure examples of single-dealer markets are rare. Examples include FX markets in some developing countries where all orders must be routed through a single dealer—the central bank (developing country markets of this type tend to be fixed-rate markets).

Multiple-dealer markets come in two main varieties—centralized and decentralized. In both cases, competition is provided via multiple competing dealers, rather than via limit orders as is the case in auction and hybrid specialist systems. In a centralized market, quotes from many dealers are available in a consolidated format, such as on a single screen (like the United States's NASDAQ), or in a single physical place (like a futures trading pit). In a decentralized market, there is generally some degree of fragmentation because not all dealer quotes are observable. One result of this fragmentation is that simultaneous transactions can occur at different prices.

The spot foreign exchange market is best described as a decentralized multiple-dealer market. (This is also true of forwards, options, and swaps markets in major currencies worldwide.) There is no physical location—or exchange—where dealers meet with customers, nor is there a screen that consolidates all executable dealer quotes in the market.[7] In this way, it is quite different from most equity and futures markets. In its structure, the spot FX market is perhaps most similar to the U.S. government bond market (bond markets have only recently attracted attention in the microstructure literature).[8]

Three characteristics in particular distinguish trading in FX from that in other markets:

1. trading volume is enormous;

2. trades between dealers account for most of this volume;

3. trade transparency is low.

Volume in the spot $/euro market alone is about $150 billion per day, dwarfing that of any other single financial instrument. Remarkably, interdealer trading currently accounts for roughly two-thirds of this volume, a much higher share than in other multiple-dealer markets (the remaining one-third is between dealers and nondealer customers).[9] Finally, the FX market has an uncommon information structure. Specifically, order flow in FX is not as transparent as in other multiple-dealer markets: in most national markets—whether equity or bonds—by law, trades must be disclosed within minutes. FX trades have no disclosure requirement, so trades in this market are not generally observable. From a theoretical perspective, this feature is quite important because order flow can convey information about fundamentals. If order flow is not generally observed, then the trading process will be less informative and the information reflected in prices will be reduced.

Let me clarify the players in the spot foreign exchange market. In addition to providing context, this will help to classify trades into types depending on who the counterparties are. (The classification of trades into types is relevant to the material in later chapters.) The three main categories are

1. dealers

2. customers

3. brokers (strictly interdealer)

Dealers provide two-way prices to both customers and other dealers. In major spot markets (like $/euro and $/yen), most dealers trade only a single currency pair. Though the number of banks that have a dealer in any major spot market is large (greater than 100 world-wide), the top ten banks handle the lion's share of the order flow, and concentration is increasing over time: Over the past 10 years, the combined market share of the top ten dealers has risen from around 40 percent to around 50 percent (BIS 1999a, 15; see also *Financial Times*, Survey: Foreign Exchange, 5 June 1998).

The customer category includes many institution types, such as nonfinancial corporations, financial firms/managers, and central banks. Chapter 9 provides some more detailed analysis of the trades of these individual customer categories. Also, chapter 8 provides analysis of the central bank category and the role of these trades in intervention. (Because it is natural to consider central banks as having superior information, this customer type receives special attention in the macro literature.)

The term "broker" is confusing to people more familiar with equity markets than the FX market. Brokers in equity markets trade for both their customers and for themselves. FX brokers do not trade for themselves; they only facilitate trades between dealers. This facilitation role is important in the spot market. To understand the FX brokers' role, note that there are two methods for dealers to trade with one another. One way is for a dealer to call another for a quote and either sell at the quoted bid or buy at the quoted offer. This is referred to as a direct interdealer trade. The other method is to trade indirectly through a broker. (In 1998, about half of all interdealer trades in the largest spot markets were direct, which implies that the total volume pie split rather cleanly into one-third customer-dealer, one-third direct interdealer, and one-third brokered interdealer. By the end of 2000, only about 10 percent of interdealer trades were direct; see BIS 2001.)

Think of brokers as a bulletin board. Brokers do not make prices themselves. They gather firm prices from dealers and then communicate those prices back to dealers. A dealer might want to post a price through a broker because he prefers not to reveal his identity before the trade is executed (revealing one's identity before the trade is a necessary consequence of trading directly). For example, one dealer may post with the broker a limit order to buy $5 million at a price of 10. Another dealer may post a limit order to sell $3 million at a price of 12. If these are the best prices the broker has received on either side, then the broker will advertise a two-way price of 10–12, and will do so without identifying the dealers posting those prices. A third dealer can choose to trade at one of those prices through the broker. (If so, after the transaction the broker reveals the counterparty, and settlement occurs directly between the counterparties; both pay the broker a small commission.) Thus, brokers are pure matchmakers—they do not take positions of their own, they only connect dealers that might not otherwise find each other. In the parlance of the three basic market structures above, brokers are running an interdealer auction market that operates concurrently with the multiple-dealer market. In this way, brokers provide a degree of centralization in an otherwise decentralized FX market.[10]

These three categories of market participants give rise to three basic types of trades. We can illustrate these trade types using three concentric rings, shown in figure 3.1.

The inner ring represents direct interdealer trading, the most liquid part of the market. In the $/euro market, current spreads in this

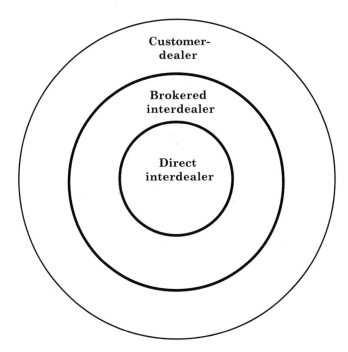

Figure 3.1
Three types of trades.

inner ring are one to two basis points (one basis point equals one one-hundredth of 1 percent) for $10 million trades (the standard size) between large banks during active trading hours (the full London trading day plus the morning hours in New York). Historically, dealers have chosen direct trading for larger interdealer trades (above $10 million). The second ring represents brokered interdealer trading. The effective spread for a $10 million trade in this ring is roughly 2–3 basis points during active trading, though this continues to fall as brokers take market share away from direct dealing. I add the word "effective" here because the inside—that is, the lowest—spread in the brokered part of the market can be less than 2–3 basis points, but that inside spread may apply to trade sizes less than $10 million; any remainder must be executed at less attractive prices, such that a $10 million trade will have price impact beyond the initial inside spread. The third ring represents customer-dealer trading. Dealers tell me that current spreads for a $10 million trade are in the 3–7 basis point range for "good" customers. ("Good" to most dealers means high volume.)

Visually, figure 3.1 reflects a common metaphor used for the foreign exchange market, namely that the market is like a pool of water, with stones being thrown in the center, where the action is most intense. The stones are the customer orders. Direct interdealer trading lies at the center. Stones landing in that center send ripple effects through the brokered interdealer trading, and, ultimately, back to the customers themselves. Why back to customers themselves? Because dealers tend not to hold positions for very long in this market, as we shall see below. This metaphor also clarifies the typical order's "life cycle."[11]

One might ask why a dealer would use a broker if direct prices are tighter (brokers also charge a commission). Part of the answer is that smaller banks often do not have access to the tighter direct spreads that large banks extend to one another. Large banks, too, have incentives to use brokers. From the large bank perspective, providing a broker with a limit order provides a wider advertisement of a willingness to trade than bilateral direct quoting provides. (Keep in mind that a large bank that provides a broker with a limit order to buy, for example, is still buying at the bid price, which is below the offer price. If a second, smaller bank hits that bid, it is the second bank that sells at this lower price.) Another reason banks—large and small alike—may choose to trade via brokers is that they provide pretrade anonymity (as noted above). In a direct interdealer trade, the dealer providing the quote knows the identity of the other dealer. (For more detail on incentives to use particular FX trading systems, see Luca 2000.)

Features for Modeling

With this more complete picture of FX market institutions, let us now consider other features of FX microstructure that influence modeling strategies. Among many cited in the literature, three in particular deserve note:

Dealers Receive Information from Their Customer Orders
As Citibank's head of FX in Europe said, "if you don't have access to the end user, your view of the market will be severely limited" (*Financial Times*, 29 April 1991). In a similar spirit, Goodhart (1988, 456) writes: "A further source of informational advantage to the traders is their access to, and trained interpretation of, the information contained in the order flow.... Each bank will also know what their own customer enquiries and orders have been in the course of the day, and will try to deduce from that the positions of others in the market, and overall market developments as they unfold." Note that banks have little information regarding the customer orders of other banks. Consequently, insofar as this order flow information helps forecast prices, it is private information (by the definition of chapter 2).

Dealers Learn about Marketwide Order Flow Largely from Brokered Interdealer Trades
Because dealers do not observe one another's customer orders, they need to gather order flow information from interdealer trading. As noted above, though, direct interdealer trading does not provide order flow information to anyone other than the counterparties. Brokered interdealer trading, on the other hand, does provide order flow information beyond the counterparties. This is important: of the three trade types (customer-dealer, direct interdealer, and brokered interdealer), the brokered interdealer trades are the only order flow information communicated to all dealers. The broker systems, which are now electronic, typically communicate this information by indicating whether incoming market orders are executed at the bid or offer side (indicated with the words "given" for a trade at the bid and "paid" for a trade at the offer) and by providing information on how

the incoming market order has changed the quantity available on the bid or offer side (information on the size of the order flow). Though there is noise in this order flow measure, on a marketwide basis it is the best measure that is available to dealers.[12]

Large Dealer Positions Are Frequent and Nontrivial

They are a natural consequence of marketmaking in a fast-paced market with tight spreads (less than 2 basis points in the interdealer $/euro market).[13] FX dealers manage these large positions intensively. The large bank dealer in the $/DM market that I tracked in 1992 (see Lyons 1995) finished his trading day with no net position each of the five days in the sample, despite trading over $1 billion each day. Within the day, the half-life of the gap between his current position and zero was only ten minutes (Lyons 1998). From the plot of that dealer's net position in figure 3.2, the strong reversion toward zero is readily apparent.[14]

Though the three features noted above are the most important from a modeling strategy perspective, let me provide a bit more perspective on what the life of a dealer in a major FX market is like.[15]

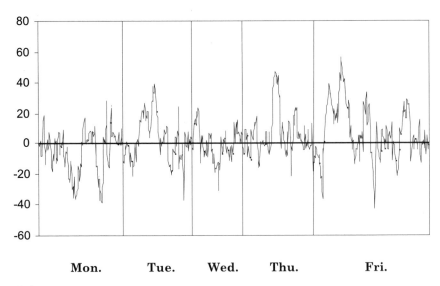

Figure 3.2
Dealer's net position (in $ millions) over one trading week. The vertical lines represent the overnight periods over which this dealer was not trading. The horizontal distance between those vertical lines is scaled by the number of transactions made by this dealer each trading day.

Two aspects of a dealer's life are particularly telling: his position sheets and his profitability. Tables 3.1 and 3.2 below provide some perspective on each of these two aspects. The position sheet is the source of the dealer position shown in figure 3.2.

Table 3.1 provides a representative position sheet from the dollar-mark dealer I tracked through one week of trading in August 1992 (see Lyons 1998 for details). The position sheets provide the dealer with a running record of his net position and the approximate cost of that position. The dealer fills the sheets in by hand as he trades (though these days it is mostly electronic and automatic). Each sheet (page) covers about fifteen transactions. The "Position" column accumulates the individual trades in the "Trade" column. Quantities are in millions of dollars. A positive quantity in the Trade column corresponds to a purchase of dollars. A positive quantity in the Position column corresponds to a net long position in dollars. The "Trade Rate" column records the exchange rate for the trade, in DM per dollar (which is the way dealers quote prices in this market). The "Position Rate" column records the dealer's estimate of the average rate at which he acquired his position. The Position and Position Rate are not calculated after every trade due to time constraints (the average intertransaction time of this dealer is 1.8 minutes over this trading week, and during especially active periods it is much shorter). The "Source" column reports whether the trade is direct over the Reuters Dealing 2000-1 system[16] (r = Reuters) or brokered (b = Broker). One dimension of actual position sheets not shown in the diagram is the names of the counterparties. Most banks are reluctant to provide these names, as they are considered confidential.

There are several take-aways. First, this dealer's trading day started around 8:30 A.M., New York time. (The New York market as a whole begins picking up liquidity around 7:30 A.M.) Second, the distinction between direct and brokered trades is evident in the way this dealer structures his sheet, with "r" capturing his direct trades and "b" capturing his brokered trades. (Beyond tracking position, one needs to track brokered trades because they involve a commission payment.) Third, trading is hectic enough that this dealer does not have time to update all information following every trade. (His average daily volume is over $1 billion, as we shall see in figure 3.3.) Fourth, each entry does not record the time, though the dealer does record the time at the beginning of every card (to the minute), and occasionally within the card, as was the case here.

Table 3.1
Diagram of Position Sheet Structure

Trade date: 8/3
Value date: 8/5

Position	Position rate	Trade	Trade rate	Source	Time
		1	1.4794	r	8:30
		2	1.4797	r	
3	1.4796				
		28	1.4795	r	
		−10	1.4797	r	
		−10	1.4797	b	
		−10	1.4797	r	
		−3	1.4797	b	
−2	1.4797				
		0.5	1.4794	r	
		0.75	1.4790	r	
		3	1.4791	r	
2	1.4791				
		−10	1.4797	r	
−8	1.4797				
		2	1.4799	b	
−6	1.4797				8:38
		5	1.4805	b	
		−7	1.4810	r	
−8	1.4808				

The "Position" column accumulates the individual trades in the "Trade" column. Quantities are in millions of dollars. A positive quantity in the Trade column corresponds to a purchase of dollars. A positive quantity in the Position column corresponds to a net long dollar position. The "Trade Rate" column records the exchange rate for the trade, in deutschemarks per dollar. The "Position Rate" column records the dealer's estimate of the average rate at which he acquired his position. The Position and Position Rate are not calculated after every trade due to time constraints. The "Source" column reports whether the trade is direct over the Reuters Dealing 2000-1 system (r = Reuters) or brokered (b = Broker). All trades on this position sheet are interdealer. First fourteen trades on Monday, August 3, 1992.

Perhaps most important, one needs to remember that this is but one dealer. In many respects, he appears to be representative; in other respects, he clearly is not. One important way in which he is not representative is that roughly 95 percent of his trades are interdealer (taking all his position cards together), compared to only about 80 percent of marketwide volume at the time (1992—the interdealer share has fallen to about two-thirds since then). Thus, the only types of trades that appear on this position sheet are either direct interdealer (r) or brokered interdealer (b) trades—no customer trades are listed (see the detailed discussion in chapter 5 of how these data compare to data on other dealers). A better understanding of heterogeneity across dealers is an important frontier for analysis in this area (see, e.g., Bjonnes and Rime 2000; Vitale 1998).

The second aspect of a dealer's livelihood that is particularly telling is profitability. It is illuminating to get a sense for the source and size of a dealer's profits (particularly given the common, and not unreasonable view, that FX trading is a zero-sum game). Table 3.2 provides some perspective on these profits, based on the same dealer whose position sheet appears in table 3.1. From the "Profit: Actual" column, we see that this dealer averages about $100,000 profit per day (on volume of about $1 billion per day). By comparison, equity dealers average about $10,000 profit per day (on volume of roughly $10 million per day).[17] So, even though this FX dealer's profit as a percentage of his volume is only one-tenth that of the average equity dealer, because his volume is hundred times as high, each day this dealer earns ten times as much.

To determine where these profits come from, first recognize that there are two possible sources: speculation and intermediation. Speculative profits come from being long on dollars, on average, when the DM price of dollars goes up (and vice versa). Intermediation profits come from the bid-offer spread: buying at the lower price (bid) and selling at the higher price (offer). The column "Profit: Spread" is an attempt to impute the profit the dealer would have earned each day purely from intermediation. It is calculated under the assumption that the dealer earns one-third of his spread on every transaction. Specifically, it is his daily dollar volume times his median quoted spread (0.0003 DM/$) times one-third, divided by the average DM/$ rate over the sample (1.475 DM/$).[18]

Let me explain the rationale behind this assumption that the dealer earns one-third of his spread on every transaction. Suppose the dealer has no net position, and quotes bid and offer prices of 1.4750 and 1.4753 DM/$, respectively (quotes apply to a standardized amount in this market, at the time $10 million). If the counterparty chooses to sell $10 million at 1.4750, then the dealer is long $10 million after the transaction. If the market has not moved, and another potential counterparty calls for a quote, this particular dealer will typically shade the price to induce the counterparty to buy—relieving the dealer of his or her long position. For example, this dealer would probably quote bid and offer prices to the next potential counterparty of 1.4749 and 1.4752 DM/$ (versus the original 1.4750 and 1.4753). Relative to the first pair of quotes, the new quote is attractive on the offer side—the 1.4752—but unattractive on the bid side. If the caller goes for the attractive offer quote and buys, then the dealer will have sold the $10 million position at 1.4752 DM/$. The net result of both transactions is that the dealer cleared two-thirds of the spread (two ticks) on two transactions—or one-third of the spread on each transaction.

From the last line of table 3.2 we can see that, under this assumption, this dealer makes most all of his profit from the spread. Of the $507,929 he made over the week, our estimate of the amount that came from intermediation is $472,496. (If I had assumed that the dealer makes half his spread from intermediation, then the profit from intermediation would have been higher than his total profit,

Table 3.2
Summary of DM/$ Dealer's Trading and Profits

	Trans-actions	Volume (mil)	Profit: Actual	Profit: Spread
Monday	333	$1,403	$124,253	$ 95,101
Tuesday	301	$1,105	$ 39,273	$ 74,933
Wednesday	300	$1,157	$ 78,575	$ 78,447
Thursday	328	$1,338	$ 67,316	$ 90,717
Friday	458	$1,966	$198,512	$133,298
Total	1,720	$6,969	$507,929	$472,496

The "Profit: Spread" column reports the profit the dealer would have realized if he had cleared one-third of his spread on every transaction. It is calculated as the dollar volume times one-third the median spread he quoted in the sample (median spread = 0.0003 DM/$), divided by the average DM/$ rate over the sample (1.475 DM/$) from Monday, August 3, to Friday, August 7, 1992.

indicating that he suffered speculative losses.) This is broadly consistent with the idea that, in terms of speculative profits, this market is a zero-sum game. However, the market need not be a zero-sum game in terms of intermediation profits. In that case, customers in this market are paying the dealers, on average, for the liquidity that the dealers provide.[19] Is that compensation inordinate? The data in table 3.2 do not allow us to answer that question because these trades are mostly interdealer trades. A hundred thousand dollars per day is not a bad day's work, though, at least not where I come from.[20]

3.2 Descriptive Statistics: The BIS Surveys

Unlike equity markets, because FX trades are not reported in most countries, marketwide volume in foreign exchange is not generally available. Every three years, however, individual central banks survey their financial institutions regarding FX trading activity (for a single month, typically April), creating a snapshot. Though the latest triennial survey was in April 2001, results are not yet available for the purposes of this book (see BIS 2002). It is useful, nevertheless, to review and interpret key results from the 1998 survey, in part as guidance for readers of future surveys (see the summary in BIS 1999a—available at ⟨www.bis.org⟩—and also individual banks' findings, e.g., Bank of England 1998 and Federal Reserve Bank of New York 1998).[21] This 1998 survey was the fifth triennial survey. Forty-three countries' central banks participated. Because these data provide institutional perspective not available from any other source, they warrant attention here.

Let us begin with the first table in the BIS (1999a) report, reproduced here as table 3.3. This table shows that the $1.5 trillion in daily volume in April 1998 is composed of $600 billion in spot trading and $900 billion in trading of outright forwards and forex swaps. However, as I noted earlier in this chapter, forex swaps have no order flow consequences in the FX market; the net demand impact from this category of FX trading is on relative short-term interest rates, not on the FX market. Of the transaction activity that corresponds to the order flow models of this book, the spot market accounts for $600 billion of $766 billion, or 78 percent. This is an important point that is easily missed by readers of BIS reports.

Table 3.3
Foreign Exchange Market Turnover

Category	April 1989	April 1992	April 1995	April 1998
Spot transactions[1]	350	400	520	600
Outright forwards and forex swaps[1]	240	420	670	900
Total "traditional" turnover	590	820	1,190	1,500
Memorandum item:				
Turnover at April 1998 exchange rates	600	800	1,030	1,500

[1] Includes estimates for gaps in reporting.
Source: BIS 1999a, table A-1, adjusted for local and cross-border double counting. Daily averages in billions of U.S. dollars.

When comparing data across surveys, it is important to keep in mind that the coverage of the survey has changed quite a bit since the first survey in 1986. Only four countries participated in that first survey. In 1989, the number rose to twenty-one (but some countries did not provide all types of information). In 1992, twenty-six countries participated, including all countries with larger FX markets. In 1995, the number of countries remained the same, but the coverage of financial activity was expanded significantly to include FX-related financial derivatives. In 1998, the number of reporting countries increased to forty-three and the coverage of derivatives activity was further expanded.[22]

Subject to the caveat of the previous paragraph, table A-1 of the BIS (1999a) report (not reproduced here) shows that spot turnover increased by 14 percent from 1989–1992, 30 percent from 1992–1995, and 15 percent from 1995–1998. Notice, though, how much the total turnover statistics change when measured at the constant (April 1998) exchange rates. The big change is in the 1995 total turnover, which falls considerably when measured at the April 1998 rates (from $1,190 to $1,030 billion). This is because the dollar was quite weak in April of 1995, particularly against the Japanese yen. Indeed, at the end of April 1995, the yen/$ rate fell to an unprecedented low of about eighty. The translation to April 1998 exchange rates means that each dollar of 1995 turnover is scaled down to reflect that a dollar in April 1995 was worth less than a dollar in April 1998 (when measured against other currencies). If one applies the same constant-rate correction to the spot growth statistics, one finds that the three growth rates cited above—14 percent, 30 percent, and 15 percent—

change to 10 percent, 15 percent, and 33 percent, respectively.[23] This changes the picture from slowing growth to accelerating growth. It will be interesting to see whether the statistics for spot turnover in the April 2001 survey continue this trend of accelerating growth. Currently, many market participants are predicting a slowing of spot-market growth, due to two factors: (1) the collapsing of many European cross markets into the euro, and (2) the more efficient inventory management that is resulting from the dominance of electronic interdealer brokers (which can dampen the hot potato process described in chapter 1).

Another key table in the BIS report is table B-4, which breaks down the turnover statistics by currency pair (reproduced here in table 3.4). As noted earlier in this chapter, the \$/DM and \$/yen spot markets are a good deal larger than any other. Although the dollar versus all other EMS currencies is listed third, most of this trading is in foreign exchange swaps, not spot. (These foreign exchange swap trades—being in fact trades on interest differentials—were probably unusually high in April 1998 due to speculation on the convergence of interest rates in the run-up to the January 1999 launch of the euro.) Note that markets in currencies against the dollar are the largest.[24] These major dollar exchange rates are floating rates (i.e., are market determined, with little intervention on the part of central banks).[25] Not until the DEM/othEMS line does one find rates that are officially pegged (though not rigidly so—these rates were allowed to vary within pre-set bands). Now that trading in the euro has been introduced, there is no need for a DEM/othEMS line in the 2001 survey table (the largest market, USD/DEM, is replaced by the USD/euro).

Table E-1 from the Statistical Annex of BIS 1999a, not reproduced here, provides statistics on spot counterparty types. The table shows an interdealer share of 60 percent (347,689/577,737). Recall that in section 3.1 I described the interdealer share as roughly two-thirds. The central bank surveys upon which the BIS draws tend to underestimate the interdealer share in total trading because the category "other financial institutions" includes some nonreporting investment banks, some of which are important in dealing. (Central banks' role in supervision and regulation applies mainly to commercial banks, so commercial banks are more thoroughly represented in the surveys than investment banks.) The evidence that dealers are included in this "other financial institutions" comes from the fact that this category includes significant brokered trading; FX brokers

Table 3.4
Reported Foreign Exchange Market Turnover by Currency Pair

April 1995

	Total amount	Percentage share		
		Spot	Outright forwards	Foreign exchange swaps
USD/DEM	253.9	56	7	37
USD/JPY	242.0	36	9	55
USD/othEMS	104.3	19	8	73
USD/GBP	77.6	33	7	60
USD/CHF	60.5	37	9	55
USD/FRF	60.0	17	9	74
DEM/othEMS	38.2	74	9	17
USD/CAD	38.2	32	11	57
DEM/FRF	34.4	86	4	9
USD/AUD	28.7	31	7	63
DEM/JPY	24.0	79	12	9
DEM/GBP	21.3	84	6	10
DEM/CHF	18.4	86	6	7
USD/XEU	17.9	11	7	82
All currency pairs	1,136.9	43	9	48

April 1998

	Total amount	Percentage share		
		Spot	Outright forwards	Foreign exchange swaps
USD/DEM	290.5	49	8	43
USD/JPY	266.6	45	10	44
USD/othEMS	175.8	14	7	79
USD/GBP	117.7	33	9	59
USD/CHF	78.6	30	7	62
USD/FRF	57.9	16	8	76
USD/CAD	50.0	25	6	68
USD/AUD	42.2	33	8	59
DEM/othEMS	35.1	75	12	13
DEM/GBP	30.7	79	10	11
DEM/JPY	24.2	77	14	9
DEM/CHF	18.4	85	7	8
USD/XEU	16.6	7	4	89
USD/SGD	17.2	71	2	27
All currency pairs	1,441.5	40	9	51

USD = U.S. dollar, DEM = Deutsche mark, JPY = Japanese yen, othEMS = other EMS (European Monetary System) currencies, GBP = British pound, CHF = Swiss franc, FRF = French franc, CAD = Canadian dollar, AUD = Australian dollar, XEU = European currency unit (a basket currency that includes all European Union members), and SGD = Singapore dollar.
Source: BIS, 1999a, table B-4. Daily averages in billions of U.S. dollars and percentage shares.

are strictly interdealer, though, so these trades belong in the interdealer category. It is difficult to know how much this biases the survey-measured interdealer share downward; my adjustment from 60 percent to two-thirds is an educated guesstimate.

Section 7 of the BIS (1999a) report provides some information on the share of interdealer trading that is brokered and the degree to which these brokered trades are handled by electronic brokers, rather than the traditional voice-based brokers.[26] Because this section is not linked to specific tables, one needs to be cautious in interpreting the data. For example, one needs to take care to distinguish statistics that apply to total FX turnover, as opposed to spot turnover. (This is important throughout the BIS report.) One particularly useful sentence in that section is the following: "Electronic brokers now handle almost one quarter of total spot transactions in the UK market."[27] That represents nearly one-half of all interdealer spot transactions (because, per above, the survey finds that interdealer transactions are roughly 60 percent of total spot transactions). To arrive at a more complete picture of the share and type of brokered trading—electronic versus voice-based—one needs to piece together data from the individual central bank reports.

3.3   Transparency of Order Flow

Any model that includes order flow as a proximate determinant of price must also specify who observes that order flow. In microstructure research, this is called transparency. The term transparency is broader than just the observability of order flow, however. It is defined to encompass the full array of information types that the trading process might transmit. The three primary categories include

1. pre-trade versus post-trade information
2. price versus order flow (quantity) information
3. public versus dealer information

Applying this three-part taxonomy to chapter two's discussion of order flow information, we see that the material of that chapter relates most directly to the (1) post-trade (2) order flow information that is (3) available to dealers. In equity markets, this issue—what post-trade order flow information is seen, and by whom—is at the heart of current policy debates.[28] Theoretically, too, post-trade order flow information is the most relevant because it is the main communicator of shifts in asset demand. When interpreting this information as shifts in asset demand, however, one needs to be precise. One cannot infer the *sign* of a shift in demand from the information that, say, ten units just traded. One needs to know whether the trade represents buying or selling pressure. The trade needs to be signed—it needs to be converted from trading volume to order flow.

Actual markets differ radically in terms of order flow transparency. In equity markets, the transparency regime is typically imposed (e.g., regimes are imposed on the London Stock Exchange, the NYSE, and NASDAQ). On the London Stock Exchange, for example, the price and size of smaller trades must be disclosed within three minutes, whereas disclosure of the largest trades can be delayed up to five business days. FX markets, in contrast, have no disclosure requirements. For this reason, FX is particularly interesting because its degree of transparency has arisen without regulatory influence.[29] With no disclosure requirements, it is perhaps not surprising that most FX trades do not generate public order flow information. But, as described earlier in this chapter, *some* trades do generate widely available order flow information. Interestingly, these trades—the brokered interdealer trades—produce a level of transparency that arises as a by-product of dealer's selective use of this trading method. The FX market is therefore not an example of purposeful transparency regime design, as is true for most equity markets.

The only other financial markets similar to FX in terms of low transparency are other nonequity OTC markets. (OTC, or over-the-counter, simply means not traded on a centralized exchange.) These include the U.S. bond markets and much of trading in derivatives. With the advent of centralized electronic trading in these other markets, however, they are on the way to becoming more transparent than the FX market.[30]

Now that we have a better sense from section 3.1 for how transparency arises in the FX market, we can examine the impact of this transparency on price determination. In markets that are highly transparent, all participants observe order flow, thereby affecting expectations—and prices—rapidly and precisely. In opaque markets, order flow is not widely observed, so the information it conveys may be impounded in price more slowly.[31] The FX market is opaque with respect to customer-dealer order flow. As noted, however, interdealer FX transactions are not completely opaque. One of the models I present in chapter 4 captures this differential dissemination of order flow information, depending on order flow type.

For market design, determining which participants see what, and when, is central. At a broad level, the key tradeoff that concerns policymakers is the following: Though greater transparency can accelerate revelation of information in price, it can also impede dealers' ability to manage risk. Full transparency may therefore not be optimal, which must be considered when designing a transparency regime. Board and Sutcliffe (1995, 2) make the point this way: "The purpose of a transparency regime is to allow marketmakers to offset inventory risk by trading before the market as a whole is aware of the large trade." It is unclear, however, whether the current low level of transparency of the FX market is optimal from the social perspective. Because low transparency has arisen without regulatory influence, a reasonable premise is that low transparency serves the interests of dealers. (Lyons 1996a provides a model in which this is true; dealers prefer low transparency because it slows the pace at which price reflects information, enabling dealers to better manage risk—in keeping with the logic of the Board and Sutcliffe passage above.)

But if low transparency is an "equilibrium" outcome in the FX market, how is that equilibrium maintained? It is unlikely to result from collusion, which is difficult to maintain in competitive, decentralized markets. More likely is that equilibrium low transparency arises as a kind of externality—a by-product of dealers' individual decisions to trade using brokers (i.e., to trade using a transparent method). A fact broadly consistent with this view is that actual transparency levels produced by brokered trading are quite similar across the world's trading centers: the share of total trading that is brokered has historically remained in the 20–40 percent range in all the major trading centers (BIS 1996). Though it is true that dealers have other reasons for using brokers, such as anonymity, brokered trading does determine transparency, so dealers are choosing transparency *de facto*. From a welfare perspective this is an important issue in institution design.

3.4 Moving Beyond Institutions

In many people's minds, there is a powerful association between the field of microstructure and the study of institutions. The association is natural, but also a bit deceptive. It is true that institution design is one of the "poles" within the microstructure literature; the material presented in this chapter is suggestive of this pole. But there is a second pole—the economics of financial market information. This book is aligned more with the second pole. To emphasize this, I presented the information framework in chapter 2, before this chapter on institutions. Later chapters, too, reflect primarily this second pole: they present models and methods that characterize how, in reality, the FX market aggregates dispersed information. The questions addressed within this second pole are of a broader nature than institution design.

Let me provide some more concrete examples of how microstructure's "information" pole extends beyond its "institutions" pole. The first example relates to order flow and the sense in which order flow's role is not about institutions. Within microstructure, order flow is an information transmission mechanism, and, crucially, it operates regardless of market structure type. Given this rather general property of order flow, it would be a mistake to attribute its information role to a specific institutional configuration. Pushing further, for reasons apart from institutions per se, order flow's information role has the potential to realign modeling strategy—at least within exchange rate economics. To understand why, recall from chapter 1 that within traditional exchange rate economics, order flow's role in transmitting information was not considered. This omission is evident from surveys of macro-style empirical work. Consider, for example, Meese's (1990, 130) survey, where he writes: "Omitted variables is another possible explanation for the lack of explanatory power in asset market models. However, empirical researchers have shown considerable imagination in their specification searches, so it is not easy to think of variables that have escaped consideration in an exchange rate equation."

It is hard to argue with Meese's point from a macro perspective. But the macro perspective considers only variables within the traditional macroeconomic set. From the microstructure perspective, there is indeed a variable that escaped macro consideration—order flow. Microstructure has opened macroeconomists' minds to the idea that order flow can serve as a real-time measure of dispersed information about changing fundamentals.

Let me illustrate further why order flow's role has little to do with institutions per se. Consider the following thought experiment: suppose spot FX markets began to trade in a completely centralized auction format (akin to the Paris Bourse or Hong Kong Stock Exchange, as described above).[32] Would the microstructure approach still be useful? Yes, because order flow would still be a determinant of prices. True, one would need to measure order flow in a different way, because the passive (noninitiating) side of each trade would now be a limit order rather than a dealer's quote (see chapter 1). But with this changed measure of order flow, one could then produce the same analysis of how order flow determines exchange rates that I present in later chapters. It is unlikely that this would change the main results in a qualitative way: the underlying information structure of this market has more to do with the properties of the asset being traded—foreign exchange—than it does with the market structure per se, particularly at lower frequencies.

Analysis of crashes and collapses is a second example of how microstructure addresses questions of a broader nature than institution design. The global stock market crash of 1987 attracted tremendous research attention, much of it set within microstructure models (see, e.g., Gennotte and Leland 1990; Jacklin, Kleiden, and Pfleiderer 1992). Note, however, that equity prices collapsed across a host of different market structure types (e.g., the specialist-market NYSE, the dealer-market NASDAQ, and several auction-type stock markets around the world as well). Because the crash was common to markets with different structures, one might argue that microstructure cannot help us understand the crash. But this would be too extreme: by providing a disciplined approach to complex information problems, microstructure models provide a useful way to understand crashes and collapses. This kind of analysis moves beyond narrow institutional concerns such as how auction and dealer markets differ.

Microstructure Effects versus Microstructure Approach

The term microstructure effects is commonly used, particularly among people who do not work in microstructure. The concept deserves attention in this chapter on institutions because its connection to institutions is quite close. People typically use the term to refer to *temporary* effects on prices that arise from specific institutional features. As such, the term pertains more to the institutions pole of microstructure than the information pole. I place emphasis on the word "temporary" because the term microstructure effects is most

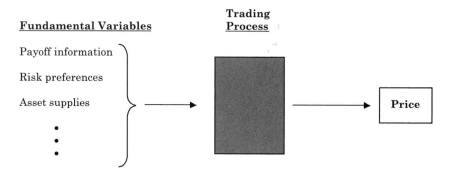

Figure 3.3
Microstructure effects question: Does trading process affect mapping?

often used to describe fleeting effects on asset prices that, at lower frequencies, are unlikely to be significant.

Figure 3.3 provides a graphic representation of microstructure effects and where they arise in the process of price determination. The lefthand column lists certain fundamental variables that might drive equilibrium prices. These variables do not, however, translate directly into price. Rather, they are inputs to the trading process, represented by the gray box. The microstructure effects "question" is whether the trading process alters the mapping from fundamental variables to price, and if so, for how long. The presumption is that it probably does, but that these effects are short-lived.

What is it that people really have in mind when they use the term microstructure effects? Though there is no explicit definition, in my judgment people use the term to refer to two particular types of effects. The first type is the temporary inventory effects described in chapter 2 (and diagrammed in figure 2.1). As an empirical matter, inventory effects in FX are indeed likely to be short-lived: As noted in section 3.1, the half-life of a dealer's inventory in FX is very short (ten minutes for the dealer whose inventory appears in figure 3.2).

The second type of microstructure effect that people often have in mind is the price effect from order flow as it accelerates the impounding of payoff information. The word "accelerate" is important here for understanding why this effect, too, might be only temporary. Consider the example of a pending earnings release by a firm and the possibility that insider trading prior to the announcement might signal the size of those earnings. Figure 3.4 provides an illus-

Price

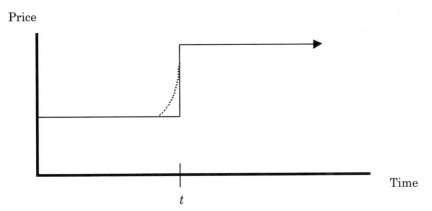

Time

t

Figure 3.4
Accelerationist view of order flow information. The solid line shows a hypothetical
price path for a stock under the assumption that price responds to a higher than
expected public earnings announcement at time t. The dotted line shows the price path
under the assumption that insider trading (buying) in advance of the announcement is
pushing price up.

tration. The solid line is the price path under the assumption that the
market responds to the (positive) public earnings announcement
only. The dotted line shows how the price path would look if, in
addition, the market were to respond to informative order flow
occurring prior to the public announcement. The difference in the
two paths is only temporary here because the announcement reveals
all the information contained in the prior order flow (and then some).
    If, as an empirical matter, order flow were conveying only infor-
mation that is on the verge of public announcement, then one would
be justified in treating its effects as temporary, in the sense portrayed
in figure 3.4. However, this is certainly not the case for the FX market. Order flow's important role in determining exchange rates—
documented in later chapters—is virtually unrelated to macroeconomic news that arrives within the subsequent year. The tight relation
between order flow and exchange rates is not, therefore, simply the
result of short-run acceleration of public information flow. Over the
longer run, whether order flow conveys information about more
distant macro policies has yet to be determined. This is an active
topic of ongoing research, one that I return to in chapter 7.
    I raise the notion of microstructure effects because depicting
the field of microstructure in this limited way can affect research

strategies. Let me provide an example that is embedded in the discussion above about analyzing crashes and collapses. In that discussion, I made the point that although the crash occurred across several different market structure types, microstructure analysis was still fruitful for specifying information problems that can lead to a crash. More generally, people less familiar with microstructure are prone to assert that microstructure cannot resolve any puzzle that (1) is common to markets with different structures or (2) is not common to markets with the same structure. As an example of the former, it might be argued that although (apparent) excess volatility is a property of both equity and FX markets, because the NYSE and FX markets have different structures, microstructure cannot help to resolve the excess volatility puzzle. This reasoning, in my judgment, is too oriented toward the institutions pole of microstructure. Effective use of information models within microstructure may indeed help to resolve puzzles in the FX market, even if the same puzzles occur in other, differently structured markets. Chapters 7 through 9 make this case.

4   Theoretical Frameworks

This chapter provides an overview of microstructure theory. It is only an overview because, in a single chapter, there simply is not enough room to present the main models in depth. Instead, my objective is to design a road map that people unfamiliar with microstructure can use for navigation. To make the map easy to follow, I present each model beginning with that model's most valuable insights. Also, I present simple—and less general—versions of each model in order to communicate the underlying economics as efficiently as possible. Clarity on the underlying economics is important for understanding the later chapters' applications.[1]

There are four distinct models in this chapter:

1. Rational expectations auction model
2. Kyle auction model
3. Sequential-trade model
4. Simultaneous-trade model

Together, these four models span the three categories of markets introduced in chapter 3: auction, single dealer, and multiple dealer. The first two models use an auction structure, whereas the third and fourth use a dealer structure. (Recall that in a dealer market, the best available price is defined by dealer quotes, in contrast to an auction market, where best available price is defined by submitted orders. Based on these differing sources of best price, dealer markets are sometimes referred to as "quote-driven" markets, whereas auction markets are sometimes referred to as "order-driven" markets.[2]) The third model—the sequential-trade model—is a single-dealer market: only one dealer sets prices. The fourth model—the simultaneous-trade model—is a multiple-dealer market: many dealers participate

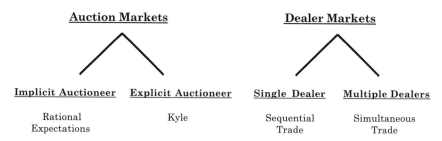

Figure 4.1
A bird's-eye view of microstructure models.

in price setting. We can organize the four models as shown in figure 4.1.

The rational expectations model of securities trading is a natural first model for this chapter, even though it is not typically classified as a microstructure model. Opening with this model clarifies how its shortcomings spurred the development of later microstructure models. Among these shortcomings is that the act of setting prices is not addressed in the model; there are no participants whose job it is to set prices. When pressed about where these prices actually come from, people who work with these models typically refer to a Walrasian auctioneer, a hypothetical agent outside the model who collects orders, sets price based on these orders, and executes the orders at the market-clearing price he sets.[3] The other models I present in this chapter, in contrast, are explicit about who sets price and what information is available for doing so (i.e., they address what really happens when the rubber meets the road). Another reason I include the rational expectations trading model within this theoretical overview is that distinguishing it from microstructure models is becoming increasingly difficult. For example, in the introduction to his paper on bilateral trading, Wolinsky (1990, 3) refers to a recent literature that "looks at the microstructure of rational-expectations equilibrium." This phrasing signals a growing connection between these literatures. Recent papers on central bank intervention in FX markets provide more evidence of connection; these papers' use of the rational expectations model fits comfortably within the microstructure approach (see chapter 8).

The Kyle (1985) model is a natural follow-up to the rational expectations model. As noted, both models have an auction structure. The key difference is that the Kyle model addresses the act of setting price explicitly. This is achieved by introducing an actual auctioneer to replace the hypothetical auctioneer of the rational expectations model. Kyle's auctioneer has privileged information about order flow and uses that information to determine the market-clearing price. In addition to his auctioneer role, he also takes speculative positions. Because the protocol that governs trading is specified in detail in the Kyle model (in contrast to the rational expectations model), the Kyle auctioneer's price setting and speculative decisions are fully specified. This produces an intimate link between trading protocol and price determination, a hallmark of microstructure modeling.

The Kyle model is not classified as a dealership market because dealer quotes do not define the best available price. The Kyle auctioneer therefore does not share a characteristic that is true of dealers—that they first provide other individuals with a quote, and then orders are submitted conditional on that quote. Rather, orders are submitted to the Kyle auctioneer before price is determined, and the Kyle auctioneer then determines a market-clearing price based on those orders.

The sequential-trade model—our third model—is the first of the two dealership models. A single optimizing dealer determines the best price before any orders are submitted. Thus, the trading protocol of this model is more "dealer-like" than the auction market models. Also, because orders are executed sequentially (one by one), this model provides a framework for analyzing individual orders. This contrasts with the Kyle model, where all orders are batched and executed simultaneously at a single market-clearing price.

The simultaneous-trade model—our fourth model—recognizes that the institutional settings of the previous three models are quite different from that in FX. All three previous models adopt a centralized market structure, which contrasts sharply with the FX market's decentralized, multiple-dealer structure. The simultaneous-trade model is designed to fit this FX market structure. It also has features that are consistent with empirical results on FX markets, such as dealer aversion to risk. (The sequential-trade and Kyle models assume the dealer/auctioneer is risk neutral.) Empirically, there is strong evidence that FX dealers behave in a risk-averse way, as we shall see in chapter 5. Introducing this feature, and the attendant management of risk by dealers, has implications for trading volume and price efficiency.

I should be clear from the outset that all four of the models I present below qualify as information models. Information models constitute one of two broad modeling approaches within microstructure theory. The other is inventory models. The purpose of information models is to explain permanent price adjustment toward a *changed* expected future payoff (payoff information was defined in chapter 2). Order flow is what induces this price adjustment—it conveys information about these future payoffs. The focus of inventory models, on the other hand, is transitory price variation around a *fixed* expected future payoff (chapter two's inventory effects). Order flow is central to inventory models as well, though in this case it affects price by influencing dealer inventories.[4] Maintaining inventories in these models is costly because it exposes the dealer to risk; the need to compensate dealers for these costs is what drives price adjustment.

Though all four models I present are information models, two are pure information models and two have both information-model and inventory-model features. The common thread, the information component, is in my judgment integral to the link between microstructure and exchange rate economics. Though both approaches are relevant, if pure inventory models were all there were to the microstructure approach—that is, transitory price variation due to changing dealer inventories—then there would be little hope of resolving the big exchange rate puzzles.[5] Consider, for example, the puzzle of what determines exchange rates at lower frequencies. Lower frequency exchange rates, by their nature, are a function of persistent variation, not transitory variation, so inventory effects alone are not sufficient for resolving this puzzle.

4.1 An Implicit Auctioneer: The Rational Expectations Model

For perspective on the rational expectations auction model, it is helpful at the outset to distinguish between two types of equilibria. These equilibrium types are

1. fully revealing equilibrium
2. partially revealing equilibrium

In a fully revealing equilibrium, all information is embedded in price, including private information (so-called strong-form efficiency). More formally, in a fully revealing equilibrium, price is a "sufficient statistic" for the underlying fundamental, making private signals redundant in an information sense.[6] Conversely, in a partially revealing equilibrium, price reflects a combination of private information and extraneous noise. The early literature on rational expectations trading focuses primarily on fully revealing equilibria. Later papers focus more on partially revealing equilibria. The secret to producing partially revealing equilibria, which are more true to life, is to add sources of noise to the trading process that make it hard to disentangle the causes of price movements. For example, consider adding noise related to asset supply to a model with private information. With the additional source of noise, when price rises people cannot tell whether the cause is more positive private information or smaller asset supply, because both would push price up. These partially revealing equilibria have important theoretical implications, as we see below.

Insights

With these equilibrium categories clarified, here is a summary of some of the key insights from the rational expectations model.

1. Price plays two roles: it clears markets *and* conveys information.

2. In a fully revealing equilibrium, an individual's asset demand depends only on price, not on any private signals received by the individual.

3. In a fully revealing equilibrium, there is no incentive to invest in costly information; this incentive is restored in a partially revealing equilibrium.

Let me comment briefly on each of these before moving to the model's specifics. Insight (1) is the most fundamental of the three. The traditional role of price in determining equilibrium is a simple market-clearing role: price changes to eliminate excess demand/supply. To clarify this traditional role, consider a financial market equilibrium based wholly on this role, that is, an equilibrium in which individuals neglect price's information role.[7] Because individuals neglect the information in price, price has no effect on expectations, so each individual's demand is a function of his own information only. The market-clearing price that would result would be a function of all these individual bits of information. That is the in-

consistency: the equilibrium price would reflect everybody's information, but individuals are acting as though price is uninformative.
Neglecting the information in price this way would be patently irrational. By bringing the information role of prices to center stage, the
rational expectations model provides a valuable framework for analyzing price as an information aggregator.

Insights (2) and (3) are related. They are often called the two
"paradoxes" of the rational expectations model. Insight (2) is a consequence of each individual's private signal being redundant when
price is fully revealing. The paradox arises when one recognizes that,
although the equilibrium price fully aggregates all private information, individual demands are conditioned wholly on that equilibrium
price—individuals neglect their own private information. But private information cannot get into price if individuals are not using
their private information in determining their demands. In a partially revealing equilibrium, this paradox does not arise because individual demands are conditioned on price *and* private information.
The second paradox, associated with insight (3), is that in a fully
revealing equilibrium there is no incentive for individuals to acquire
their own private information—it would be reflected in price before
a profitable position could be opened. So if private information can
only be acquired at a cost (e.g., by investing in better research), then
nobody will acquire it, and there will be no private information
to aggregate. This paradox, too, does not arise in a partially revealing equilibrium because when one acquires private information, a
profitable position can be opened before price can fully reflect that
information.

The Model

The following Grossman-Stiglitz (1980) version of the rational
expectations auction model is widely used. Because it includes both
private information and noise in asset supply, its equilibrium only
partially reveals private information. The model has two traders,
both of whom are risk averse and nonstrategic (nonstrategic meaning that they act as perfect competitors and take market prices as
given). There is a single risky asset and a single trading period.[8]
Within the single trading period, there are three events, shown in
figure 4.2.

The value of the risky asset's end-of-period payoff is denoted here
as V, a Normally distributed random variable with mean zero and

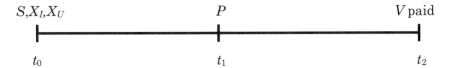

S, X_I, X_U $\qquad\qquad\qquad\qquad\qquad$ P $\qquad\qquad\qquad\qquad\qquad$ V paid

t_0 $\qquad\qquad\qquad\qquad\qquad\qquad\quad$ t_1 $\qquad\qquad\qquad\qquad\qquad\quad$ t_2

Figure 4.2
Timing of rational expectations model.

variance σ_V^2.[9] Before V is paid or observed, the risky asset is traded at price P. Initially, before trading at price P, one of the two traders is "informed," meaning that he receives private information about V in the form of a signal S. Though only the informed trader observes the signal S, both traders know that S is Normally distributed, with mean V and variance σ_S^2. We specify this signal as

$$S = V + \varepsilon,$$

where the noise in the signal S, denoted ε, has a mean of zero and a variance denoted as σ_ε^2. The other trader is "uninformed," meaning that he has not observed S and therefore does not have an information motive for trading.

The uninformed trader does, however, have a hedging motive for trading. In fact, both traders have a hedging motive for trading. Each trader initially receives a random endowment in units of the risky asset—for example, shares or euros—which we denote X_I and X_U (I and U denote the informed and uninformed trader, respectively). Each endowment is Normally distributed, with mean zero and variance σ_X^2.[10] We denote the aggregate supply of the risky asset by X, where $X = X_I + X_U$. (If $X_I > X_U$, then based purely on hedging motives, one would expect the informed trader to be selling to the uninformed trader, other things equal.) X_I and X_U are distributed independently of one another and independently of the signal S and the payoff V.

The exponential utility function we use here is used throughout microstructure theory. This utility function is so prominent in the literature that a good portion of the appendix to this chapter is dedicated to explaining its properties and appeal. It is defined over end-of-period dollar wealth W:[11]

$$U(W) = -\exp(-W). \tag{4.1}$$

This utility function has two convenient properties. First, the risky-asset demands that it implies do not depend on wealth, so realloca-

Players:	• 1 informed trader (risk averse, perfect competitor)
	• 1 uninformed trader (risk averse, perfect competitor)

Players:
- 1 informed trader (risk averse, perfect competitor)
- 1 uninformed trader (risk averse, perfect competitor)

Information:
- final payoff V of risky asset distributed Normal(0, σ_V^2)
- informed trader has private information about V
- uninformed sees only market-clearing price P

Institutions:
- single trading period
- batch clearing: all trades cleared at single price
- consistency of conjectured and actual pricing rule

Figure 4.3
Summary of rational expectations auction model.

tion of wealth in the trading process does not affect equilibrium. This obviates the need to keep track of individuals' trading gains/losses. Second, when coupled with the assumption that returns are Normally distributed, this exponential utility function produces a demand function for the risky asset that takes a simple linear form.

At the center of rational expectations models is the pricing rule, which describes how the model's random variables determine equilibrium price. All traders know the pricing rule. (An implication of knowing the rule is that the uninformed trader can use the rule, together with the market price, to back out information about the informed trader's signal.) In rational expectations equilibrium, the pricing rule must meet two conditions: the first is the "rational expectations" part and the second is the "equilibrium" part:

Conditions for Rational Expectations Equilibrium

1. Expectations of the payoff V are consistent with the equilibrium pricing rule.
2. Markets always clear, that is, excess demand equals zero for all random variable realizations.

When solving for equilibrium below, I will show that the proposed equilibrium conforms to these rational expectations conditions. (See figure 4.3 for a summary of the model's key features.)

Solving for Equilibrium
We solve for equilibrium in this type of model "by construction," that is, by proposing a pricing rule and then verifying that it meets

the two conditions above. Our assumptions about utility and Normal distributions give us a basis for proposing a linear pricing rule. As usual, though, it is not a priori clear what the content of that linear rule should be (or that an equilibrium rule need even be linear). The initial conjecture is a matter of judgment and experience. The following conjectured rule does in the end meet the two equilibrium conditions, but this is far from obvious at this stage:

$$P = \alpha S - \beta X \qquad (4.2)$$

The key components are the realized signal S and the realized risky-asset supply X. These are natural choices for the proposed rule: they are the random variables on which asset demands are based. The remaining random variable V is not a candidate because the payoff V is not observable at the time of trading. Values for the constants α and β are determined at the end of the solution process in a manner that makes them consistent with optimizing behavior of both traders.

There are three additional steps to solving for equilibrium. First, we need expressions for each trader's expectation of the payoff V; these must be consistent with the equilibrium pricing rule. Second, based on these expectations of V from step one, we need expressions for each trader's risky-asset demand. Finally, we use those demands to find a market-clearing price that matches the proposed pricing rule in equation (4.2). Then we will have our rational expectations equilibrium, because it conforms to equilibrium condition (2). In that equilibrium, expectations are formed using the correct pricing rule, conforming to condition (1).

Expectations
Expressions for traders' expectations are not difficult to produce in this setting. This is particularly true in the case of the informed trader because the informed trader learns only from his own signal —he knows the other trader is uninformed. In the appendix to this chapter, I show why we can write the informed trader's posterior beliefs about the payoff V conditional on his signal S as *Normally distributed* with

$$E[V\,|\,S] = \left(\frac{\sigma_S^{-2}}{\sigma_S^{-2} + \sigma_V^{-2}}\right)S \quad \text{and} \quad \mathrm{Var}[V\,|\,S] = \left(\frac{1}{\sigma_S^{-2} + \sigma_V^{-2}}\right).$$

These expressions make intuitive sense. As σ_S^2—the variance of the signal S about V—goes to infinity (a weaker signal), $E[V\,|\,S]$ goes to the unconditional expectation of V, or $E[V] = 0$, and $\text{Var}[V \mid S]$ goes to the unconditional variance of V, or σ_V^2. These are the unconditional mean and variance of V. As σ_S^2 goes to zero (a stronger signal), $E[V \mid S]$ goes to S and $\text{Var}[V \mid S]$ goes to zero.

The uninformed trader's expectation is, by definition, not based on any private signal. Rather, the uninformed trader extracts all his information from price, which, in equilibrium, will embed information from the informed trader's trades.[12] Equilibrium price thus becomes a kind of "signal" for the uninformed. What the uninformed trader would like to know is the additional information observed by the informed trader, the signal S. To use price to make inferences about S, the uninformed trader can use the proposed pricing rule—in particular its parameters α and β—to transform price P into a second signal that is distributed about S. Specifically, starting from the pricing rule

$$P = \alpha S - \beta X,$$

the uninformed trader can divide the price P that he observes by α to yield:[13]

$$P/\alpha = S - (\beta/\alpha)X.$$

This variable P/α is distributed around a mean of S—the information the uninformed trader wants to know. (Neither the informed nor the uninformed know the value of X, a point I return to below.) For notational convenience, I will use Z to denote this second signal:

$$Z = P/\alpha = S - (\beta/\alpha)X.$$

Because $S \sim N(V, \sigma_S^2)$, $X \sim N(0, 2\sigma_X^2)$, and S and X are independent, we know that Z is distributed Normally about V with variance $\sigma_Z^2 = \sigma_S^2 + 2(\beta/\alpha)^2 \sigma_X^2$. (I have introduced the notation "$\sim$" to denote "distributed.") With this value for σ_Z^2, the uninformed trader's posterior distribution is Normally distributed about V with

$$E[V \mid P, \alpha, \beta] = \left(\frac{\sigma_Z^{-2}}{\sigma_Z^{-2} + \sigma_V^{-2}} \right) Z \quad \text{and} \quad \text{Var}[V \mid P, \alpha, \beta] = \left(\frac{1}{\sigma_Z^{-2} + \sigma_V^{-2}} \right).$$

Knowledge of the pricing-rule coefficients α and β is clearly vital to the uninformed trader's inference. I recognize them explicitly as conditioning information to highlight that fact. Note too that neither the informed trader nor the uninformed trader conditions on the realization of his own endowment—X_I and X_U, respectively—because they are assumed to be nonstrategic (i.e., to take price as given). (Below I address this assumption of nonstrategic behavior in more detail.)[14]

Demand

Expressions for traders' demand are not difficult to produce as long as expected returns conditional on available information are still Normally distributed. From the analysis above, we know that both trader's posterior distributions are Normal. Given this, and our exponential utility specification, the demand functions for the informed trader D^I and the uninformed trader D^U—in units of the risky asset, for example, shares or euros—take the following form (see appendix for details):

$$D^I = \frac{E[V \mid S] - P}{\text{Var}[V \mid S]}$$

$$D^U = \frac{E[V \mid P, \alpha, \beta] - P}{\text{Var}[V \mid P, \alpha, \beta]}. \tag{4.3}$$

Note the information role that price plays in the demand of the uninformed trader (it enters in the conditional expectation and conditional variance).

Inserting the values above for $E[V \mid S]$ and $\text{Var}[V \mid S]$ into this expression for D^I and D^U yields the following:

$$D^I = (\sigma_S^{-2})S - (\sigma_S^{-2} + \sigma_V^{-2})P$$

$$D^U = (\sigma_Z^{-2})Z - (\sigma_Z^{-2} + \sigma_V^{-2})P. \tag{4.4}$$

Market-Clearing Price

Market-clearing price is determined by equating demand with supply so that excess demand is zero:

$$D^I + D^U = X.$$

Inserting our expressions from equation (4.4) for D^I and D^U in this market-clearing condition yields a price of

$$P = \alpha S - \beta X, \tag{4.5}$$

where

$$\alpha = \left(\frac{\sigma_Z^{-2} + \sigma_S^{-2}}{\sigma_Z^{-2} + \sigma_S^{-2} + 2\sigma_V^{-2}} \right)$$

$$\beta = \left(\frac{1}{\sigma_Z^{-2}(1 - \alpha^{-1}) + \sigma_S^{-2} + 2\sigma_V^{-2}} \right).$$

(Recall that σ_Z^2 was defined above as $\sigma_S^2 + 2(\beta/\alpha)^2 \sigma_X^2$.) These values for α and β insure that excess demand equals zero for all random-variable realizations, which fulfills condition (2) above for rational expectations equilibrium. Further, we imposed in our derivation of these coefficient values that the pricing rule used to form expectations is the actual rule used to determine price. This fulfills equilibrium condition (1) above. Thus, we have verified what we set out to verify: that the conjectured pricing rule in equation (4.2) describes a rational expectations equilibrium.

This equilibrium is partially revealing, a fact evident from the uninformed trader's expectation. Specifically, the uninformed trader does not know as much in equilibrium as the informed trader, as shown by the distributions of posterior expectations. Recall that the variance of the informed trader's posterior expectation is

$$\text{Var}[V \mid S] = \left(\frac{1}{\sigma_S^{-2} + \sigma_V^{-2}} \right),$$

and the variance of the uninformed trader's posterior expectation is

$$\text{Var}[V \mid P, \alpha, \beta] = \left(\frac{1}{\sigma_Z^{-2} + \sigma_V^{-2}} \right).$$

The only difference is the replacement of σ_S^2 with σ_Z^2, where σ_Z^2 has a value of $\sigma_S^2 + 2(\beta/\alpha)^2 \sigma_X^2$. Because $2(\beta/\alpha)^2 \sigma_X^2$ must be positive, σ_Z^2 must be larger than σ_S^2, so the variance of the uninformed trader's posterior expectation is larger.

The Implicit Auctioneer
I began this chapter by framing the two auction-market models—rational expectations and Kyle—as the difference between an implicit auctioneer and an explicit auctioneer. Yet the model description above makes no reference to an implicit auctioneer, so let me clarify. Strictly speaking, the rational expectations model does not require an auctioneer, which is why the specification above contains no reference to one. Nevertheless, the fiction of an implicit, Walra-

sian auctioneer is the traditional way to envision how prices are actually set in rational expectations models. The implicit auctioneer collects the "preliminary orders" (described in chapter 1), and uses them to find the model's market-clearing price. Without a story like this in the background, there is no way to understand how price is actually determined in real time—the model requires only that price clears the market and is consistent with expectations. By introducing an explicit auctioneer, the Kyle auction model brings this process of price determination from a background abstraction to the foreground.

Discussion

I close this section with four drawbacks of standard rational expectations modeling.[15]

Generality

A common concern in this literature is that examples like the one used above cannot be generalized to more complex model settings. The problem is that for a given model, a rational expectations equilibrium may not exist (i.e., the two conditions for rational expectations equilibrium cannot be met). This is important: models without an equilibrium are not very useful. Whether an equilibrium exists, and what properties it has if it does exist, depends on a particular feature of the model's specification: the number of signals relative to the number of assets. In the simple specification I present here, the number of signals and the number of assets are the same, namely one. When these numbers are not the same, the existence of an equilibrium becomes more fragile. Accordingly, some concern about generality is warranted.

Nonstrategic Behavior

Notice from the demand function in equation (4.3) that the informed trader takes the current price as given. Thus, he does not exploit the fact that his trade has a direct effect on that price (though, by definition, expectations are validated in equilibrium). This is often referred to as the "schizophrenia problem" inherent in these models: the effect that individuals' trades have on price is not negligible, but these traders behave like perfect competitors (price takers) nonetheless.

Knowledge of Pricing Rule

As noted above, the uninformed trader needs to condition his demand on the pricing rule—in this case the values of α and β. As a practical matter, it is not clear how he acquires such knowledge; this is not specified within this modeling approach. Individuals may be able to learn the rule over time, in which case the rational expectations equilibrium might be considered a long-run steady state. Research on learning to form such pricing rules shows this can be problematic, however.

Order Flow

The pricing rule at the center of the rational expectations model treats demands (orders) symmetrically. Consequently, trades cannot be split into an active (or initiating) side and a passive side (recall the definition of order flow in section 1.2). The model therefore provides no guidance for empirical work on the links among order flow, information, and price. It is this feature, more than any other, that makes this model less of a "microstructure" model than the other models of this chapter.

The four drawbacks above are at least partially addressed in the models to come. There is no question that the models to come have their own generality problems, so I have little to add on that count. The second and third drawbacks, however, are largely assuaged by the other models. For example, they incorporate strategic behavior. Also, the models below do not rely on a pricing-rule conjecture. Rather, they introduce an explicit price setter, who optimizes subject to the constraints imposed by the model. The fourth drawback is a nonissue in the other models because they provide a clear means of signing order flow according to which counterparty initiates the trade.

4.2   An Explicit Auctioneer: The Kyle Model

The Kyle (1985) model and the rational expectations model are close cousins. Both have an auction market structure, and at the heart of both is an expectations-consistent pricing rule. The key conceptual difference is that the Kyle model includes an explicit auctioneer rather than an implicit one. This changes the nature of the pricing rule because the act of price setting is now assigned to a player within the model. Introducing an explicit auctioneer also introduces an information dimension that is missing in the rational expectations model. Specifically, the auctioneer can only use available information for determining price, but the information available to the auctioneer is determined by the trading protocol itself. This produces an intimate link between trading protocol and price.

Before presenting the model, let me clarify my use of the term auctioneer. The presence of an auctioneer in the Kyle model provides a link to the Walrasian auctioneer that is implicit in the rational expectations model. The term also reminds us that both of these models are auction models. However, the Kyle auctioneer does more than just set prices: he also takes trading positions and has privileged access to order flow information. In many ways, then, he shares features commonly associated with dealers (even though this is not a dealer-market setting). The literature commonly uses the term marketmaker for hybrid cases like this. Henceforth, I will also use the term marketmaker in the context of the Kyle model.

Insights

The Kyle model presented below generates many insights. Relative to the rational expectations model, three of the most important include:

1. Marketmakers are vote counters, not analysts of fundamentals. The votes they count are the order flow.

2. Marketmakers cannot separate informative orders from uninformative ones, and informed traders can use this to their advantage.

3. Liquidity and market efficiency are deeply related: In efficient markets, there are forces that drive liquidity (depth) toward a constant, unchanging level.

Though the model itself will enrich each of these, let me offer a few thoughts at this stage. Insight (1) comes out of the feature common to microstructure models that information processing has two stages. The first stage is the analysis or observation of fundamentals by market participants other than marketmakers (fund managers, proprietary traders, analysts, etc.). The second stage is the marketmaker's —that is, the price setter's—interpretation of analysis/observation from the first stage. That interpretation comes from reading the order flow, as figure 4.4 illustrates.

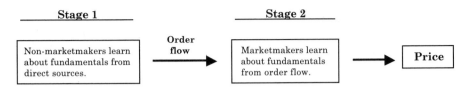

Figure 4.4
Two stages of information processing.

Order flow communicates information about fundamentals because it contains the trades of those who analyze/observe fundamentals. Naturally, though, these informative trades are mixed with uninformative trades, making the task of "vote counting" more complex than the term might suggest. Note too that in the Kyle model the marketmaker can only learn about fundamentals from order flow. This is clearly too strong. This complete dependence on learning from order flow arises in the model because the information being learned is not public information (by public information I mean information that is shared by everyone, and whose implication for the exchange rate is agreed upon by everyone).[16] In the case of public information, marketmakers obviously do not need to learn from order flow. Though some information relevant to FX is public, much is not, so learning from order flow is important.

Insight (2) introduces strategic behavior that is not present in the rational expectations model. There is room for informed traders to be strategic because marketmakers cannot separate informative and uninformative orders. The strategic behavior of the informed traders takes the form of camouflaging their trades using the uninformed order flow. This hides their information from the marketmaker, thereby reducing the degree to which price moves against them (e.g., price rises less as a result of their trying to buy).

Insight (3)—that there is a deep relation between liquidity and market efficiency—is a fascinating message. The basic idea is that in efficient markets there are forces pushing to keep liquidity from moving predictably over time. Although defined inconsistently in the literature, liquidity refers here to an order's *price impact*— what Kyle (and practitioners) calls depth. To understand the stable-liquidity insight, let us suppose that liquidity is not constant, and that we can predict how it will change. A simple example shows that

V observed by D^I, D^U P   V paid
informed trader

Figure 4.5
Timing of Kyle Model.

this predictable liquidity change can result in an inefficiency—a
trading opportunity. Suppose the $/yen market will be especially
illiquid this morning, but this afternoon it will be very liquid. If I
buy $1 billion this morning, this will push the yen price of dollars
upward. (If my trades can communicate information about fundamentals—as in the Kyle model—then these price increases from my
buy orders should persist.) In the extreme, suppose liquidity is so
high in the afternoon that unwinding my position by selling $1 bil-
lion will not have any price impact. I expect to make money because
I expect to sell at a price greater than my average buying price. In an
efficient market, this opportunity should not exist. More precisely,
predictable variation in liquidity in an efficient market should not be
large enough to generate excessive risk-adjusted returns.[17]

The Model

The following one-period version of the Kyle (1985) auction model
is a workhorse within the microstructure literature. The model has
three types of traders: a risk-neutral informed trader, a risk-neutral
marketmaker, and many uninformed traders. The uninformed traders are nonstrategic and trade for motives other than information
(such as hedging). There is a single risky asset, and a single trading
period. Within the single trading period there are four events, detailed in figure 4.5.

The value of the risky asset's end of period payoff is V, a Normally
distributed random variable with mean zero and variance σ_V^2.[18] The
informed trader observes the realization of this random payoff V
before trading, but the marketmaker does not.[19] After the informed
trader observes V, he and others submit market orders to the marketmaker to be executed at a single market-clearing price P. These
submitted orders are of two kinds: the order from the informed
trader, D^I, and orders from the uninformed traders, which sum to

D^U. (If D^U is negative then the uninformed are, on balance, selling.) D^U is a Normally distributed random variable that is independent of V, with mean zero and variance σ_U^2. The informed trader does not observe D^U before submitting his order D^I. (Effectively, this precludes the informed trader from conditioning on the market-clearing price, a stark contrast from rational expectations models, where all trades are conditioned on the market-clearing price.) For setting the price P, the marketmaker observes only the sum of the two types of orders, $D^I + D^U$.

The marketmaker's pricing rule is pinned down by the assumption that he expects to earn a profit of zero. This assumption is consistent with free entry of competing marketmakers, a condition under which the single marketmaker cannot exercise monopoly power. (This zero profit condition is important to the model and is shared by many other models within microstructure.) Expected profit of zero implies that the marketmaker sets price P as a function of the sum $D^I + D^U$ such that

$$P = E[V \mid D^I + D^U]. \tag{4.6}$$

Price depends on the sum because the marketmaker does not observe D^I and D^U individually. The D^U component of that sum is exogenous in this simple version of the model, which simplifies inference. The complication comes from the D^I component, which depends on the trading strategy of the informed trader.

An important feature of the Kyle model is that the informed trader trades strategically, meaning that he takes into account the effect of his orders on price. This involves conditioning on the behavior of both other player types—uninformed traders, whose trades are exogenous, and the marketmaker. Recall that in the rational expectations model the informed trader does not trade strategically. In that model the demand of the informed trader, D^I in equation (4.3), takes the market price P as given, and thus does not consider the effect that D^I has on equilibrium price. Because the informed trader in the Kyle model is risk neutral (recall the discussion in the introduction to this chapter), he will choose a trading strategy that maximizes his expected profit. That is, he chooses a demand D^I that maximizes the following:

$$E[D^I(V - P) \mid V], \tag{4.7}$$

Players:
- 1 marketmaker (risk neutral)
- 1 informed trader (risk neutral and strategic)
- many uninformed traders (non strategic)

Information:
- final payoff V of risky asset distributed Normal$(0, \sigma_V^2)$
- informed trader sees V
- informed trader does not see uninformed orders (but knows distribution)
- marketmaker only sees total orders, not the individual traders' components

Institutions:
- single trading period
- batch clearing: all trades cleared at single price
- marketmaker pricing such that expected profit equals zero

Figure 4.6
Summary of Kyle Auction Model.

for each possible realization of V. The interaction between the marketmaker's problem and the informed trader's problem is clear from these last two equations. The marketmaker's pricing rule depends on the contribution of D^I to order flow, but the informed trader's choice of D^I depends on the impact orders have on the marketmaker's price P. In equilibrium, this circularity is resolved. (See figure 4.6 for a summary of the model's key features.)

The pricing and trading rules that produce equilibrium convey the model's essential lessons. The equilibrium analyzed by Kyle is the unique linear equilibrium, with a marketmaker pricing rule

$$P = \lambda(D^I + D^U), \tag{4.8}$$

and a trading rule for the informed trader of[20]

$$D^I = \beta V \tag{4.9}$$

with strictly positive parameters λ and β that take the following form (not derived here):

$$\lambda = \tfrac{1}{2}(\sigma_V^2/\sigma_U^2)^{1/2}$$
$$\beta = (\sigma_U^2/\sigma_V^2)^{1/2}. \tag{4.10}$$

Notice that the pricing and trading rules depend on the same two parameters—the variance of the uninformed order σ_U^2 and the variance of the payoff σ_V^2. This is a natural consequence of being determined jointly and is analogous to the consistency criterion that governs the pricing rule in the rational expectations model. Notice also that the ratio of these two parameters is inverted in the two rules. This too is quite natural: When λ is high, meaning orders have high price impact, then β is low, meaning the informed trader trades less aggressively (to avoid the impact of his own trades). The constituent variance parameters are also easily interpreted. When σ_V^2 is high, other things equal, the informed trader's information is more likely to be substantial, inducing the marketmaker to adjust price more aggressively. When σ_U^2 is high, the informed trader's order is a less conspicuous (better camouflaged) component of the total order flow, inducing him to trade more aggressively.

Some Intuition for the Equilibrium

One way to provide some intuition for the equilibrium described above is to show that a marketmaker who faces an insider with the trading strategy in equation (4.9) would indeed set price according to the pricing rule in equation (4.8). To show this, we need to examine the learning problem the marketmaker faces. The marketmaker starts with a prior belief about the true value V that is the unconditional distribution of V, or $N(0, \sigma_V^2)$. The marketmaker then updates his belief using information in the order flow $D^I + D^U$ and sets price equal to his best estimate of V. The marketmaker knows that the D^U component of $D^I + D^U$ is exogenous and is distributed $N(0, \sigma_U^2)$. The informative component D^I depends on the informed trader's strategy. Suppose the marketmaker conjectures that the informed trader's trading rule will be the linear rule in equation (4.9): $D^I = \beta V$. We want to show that an optimizing marketmaker would indeed set price according to the pricing rule in equation (4.8).

If the informed trader trades according to $D^I = \beta V$, then we can write the total order flow as

$$D^I + D^U = \beta V + D^U.$$

We can now employ a technique introduced in the previous section: we can transform the marketmaker's signal into a new signal, one distributed about the variable of interest—the value V. The marketmaker divides $D^I + D^U$ by β to yield

$$(D^I + D^U)/\beta = V + D^U/\beta. \tag{4.11}$$

As in the last section, we call this transformed signal Z, as in

$$Z = V + D^U/\beta.$$

Note that Z is distributed Normally about V with a variance of σ_U^2/β^2 (from the second term). Using the updating tools in the appendix to this chapter makes it is easy to show that after seeing Z, the market-maker's best estimate of V is proportional to Z:

$$E[V \mid Z] = \left(\frac{\beta^2 \sigma_U^{-2}}{\beta^2 \sigma_U^{-2} + \sigma_V^{-2}}\right) Z.$$

Inserting the value of β from equation (4.10) yields

$$E[V \mid Z] = Z/2.$$

The risk-neutral marketmaker then sets his price equal to his best estimate of V:

$$P = E[V \mid Z] = Z/2 = (V + D^U/\beta)/2 = [1/(2\beta)](D^I + D^U),$$

where the last step uses equation (4.11). Note that this exactly matches the pricing rule in equation (4.8) because

$$1/(2\beta) = \tfrac{1}{2}(\sigma_V^2/\sigma_U^2)^{1/2} = \lambda.$$

We have therefore shown what we set out to show: Faced with the trading rule in equation (4.9), the marketmaker does indeed set price according to the pricing rule in equation (4.8). Though this is not a proof of equilibrium—we have not shown that the β we inserted corresponds to optimal trading on behalf of the informed trader—this intuition for the marketmaker's problem provides valuable perspective on how he learns. Learning from the order flow is also an essential feature of the two remaining models of this chapter.

Another interesting result is the degree to which the informed trader's information is revealed by the equilibrium price. A common way to measure this is from the market's expectation of V. Specifically, after observing price, how much more precise is the market's expectation? (In the context of the model, the "market" is the uninformed traders because they have no information other than that conveyed by price.) Initially the market—and the marketmaker—have an expectation that is distributed about V with a variance I will denote as σ_0^2. After seeing $D^I + D^U$, the marketmaker's expectation is distributed about V with a variance σ_1^2 of

$$\sigma_1^2 = \tfrac{1}{2}\sigma_0^2,$$

a fact that is easy to show using the tools in the appendix for updating conditional variances. This is a striking result: Regardless of the realizations of V and D^U, the updated variance is exactly one-half of the prior variance. The informed trader's strategy results in exactly half of his information being revealed by the market price. Intuition for this result starts with the fact that one would not expect σ_1^2 to collapse to zero: in that case, the informed trader would make no profit, because all the trades would clear at the perfectly revealing price V. Nor would one expect σ_1^2 to remain at σ_0^2: In that case, the marketmaker learns nothing, and the informed trader could make infinite profits. That σ_1^2 should settle at precisely $\tfrac{1}{2}\sigma_0^2$ is not obvious, but it certainly is appealing on aesthetic grounds.

We have not yet addressed the link between liquidity and market efficiency—the topic of this model's insight (3). Recall that we defined liquidity as the sensitivity of price to order flow, which in the model is measured by λ (the coefficient that relates order flow to price in the marketmaker's pricing rule). Recall too that the point of insight (3) is the constancy of liquidity over time, as opposed to liquidity at a point in time. Addressing liquidity over time clearly requires something more than the one-period Kyle model. The original Kyle (1985) paper also presents a multiple-period version of the model, which consists of a sequence of batch auctions; Kyle examines the limit as the number of trading rounds within a fixed time interval goes to infinity. In this version of the model, the informed trader must consider the effects of current trades on future trading opportunities: if the informed trader trades too much too soon, price will adjust rapidly, and his total profit will be smaller. Instead, the trader chooses to trade gradually, hiding trades among the uninformed trades as they arrive over time. Though not obvious at first blush, this generates the constant-liquidity property noted in insight (3). To understand why, note that the informed trader simply wants to trade with as little price impact as possible. If price impact is not constant, however, the informed trader could earn higher profit by trading more when impact is low and less when it is high. This incentive to reallocate trading across time will persist until the marginal price impact is equalized. The result in equilibrium is constant liquidity.

Discussion

The Kyle (1985) model has been extended in many directions (e.g., allowing the informed trader to be risk averse, allowing uninformed traders to be strategic, and allowing multiple informed traders).[21] It is designed to capture the strategic trading of traders with superior information, and it does that very well. Naturally, though, there are aspects of markets about which it has less to say. For analyzing the FX market (and most other asset markets for that matter), three features of the Kyle model limit its applicability.

No Marketmaker Risk-Aversion

The Kyle model is a pure information model. It has none of the features that can produce price effects from marketmaker inventory or imperfect substitutability (per chapter 2).[22] Because the marketmaker is risk neutral, he always sets price at his conditional expectation of V (i.e., this story is purely about expected future payoffs). Not only does this preclude inventory or portfolio balance effects on price, it also precludes any interaction between information effects and these other effects. Empirically, there is evidence that FX dealers manage inventory intensively. One consequence is that this can alter the composition of order flow: if a greater share of order flow is unrelated to expectations of V—due to intensive inventory management—then the order flow's signal-to-noise ratio is lowered.

No Spread

Because all orders in the batch auction are executed at the single auction-clearing price, the Kyle model does not generate a bid-ask spread. The major FX markets are dealership markets, which do generate spreads, so the Kyle model is not directly useful for analyzing those spreads. One way researchers have used the model for spread analysis is by calculating an "implicit" spread (e.g., Madhavan 1996). The implicit spread is calculated from the marginal price impact of a single-unit trade, captured in the model by the parameter λ (equation 4.8). If the one-way price impact is λ, then the roundtrip price impact—the implicit spread—can be measured as 2λ. This estimate raises its own issues, however, because the equilibrium value of λ is not derived under the possibility that additional trades can be executed.

No Individual Trades

Another consequence of the batch auction format of this model is that the impact of individual orders cannot be analyzed. This is unfortunate because the trade data available for major FX markets include individual orders. One might apply the insights of the Kyle model by attempting to "batch" the individual orders by aggregating over time. However, the economics of aggregating orders over time is potentially different from the batching of orders at a point in time.

4.3   Single Dealer: The Sequential-Trade Model

The Kyle model and the sequential-trade model share many features, primarily involving the specification of dealers. First, both models include a single optimizing dealer whose prices are conditioned on information available specifically to him or her.[23] Second, in both models the dealer is risk-neutral. Third, in both models the dealer learns from order flow and has no other source of fundamental information.

The Kyle and sequential-trade models also have several important differences that primarily involve the trading protocol. Unlike the auction market of the Kyle model, the sequential-trade model describes a dealership market. All trades in a pure dealership market have a dealer on one side of the transaction. In the sequential-trade model, this takes the form of individual traders who, sequentially, are selected from a "pool" and given a chance to trade at the dealer's posted bid and offer. This protocol implies three important differences from the Kyle model. First, an explicit bid-offer spread arises in the sequential-trade model, as opposed to the single market-clearing price of the Kyle model. This is an attractive feature, particularly for empirical implementation, because the spread is readily measured in most markets. Second, the information content of individual orders can be analyzed in a way not possible with the Kyle model because in the Kyle model, all orders clear in a single batch. Third, and not so attractive, the process of selecting traders from a pool in the sequential-trade model is random. Random selection means that informed traders have no ability to adjust their trading intensity the way the informed trader does in the Kyle model. Indeed, incorporation of strategic trading was an important advantage of the Kyle model.

Insights

The sequential-trade model presented below generates many insights. Relative to the single-auction version of the Kyle model above, three of the most important include:[24]

1. Spreads arise even with competitive risk-neutral dealers

2. Price discovery is a gradual process by which price adjusts over time to impound all private information (i.e., to become strong-form efficient)

3. Dealers learn about private information from the sequential arrival of distinct orders.

Insight (1) is truly fundamental. The equilibrium spread in this model is such that when the dealer happens to trade with an informed trader he loses money (as in the Kyle model, here the informed trader knows the true value exactly). To prevent overall losses, the dealer must offset these losses with gains from trading with uninformed traders. The equilibrium spread balances these losses and gains exactly so that expected profit is zero. Information alone is thus sufficient to induce spreads; it is not necessary that the dealer be risk-averse, face other dealing costs, or have monopoly power in order to generate positive spreads.

The term "price discovery" used in insight (2) is not common outside microstructure; this model is a nice illustration of its meaning. (The Kyle model in its multiple-auction version also generates this insight.) In macro exchange rate models, it is traditional to use the term "price determination." All information is public in these models so price is not really discovered—it is determined by a consensus linear combination of fundamentals. In contrast, when a dealer is trading with individuals with private information, the task is indeed one of discovery—discovery of the private information. These models capture the process by which this private information is embedded in price. (Recall that strong-form efficiency means that all information, including private information, is embedded in price.)

Dealers' learning about private information from individual orders—insight (3)—is at the center of this model. Though the Kyle auction model also focused on learning from order flow, it could not address the link between learning and individual orders. In most financial markets, this individual-order process is much closer to reality than the batch trading described in the Kyle model. If a trader wants to sell, the reason could be that the trader knows something negative that the dealer does not. However, it could also be that the trader is selling for reasons unrelated to fundamentals (such as when the trader is a pension fund selling to meet pension obligations). The dealer cannot identify which is the case for any individual trade. But if a preponderance of sales occurs over time, the dealer adjusts his or her beliefs and prices downward—it is unlikely so many sales could occur for non-fundamental reasons. In this way the dealer's price gradually embeds the private information in order flow.

The Model

The following simple version of the Glosten and Milgrom (1985) model is—like the Kyle model—a workhorse within the micro-structure literature. The model has three familiar trader types: risk-neutral informed traders, a risk-neutral dealer, and uninformed traders. There is a single risky asset, whose terminal payoff is either high V^H or low V^L. All informed traders initially observe whether the terminal payoff is high or low. Initially, the dealer knows only the unconditional probability of V^H and V^L, which we denote as p and $(1 - p)$, respectively.

The model organizes trading as a sequence of bilateral trading opportunities. Each trading opportunity involves a single potential trader selected at random from an unchanging pool of potential traders. The dealer knows that q percent of the traders in the pool are informed, and $(1 - q)$ percent are uninformed. The dealer then presents the selected trader with bid and offer prices that are good for a single transaction of one unit. The selected trader can buy at the offer, sell at the bid, or choose not to trade (figure 4.7 presents the model's time line). For simplicity, I will assume that when an uninformed trader is selected, the probability of buying and selling are equal at 0.5 (arising, for example, from idiosyncratic hedging demands).

Trader selected   Dealer quotes   Trader acts   Dealer updates

Figure 4.7
Timing of a single trade in sequential-trade model.

This trading protocol is more elaborate than that for the previous two models. The sequential-trade model's more explicit dealership setting requires more structure (in much the same way that the Kyle model's explicit auctioneer required more structure than the rational expectations model). This sequential protocol is what allows us to analyze trades individually. It also prevents the informed traders from trading aggressively when prices do not yet reflect all information.

The dealer's pricing rule is the essence of the model. Two key features pin it down—risk neutrality and zero profits. (The zero profit condition can be supported by incipient entry of competing dealers, as in the Kyle model.) These features mean the dealer will provide bid and offer prices to the next trader that conform to

$$\text{Bid} = E[V \,|\, \text{next trader sells}]$$
$$\text{Offer} = E[V \,|\, \text{next trader buys}].$$

(4.12)

These expectations internalize the effect that a sell/buy of one unit would have on the dealer's expectation of the payoff V. They are therefore regret free in the sense that the dealer does not regret having done (or not done) the transaction after the fact in either case. Figure 4.8 summarizes the model's key features.

The tree diagram in figure 4.9 clarifies how these expectations are determined. The protocol of the model provides just enough struc-

Players:
- 1 dealer (risk neutral)
- many informed traders (risk neutral and nonstrategic)
- many uninformed traders (nonstrategic)

Information:
- final payoff V of risky asset is either high V^H or low V^L
- all informed traders know whether payoff is V^H or V^L
- dealer knows unconditional probability of V^H (p)
- dealer knows probability that next trader is informed (q)
- dealer sees sequence of incoming orders

Institutions:
- sequence of trading periods, 1 trade maximum per period
- dealer participates in all trades
- trade size limited to one unit
- potential trader randomly selected from pool each period
- dealer presents bid and offer price to potential trader
- dealer sets prices such that expected profit equals zero

Figure 4.8
Summary of sequential-trade model.

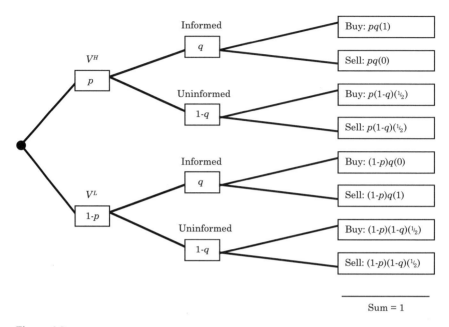

Sum = 1

Figure 4.9
Probability of different trade types: Sequential-trade model. There are eight possible trade types. The probability of each occurring appears in the far right column (the sum of the eight probabilities equals 1). Each of these probabilities has three components. First, nature produces either a high payoff value V^H or a low payoff value V^L, with probabilities p and $(1-p)$ respectively. Then a trader is selected from a pool who is either informed or uninformed, with probabilities q and $(1-q)$ respectively. Informed traders know whether the realized value is V^H or V^L. Finally, the selected trader chooses to buy or sell. If the selected trader is uninformed he buys with probability $\frac{1}{2}$ and sells with probability $\frac{1}{2}$. If the selected trader is informed he buys with probability 1 if payoff value is high and sells with probability 1 if payoff value is low.

ture to make this easy. There are eight possible trade types, which are the product of two different states of the world, two different trader types, and two different transaction directions ($2 \times 2 \times 2$). The far right column shows the probability of each trade type occurring. Because these eight types span all possibilities, the sum of the eight probabilities must equal one. Each of these probabilities has three components. First, nature produces either a high payoff value V^H or a low payoff value V^L, with probabilities p and $(1-p)$, respectively. Then a trader is selected from the pool who is either informed or uninformed, with probabilities q and $(1-q)$, respectively. Informed traders know whether the realized value is V^H or V^L. Finally, the

selected trader chooses to buy or sell. If the selected trader is uninformed he buys with probability $\frac{1}{2}$ and sells with probability $\frac{1}{2}$ (one
can think of the uninformed in this model as trading for idiosyncratic
hedging purposes). If the selected trader is informed he buys with
probability 1 if the realized value is high and sells with probability 1
if the realized value is low.

Setting Bid and Offer Prices

Let us walk through an example of how the dealer would set the
offer price shown in equation (4.12). We can expand that equation to

$$\text{Offer} = E[V \mid \text{buy}] = (V^L)\text{Prob}\{V^L \mid \text{buy}\} + (V^H)\text{Prob}\{V^H \mid \text{buy}\}, \quad (4.13)$$

where $\text{Prob}\{V^L \mid \text{buy}\}$ denotes the probability that $V = V^L$ conditional on the next trader choosing to buy. The dealer knows the val-
ues of V^L and V^H; he just does not know which nature has selected.
We need expressions for $\text{Prob}\{V^L \mid \text{buy}\}$ and $\text{Prob}\{V^H \mid \text{buy}\}$. These
two probabilities are calculated using the same method. Going
through the first only, $\text{Prob}\{V^L \mid \text{buy}\}$, is therefore sufficient for understanding the complete solution.

To calculate the probability $\text{Prob}\{V^L \mid \text{buy}\}$, we need to use a
handy rule called Bayes Rule. The appendix to this chapter provides
a review of Bayes Rule and its underlying intuition. Let me simply
assert here that applying Bayes Rule provides us with the following
expression:

$$\text{Prob}\{V^L \mid \text{buy}\}$$

$$= \frac{\text{Prob}\{V^L\}\text{Prob}\{\text{buy} \mid V^L\}}{\text{Prob}\{V^L\}\text{Prob}\{\text{buy} \mid V^L\} + \text{Prob}\{V^H\}\text{Prob}\{\text{buy} \mid V^H\}} \quad (4.14)$$

The dealer knows $\text{Prob}\{V^L\}$ and $\text{Prob}\{V^H\}$ are p and $(1-p)$ respectively. The only other components to the dealer's problem are
$\text{Prob}\{\text{buy} \mid V^L\}$ and $\text{Prob}\{\text{buy} \mid V^H\}$. These are easily determined
from the probabilities in the righthand column of the tree diagram.
For example, $\text{Prob}\{\text{buy} \mid V^L\}$ is the sum of the buy probabilities in the
fifth and seventh cells, divided by $(1-p)$. The $(1-p)$ comes from the
sum of the probabilities in the fifth through eighth cells—the probability of V^L.

The determination of expectations and prices for subsequent periods follows the same procedure. The dealer uses all available infor-

mation to update these expectations over time in a Bayesian manner. The resulting prices follow a Martingale with respect to that information. (Following a Martingale means that unless one had more information than the dealer, the best estimate of the future price is the current price.[25]) Note too that over time, trading and price adjustment occur even though there is no news beyond that in the trading process itself. This point should speak to anyone who has observed hours of frenzied FX trading with no apparent changes in macro fundamentals (see also Romer 1993 on this issue).

Discussion

Like the Kyle model, the sequential-trade model has been used extensively within microstructure and has been extended in many directions (e.g., allowing different trade sizes, allowing the possibility of no new information, and allowing the intensity of trading by informed traders to vary with the amount of information).[26] It is designed to capture how price—both bid and offer—evolves in a dealership market as orders arrive in sequence. This ability to characterize the spread is a big advantage as a guide for empirical work. Like any model, though, the sequential-trade model has its drawbacks. Three in particular deserve mention.

Order Arrival Process
The sequential-trade model's fiction of random draws from a pool of potential traders is a powerful simplifying assumption. The cost, of course, is that it does nothing to explain the process of order arrival. The timing and sequencing of trades are important choice variables in actual markets.

No Strategic Behavior
This drawback is directly related to the first. Informed traders in the basic sequential-trade model have no ability to vary their trading frequency. In the Kyle model, in contrast, strategic variation of trading intensity is the focus. This point applies to uninformed traders as well: Though the uninformed have no information advantage, in actual markets they may be able to lower their trading costs by trading at particular times (see, e.g., the Kyle-type model analyzed by Admati and Pfleiderer 1988).

No Dealer Risk Aversion

Like the Kyle model, the sequential-trade model is a pure information model. Because the dealer is risk neutral (but has no monopoly power), he always sets price at his conditional expectation of V. It is therefore a story purely about expected future payoffs—there is no possibility of price effects from inventory or imperfect substitutability. For FX markets, however, this does not square with empirical work showing that dealers do adjust prices based on their inventory. In addition, in multiple-dealer markets, if the intensity of inventory control trading by dealers varies over time, this will affect the composition of the "pool" of potential trading partners.

4.4   Multiple Dealers: The Simultaneous-Trade Model

This section of chapter 4 is more extensive than the previous three for several reasons. First, the simultaneous-trade model, with its multiple-dealer structure, is a better proxy for FX market institutions than the other models, so it provides perspective on FX trading that the others cannot provide (see also Lyons 1997a). Second, many papers in the literature extend the simple versions of the three models presented above. Readers therefore have ample references for these models. Because the simultaneous-trade model is more recent, references are few. Indeed, the theory of multiple-dealer trading is, on the whole, rather underdeveloped.[27] Third, I employ variations on the simultaneous-trade model to guide much of the empirical analysis in later chapters; a solid introduction to how it works will provide background for understanding those empirical models.

Of the FX market features reviewed in chapter 3, there are three in particular that the preceding models do not address, but which the simultaneous-trade model is designed to capture. The first of these is interdealer trading. Most trading in the foreign exchange market is interdealer—roughly two-thirds. Single-dealer (and dealerless) models cannot address the causes and implications of such trades. The second feature is the way in which private information arises. Customer order flow in FX is an important source of information advantage that accrues to dealers. That said, it is not the case that all information about payoffs is revealed to the dealers who enjoy this advantage. Dealers therefore have less information than the informed traders in the preceding single-dealer frameworks. The third feature is dealer risk aversion, which makes inventory imbalances less acceptable to dealers. FX dealers manage inventory quite intensely. The dealers in the Kyle and sequential-trade models, however, are risk-neutral. Risk neutrality is a powerful simplifying assumption for analyzing information revelation, but it also rules out the possibility that information revelation and dealer risk management interact. This interaction can be analyzed within the simultaneous-trade model.

Modeling multiple-dealer interaction necessarily involves game theory. The simultaneous-trade model draws from a class of games called simultaneous-move games (versus sequential-move games). There are two key effects of the simultaneous-trade feature. The first is to constrain dealers' conditioning information: Dealers cannot condition on other dealers' trades when they occur simultaneously. The second key effect of the simultaneous-trade feature is that it introduces inventory shocks. Because dealers cannot condition on incoming trades when simultaneously placing their own orders, these incoming orders can alter the dealers' inventory in unpredictable ways. The inventories these shocks engender are integral to the hot potato phenomenon described in chapter 1. Our three other microstructure models cannot capture this hot potato phenomenon because undesired inventories do not arise. (They do not arise because in the two single-dealer models the dealer is risk-neutral, and in the rational-expectations model all trades are conditioned on the market-clearing price.) Empirically, undesired inventories are crucial for understanding the immense trading volume in FX, a point echoed by Flood (1994, 147): "The large volume of interbank trading is not primarily speculative in nature, but rather represents the tedious task of passing undesired positions along until they happen upon a marketmaker whose inventory discrepancy they neutralize."

Insights

Multiple-dealer models of the FX market present many challenges, but also produce insights not accessible with the simpler single-dealer models. Relative to the two preceding single-dealer models, three of the most important insights from the simultaneous-trade model are as follows:

1. Dealer inventories and customer order flow are sources of private information that drive dealer speculation.

2. Private information and strategic dealer behavior have interacting effects that reduce the information revealed by price.

3. Private information and dealer risk-aversion have interacting effects that reduce the information revealed by price.

The model provides further perspective on these, but let me offer a few initial thoughts. To appreciate the significance of insight (1), recall that within exchange rate economics it is common to view exchange rates as entirely determined by publicly available macro-economic information. A corollary is that private information is irrelevant. Taken literally, this view has profound implications for the plausibility of various modeling approaches. The simultaneous-trade model provides examples of types of information that are not publicly available and shows that this information can help individuals forecast prices (e.g., the dispersed information about current account balances noted in chapter 2). This information is different than in the three preceding models. In particular, there are no traders with the type of "inside" information associated with the preceding models. In the FX market, this type of concentrated information about, say, future interest rates, is not plausible. Instead, superior information in the simultaneous-trade model concentrates itself at the dealer level and derives from the order flow each dealer observes. It is therefore the dealers who have information advantages in this model, which they use as a basis for speculation. Because the number of dealers is not large, strategic behavior naturally arises. The strategic trading is between dealers, however, not between dealers and an informed nondealer as in the Kyle model.

Insight (2)—that private information and strategic dealer behavior interact—is a fascinating aspect of multiple-dealer markets. In effect, dealers play two conflicting roles in the market. On one hand, they are information intermediaries, standing between the information in their customer order flow and subsequent market prices. On the other hand, they are also rational speculators. Their speculative behavior distorts information intermediation, reducing the informational efficiency of price.

Insight (3) relates directly to hot potato trading, which arises out of dealer risk aversion. When coupled with private information, though, this trading is not innocuous—it reduces the information revealed by price. This result follows from two underlying points. First, hot potato trading reduces the information in interdealer trades because it lowers those trades' signal-to-noise ratio. Second, it is precisely these interdealer trades that determine price: price cannot depend directly on customer-dealer trades because in the FX market—and as modeled in the simultaneous-trade model—dealers cannot observe each others' customer trades (i.e., transparency of this type of trade is zero, whereas transparency of interdealer trades is not zero).

Consider an example that illustrates the first of these two points—that hot potato trading lowers the signal-to-noise ratio in interdealer trades. There are two dealers, A and B. Dealer A receives two signals of the value of the asset (denote this value V). One of dealer A's signals is in the form of a customer trade, C, and the other is a signal S that is not directly related to order flow (but may be indirectly related; for example, it may be a signal that helps dealer A better interpret the information in the customer trade C). For simplicity, suppose the best estimate of V conditional on these signals is $C + S$. Now suppose A trades with B, and A's rule for determining demand is $D^A = (1 + \beta)C + S$, where β is known by B. Think of β as the additional weight put on the customer trade C to reflect the laying off of that trade to reduce inventory risk (the unit weights on C and S reflect speculative demand based of information advantage). Because B knows the weight β and observes A's demand D^A, if $\beta = 0$ then D^A communicates $C + S$ exactly—the best estimate of V. In contrast, if $\beta \neq 0$, then B does not learn the best estimate of V exactly; the demand D^A is now a noisy signal of $C + S$. In the simultaneous-trade model—as in the preceding models—all dealers know the weights in the optimal trading rule. Hot potato passing of inventories causes these weights to differ from weights based on fundamental information alone. This makes signal extraction less precise, thereby reducing the information in price.

The Model

The model is a two-period game with N dealers. Like previous models, this model includes one risky asset. Each dealer has an equal-sized customer base composed of a large number of competitive customers (e.g., fund managers, speculators, corporate treasurers, liquidity traders, central banks, etc.). All dealers and customers have

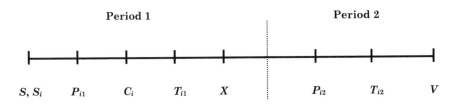

Period 1   **Period 2**

S, S_i P_{i1} C_i T_{i1} X P_{i2} T_{i2} V

Notation
S: common signal received by all dealers
S_i: private signal received by dealer i
P_{i1}:   dealer i's quote in period one
C_i: net customer order received by dealer i
T_{i1}:   dealer i's net outgoing order to other dealers in period one
X: net interdealer order flow in period one
P_{i2}:   dealer i's quote in period two
T_{i2}:   dealer i's net outgoing order to other dealers in period two
V: payoff on the risky asset

Figure 4.10
Timing in the simultaneous-trade model.

identical negative exponential utility defined over nominal wealth at the end of period two. Figure 4.10 provides the timing of the model and introduces some notation.

Let us turn to the information available to dealers. Before quoting in period one, each dealer (indexed by i) receives a private signal S_i and all dealers receive a common signal S.[28] Both signals are distributed about V—the final payoff on the risky asset. After quoting in period one, each dealer receives orders from his own customers that aggregate to C_i. These customer orders C_i are distributed Normal $(0, \sigma_C^2)$. I will use the convention that C_i is positive for net customer purchases and negative for net sales. Importantly, each dealer's C_i is not observed by other dealers (and will be a source of superior information available to dealer i). The variables S_i, S, and C_i are all independently distributed.

The rules governing the quotes P_{it} are outlined in the model summary in figure 4.11 (under Institutions). The most important to note is that there are no spreads—quotes are single prices.[29] Note that simultaneous moves are consistent with interdealer FX transactions being initiated electronically rather than verbally, providing the capacity for simultaneous quotes, trades, or both. The assumption that quotes are observable is tantamount to assuming that quote search is costless. The last quoting rule (that dealers must take the other side of any trade at the single quote) prevents a dealer from exiting the

Players: • a continuum of "customers" (risk-averse and nonstrategic)
                        • N dealers (risk-averse and strategic)

Information: • final payoff V of risky asset distributed Normal$(0, \sigma_V^2)$
                        • each dealer receives a signal S_i distributed Normal$(\sigma V, \sigma_{Si}^2)$
                        • all dealers receive a signal S distributed Normal(V, σ_S^2)
                        • each dealer i receives customer orders that aggregate to C_i, distributed Normal$(0, \sigma_C^2)$
                        • after trading dealers observe a signal of interdealer order flow X

Institutions: Quoting
                        • dealer quoting is simultaneous, independent, and required
                        • quotes are available to all dealers
                        • a quote is a single price at which the dealer agrees to buy and sell any amount
                        Trading
                        • trading is simultaneous and independent
                        • trading with multiple partners is feasible

Figure 4.11
Summary of simultaneous-trade model.

game at times of informational disadvantage. Regarding this last rule, in actual FX markets dealers who choose not to quote during trading hours are viewed as breaching the implicit contract of quote reciprocity and are punished by other dealers (e.g., breaches are met with subsequent refusals to provide quotes, or by quoting large spreads to that dealer).

The rules governing interdealer trading are also outlined in the model summary in figure 4.11. Let T_{it} denote the net of outgoing interdealer orders placed by dealer i in period t; let T_{it}' denote the net of incoming interdealer orders received by dealer i in period t, placed by other dealers. Simultaneous and independent trading generates an important role for T_{it}' as an unavoidable disturbance to dealer i's position in period t that must be carried into the following period.

For consistency with our previous definition of C_i as positive for net customer purchases, orders will always be signed according to the party that initiates the trade. Thus, T_{it} is positive for dealer i purchases, and T_{it}' is positive for purchases by other dealers from dealer i. Consequently, a positive C_i or T_{it}' corresponds to a dealer i sale. Letting D_{it} denote dealer i's desired position in the risky asset (net of customer and dealer orders received), we can write each period's interdealer trade as follows:

$$T_{i1} = D_{i1} + C_i + E[T'_{i1} \mid \Omega_{T_{i1}}] \tag{4.15}$$

$$T_{i2} = D_{i2} + E[T'_{i2} \mid \Omega_{T_{i2}}] - D_{i1} + T'_{i1} - E[T'_{i1} \mid \Omega_{T_{i1}}], \tag{4.16}$$

where Ω_{Ti1} and Ω_{Ti2} denote dealer i's information sets at the time of trading in periods one and two, respectively. From equation (4.15) it is clear that customer purchases (sales) must be repurchased (resold) in interdealer trading to establish the desired position D_{i1} (we assume an initial position of zero). In addition, to establish D_{it}, dealers must factor the expected value of the interdealer orders received T'_{it} into each period's trade. Turning to equation (4.16), in period two, the realized period-one position must be reversed, which has the three components: D_{i1}, T'_{i1}, and $E[T'_{i1} \mid \Omega_{t_{i1}}]$ (recall that $T'_{i1} > 0$ corresponds to a dealer i sale in period one). The term $T'_{i1} - E[T'_{i1} \mid \Omega_{ti1}]$ is the unexpected incoming order—the inventory shock.

At the close of period one, dealers observe period-one interdealer order flow:

$$X \equiv \sum_{i=1}^{N} T_{i1}. \tag{4.17}$$

This summation over the signed interdealer trades T_{i1} measures the difference between buy and sell orders (i.e., net buying) because T_{i1} is negative in the case of a sale. The empirical analogue of X is the signed order flow information communicated by interdealer brokers, a statistic common to all dealers. Specifying this order flow statistic X as an exact measure (i.e., without noise) maximizes the transparency difference across trade types because the model's customer-dealer trades are unobservable to noncounterparties. As noted in chapter 3, trades between dealers and their customers do indeed have zero transparency. However, the actual transparency of interdealer trades is not complete. I address the role of noise in this equation in Lyons 1996a, a paper that examines the effects of changing transparency.

Before proceeding, recall that one of the objectives of this model is to capture the effect of different transparency levels across trade types, customer-dealer versus interdealer. Because customer-dealer trades are not generally observable, they are not aggregated in price until they are later reflected in interdealer trades—which are observable. The result is a "two-stage" process of information aggregation, with interdealer trading as the second, crucial stage (see also Gersbach and Vogler 1998).

Dealer Objectives and Information Sets

Each dealer determines his or her quotes and demands for the risky asset by maximizing a negative exponential utility function defined over nominal wealth at the close of period two. Letting W_{it} denote the end-of-period t wealth of dealer i, we have:

$$\underset{\{P_{i1},P_{i2},D_{i1},D_{i2}\}}{\text{MAX}} E[-\exp(-\theta W_{i2} \mid \Omega_i)] \tag{4.18}$$

s.t.

$$W_{i2} = W_{i0} + C_i(P_{i1} - P'_{i1}) + (D_{i1} + E[T'_{i1} \mid \Omega_{Ti1}])(P'_{i2} - P'_{i1})$$
$$+ (D_{i2} + E[T'_{i2} \mid \Omega_{Ti2}])(V - P'_{i2}) - T'_{i1}(P'_{i2} - P_{i1}) - T'_{i2}(V - P_{i2}),$$

where P_{i1} is dealer i's period-one quote, a prime ($'$) denotes a quote or trade received by dealer i, and V is the payoff value of the risky asset at the end of period two. The second term in final wealth is the dealer's roundtrip profit on his customer order—if C_i is positive, then the dealer sold to the customer at P_{i1}, and bought the same amount back from other dealers at P'_{i1}. The third term in final wealth is the capital gain on the dealer's period-one speculative and hedging demands (recall that $E[T'_{i1} \mid \Omega_{ti1}]$ is the dealer's hedge against incoming orders). The fourth term in final wealth is the same as the third term, but defined for the second period. The last two terms in final wealth capture the position disturbances that arise due to the simultaneous trade feature: dealer i does not know the value of the order he receives T'_{i1} when he chooses his trade T_{i1} (similarly for period two). The conditioning information Ω_i at each decision node (two quotes and two trades) is as follows:

Quoting P_{i1}: $\{C_i, S_i, S\}$

Trading T_{i1}: $\{C_i, S_i, S, P_{11}, \ldots, P_{N1}\}$

Quoting P_{i2}: $\{C_i, S_i, S, P_{11}, \ldots, P_{N1}, T_{i1}, T'_{i1}, X\}$

Trading T_{i2}: $\{C_i, S_i, S, P_{11}, \ldots, P_{N1}, T_{i1}, T'_{i1}, X, P_{12}, \ldots, P_{N2}\}$

Equilibrium Quoting Strategies

In this model, rational quotes must be the same across dealers at any given time. If not common across dealers, arbitrage opportunities would exist (quotes are single prices, are available to all dealers, and are good for any size). Further, given that quotes are common, then they must be based on common information. Because there is only one piece of common information—the signal S—this yields a linear quoting strategy:

$$P_1 = \Lambda_s S \tag{4.19}$$

where the constant Λ_s is a signal-extraction coefficient that produces an unbiased estimate of the value V conditional on S.

Given that dealers' quotes are common, I need to introduce a rule for how interdealer trades are assigned. It is simplest to think of the dealers as arranged in a circle and to assume that each dealer directs his trade to the dealer on his left. This assumption is not substantive. Relaxing it, for example, by allowing a split into $m < n$ equal fractions is straightforward as long as m is known.[30] Given this assumption, then, each dealer receives exactly one order in period one from another dealer, from the dealer on his right. This order corresponds to the position disturbance T'_{i1} in the dealer's problem in equation (4.18).

Period-two quotes are also common across dealers. In this case they depend on two pieces of common information:

$$P_2 = \Lambda_2 S + \Lambda_X X. \tag{4.20}$$

The no-arbitrage argument for why these quotes must be common across dealers is the same as that for period one. And like P_1, P_2 is pinned down by public information because common quotes cannot be based on information that is not common. The public information available in period two includes the interdealer order flow X in addition to the public signal S. Intuition for the effect of X on P_2 is important. Because X is the sum of interdealer orders, it conveys some information embedded in those orders that is not yet public (i.e., X is correlated with the individual customer orders C_i and the private signals S_i). Order flow X does not convey all of the information in the C_i's and the S_i's, however, so P_2 does not fully impound all of that information. Any private information not reflected in P_2 becomes a basis for speculative dealer demands in period two.

Equilibrium Trading Strategies

Given the quoting strategies above, the optimal trading strategy in periods one and two for all dealers is the following:

$$T_{i1} = \beta_{11}C_i + \beta_{21}S_i + \beta_{31}S - \beta_{41}P_1$$
$$T_{i2} = \beta_{12}C_i + \beta_{22}S_i + \beta_{32}S + \beta_{42}T'_{i1} + \beta_{52}X - \beta_{62}P_2.$$

(4.21)

Though busy, these two trading rules have a convenient linear structure that is familiar from the earlier models, deriving from the assumption of exponential utility and Normally distributed returns. For readers interested in a detailed derivation, see Lyons (1997a).

Hot Potato Trading

Due to the simultaneous-trade feature, the model produces hot potato trading of the kind introduced in chapter 1. Inventory imbalances are passed from dealer to dealer, independently of whether or not they offset the imbalance of the receiving dealer. This hot potato property arises because dealers have no knowledge, ex-ante, of which dealers are long and which dealers are short, and they cannot condition on other dealers' trades in any given trading round. Consequently, perfectly efficient risk sharing between dealers is not possible. This property is in sharp contrast to the rational expectations model (which is the only model of the preceding three that is relevant in this respect because agents in that model are also risk averse). In the rational expectations model, inventory imbalances are impossible at the close of trading because agents condition on market-clearing prices—there are no surprises.

I view these imbalances as an important dimension of any model that addresses trading in FX. By producing hot potato trading in equilibrium, the simultaneous-trade model provides a rationale for the skeptic who asks "Why doesn't price simply adjust?" In equilibrium, price does adjust, but only to reflect the aggregate inventory imbalance. Idiosyncratic imbalances remain because arbitrage limits idiosyncratic dispersion in price, and dealers cannot condition on other dealers' trades at ultra-high frequencies. Though people have attributed the extraordinary volume in FX to the repeated passing of inventory imbalances, this process had never before been modeled in the context of rational agents.

The Information in Price

The hot potato passing of inventories is not innocuous; rather, it hampers information aggregation because the passing of inventories dilutes the information content of order flow, which reduces the information in the period-two price (insight 3 from this model). This is true even if dealers behave competitively. To see why, recall that information is aggregated on the basis of signal extraction applied to X, the interdealer order flow. The greater the noise relative to signal, the less effective the signal extraction. Passing hot potato liquidity trades increases the noise in the interdealer order flow.

On top of this hot potato effect, strategic dealer behavior causes a further reduction of information in period-two price (insight 2). This result comes from dealers recognizing that their own orders will have a subsequent price impact. This induces each to alter speculative demand to profit from the forecastable effect on price. These altered speculative demands exacerbate the reduced efficiency of signal extraction due to hot potato trading.

Let me return to the earlier example I used to illustrate these insights (2) and (3), using the model's specifics to make it more concrete. Suppose that dealer i receives a combination of signals and customer order flow $\{S, S_i, C_i\} = \{0, 0, 1\}$, where S is the public signal, S_i is the private signal, and C_i is dealer i's customer order (the latter being uncorrelated with the payoff V). Because the value of the public signal S pins down the first period price P_1 at $\Lambda_s S$, that $S = 0$ implies that $P_1 = 0$. Further, because both signals S and S_i are zero, the expected value of the payoff $E[V \mid S, S_i, C_i] = 0$ and the incoming interdealer trade that dealer i expects $E[T'_{i1} \mid S, S_i, C_i] = 0$. (The latter relation holds because the customer orders C_i each dealer receives are uncorrelated across dealers; thus, using equation (4.21), dealer i's realization of $\{S, S_i, C_i\}$ gives him no information useful for forecasting the incoming interdealer trade.) Despite the realization $\{0, 0, 1\}$, however, dealer i's speculative demand is not zero. To see this, note that dealer i's interdealer trade T_{i1} includes his customer order C_i one-for-one due to inventory control. Note also—from the pricing rule in equation (4.20)—that P_2 will move in the same direction as the sign of interdealer flow X, one component of which is T_{i1}. Dealer i can therefore forecast the effect that the passing along of his customer order C_i will have on the price P_2. This induces him to take a positive (long) position in order to profit from the forecastable market move. Part of what dealer i is able to forecast is the market's misinterpretation of dealer i's interdealer trade T_{i1}: The market can only presume that a positive T_{i1} partly reflects a positive S_i, which, in this example, it does not. Note that the added weight that dealer i

puts on his customer order C_i in determining his speculative demand is not an artifact of the specific realization $\{0, 0, 1\}$: The weights in the trading rule are not realization dependent. To summarize, the dealer alters his speculative demand to profit from the forecastable error in price. This behavior makes it more difficult for the market to extract information from order flow.

Discussion

The simultaneous-trade model captures several FX market features not captured in the three other models of this chapter.[31] At the same time, introducing multiple dealers makes the analysis much more complicated. Tractability necessitates leaving out some important features. Three in particular deserve mention.

No Spread
Like the Kyle and rational expectations models, this model is unable to characterize the bid-ask spread. It is straightforward to add a spread or commission for the initial customer trade (which provides a means of determining the number of dealers endogenously). Adding a spread to interdealer trading, however, means that potential arbitrage no longer rules out price dispersion. This would add considerably to the model's technical complexity.

No Signaling via Price
In the model, the only way dealers learn about others' private information is through observing interdealer order flow, so private information is reflected in price only if first reflected in interdealer orders. In theory, dealers might also communicate information through their quoted prices. Signaling via quotes does not arise in this model because dispersion in price with no spread would produce arbitrage. As an empirical matter, individuals in multiple-dealer markets surely learn about private information through both order flow and dispersion in prices (see Chakrabarti 2000).

Brokered Trading Is Unmodeled
Brokered interdealer trading is an important category of trading in the foreign exchange market but remains unmodeled. One might be tempted to sweep this under the models-cannot-capture-everything rug. The omission is more egregious here, though, because the order

flow signal that drives the model parallels most closely that provided by brokered trading. How individuals choose a particular trading mechanism in markets where there is choice is a burgeoning area of research (for empirical work in FX, see Bjonnes and Rime 2000; for theoretical work on modeling brokers, see for example Werner 1997.) Direct versus brokered interdealer trading in FX has particularly interesting implications given the difference in transparency across trading mechanisms.

4.5 Appendix: A Tool Kit

There are many standard results useful for working with micro-structure models. In this appendix I present three of the most useful. Before launching into details, however, I begin at a more general level by providing some perspective on the so-called CARA-Normal framework, a norm within microstructure. In this framework, utility exhibits constant absolute risk aversion (CARA) and random variables are Normally distributed. Then I turn to the three specific results: the first is that in the standard CARA-Normal framework, preferences are mean-variance, which makes them particularly easy to work with; the second is that in the CARA-Normal setting, demands for risky assets take a particularly simple form; third, I show that in the CARA-Normal setting, conditional expectations, too, take a particularly simple form. For each of the last three results I provide derivations, with the intention to alert readers that the techniques used in the derivations are themselves quite useful for solving more complex models. Another good reference for useful tools used in microstructure analysis is O'Hara 1995, in particular the appendix to chapter 3, where she addresses Bayesian learning with discretely distributed random variables.

The CARA-Normal Setting: Exponential Utility and Normal Returns

The negative exponential utility function I introduce in equation (4.1) of this chapter is a standard feature of trading models. It produces simple expressions for risky asset demand as long as returns are conditionally Normally distributed. The word conditionally is important: it is not enough that all random variables in the model are Normally distributed. There are many cases in which Normally distributed random variables do not produce conditionally Normal returns. Examples of non-Normal returns include products of (discrete) Normal random variables and mixtures of Normal random variables. (An example of a mixture of Normals X_1 and X_2 is $pX_1 + (1-p)X_2$, where p is a probability between zero and one. Specifications with a mixture of Normals are intuitively appealing, but technically more complex.) Trading model specifications rely heavily on the fact that the sum of two Normally distributed variables is itself Normally distributed.

It may be helpful to review the definition of the coefficient of absolute risk aversion, θ:

$$\theta(W) = -\frac{U''(W)}{U'(W)},$$

where the utility function $U(W)$ is defined over wealth W, and "'" denotes derivative. With risk aversion, $U''(W) < 0$, which implies that $\theta(W) > 0$ (because $U' > 0$). When the coefficient of absolute risk aversion is constant—that is, independent of wealth W—then we have CARA.

Utility functions that satisfy CARA can be represented by the negative exponential

$$U(W) = -\exp(-\theta W),$$

where here θ is a positive constant, and therefore not a function of wealth (assumed equal to 1 in equation 4.1).

For those who prefer a graphic representation for this utility specification, note that the function $U(W) = -\exp(-W)$ is simply the graph of $U(W) = \exp(W)$ rotated twice: once around the x-axis to account for the minus sign in front of the exponential, and then again around the y-axis to account for the minus sign in front of wealth W (see figure 4.12). The curvature of this graph is a measure of risk aversion; it increases with the coefficient θ.[32]

I should note before moving on that a common critique of CARA-Normal modeling is that the assumption of a Normally distributed payoff on the risky asset implies prices are not bounded. This implies unlimited downside liability, which may not be appropriate for analyzing certain issues. Also, the specification implies that prices can be negative. However, by increasing the mean of the payoff's distribution, the probability of a negative price becomes arbitrarily small.

Let us return to the three specific results noted above. I will state all three at the outset, followed by derivations.

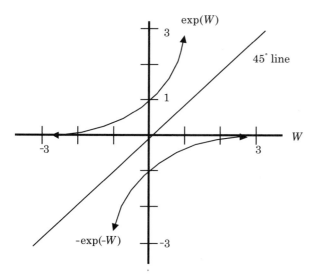

Figure 4.12
Negative exponential utility.

Result 1: Mean-Variance Preferences

In the CARA-Normal setting, with utility $U(W)$ defined over wealth W, and $W \sim N(\mu, \sigma^2)$, agents' preferences can be represented as a function of the mean and variance of wealth:

$$g(\mu, \sigma^2) = \mu - \tfrac{1}{2}\theta\sigma^2,$$

where θ is the (constant) coefficient of absolute risk aversion.

Result 2: Risky Asset Demand

In a one-period CARA-Normal setting, with one risky asset whose payoff V is distributed $N(\mu, \sigma^2)$, agents' demand for the risky asset is given by

$$D(P) = \frac{\mu - PR}{\theta\sigma^2},$$

where P is the price of the risky asset, $D(P)$ is the number of units demanded, and R is the gross return on the riskless asset (i.e., 1 plus the net return; the net return is set equal to 0 in most work). Note that this demand is not a function of the level of wealth. An implication is that redistributions of wealth do not affect aggregate risky-asset demand—a useful property because it means that one does not have to keep track of the wealth of individual participants when modeling.[33]

Result 3:   Conditional Expectations

With Normally distributed random variables, conditional expectations are Normally distributed and take a convenient form. Specifically, define the following:

$$y = \bar{y} + \varepsilon_0$$

$$x_i = y + \varepsilon_i \quad i = 1, \ldots, n,$$

where the variable y is the variable of interest and the variables x_i are signals of y. Let each ε_i, $i = 0, \ldots, n$, be distributed independently and Normally $N(0, \sigma_i^2)$. Then

$$E[y \,|\, x_1, \ldots, x_n] = \frac{\bar{y}\sigma_0^{-2} + x_1\sigma_1^{-2} + \cdots + x_n\sigma_n^{-2}}{\sigma_0^{-2} + \sigma_1^{-2} + \cdots + \sigma_n^{-2}},$$

and

$$V[y \,|\, x_1, \ldots, x_n] = \frac{1}{\sigma_0^{-2} + \sigma_1^{-2} + \cdots + \sigma_n^{-2}},$$

and these two moments fully characterize the conditional expectation because the conditional distribution is Normal. Note the simplicity: The mean of the posterior distribution is the sum of the prior and signals, each weighted by its own precision (the inverse of its own variance), divided by the sum of the precisions. The conditional variance is just one over the sum of the precisions.

Derivation of Result 1:   Mean-Variance Preferences

To derive the result that preferences are mean-variance, start from first principles with

$$E[U(W)] = \int_{-\infty}^{\infty} -\exp(-\theta W)\phi(W)\,dW,$$

where $\phi(W)$ is the Normal density function:

$$\phi(W) = \frac{1}{\sqrt{2\pi\sigma^2}} \exp\left(-\frac{(W-\mu)^2}{2\sigma^2}\right).$$

The trick to solving this is to factor the integral into two parts, one part that depends on the random variable W and one part that does not. Once factored, we will find that maximizing $E[U(W)]$ is as simple as maximizing the part that does not depend on W.

Now, substituting in the Normal density $\phi(W)$ and rearranging slightly, we get

$$E[U(W)] = -\int_{-\infty}^{\infty} \frac{1}{\sqrt{2\pi\sigma^2}} \exp\left(-\frac{z}{2\sigma^2}\right) dW,$$

where

$$z = (W - \mu)^2 + 2\theta W\sigma^2$$

and z can be rewritten as

$$z = (W - \mu + \theta\sigma^2)^2 - \theta(\theta\sigma^4 - 2\mu\sigma^2).$$

This is the key step in factoring the integral into two parts: the second of these two parts does not depend on random wealth W. We can now write the problem as

$$E[U(W)] = -\exp\left(-\theta\left(\mu - \frac{\theta\sigma^2}{2}\right)\right)$$

$$\times \left(\int_{-\infty}^{\infty} \frac{1}{\sqrt{2\pi\sigma^2}} \exp\left(-\frac{(W - (\mu - \theta\sigma^2))^2}{2\sigma^2}\right) dW\right),$$

where I have divided the term $-\theta(\theta\sigma^4 - 2\mu\sigma^2)$ by $2\sigma^2$ and multiplied by -1 in order to bring this term outside the second exponential. Notice that the integral on the right-hand side is just the integral over a Normal density (with mean $\mu - \theta\sigma^2$ and variance σ^2), and is therefore equal to one. This reduces the problem to maximizing the simple exponential expression to the left of the integral. Given the behavior of the negative exponential function illustrated in figure 4.12, it should clear that this expression is maximized when $\mu - \frac{1}{2}\theta\sigma^2$ is maximized.

Derivation of Result 2: Risky-Asset Demand

Again, let us start from first principles. We will find that the solution method is quite similar in spirit to the derivation of result 1. For notation, recall that I defined V as the risky-asset payoff, with $V \sim$

$N(\mu, \sigma^2)$, P as the price of the risky asset, $D(P)$ as the number of units demanded, and R as the (gross) return on the riskless asset. Further, let W_0 and W_1 denote beginning and final wealth, respectively. With these definitions, we can write the budget constraint as

$$W_1 = R(W_0 - DP) + DV = RW_0 - DRP + DV.$$

Using the fact that V is Normally distributed, we can write the problem as

$$E[\dot{U}(W_1)] = \int_{-\infty}^{\infty} (-\exp(-\theta(RW_0 - DRP + DV))) \frac{1}{\sqrt{2\pi\sigma^2}}$$

$$\times \exp\left(-\frac{(V-\mu)^2}{2\sigma^2}\right) dV.$$

Now, like in the derivation of result 1, we want to factor the integral into two parts, one part that depends on the random variable (in this case V) and one part that does not. Once factored, maximizing $E[U(W)]$ will be equivalent to maximizing the part that does not depend on V.

Rearranging the previous equation we have

$$E[U(W_1)] = (-\exp(-\theta(RW_0 - DRP)))$$

$$\times \left(\int_{-\infty}^{\infty} \frac{1}{\sqrt{2\pi\sigma^2}} \exp\left(-\frac{(V-\mu)^2}{2\sigma^2} - \theta DV\right) dV\right).$$

To factor the integral, we need to factor

$$-\frac{(V-\mu)^2}{2\sigma^2} - \theta DV$$

into one part that depends on V and another that does not. Simple algebraic manipulation yields

$$-\frac{(V-\mu)^2}{2\sigma^2} - \theta DV = -\left(\frac{1}{2}\right)\left(\frac{(V-(\mu-\theta D\sigma^2))^2}{\sigma^2}\right) - \left(\frac{1}{2}\right)(2\mu\theta D - \theta^2 D^2 \sigma^2).$$

The second of these two terms does not depend on the random pay-off V. Accordingly, we can write the problem as

$$E[U(W_1)] = (-\exp(-\theta(RW_0 - DRP) - (1/2)(2\mu\theta D - \theta^2 D^2 \sigma^2)))$$

$$\times \left(\int_{-\infty}^{\infty} \frac{1}{\sqrt{2\pi\sigma^2}} \exp\left(-\frac{(V-(\mu-\theta D\sigma^2))^2}{2\sigma^2}\right) dV\right).$$

As was the case for result 1, the integral on the right-hand side is just the integral over a Normal density (with mean μ-$\theta D\sigma^2$ and variance σ^2), and is therefore equal to one. This reduces the problem to maximizing the following expression:

$\theta(RW_0 - DRP) + (1/2)(2\mu\theta D - \theta^2 D^2\sigma^2)$.

The first order condition is

$-\theta RP + \mu\theta - D\theta^2\sigma^2 = 0$,

or

$$D(P) = \frac{\mu - PR}{\theta\sigma^2},$$

which is what we set out to show.

Before moving on to the derivation of result 3, let us return to the budget constraint because it clarifies the role played by the risk-free asset in all the models of this chapter. Because risky-asset demand is independent of wealth, in order for each individual's demand to be feasible, then each individual must be able to borrow and lend at the risk-free interest rate without constraint. If risky-asset demands were constrained by borrowing constraints, trading limits, and so on, then actual demand would differ from desired demand, which would in general affect price.

Derivation of Result 3: Conditional Expectations

Result 3 follows quite directly from Bayes Theorem for updating beliefs with continuously distributed random variables. I will go through it in the case of a prior and one signal; the extension to multiple signals is straightforward. Suppose that the probability density function describing an agent's prior belief about a payoff V is Normally distributed, with mean μ and variance σ_V^2. We can write this density function as

$$f(V) = \frac{1}{\sqrt{2\pi\sigma_V^2}} \exp\left(-\frac{(V - \mu)^2}{2\sigma_V^2}\right).$$

Suppose one observes a random variable X (e.g., order flow) that is jointly Normally distributed with V. What we are interested in is the density of $f(V \mid X)$.

Because X and V are jointly Normally distributed, the conditional density of observing X given V is also Normally distributed (not shown here). Let that conditional density function of observing X given V be denoted $g(X \mid V)$:

$$g(X \mid V) = \frac{1}{\sqrt{2\pi\sigma_x^2}} \exp\left(-\frac{(X-V)^2}{2\sigma_x^2}\right).$$

Now we simply need to apply Bayes Theorem. This theorem is proved in most statistics textbooks, so I use it here without derivation:

$$f(V \mid X) = \frac{f(V)g(X \mid V)}{\int_{-\infty}^{\infty} g(X \mid V)f(V)\,dV}.$$

If we make the substitutions for $f(V)$ and $g(X \mid V)$, we find that

$$f(V \mid X) = \left(\frac{1}{\sqrt{2\pi(\sigma_V^{-2} + \sigma_x^{-2})^{-1}}}\right)$$

$$\times \exp\left(-\left(\frac{1}{2\pi(\sigma_V^{-2} + \sigma_x^{-2})^{-1}}\right)\left(V - \frac{\mu\sigma_V^{-2} + X\sigma_x^{-2}}{\sigma_V^{-2} + \sigma_x^{-2}}\right)\right).$$

This is simply a Normal distribution with

$$\text{Mean} = \frac{\mu\sigma_V^{-2} + X\sigma_x^{-2}}{\sigma_V^{-2} + \sigma_x^{-2}}$$

and

$$\text{Variance} = (\sigma_V^{-2} + \sigma_x^{-2})^{-1}.$$

This is what we set out to show: the mean of the posterior distribution is the sum of the prior and signal, each weighted by its own precision (the inverse of its own variance), divided by the sum of the precisions. The conditional variance is just the inverse of the sum of the precisions.

5

Empirical Frameworks

This chapter covers key topics of empirical interest in FX micro-structure research. Order flow features prominently, as it does in later chapters that cover work that is more macro-oriented. This is because, as we have seen, order flow plays a crucial role in micro-structure models. The chapter begins with a survey of data sets; recent advances in available FX data—due largely to the advent of electronic trading—have opened new doors for empiricists. Then I introduce the main empirical approaches within the field of micro-structure and how they are applied in FX. The closing sections review important empirical results. In particular, I present results bearing on central questions from the previous theory chapter such as "Does FX order flow convey private information?" Confirming empirical evidence supports this book's continuing use of information models. Another key question is, "Does incomplete risk sharing affect exchange rates?" Confirming evidence here supports the use of inventory models as well.

For perspective, consider how the data available for research in FX microstructure have evolved over the last twenty years. The earliest work used futures data because those data are available at high frequencies (Grammatikos and Saunders 1986; Jorion 1996.) In FX, however, the futures market is much smaller than the spot market; it is unlikely that a significant share of price determination occurs there (Dumas 1996). Moreover, early futures data sets did not have sufficient granularity to capture agent heterogeneity, a hallmark of the microstructure approach. Work on the spot market itself grew in the early 1990s with the availability of quotes on an intraday basis (specifically, the indicative quotes from Reuters called FXFX).[1] These quotes provide a quite accurate picture of price dynamics. More importantly, they also speak to heterogeneity issues because the names and locations of the quoting banks are available. Thus, a number of interesting questions can be addressed that earlier data did not permit. The FXFX data did not, however, leave much room for direct testing of theory because they provide no measures of order flow (i.e., signed quantities traded). As we saw in previous chapters, order flow's role in determining price is central to microstructure theory. As order flow data became available, more direct tests became possible.[2]

More recently, empirical work in FX microstructure has entered an exciting new phase. Within the last few years, the availability of transaction data on a *marketwide* basis has opened important new terrain. In equity microstructure, an analogous opening of new empirical terrain occurred in the early 1990s when then NYSE made available its Trades, Orders, and Quotes (TORQ) and Trades and Quotes (TAQ) databases (see Hasbrouck 1992 for more on these equity databases). These new FX data allow us to test theory and measure price determination in ways not possible only five years ago.

Nevertheless, it remains true that the microstructure approach to exchange rates suffers from a lack of publicly available data. Decades of macro data are readily accessible to researchers from sources like Datastream or the International Monetary Fund's *International Financial Statistics*. Not so of microstructure data. It is my hope that this book might stimulate further availability by promoting awareness among official and private institutions of the importance of these data. For my part, I have collected some of the publicly available data sets described in the next section for downloading from my Web site: ⟨www.haas.berkeley.edu/~lyons⟩. The Web site also provides information on how to obtain other data sets from various sources that charge fees for public use.

5.1   FX Data Sets

Before reviewing FX data sets in detail, it may be helpful to look at the big picture. These data sets can be grouped into three basic types, corresponding to the three trade types reviewed in chapter 3:

1. customer-dealer trades (roughly 1/3 of total trading in $/euro and $/yen in the late 1990s)

2. direct interdealer trades (roughly 1/3)

3. brokered interdealer trades (roughly 1/3)

Let us consider each of these in turn. Data on customer-dealer trades have been unavailable until recently. These data are difficult to obtain because banks consider their trades with customers highly confidential. (Recall from chapter 3 that banks have no regulatory obligation to disclose this information.) One recent data set that makes progress on this front includes all the signed customer-dealer trades at a single bank (Fan and Lyons 2000) over a sample period of seven years. The bank (Citibank) is one of the top three banks in the world in terms of trading volume, handling more than 10 percent of worldwide customer order flow in the major FX markets. Another available data set that relates to customer-dealer trading is FXFX. As noted above, FXFX data are indicative quotes (no trades) that provide nondealer customers with real-time information about current prices. It is believed that dealers provide these prices to attract customer business. Because the quotes are indicative—meaning they are not committed prices—they are in effect a form of advertising. These indicative quotes lag the interdealer market slightly, and spreads are roughly twice the size of interdealer spreads. Consequently, from a dealer's perspective, the price information the FXFX quotes convey is dominated by the firm prices observable from interdealer brokers.

Data covering the second of the three categories—direct interdealer trades—were limited until recently to the trades of individual dealers (versus summarizing the trades of all dealers, or some large subset). In contrast to customer-dealer trades, data on direct interdealer trades are available because dealers trade directly with one another using a bilateral electronic trading system called Dealing 2000-1 (a Reuters product). Because quotes and trades are executed electronically, an electronic record is produced that can be used for empirical analysis. In this case, researchers get their data directly from individual banks (the banks keep these electronic records on hand, temporarily, to help resolve trading disputes, etc.). Evans (1997) introduced a data set, obtained from Reuters, that includes all the interdealer trades executed through D2000-1 during four months in 1996. This data set spans a much larger slice of the total trading pie than any preceding it.

Brokered interdealer trading has also recently become measurable. The newfound accessibility of this data category corresponds to the shift in brokered trading from voice-based systems to electronic systems (see chapter 3 for details). Early data from brokered trades over the voice-based system was rather spotty (e.g., Lyons 1995). More recently, data sets have emerged from the records of the newer electronic brokers (e.g., Goodhart, Ito, and Payne 1996; Goodhart and Payne 1996; Killeen, Lyons, and Moore 2000a). The main electronic brokers in the major spot markets are EBS and Dealing 2000-2. (Dealing 2000-2 is Reuters product for brokered interdealer trading; Dealing 2000-1 is for direct interdealer trading.) These electronic broker data have the advantage that they reflect the activities of multiple dealers who are trading simultaneously. At present, however, the available data sets do not span the full brokered interdealer segment because they reflect only the trading on either Dealing 2000-2 or EBS, but not both.

With this as background, figure 5.1 offers a model for organizing one's thinking regarding available data.

The inner ring in figure 5.1 represents direct interdealer trading, the most liquid part of the market. Dealing 2000-1 data is from this inner ring. The middle ring contains brokered interdealer trading.

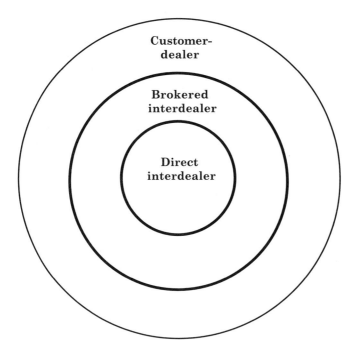

Figure 5.1
Three data groupings.

EBS and D2000-2 data are from this middle ring. The outer ring represents customer-dealer trading. Data from this ring come directly from banks' own order flow records.[3]

The Inner Ring: Direct Interdealer Transactions and D2000-1

Data Set 1: Lyons 1995

The Lyons data set, like others from this inner ring of the market, comes from Dealing 2000-1 trading records. For direct interdealer trading in the major currencies, the Dealing 2000-1 system dominates the market: it is believed to account for about 90 percent of the world's direct interdealer volume.[4] Trades on this system take the form of electronic bilateral conversations initiated when one dealer calls another dealer on the system, asking for a quote. Users of the system are expected to provide a fast quote with a tight spread, which is in turn accepted or declined quickly (i.e., within seconds). Acceptance of a quote constitutes a trade.

The Lyons data set chronicles the activity of a dealer in the $/DM market at a major New York investment bank. The sample spans five trading days over the week August 3–7, 1992 (from 8:30 A.M. to on average 1:30 P.M., Eastern Standard Time). These data come from the bank's own dealing records from the Dealing 2000-1 system. This dealer uses Dealing 2000-1 for more than 99 percent of his non-brokered interdealer trades.

Each record from the Dealing 2000-1 system includes the first five of the following seven variables. The last two are included only if a trade takes place:

1. a time stamp (to the minute)
2. which of the two dealers is requesting the quote
3. the quote quantity
4. the bid quote
5. the ask quote
6. the quantity traded
7. the transaction price

Note that these records provide firm bilateral quotes rather than just transaction prices. They also identify which counterparty is the aggressor. As such, they allow one to measure signed order flow precisely (rather than simply unsigned trading volume). Finally, these records also include firm bilateral quotes that do not generate trades. These nondealt quotes account for roughly 80 percent of all quotes over the week.

In addition to these direct interdealer records from D2000-1, the Lyons data set also includes data from the dealer's position sheets. These sheets include all his trades (i.e., in addition to his direct trades with dealers, they include his trades with customers and his brokered trades with dealers). Because the position sheets include all transactions, they provide an exact measure of the dealer's position through time. For every trade these sheets provide the following:

1. the signed quantity traded

2. the transaction price

3. the trade type: direct, brokered, or customer

4. the counterparty name

Note that the bid-ask quotes at the time of the transaction are not included on the position sheets. This part of the data set includes all 1,720 of the dealer's transactions over the week-long sample, amounting to $7 billion, or $1.4 billion per day on average.

The following two figures help make these data more concrete. Figure 5.2 provides an example of a Dealing 2000-1 communication, with details provided in the notes to the figure. Figure 5.3 provides a diagram of the data flow from the 2000-1 communications through time. (I do not include a figure with the position sheet's structure here because that was presented in chapter 3—table 3.1.)

Data Set 2:   Yao 1998a
The Yao data set is similar in its structure to that of Lyons but has two important advantages. Like Lyons's, it includes the D2000-1 records and position sheets of a spot $/DM dealer who trades in New York. The two advantages over the Lyons data are that the Yao data set covers

1. 25 trading days (November 1 to December 8, 1995)

2. a dealer with substantial customer order flow

The Yao data set thus covers five times the number of trading days. In terms of daily average volume, the Yao and Lyons dealers are similar: $1.5 billion versus $1.4 billion per day, respectively (note,

```
From CODE    FULL NAME HERE    *1250GMT  030892  */1080
Our Terminal: CODE    Our user: DMK
      SP DMK 10
# 8891
      BUY

# 10 MIO AGREED
# VAL 6AUG92
# MY DMK TO FULL NAME HERE
# TO CONFIRM AT 1.5891 I SELL 10 MIO USD
#
      TO CONFIRM AT 1.5891 I SELL 10 MIO USD
      VAL 6AUG92
      MY USD TO FULL NAME HERE AC 0-00-00000
      THKS N BIFN
#
#      #END LOCAL#
#
##WRAP UP BY DMK DAMK 1250GMT 3AUG92
#END#
```

Figure 5.2
Example of Dealing 2000-1 Communication. The opening word, "From," establishes this as an incoming quote request (outgoing quote requests begin with "To"); this information is crucial for signing trades. The caller's four-digit code and institution name follow; "GMT" denotes Greenwich Mean Time; the date follows, with the day listed first; the "1080" at the end of line one is simply a record number. "SP DMK 10" identifies this as a request for a spot DM/$ quote for up to $10 million; "8891" denotes a bid of 88 and an offer of 91. Only the last two digits are quoted because it involves fewer keystrokes; dealers are well aware of the first digits of the price—sometimes called the "handle." From the confirmation that follows, one can see that the earlier bid quote was in fact 1.5888 DM/$ and the offer quote was 1.5891 DM/$. The confirmation also provides the transaction price and verifies the transaction quantity. "THKS N BIFN" is shorthand for "thanks and bye for now."

though, that roughly three years separate these data, and the $/DM spot market grew in dollar terms by about 50 percent over those three years).

The more important difference between the two data sets is the composition of these trades; in particular, the extent to which the two dealers trade with non-dealer customers differs dramatically. About 14 percent of the Yao dealer's volume comes from customer trades, whereas less than 1 percent of the Lyons dealer's volume comes from customers. In this respect, the mix of trades executed by the Yao dealer is more representative of market averages (in 1995, roughly 25 percent of total trading was customer-dealer). The fact that the Yao dealer is from a commercial bank rather than an investment bank helps explain why his customer order flow is so much

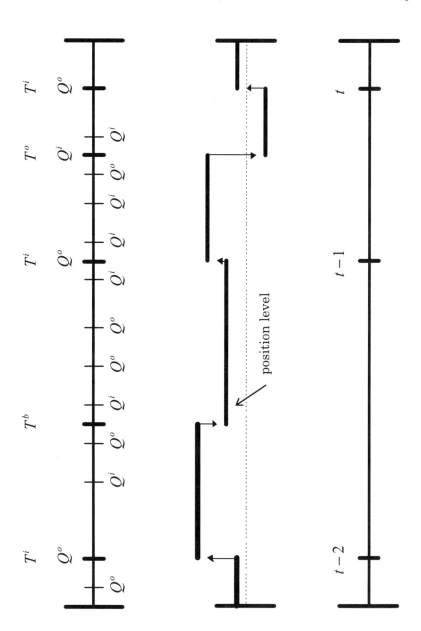

heavier: for spot FX, commercial banks have a more natural customer base than investment banks.

Data Set 3:   Evans 1997

The data set introduced by Evans (1997) covers direct interdealer
trading over a four-month period (May 1–August 31, 1996). It contains time-stamped tick-by-tick data on all transactions for nine currencies against the U.S. dollar. These data were collected from the
Dealing 2000-1 system via a customized feed at the Bank of England.
Reuters keeps a temporary archive of all conversations on the system
to settle disputes; this archive is the source of these data. For every
D2000-1 transaction, the data set includes

1. a time-stamp

2. the transaction price

3. a bought or sold indicator (for signing the trade)

For confidentiality reasons, Reuters was unable to provide the identity of the trading partners. The following list shows the nine currencies covered and the number of transactions for each over the
four-month period:

German Mark	257,398
Japanese Yen	152,238
Swiss Franc	67,985
British Pound	52,318
French Franc	20,553
Italian Lira	8,466

Figure 5.3
Diagram of data structure. Definitions: Q^o is an outgoing interdealer quote (i.e., a
quote made) and, if the quote is hit, T^i is the incoming direct dealer trade. Q^i is an
incoming interdealer quote (i.e., a quote received) and, if the quote is hit, T^o is the
outgoing direct trade. T^b is a brokered interdealer trade. Brokered trades do not align
vertically with a quote because the data for brokered trades in the Lyons (1995) data
set come from the dealer position sheets, and the broker-advertised quotes at the time
of the transaction are not recorded. "|" appears whenever a trade occurs; "|" appears
whenever a nondealt quote occurs. The disjoint segment below the top timeline presents a hypothetical path of the dealer's position over the same interval; it changes with
trades only. The timeline at the bottom clarifies the definition of "periods" within the
Lyons (1995) analysis: incoming trades define an event, not all trades (that model is
presented in chapter 5).

Belgian Franc   5,256
Dutch Guilder   3,646
Danish Krona   1,488.

Several features of the data are noteworthy. First, they provide transaction information for the whole interbank market over the full twenty-four-hour trading day. This contrasts with earlier transaction data sets covering individual dealers over some fraction of the trading day (Lyons 1995; Yao 1998a). Such a comprehensive data set makes it possible, for the first time, to analyze order flow's role in price determination at the level of "the market." (Recall that roughly half of interdealer trading is direct, and, for the largest spot markets, roughly 90 percent of the world's direct interdealer transactions take place through the 2000-1 system.)

Second, these marketwide transactions data are not observed by individual FX dealers as they trade. Though dealers have access to their own transaction records, they do not have access to others' transactions on the system. These transactions data therefore represent a history of market activity that market participants can only infer indirectly (a kind of latent variable that *is* observed by the econometrician). This provides extra power for econometric analysis of how dealers learn about pressure for price adjustment.

Third, the data cover a relatively long time span (four months). This is important for two reasons. First, with a longer time span and multiple currencies, the data set can address exchange rate determination from more of an asset-pricing perspective than previously had been possible. Second, the longer time span permits estimation of intraday patterns in transaction activity with much more precision than is possible from other transaction data sets. Existing studies using the FXFX quote data have noted the importance of controlling for these intraday patterns when analyzing other features of the data (see, e.g., Baillie and Bollerslev 1991; Dacorogna et al. 1993, Guillaume et al. (1995), and Andersen and Bollerslev 1998).

Against all these positive features one needs to acknowledge two drawbacks. First, unlike the Lyons and Yao data sets, the Evans data set does not include firm bilateral quotes communicated between dealers, but instead has only the transaction prices. This prevents direct observation of spreads. As such, the Evans data set does not help us understand the "search" process behind the trade. The fact that bilateral quotes typically do not generate a transaction is informative from the perspective of analyzing price discovery. (As noted above, in the Lyons data set, for example, roughly 80 percent of all bilateral quote requests over D2000-1 did not generate a trade.) The second drawback is that the Evans data set does not provide the inventory positions of the trading dealers. This precludes direct analysis of inventory control at the individual level. It also precludes estimation of the type of "structural" models of dealer behavior that I introduce in section 5.2.

The Middle Ring: Brokered Interdealer Transactions and D2000-2

The second type of trading for which data sets are available is brokered interdealer trading. Like the Evans data set, these data sets cover the trading activity of multiple dealers.

Data Set 4:   Goodhart et al. 1996 and Payne 1999
The first data set of this kind, introduced by Goodhart, Ito, and Payne (1996), covers only a single day and accounts for only a small fraction of daily trading volume. The authors' source was a screen from Dealing 2000-2, a system that at the time was relatively new to the market (June 1993). A later data set, used by Payne (1999), is also from the Dealing 2000-2 system, but spans a longer period (one trading week) and represents a larger fraction of brokered inter-dealer trading.

Recall from chapter 3 that interdealer broking systems provide prices that are advertised to dealers generally. Dealers have a choice of submitting a quote—typically on one side of the market only—or hitting the quote of another dealer. (Remember that brokers in the FX market are interdealer only; customers cannot trade on these prices, and cannot in general observe them because their access to screens is restricted by EBS and Reuters.)[5]

Data Set 5:   Killeen, Lyons, and Moore 2000a, b
More recently, a new data set has appeared that includes two years of data from the larger of the two electronic interdealer brokers— EBS (at least, it is larger in the two largest FX markets, $/euro and $/ yen). This data set includes, on a daily basis, all the order flow pass-ing through the EBS system from January 1998 to December 1999. This is an important period because it spans both the year preceding the launch of the euro and the year following the launch. The first

year of the sample includes order flow for \$/DM, \$/FF, and DM/FF. The second year includes order flow for \$/euro. These order flow series are valuable for addressing hypotheses about the launch of the new currency.

The Third Ring: Customer-Dealer Trades and Indicative Quotes

Data Set 6:   Customer Orders (Fan and Lyons 2000)
This data set includes all the customer-dealer trades—signed according to the customer's direction—received by Citibank over a period of seven years (1993–1999). Citibank is among the top three banks in the world in terms of trading volume (handling more than 10 percent of worldwide customer order flow in the major FX markets).

Traditionally, banks have been reluctant to provide researchers access to this kind of data, given its proprietary nature. One reason Citibank was more accommodating is that the data are aggregated to daily totals (i.e., individual transactions are not available). These time-aggregated order flows are valuable for examining the link between order flows and lower frequency price dynamics.

Because these order flows come from underlying customers, they provide a direct connection to the underlying sources of demand in the economy. The data set includes the \$/yen market and the \$/euro market (order flow for the euro before its launch is synthesized from its constituent currencies). These data are the basis for the material I present in chapter 9.[6]

Data Set 7:   FXFX Quotes (Goodhart and Figliuoli 1991)
As noted above, FXFX is a second type of data that relates to customer-dealer trading. These data are indicative quotes that provide customers (i.e., nondealers) with real-time information about current prices. This source of data has many strengths. First, the data are available over long periods—from the late 1980s to the present. Second, they are available for many currency pairs. Third, they are available on a tick-by-tick basis (typically with thousands of ticks per day in a major currency pair). Fourth, each quote is time-stamped to the second. Fifth, the bank that input each quote can be identified.

These data also have several drawbacks. First, and most important, these data do not include order flow—they are quotes only. This precludes direct testing of models like those in chapter 4 because order flow is central to those models.[7] (Some authors have

used the rate at which quotes arrive to proxy for trading volume—
i.e., unsigned order flow—but the proxy is rather loose; see Goodhart, Ito, and Payne 1996 and Evans 1997. Hartmann 1998a, on the
other hand, finds that quote arrival provides a good proxy for volume over longer horizons.) Second, the spreads in these indicative
quotes tend to be clustered at specific spread sizes, whereas firm
quotes in the market do not exhibit such clustering (see Goodhart,
Ito, and Payne 1996; Evans 1997). Third, a displayed indicative quote
cannot be replaced with a new quote until five seconds have passed
(Evans 1997). Fourth, the raw data are rather noisy (Zhou 1996),
and even after applying the standard filter used in the literature
(Dacorogna et al. 1993), significant outliers remain (Andersen, Bollerslev, and Das 2001).

Closing Thoughts

It is important to note that FX microstructure is evolving rapidly
in terms of available state of the art data. In the future, sample
lengths will surely be extended, and I anticipate further integration
of data from all three market segments (direct interdealer, brokered
interdealer, and customer-dealer).[8] Thus, the data sets above are
perhaps best thought of as a guide to measurable variables and their
sources. At present, the customer-dealer segment is still thinly covered. This segment is important, though, because these trades represent the outside "shocks" to the interdealer trading at the market's
core.

  I chose in this section to present FX data sets as they appear in the
literature. This provides easy reference to additional detail in the
corresponding papers. Another way to organize the data is according to information sets, that is, according to which participants observe which data in real time, and how data that are not available in
real time are disseminated. This would have been a more difficult
task. Consider, for example, the Evans 1997 data set that contains all
the direct interdealer trading from the 2000-1 system. In that case, it
is most appropriate to think of individual dealers as observing only
part of those data, the part that corresponds to their own trading
(both prices and order flow). But individual FX dealers do not observe these marketwide data in their entirety, and nondealer customers do not observe any of these data. Turning to the data sets on
brokered interdealer trading (EBS and D2000-2), to organize those

data according to participants' information sets one would have to distinguish between the observability of transaction prices and the observability of order flow. Recall from section 3.1 that although transaction prices from brokered trades are observable, the order flow information that all dealers receive from these trades is noisy. Nondealer customers do not in general observe these data. As for data on dealer trading with their customers, these data are quite bank-specific. Dealers at other banks do not observe them directly; other bank dealers can at best make inferences based on a given dealer's behavior and any information gleaned from interacting with common customers.

5.2 Statistical Models and Structural Models

This section presents the main empirical approaches within micro-structure and relates them to the FX market. My objective is to introduce readers who are new to microstructure to some of the empirical tools. It is, however, exactly that—an introduction. It is not possible to cover these approaches in depth. Ample references to key papers will help guide those who desire more detail.

There are two broad approaches to empirical microstructure: statistical models and structural models. Not surprisingly, the split mirrors that in economics more generally. All of these models are designed to characterize the joint behavior of order flow and price. The statistical models have the benefit of modest data requirements. They also are more generally applicable across different market structures (i.e., dealer versus auction markets). Their lack of structure makes their reduced form results more difficult to interpret, however. Structural models are grounded more explicitly in the economic decisions that dealers face. Accordingly, they are most appropriate for dealer markets, including the FX market.

There are three specific approaches I will cover here, the first two statistical, and the third structural. They are

1. The Vector Auto-Regression (VAR) Approach
2. The Trade-Indicator (TI) Approach
3. The Dealer-Problem (DP) Approach

Naturally, summarizing empirical microstructure with these three approaches runs the risk of oversimplification. Although microstructure empiricists are sure to feel that much has been left out, I believe they would agree that these are the three most important of the basic approaches.[9] Each has been applied in the microstructure literature for more than a decade now, across many different market structures and asset types.

In essence, all three approaches are a means of relating changes in price to order flow. The status awarded to order flow in these approaches is in keeping with the leading role played by order flow in microstructure theory (per the previous chapter). Naturally, then, all three approaches depend crucially on having signed trade data. (It is not enough to know the size of a trade; one must also know its direction.) In dealer markets, the initiator of the trade establishes the direction: a customer selling 10 units at a dealer's bid generates an order flow observation of -10 (exactly analogous to the Bayesian learning problem featured in the sequential-trade model of the previous chapter). In auction markets, trades are signed according to the direction of the incoming market order (which is executed against the most competitive limit order).

In some markets, access to signed trade data is difficult to obtain. Instead, one might have access only to the sequence of trade sizes and the transaction prices at which each trade is executed. Though certainly less desirable than having signed order flow data, there are techniques in the literature that are commonly used to convert unsigned trade data into signed order flow data. The conversion can be noisy, but for many empirical purposes it is adequate (see, e.g., Lee and Ready 1991).

All three of these empirical approaches are estimated at the transaction frequency (i.e., observations are the realizations of individual trades, which are matched to the prices that correspond to those trades). For work in empirical microstructure, this is the natural data frequency. More recently, however, estimation of microstructure-inspired models has been effected at much lower frequencies (e.g., daily, weekly, and monthly). We review these lower frequency applications in chapters 7 and 9.

Statistical Model 1:   The Vector Auto-Regression (VAR) Approach

The VAR approach was pioneered by Hasbrouck (1991a, b) and has been successfully applied to FX markets by Payne (1999) and Evans (2001).[10] The approach is not predicated on any particular microstructure model, so it is particularly flexible in its use. Its applications by Hasbrouck and Payne correspond to trading in an auction setting with a limit order book. The application by Evans corresponds to trading in a multiple-dealer setting.

The model's inferences about the information content of order flow are drawn from two main sources. First, the model identifies informed trades from impulse responses of prices to order flow. Specifically, informed order flow is that which induces a positive long-run response in price. Second, variance decompositions allow one to determine what proportion of all information that enters price is accounted for by order flow. This attribution statistic represents the overall contribution of order flow to price determination.

There are two important economic assumptions that underlie the typical application of this framework:

Assumption 1: Public information is immediately reflected in prices.
This assumption is tantamount to assuming that the underlying market is semi-strong-form efficient (i.e., prices embed all information that is publicly available).

Assumption 2: Trades strictly precede quote revisions.
In the VAR, order flow is allowed to affect price contemporaneously; reverse causality is prohibited. This is consistent with the general tack of microstructure theory, under which order flow innovations drive price innovations, but not the reverse, with subsequent prices impounding the information that order flow conveys. With contemporaneous order flow in the price equation, one can interpret innovations in the price equation as reflecting effects from public information.[11]

Let us turn now to the specification of the VAR model. Let r_t denote the percentage change in the spread midpoint and let x_t denote the incoming signed order, where t is a transaction-time observation counter:[12]

$$r_t = \sum_{i=1}^{p} \alpha_i r_{t-i} + \sum_{i=0}^{p} \beta_i x_{t-i} + \varepsilon_{1t} \tag{5.1}$$

$$x_t = \sum_{i=1}^{p} \gamma_i r_{t-i} + \sum_{i=1}^{p} \delta_i x_{t-i} + \varepsilon_{2t}. \tag{5.2}$$

Beyond the two assumptions described above, identification also requires the following restrictions on the innovations:

$$E(\varepsilon_{1t}) = E(\varepsilon_{2t}) = E(\varepsilon_{1t}\varepsilon_{2t}) = 0 \tag{5.3}$$

$$E(\varepsilon_{1t}\varepsilon_{1s}) = E(\varepsilon_{1t}\varepsilon_{2s}) = E(\varepsilon_{2t}\varepsilon_{2s}) = 0 \quad \forall t \neq s. \tag{5.4}$$

From this specification, the effects of order flow information on prices are easily retrieved. Inverting the VAR representation yields the following vector moving-average model:

$$\begin{pmatrix} r_t \\ x_t \end{pmatrix} = \begin{pmatrix} a(L) & b(L) \\ c(L) & d(L) \end{pmatrix} \begin{pmatrix} \varepsilon_{1t} \\ \varepsilon_{2t} \end{pmatrix} \tag{5.5}$$

The coefficients of the lag polynomials in this moving average representation are the impulse response functions implied by the VAR model (see, e.g., Hamilton 1994).

Most important among these lag polynomials is $b(L)$, which captures the impact of order flow information on subsequent prices. The individual coefficient b_i, for example, measures the effect of a unit order flow innovation on the price change at the i period horizon. If we sum these price effects over all horizons, we get a measure of the cumulative impact of order flow on the level of price. Within this approach, these cumulative (i.e., persistent) effects are identified as information:

$$\sum_{i=0}^{\infty} b_i = \text{information content of order flow.} \tag{5.6}$$

By defining information content as persistent effects, the definition includes the two persistent categories outlined in chapter 2: (1) information about future payoffs, and (2) information about portfolio balance effects. If, on the other hand, the price impact of order flow reverses over the long run, then by equation (5.6), that order flow conveys no information. This definition of information therefore does not include the transitory category outlined in chapter 2—information about transitory inventory effects.[13]

To assess the overall importance of order flow information, we want to know the share of price variance that is due to order flow. Within the VAR framework, this is a straightforward task of variance decomposition (Hasbrouck 1991b). More formally, decompose the (logarithm) of the spread midpoint, denoted p_t, into a random-walk component m_t and a stationary component s_t:

$$p_t = m_t + s_t, \tag{5.7}$$

where

$$m_t = m_{t-1} + v_t \tag{5.8}$$

and $v_t \sim N(0, \sigma_v^2)$, with $E[v_t v_s] = 0$ for $t \neq s$. We shall refer to the random-walk component (m_t) as the permanent component; we refer to the stationary component (s_t) as the transitory component. Now, defining $\sigma_{\varepsilon 1}^2 = E[\varepsilon_{1t}^2]$ and $\sigma_{\varepsilon 2}^2 = E[\varepsilon_{2t}^2]$ from the VAR innovations, we can further decompose the variance of the permanent component σ_v^2 into a part due to public information and a part due to order flow information:

$$\sigma_v^2 = \left(\sum_{i=0}^{\infty} a_i \right)^2 \sigma_{\varepsilon 1}^2 + \left(\sum_{i=0}^{\infty} b_i \right)^2 \sigma_{\varepsilon 2}^2 \tag{5.9}$$

The second term captures the information impounded in price through order flow.

With estimates of these parameters, one can pin down the *share* of variance that comes from order flow innovations. The findings in the literature are quite comparable across equities and FX. For NYSE stocks, order flow accounts on average for about 33 percent of all permanent price variation (Hasbrouck 1991b). The same statistic for French stocks is 40 percent (De Jong, Nijman, and Roell 1996). For the $/DM market, the statistic is 40 percent (Payne 1999).[14]

Statistical Model 2: The Trade-Indicator Approach

The second of the two statistical models I present here is the Trade-Indicator (TI) approach, pioneered by Glosten and Harris (1988) and recently generalized by Huang and Stoll (1997). This model, like the other two approaches presented here, addresses the link between order flow and prices. The focus in this case, however, is a bit narrower than it is under either the VAR or DP approaches. It is narrower in two ways. First, order flow is not measured from signed trade size, but rather as a direction indicator variable, say D_t, that takes on a value of -1 if the previous trade is a sell, and a value of $+1$ if the previous trade is a buy. This makes the approach less applicable to questions that revolve around trade size.[15] Second, the TI approach is primarily concerned with decomposing the bid-ask spread.

In chapters 1 and 2, I hinted at the idea that spreads have different components; now it is time to be explicit. There are three basic costs that go into determining bid-ask spreads: adverse selection costs, inventory costs, and order processing costs. To understand the first —adverse selection costs—consider the sequential trade model presented in chapter 4 (Glosten and Milgrom 1985). In that model, the dealer faces a pool of potential counterparties, some of whom have superior information. Because the dealer cannot distinguish those who are better informed from those who are not, the dealer quotes a spread that is wide enough so that his losses to informed traders are balanced against the spread revenues he generates from uninformed traders. The spread arises in that model strictly because of this information asymmetry; there are no other reasons for a spread (the dealer is assumed risk neutral and faces no other costs, such as settlement costs, back-office costs, cost of this time, etc.). This information asymmetry is what leads to adverse selection costs.

The inventory cost component of the spread is best understood using models from the inventory-control branch of microstructure theory (see, for example, the multiple-dealer inventory model of Ho and Stoll 1983). In these models, dealers are not risk neutral as they are in the sequential trade model, and therefore have to be compensated for temporarily absorbing risky positions (temporary mismatches in market supply and demand). The spread that arises in these models is entirely due to this compensation for taking risk; there are no information asymmetries (by assumption), and no other costs of marketmaking. (For technical convenience, some models replace risk-averse dealers with risk-neutral dealers who face some unspecified "inventory holding" cost; qualitatively, the results are quite similar.)

The third component, order processing cost, is more of a catch-all category than a specific type of cost. The earliest models of dealers focus on costs in the traditional sense of production costs: labor costs, input costs such as back-office services, and so on (e.g., Demsetz 1968). Spreads arise in these models in order to produce the revenues that cover these costs. This cost category is a catch-all in that a dealer's production function can involve many different types of input cost (some fixed, some variable). Moreover, if the dealing "industry" is not perfectly competitive, then spreads (revenues) will also include some monopoly profit ("rents"). This, too, is lumped into the order processing cost category.

Empiricists do not have the luxury of considering spread components in isolation: their methods have to accommodate all the components, and, to the extent possible, to distinguish among them. Enter the TI approach. Perhaps the best way to communicate how the TI approach accomplishes this is to do so graphically. Suppose the only cost component that enters the spread is the order processing cost. Consider how the sequence of transaction prices would look if this were the only component. Panel 1 of figure 5.4 provides an illustration. A_t is the ask price (often called the offer price in FX), B_t is the bid price, and M_t is the spread midpoint. Because order flow conveys no information in this case, nor is there any inventory cost, the only connection between transaction prices and order flow is the bouncing of transaction prices from bid to ask (so-called bid-ask bounce).[16]

Now consider the case in which the spread arises because of inventory costs only. In this case, following the customer buy order, the dealer's bid and offer prices change (panel 2 of figure 5.4). This is the inventory effect described in chapter 2: after the customer sell order, the dealer is long (or at least longer than before), so to restore the previous position the dealer lowers his or her quotes. This induces subsequent customer purchases at those lower prices (not shown with asterisks), which brings the dealer's position gradually back to its previous level.[17] Once the original position is restored, the original prices are restored, illustrating the transitory nature of inventory effects.

Finally, consider the case in which the spread arises because of adverse selection costs only. Now the customer sell order pushes prices down, but the price adjustment is persistent (panel 3 of figure 5.4). This reflects the information conveyed by the order flow. This information can be either of the two types presented in chapter 2 that have persistent effects: payoff information or information about persistent changes in discount rates (portfolio balance effects).

Equation (5.10) presents the basic Trade-Indicator specification. The change in the midpoint of the spread, ΔM_t, is the change between two transactions; S_{t-1} is the quoted bid-ask spread at the time of the previous transaction at $t-1$; D_{t-1} is the indicator variable introduced above, which takes values of -1 or $+1$, depending on the direction of the previous trade.[18] The residual ε_t represents a random (iid) public information shock at time t:

$$\Delta M_t = (\alpha + \beta) \frac{S_{t-1}}{2} D_{t-1} + \varepsilon_t \tag{5.10}$$

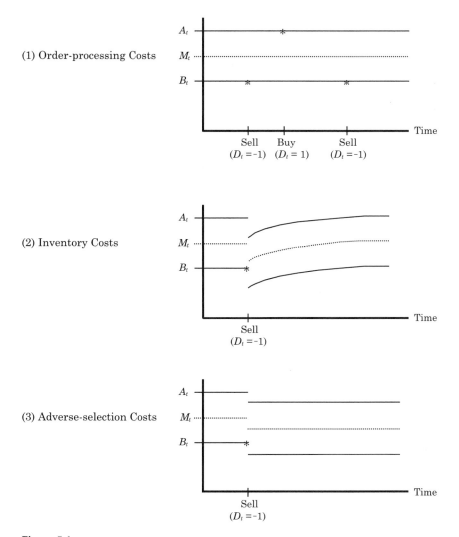

Figure 5.4
An illustration of the three spread components: order processing, inventory, and adverse selection. Transactions are marked with an asterisk. A_t, M_t, and B_t denote ask price, midpoint, and bid price, respectively (at time t). The indicator variable D_t is 1 if the trade is buyer-initiated and -1 if seller-initiated.

The coefficients α and β capture adverse selection and inventory costs, respectively. The sum $\alpha + \beta$ measures the share of the spread stemming from these two costs. (More precisely, this is the share of the half spread, which is what is relevant here because it is the cost faced by a one-way transaction captured by the indicator D_{t-1}. The whole spread would be relevant for a roundtrip transaction.) The remaining share of the spread, $(1 - \alpha - \beta)$, stems from order-processing costs. Figure 5.4 is helpful for understanding why this decomposition makes sense. In response to a trade, the mid-quote is adjusted to reflect the inventory cost of the last trade (panel 2) and the information revealed by the last trade (panel 3). If changes in the midpoint are unrelated to the direction of the last trade, then the spread is arising from the order processing cost only.

To separate the adverse selection component of the spread from the inventory component, Huang and Stoll (1997) extend the basic model in equation (5.10) to account for the fact that inventory effects on the mid-quote are transitory, whereas information effects on the mid-quote are permanent (see their paper for specifics). What do Huang and Stoll find in the end? On average for NYSE stocks, the order processing component of the spread is about 60 percent, the inventory component is about 30 percent, and the adverse selection component is 10 percent. To my knowledge, the TI approach has not yet been applied to FX markets, though there is certainly scope for doing so in the future.[19]

Structural Model: The Dealer-Problem Approach

The structural dealer-problem (DP) approach focuses explicitly on the dealers' decision problem. The solution to that problem generates the equation to be estimated. Though the DP approach draws heavily on existing theory, the pioneering empirical implementation is due to Madhavan and Smidt (1991), who examine NYSE stocks.[20] The variation I present here for the FX market is in Lyons 1995. The variation makes a change to account for the multiple-dealer setting of FX: the model introduces a role for marketwide order flow of the kind produced by interdealer brokers.[21]

The DP model includes features from both the information-model and inventory-model branches of microstructure theory. Let me address the information-model features now (the inventory-model features are introduced within the specification of the model). In the model, dealers recognize that they will sometimes be trading with counterparties who are better informed. The dealers are assumed to have rational expectations, in the sense that transactions are ex post regret free (see chapter 4 for a definition). This means that when, for example, dealer i quotes an offer price for quantity 10, built into that quote is an answer to the question: How would my expectation of value change if my counterparty bought 10, given that he may have private information? Similarly, the bid price rationally incorporates any updating a counterparty sale of 10 would engender. To accommodate all possible order sizes, the dealer needs to quote a schedule of prices, one for each quantity, buy or sell. This schedule therefore internalizes the proper inference for any potential order and ensures the quoting dealer will not regret the quote ex post. I provide an illustration of this schedule below, once the structure of the model is clear.

The basic idea of the model is the following. Consider the decision faced by an individual FX dealer, dealer i, when determining what prices (bid and offer) to quote to another dealer. This decision will depend on many variables. The model is designed to determine which variables those are and how each should be weighted in determining the appropriate prices. Importantly, the model also needs to account for how the dealer's beliefs and his position (inventory) vary across time. The model will include T trading periods, indexed by $t = 1, \ldots, T$, to allow for this across-time aspect of the decision.

I present the model in three parts. The first part is the information environment. The second part is the formation of expectations conditional on the information environment. The third part is the determination of bid-offer quotes as a function of expectations and current inventory.

The Information Structure

The payoff to holding FX at time T is denoted by V, which is composed of a series of increments—for example, interest differentials—so that:

$$V = \sum_{i=0}^{T} R_i,$$

where R_0 is a known constant. The increments are i.i.d. Normal with mean zero. Each increment R_t is realized immediately after trading in period t. Realizations of the increments represent the flow of public information over time. The value of FX at t is thus defined as $V_t = \sum_{i=0}^{t} R_i$. At the time of quoting and trading in period t, that is, before R_t is realized, V_t is a random variable. Given this structure, without transaction costs or further information, the quoted price of FX at time t would equal V_{t-1}, which is the expected value of the asset conditional on public information at t.

The following three signals define each period's information environment prior to dealer i's quote to another dealer, dealer j. The first two are received simultaneously, prior to the third. The first and third are observed by all dealers; the second is observed only by dealer j (this second signal is the source of adverse selection faced by the quoting dealer, dealer i):

$$S_t = V_t + \eta_t \tag{5.11}$$

$$S_{jt} = V_t + \omega_{jt} \tag{5.12}$$

$$B_t = V_t + \xi_t \tag{5.13}$$

The noise terms η_t, ω_{jt}, and ξ_t are Normally distributed about zero, are independent of one another and across periods, and have variances σ_η^2, σ_ω^2, and σ_ξ^2, respectively. At the outset of each period t, all dealers receive a public signal S_t of the full information value V_t. Also at the outset of each period t, dealer j receives a private signal S_{jt} of V_t. One potential source of private signals at the dealer level is order flow from nondealer customers, as described in chapter 3.

The third signal, B_t, is an additional public signal that reflects the institutions of the FX market. It is distinct from S_t in that it is directly measurable. In particular, B_t represents a signal of marketwide order flow. As indicated in chapter 3, there is one source of information on marketwide order flow that provides transparency in an otherwise opaque FX trading process: interdealer brokers.

The last variable dealer i uses to determine his quote schedule is dealer j's signed trade, denoted X_{jt}. That is, consistent with the regret-free property discussed above, dealer i quotes a schedule of prices that protects him from the information in X_{jt}. To determine the information in X_{jt}, dealer i needs to think through dealer j's trading incentives. Under the usual assumptions (exponential utility defined over end-of-period wealth), the quantity dealer j chooses to trade is linearly related to the deviation between dealer j's expectation and

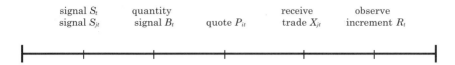

Figure 5.5
Timing in each period of the DP model.

the transaction price, plus a quantity representing liquidity demand L_{jt} that is uncorrelated with V_t (e.g., inventory adjustment trading):

$$X_{jt} = \theta(\mu_{jt} - P_{it}) + L_{jt} \tag{5.14}$$

where μ_{jt} is the expectation of V_t conditional on information available to dealer j at t, and the value of X_{jt} is known only to dealer j. Note that X_{jt} can be either positive or negative.

Figure 5.5 summarizes the timing of the model in each period.

Formation of Expectations

Dealer i's quote schedule is a function of his expectation of V_t, which is denoted μ_{it}. This expectation, in turn, is conditioned on the signals described above: S_t, B_t, and X_{jt} (the fourth variable described above, S_{jt}, is the signal embedded in X_{jt}).

The first public signal, S_t, summarizes dealer i's prior belief regarding V_t. After observing the second public signal B_t, dealer i's posterior belief, denoted μ_t, can be expressed as a weighted average of S_t and B_t:

$$\mu_t = \rho S_t + (1 - \rho)B_t, \tag{5.15}$$

where $\rho = \sigma_\xi^2/(\sigma_\xi^2 + \sigma_\eta^2)$. These posterior beliefs μ_t are Normally distributed with mean V_t and variance $\sigma_\mu^2 = \rho^2\sigma_\eta^2 + (1 - \rho)^2\sigma_\xi^2$.

After observing B_t, dealer i then considers what he would learn from various possible realizations of X_{jt} (and the schedule he quotes internalizes what he would learn from each possible realization). In particular, dealer i can form the statistic Z_{jt}:

$$Z_{jt} = \frac{(X_{jt}/\theta) + P_{it} - \lambda\mu_t}{1 - \lambda} = V_t + \omega_{jt} + \left(\frac{1}{\theta(1 - \lambda)}\right)L_{jt}, \tag{5.16}$$

where $\lambda = \sigma_\omega^2/(\sigma_\mu^2 + \sigma_\omega^2)$. This statistic is also Normally distributed, with mean V_t and variance equal to the variance of the last two terms, both of which are orthogonal to V_t. Let σ_{Zj}^2 denote this variance. Note that Z_{jt} is statistically independent of μ_t, because Z_{jt} is orthogonal to both S_t and B_t. Thus, dealer i's posterior μ_{it}, expressed as a function of any X_{jt}, takes the form of a weighted average of μ_t and Z_{jt}:

$$\mu_{it} = k\mu_t + (1-k)Z_{jt}, \tag{5.17}$$

where $k = \sigma_{Zj}^2/(\sigma_{Zj}^2 + \sigma_\mu^2)$. This expectation plays a central role in determining dealer i's quote.

Quote Determination

Consider a prototypical inventory control model in which the transaction price P_{it} is linearly related to the dealer's current inventory:

$$P_{it} = \mu_{it} - \alpha(I_{it} - I_i^*) + \gamma D_t, \tag{5.18}$$

where μ_{it} is the expectation of V_t conditional on information available to dealer i at t, I_{it} is dealer i's current inventory position, I_i^* is i's desired position,[22] and D_t is a direction indicator that picks up bid-offer bounce in the model. The inventory control effect, governed by α, will in general be a function of firm capital, relative interest rates, and other inventory carrying costs. The direction indicator D_t equals 1 when the transaction price P_{it} is the offer price and -1 when P_{it} is the bid price. For a given expectation μ_{it}, D_t picks up half the spread. (D_t should be viewed as half the spread for quantities close to zero; for other quantities, the quoted spread widens to protect against adverse selection—through the effects on μ_{it}.) This term measures the catch-all order-processing costs described in the presentation of the trade-indicator (TI) model.

Consistent with the regret-free property of quotes, I substitute dealer i's expectation μ_{it} in equation (5.17) into equation (5.18), yielding:

$$P_{it} = k\mu_t + (1-k)Z_{jt} - \alpha(I_{it} - I_i^*) + \gamma D_t \tag{5.19}$$

which is equivalent to

$$P_{it} = (1-\rho)B_t + \rho S_t + \left(\frac{1-\phi}{\phi\theta}\right)X_{jt} - \left(\frac{\alpha}{\phi}\right)(I_{it} - I_i^*) + \left(\frac{\gamma}{\phi}\right)D_t, \tag{5.20}$$

where the parameter $\phi = (k - \lambda)/(1 - \lambda)$ and $0 < \phi < 1$ because $0 < k < 1$, $0 < \lambda < 1$, and $k < \lambda$.

An Estimable Equation

Equation (5.20) is not directly estimable because the public signal S_t is not observable to the econometrician. Fortunately, though, the assumptions about the model's signals and the evolution of V_t allow one to express the period t prior as equal to the period $t-1$ posterior from equation (5.18) lagged one period, plus an expectational error term ε_{it}:

$$S_t = \mu_{it-1} + \varepsilon_{it} = P_{it-1} + \alpha(I_{it-1} - I_i^*) - \gamma D_{t-1} + \varepsilon_{it}. \qquad (5.21)$$

Substituting this expression for S_t into equation (5.20) and taking the first difference yields:

$$\Delta P_{it} = \left(\frac{\alpha}{\phi} - \alpha\right) I_i^* + \left(\frac{1-\phi}{\phi\theta}\right) X_{jt} - \left(\frac{\alpha}{\phi}\right) I_{it} + \alpha I_{it-1}$$

$$+ \left(\frac{\gamma}{\phi}\right) D_t - \gamma D_{t-1} + (1-\rho)B_t + \varepsilon_{it} \qquad (5.22)$$

This corresponds to a reduced-form estimating equation of:[23]

$$\Delta P_{it} = \beta_0 + \beta_1 X_{jt} + \beta_2 I_{it} + \beta_3 I_{it-1} + \beta_4 D_t$$

$$+ \beta_5 D_{t-1} + \beta_6 B_t + \beta_7 v_{it-1} + v_{it}. \qquad (5.23)$$

The structural model predicts that $\{\beta_1, \beta_3, \beta_4, \beta_6\} > 0$, $\{\beta_2, \beta_5, \beta_7\} < 0$, $|\beta_2| > \beta_3$, and $\beta_4 > |\beta_5|$, where the latter inequalities derive from the fact that $0 < \phi < 1$. The following section presents results from estimating equation (5.23) in the \$/DM market.

Figure 5.6 provides an illustration of the qualitative features of the DP model's quote schedule. Note the similarity to the net-supply figures presented in chapter 2.

5.3 Findings: Informative Orders and Imperfect Risk Sharing

Table 5.1 presents results from estimating the DP model in equation (5.23) over the five-day sample in Lyons (1995). The sample size is the number of incoming direct interdealer transactions received by the dealer being tracked (dealer i in the model), for a total of 839 observations. (The four overnight price changes are excluded because the model is intended to explain intraday quoting dynamics, not price changes over periods when the dealer is not active.) The

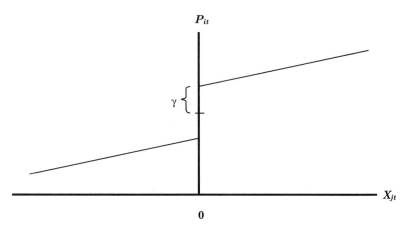

Figure 5.6
Dealer i's quote schedule in the DP model. The slope of the quoted price schedule is determined by β_1 and reflects the information conveyed by order flow X_{jt} (X_{jt} is negative if the incoming order is a sell). Inventory is a shift variable: the larger I_{it} is relative to the desired position I_i^*, the lower the price schedule throughout (to induce inventory decumulating purchases by counterparties). The bid-offer spread at quantities near zero is pinned down by the parameter γ, which multiplies the direction-indicator variable D_t in the pricing rule of equation (5.18).

Table 5.1
Structural Model Estimates

$$\Delta P_{it} = \beta_0 + \beta_1 X_{jt} + \beta_2 I_{it} + \beta_3 I_{it-1} + \beta_4 D_t + \beta_5 D_{t-1} + \beta_6 B_t + \beta_7 v_{it-1} + v_{it}$$

β_0	β_1	β_2	β_3	β_4	β_5	β_6	β_7	R^2
−1.30	1.44	−0.98	0.79	10.15	−8.93	0.69	−0.09	0.23
(−0.96)	(3.10)	(−3.59)	(3.00)	(4.73)	(−6.12)	(2.21)	(−2.55)	
−1.34	1.40	−0.97	0.78	10.43	−9.16		−0.09	0.22
(−0.99)	(3.03)	(−3.56)	(2.95)	(4.86)	(−6.28)		(−2.61)	
>0	<0	>0	>0	<0	>0		<0	

T-statistics in parentheses. The last row indicates the signs predicted by the structural model. ΔP_{it} is the change in the incoming transaction price (DM/$) from $t-1$ to t. X_{it} is the incoming order transacted at dealer i's quoted prices, positive for purchases (i.e., effected at the offer) and negative for sales (at the bid). The units of X_{it} are such that $\beta_1 = 1$ implies an information effect on price of DM0.0001 for every $10 million. I_t is dealer i's inventory at the end of period t. D_t is an indicator variable with value 1 if the incoming order is a purchase and value −1 if a sale. B_t is the net quantity of third-party brokered trading over the previous two minutes, positive for buyer-initiated trades and negative for seller-initiated trades. All quantity variables are in $ millions. All coefficients are multiplied by 10^5. Sample: August 3–7, 1992, 839 observations.

first row presents estimates of the full reduced form, that is, including the information effects of brokered order flow. The second row excludes the brokered order flow variable to make it directly comparable to results from work on the stock market (Madhavan and Smidt 1991). Row three indicates the signs of the coefficients predicted by the structural model under the null that both information and inventory control effects are present.

The main results from table 5.1 are the significant and properly signed coefficients on the information (order flow) variables X_{jt} and B_t, and the inventory variables I_{it} and I_{it-1}. The size of β_1 implies that the dealer being tracked widens his spread about 2.8 pips (0.00028 DM, or 1.4 doubled—adjusted for units) per \$10 million to protect against adverse selection. The size of the inventory control coefficient β_3 (which equals α in equation 5.18) implies that the dealer motivates inventory decumulation by shading his DM price of dollars by 0.8 pips for every \$10 million of net open position.

The coefficients on the indicator variables D_t and D_{t-1}, which measure the effective spread when X_{jt} close to zero, are significant, and have the predicted relative size as well, $\beta_4 > |\beta_5|$. (Recall that there is a one to one correspondence between D_t and the sign of X_{jt}, so D_t controls perfectly for whether X_{jt} is at the bid or the offer.) The coefficient β_4 suggests that once one controls for the information and inventory effects, the baseline spread for this dealer is about two pips $(2\beta_4/10^5)$. Note too that the moving average coefficient β_7 is significant and properly signed, providing further support for the model. Finally, the levels of the R^2's reflect that X_{jt} and B_t together account for only a small fraction of the trading activity in the wider market.

Qualitatively, the main difference in the results from those for NYSE stocks (Madhavan and Smidt 1991) is the significance of the inventory effect on price, captured by β_2 and β_3. Despite a large theoretical literature on price effects from inventory, work on equity marketmakers does not detect it. In this respect, the model fits better in FX.[24] From the perspective of exchange rate economics, however, the more striking result is the finding of a significant β_1—the private information conveyed by order flow. It is more striking because most exchange rate economists are quite comfortable with the idea that there is private information in stock markets. At the same time, they were not taught to believe that private information is relevant in the FX market.

The results in table 5.1 belong in the category of traditional microstructure analysis in the sense that they arise at the transaction frequency. Despite their high-frequency nature, we have seen that these results—as well as other high-frequency results noted in this chapter—point toward some larger lessons. I want to highlight two in particular that will resurface in later chapters.

1. Asymmetric information is present in the FX market. There is a long-standing convention within exchange rate economics to treat all relevant information as common knowledge among market participants (central banks excepted). The results of empirical papers described in this chapter—and in chapter 2—suggest that this common knowledge paradigm is incomplete. Moving away from this paradigm is a realignment of how we think about this market's information environment.

2. Order flow is an important proximate determinant of exchange rates. The biggest puzzle in exchange rate economics for nearly two decades now has been the fact that hypothesized macroeconomic determinants have little explanatory power. The microstructure analysis described in this chapter suggests that order flow, in contrast, has considerable explanatory power (e.g., Payne 1999; Evans 2001). Moving toward the idea of order flow as a proximate cause of exchange rates is another realignment of how we think about this market; the traditional macro paradigm does not recognize the concept of order flow.

Before turning to microstructure analysis of a more macro sort (in chapters 7–9), let us consider another more "micro" question: Where is all that trading volume coming from?

5.4 Why Is Volume So High in FX?

Trading volume in FX markets—at $1.5 trillion per day—is extremely high. It is high relative to other asset markets, high relative to underlying trade in goods and services, and high relative to what standard theories would predict (be they micro theories or macro theories).

Why, some might ask, should we care? After all, it's not clear this volume affects prices, and if it does not affect prices, it may not have important welfare consequences. But there are several ways in which inexplicably high FX volume can have important consequences. For example, misunderstanding the causes of high volume can lead to bad policy. Consider the issue of transaction taxes. Proponents of levying transaction taxes tend to associate high volume with excessive speculation. If instead much of this volume reflects dealer risk management, then a transaction tax would—unintentionally—impede that risk management. Another way for high volume to have important consequences is that it can impede order flow's information role. Per the models of chapter 4, the precision of the information that order flow conveys is a function of the underlying causes of that order flow. It is important to understand whether those causes contribute to, or detract from, informational precision. A third way for volume to have important consequences is that misunderstanding its causes can lead to bad theory. The volume puzzle indicates that the asset approach to the FX market is missing key features. These features may not be important, but to be confident that they are unimportant requires a tremendous leap of faith.[25]

Microstructure analysis suggests that resolving the volume puzzle should rest on two features missing from the macro-asset approach:

1. Inventory control
2. Asymmetric information

Take inventory control first. On the inventory control side, the key mechanism is hot potato trading—passing unwanted positions from dealer to dealer following an initial customer trade. Burnham (1991, 135) provides a clear link between this hot potato and the volume puzzle when he writes: "A game of 'hot potato' has begun.... It is this search process for a counterparty who is willing to accept a new currency position that accounts for a good deal of the volume in the foreign exchange market." The simultaneous-trade model of the previous chapter provides some rigor to this descriptive account of volume amplification.

Asymmetric information contributes to resolution of the volume puzzle by furnishing an additional and important motive for speculative trade that is not present within the macro-asset approach: Because all information is assumed to be common knowledge under the macro-asset approach, no agent can have an information advantage on which to trade.

Do hot potato trading and asymmetric information together fully account for the volume puzzle? They certainly both contribute, but we do not yet know enough to be confident that we have a full accounting. In fact, as an empirical matter, there is very little work on hot potato trading.[26] The one paper that addresses hot potato trading head on is Lyons 1996b. The remainder of this section reviews the methodology and results from that paper.

Volume: Sound and Fury Signifying Nothing?

Lyons 1996b addresses hot potato trading by examining when—as opposed to whether—trades are informative. Specifically, I use transaction data to test whether trades occurring when trading intensity is high are more informative—dollar for dollar—than trades occurring when trading intensity is low. Theory admits both possibilities, depending on the posited information structure. I present what I call a hot potato model of currency trading, which explains why low-intensity trades might be more informative. In the model, the wave of inventory management trading among dealers following innovations in order flow generates an inverse relationship between intensity and information content. Empirically, I find that low-intensity trades are more informative, supporting the hot potato hypothesis.

To clarify the hot potato process, consider the following crude, but not unrealistic example. Suppose there are ten dealers, all of whom are risk averse, and each currently with a zero net position. One dealer accommodates a customer sale of $10 million worth of DM. Not wanting to carry the open position, the dealer calculates his share of this inventory imbalance—or 1/10th of $10 million— calls another dealer, and unloads $9 million worth of DM. The dealer receiving this trade then calculates his share of this inventory imbalance—or 1/10th of $9 million—calls another dealer, and unloads $8.1 million worth of DM. The hot potato process continues. In the limit, the total interdealer volume generated from the $10 million customer trade is $9m$/(1 − 0.9) = $90 million. The resulting share of wholesale trading that is interdealer is therefore $90m/$100m, or 90 percent. This is a bit high relative to an interdealer share these days of about two-thirds, but 10 years ago, the total share of interdealer FX trading was close to 90 percent.

Here are two possible reactions to the example above, neither of which vitiates its message. Reaction one: Shouldn't the multiplier be infinite because risk-averse dealers would not choose to retain any of the imbalance? The answer is this: In equilibrium, price will adjust to induce dealers to hold some of the perceived excess supply. (The 10 percent rule of the example is a crude approximation of a much richer trading process, e.g., that in the simultaneous-trade model of chapter 4.) Reaction two: Interdealer trades can reduce idiosyncratic inventory imbalances—which reduces idiosyncratic risk rather than simply bouncing it—which will mute the multiplier. This is true, particularly if the trades are brokered. It is therefore more reasonable to think about the example in terms of net customer order flow (i.e., after offsetting buys and sells have been netted out).

As I noted above, theory admits the possibility that trades are in fact *more* informative when trading intensity is high—the opposite of the hot potato prediction. This arises in a model by Easley and O'Hara (1992). In contrast to earlier models where private information is known to exist, in Easley and O'Hara (1992) there is simply a probability that private information exists (which they call event uncertainty). If private information does exist, there is some probability, say q, that an informed trader has received good news, and probability $(1 - q)$ that he has received bad news. They demonstrate that if there is active trading at time t, then a rational dealer raises the probability he or she attaches to the existence of private information and lowers the probability of no private information. If trading intensity is high, an incoming trade of a given size induces a larger update in beliefs because it is more likely to be signaling news. On the flipside, trades occurring when intensity is low should induce a smaller update in beliefs.

Before turning to the empirical model, I should note that the role of time in empirical microstructure has only recently emerged. Two important contributions are papers by Hausman, Lo, and MacKinlay (1992) and Engle and Russell (1998). Working with stocks, Hausman, Lo, and Mackinlay test for exogeneity of the length of time between transactions, which they reject at conventional significance levels. However, they also find that their estimates do not change appreciably when they use instrumental variables to control for endogeneity. This finding motivates them to perform the rest of their analysis under the assumption of exogenous intertransaction times. Engle and Russell (1998) meet the role of time head on by modeling it explicitly. Their statistical model of irregularly spaced transactions data treats the time between transactions as a stochastic process. (They refer to the model as an "autoregressive conditional duration" model.) Applying the model to stock data, they find evidence of clustering in intertransaction times, which they relate to underlying market conditions.

The Model

We introduce a role for time in the DP model of the previous section via the liquidity demand L_{jt}. Equation (5.14) described the role of that liquidity demand in dealer j's trade, which I note again here for reference:

$$X_{jt} = \theta(\mu_{jt} - P_{it}) + L_{jt} \tag{5.14}$$

The hot potato hypothesis of order flow information associates liquidity demand L_{jt} with inventory adjustment trading. In FX—according to the hypothesis—innovations in nondealer order flow spark repeated interdealer trading of idiosyncratic inventory imbalances. This rapid passing of the hot potato generates a relatively large role for liquidity trades in periods of short intertransaction times. The event uncertainty hypothesis, in contrast, associates short intertransaction times with a relatively large role for informative trading: in the presence of event uncertainty, intense trading is a signal that an information event has occurred. To summarize, for given precisions of the signals S_{jt} and S_t, we can characterize these views as:

Hot potato hypothesis

$\sigma_{Lj}^2 \begin{cases} \text{High when intertransaction times are short} \\ \text{Low when intertransaction times are long} \end{cases}$

Event uncertainty hypothesis

$\sigma_{Lj}^2 \begin{cases} \text{Low when intertransaction times are short} \\ \text{High when intertransaction times are long} \end{cases}$

This change in the relative intensity of liquidity trading will alter the signal extraction problem faced by the quoting dealer. The implications within the DP model follow immediately from the analysis in section 5.2: The hot potato hypothesis predicts that the information effect of order flow on price will be smaller when trading is intense; the event uncertainty hypothesis predicts the opposite, that the information effect of order flow on price will be larger when trading is intense.

Table 5.2
Testing the Hot Potato Hypothesis: Is Order Flow Less Informative When Inter-transaction Time Is Short?

$$\Delta P_{it} = \beta_0 + \beta_1 s_t X_{jt} + \beta'_1 l_t X_{jt} + \beta_2 I_{it} + \beta_3 I_{it-1} + \beta_4 D_t + \beta_5 D_{t-1} + \varepsilon_{it}$$

	β_1 (short)	β'_1 (long)	Fraction short	$\beta_1 = \beta'_1$ P-value
Intertransaction time short if:				
Less than 1 minute	−0.01	2.20	262/842	0.000
	(−0.01)	(3.84)		
Less than 2 minutes	0.76	2.60	506/842	0.009
	(1.63)	(3.40)		

T-statistics in parentheses. The coefficient β_1 measures the information effect of orders for which the time from the previous transaction is short ($s_t = 1$ and $l_t = 0$ in the equation in the heading), where short is defined in the first column. The coefficient β'_1 measures the information effect of those orders for which the time from the previous transaction is long ($s_t = 0$ and $l_t = 1$), where long is defined as not short. The "Fraction short" column presents the fraction of observations satisfying the corresponding definition of short intertransaction times. In each case, the remaining observations fall into the long category. The P-value column presents the significance level at which the null $\beta_1 = \beta'_1$ can just be rejected. ΔP_{it} is the change in the incoming transaction price (DM/ $) from $t - 1$ to t. X_{it} is the incoming order transacted at dealer i's quoted prices, positive for purchases (i.e., effected at the offer) and negative for sales (at the bid). The units of X_{it} are such that $\beta_1 = 1$ implies an information effect on price of DM0.0001 for every $10 million. I_t is dealer i's inventory at the end of period t. D_t is an indicator variable with value 1 if the incoming order is a purchase and value −1 if a sale. Sample: August 3–7, 1992. Estimated using OLS with autocorrelation consistent (first order) standard errors.

Results

Table 5.2 presents estimates of the information content of order flow, distinguishing between short and long intertransaction times. This is achieved via the introduction of dummy variables s_t and l_t (see the equation heading the table). The dummy s_t equals 1 if intertransaction time is short, 0 otherwise; the dummy l_t equals 0 if intertransaction time is short, 1 otherwise. Short intertransaction times are defined two ways: less than 1 minute from the previous transaction and less than 2 minutes. (The time stamps on the Lyons 1995 data are very precise, because they are assigned by the computer; however, they do not provide precision beyond the minute. Hence, less than 1 minute includes trades with the same time stamp; less than 2 minutes includes trades with time stamps differing by 1 or 0 minutes.) These categories bracket the mean intertransaction time of 1.8 minutes. The second category corresponds to a break at the median intertransaction time.

The results support the hot potato hypothesis over the event uncertainty hypothesis. The coefficient β_1—which measures the information effect of incoming trades with short intertransaction times—is insignificant at conventional levels. In contrast, the coefficient β'_1—which measures the information effect of incoming trades with long intertransaction times—is significant. (The model's other coefficients—not presented—are little changed from those reported in table 5.1.) Moreover, a test of the restriction that $\beta_1 = \beta'_1$ is rejected at the 1 percent level in both cases. In summary, trades occurring when transaction intensity is high are significantly less informative than trades occurring when transaction intensity is low, as the hot potato hypothesis predicts.

Table 5.3
Testing the Hot Potato Hypothesis: Is Order Flow Less Informative When Transactions Follow In the Same Direction?

$$\Delta P_{it} = \beta_0 + \beta_1 s_t X_{jt} + \beta'_1 o_t X_{jt} + \beta''_1 l_t X_{jt} + \beta_2 I_{it} + \beta_3 I_{it-1} + \beta_4 D_t + \beta_5 D_{t-1} + \varepsilon_{it}$$

β_1 (short and same)	β'_1 (short and opposite)	β''_1 (long)	Fraction short and same	Fraction short and opposite	$\beta_1 = \beta'_1$ P-value
−0.06	1.90	2.64	276/842	230/842	0.009
(−0.11)	(3.01)	(3.46)			

T-statistics in parentheses. The coefficient β_1 measures the information effect of orders that have (1) short intertransaction times, defined as less than the median of two minutes, and (2) the same sign (direction) as the previous order ($s_t = 1$, $o_t = 0$, and $l_t = 0$ in the equation in the heading). The coefficient β'_1 measures the information effect of orders that have (1) short intertransaction times, defined as less than the median of two minutes, and (2) the opposite sign (direction) of the previous order ($s_t = 0$, $o_t = 1$, and $l_t = 0$). The coefficient β''_1 measures the information effect of orders that have long intertransaction times, defined as greater than or equal to the median of two minutes ($s_t = 0$, $o_t = 0$, and $l_t = 1$). The "Fraction short and same" column presents the fraction of observations satisfying the corresponding definition of short and same (similarly for the "Fraction short and opposite" column). The remaining observations fall into the long category. The P-value column presents the significance level at which the null $\beta_1 = \beta'_1$ can just be rejected. ΔP_{it} is the change in the incoming transaction price (DM/$) from $t − 1$ to t. X_{it} is the incoming order transacted at dealer i's quoted prices, positive for purchases (i.e., effected at the offer) and negative for sales (at the bid). The units of X_{it} are such that $\beta_1 = 1$ implies an information effect on price of DM0.0001 for every \$10 million. I_t is dealer i's inventory at the end of period t. D_t is an indicator variable with value 1 if the incoming order is a purchase and value −1 if a sale. Sample: August 3–7, 1992. Estimated using OLS with autocorrelation consistent (first order) standard errors.

There is an additional testable implication of the hot potato hypothesis that follows directly from inventories being repeatedly bounced from dealer to dealer. These inventory management trades will tend to be in the same direction (i.e., have the same sign). The test presented in table 5.3 addresses this question: In periods of intense trading, is order flow less informative when transactions follow the same direction? Again, we introduce dummy variables, in this case s_t, o_t, and l_t (see the equation heading the table). The dummy s_t equals 1 if (1) intertransaction time is short and (2) the previous incoming trade has the same direction, 0 otherwise; the dummy o_t equals 1 if (1) intertransaction time is short and (2) the previous incoming trade has the opposite direction, 0 otherwise; the dummy l_t equals 0 if intertransaction time is short, 1 otherwise. A short intertransaction time is defined as less than the median of 2 minutes.

Once again, the results are consistent with the hot potato hypothesis. The coefficient β_1—short intertransaction times and same direction—is insignificant. In contrast, the coefficient β'_1—short intertransaction times and opposite direction—is significant. A test of the restriction that $\beta_1 = \beta'_1$ is rejected at the 1 percent level. To summarize, in periods of intense trading, trades occurring in the same direction are significantly less informative than trades occurring in the opposite direction.

It should be noted, however, that although the hot potato and event uncertainty hypotheses make opposite predictions regarding the relation between information and trading intensity, they are not necessarily exclusive hypotheses. That is, both effects could be operative: hot potato trading may simply dominate when trading is most intense in this market. We will see in chapter 8 that both effects are indeed operative in the data.

6

Exchange Rate Models: Macro to Micro-foundations

This chapter reviews the traditional models in exchange rate economics, all of which are macroeconomic in orientation. My objective is to provide perspective for people working in mainstream finance who are interested in FX markets, but do not feel they know enough exchange rate economics to work in the area. (There remains, in my judgment, much room for intellectual arbitrage, if working on the world's largest and arguably most important financial market is not motivation enough.) Accordingly, presentation of individual models is rather compact. Fuller treatment is available in the surveys of Frankel and Rose (1995), Isard (1995), and Taylor (1995).

Before presenting the models, though, I include a section on defining the term "fundamentals" as used in exchange rate economics. Reviewing how exchange rate economists think about fundamentals should help readers whose perspective on asset valuation comes primarily from equity markets. At the end of the chapter, I offer a discussion designed to help loosen the dichotomy in exchange rate economics between "micro" issues and "macro" issues. I provide examples of the sweep of issues—micro to macro—to which one can apply microstructure tools.

Sections 6.3 and 6.4 address microfoundations. Because traditional exchange rate models are macroeconomic, to many people their lack of microeconomic foundations is problematic. Shoring up these microfoundations is the aim of much recent work in exchange rate economics. The microstructure approach, too, is an effort to bring microfoundations to exchange rate economics. However, it does so in a qualitatively different way because it emphasizes a different set of microfoundations. Recent work within the asset market approach emphasizes microfoundations that mirror those emphasized in macroeconomics more generally. These microfoundations are rooted in the "two T's": tastes and technology. In macroeconomics, a model built from tastes and technology is a model with well-defined preferences defined over consumption goods (tastes) and well-defined technology for producing those consumption goods. The microstructure approach is grounded instead in what I call the "two I's": information and institutions. By information I mean that microstructure models incorporate a greater variety of information types (most of which are ruled out in most asset-approach models, such as information types that are not public). By institutions I mean these models recognize the effect of market organization on how non-public information is learned and aggregated.

6.1 Fundamentals in FX: Goods Market and Asset Market Views

Before I survey exchange rate theory, it may be helpful to relate that theory to the broader context of asset valuation. What, in particular, are the fundamentals that drive valuation in FX markets? In equity markets, the fundamental payoffs that drive valuation are future dividends (cash flows). In bond markets, the fundamental payoffs that drive valuation are coupons (and principal). Let me offer some perspective on the analogue in FX markets to dividends and coupons.

I offer two core notions of FX fundamentals, one from each of the two macro approaches introduced in chapter one. From the goods market approach, the core notion of fundamentals comes from a relation called Purchasing Power Parity, or PPP, which is the idea that a given currency should have the same purchasing power over goods everywhere in the world. The core notion of fundamentals from the asset-market approach comes from a relation called Uncovered Interest Parity, or UIP, which is the idea that the returns on assets that differ only in their currency denomination should be equal (when expressed in the same currency). Let us consider each of these in turn.

FX Fundamentals: The Goods Market View and PPP

Purchasing Power Parity is perhaps the oldest and most venerated relation in exchange rate economics. It can be motivated intuitively with the "law of one price"—a no-arbitrage condition, applied in this case to international goods markets. (For a recent treatment of goods market arbitrage, see Obstfeld and Taylor 1997.) This close link to goods markets is what ties this PPP notion of fundamentals to the goods market approach. In the absence of friction, the law of one price says that the dollar price of a good in the United States should be the same as the dollar price of the same good in another country, say Britain:

$$P_{i,\mathrm{US}} = P_{\$/\pounds} P_{i,\mathrm{UK}} \tag{6.1}$$

where $P_{i,\mathrm{US}}$ is the dollar price of good i in the United States, $P_{i,\mathrm{UK}}$ is the pound sterling price of good i in Britain, and $P_{\$/\pounds}$ is the spot exchange rate (dollars per pound).[1] PPP simply generalizes this one-good relation to a price index representing multiple goods, like the consumer price index:

$$P_{\mathrm{US}} = P_{\$/\pounds} P_{\mathrm{UK}}, \tag{6.2}$$

where P_{US} is the dollar price of a basket of goods in the United States and P_{UK} is the pound price of a comparable basket in Britain. Rearranging yields an expression for exchange rate fundamentals:

$$P_{\$/\pounds} = P_{\mathrm{US}} / P_{\mathrm{UK}}. \tag{6.3}$$

This goods market view of fundamentals is an important conceptual anchor within exchange rate economics. The PPP relation is simple and appealing: the exchange rate equals the ratio of the two national price levels. Now, empirically this relation does not hold at all times, and departures can be substantial (departures in excess of 30 percent in major U.S. dollar markets are not uncommon). Nevertheless, there is ample evidence that departures dissipate over time, with a half-life on the order of five years.[2] Thus, in terms of providing a "center of gravity" for thinking about exchange rate fundamentals, the PPP relation remains quite valuable.[3]

FX Fundamentals: The Asset Market View and UIP

Though fundamentals as described by PPP are an important conceptual anchor, this notion of fundamentals is a far cry from the dividend-discount valuations common in equity markets. The asset-market approach to exchange rates provides a more comforting analogue. Within the asset approach, a good way to illustrate fundamentals is with the relation Uncovered Interest Parity.

UIP describes the relationship between expected returns on short-term, interest-bearing assets denominated in different currencies.

(For simplicity, I refer to this asset class as "deposits.") The relation implies that, when measured in dollars, the expected returns on pound sterling deposits and dollar deposits are equal. One would expect this to hold, for example, in a risk-neutral world without capital controls because any disparity would be immediately exploited. In its exact version, UIP implies that

$$(1 + i_{\$,t}) = (1 + i_{£,t}) \left(\frac{E[P_{\$/£,t+1} \,|\, \Omega_t]}{P_{\$/£,t}} \right),$$

where $i_{\$,t}$ and $i_{£,t}$ are the one-period nominal interest rates in dollars and pounds at time t, respectively, and $E[P_{\$/£,t+1} \,|\, \Omega_t]$ is the expected future spot rate. The expected spot rate is conditional on information available at t, which I denote by "$|\Omega_t$", where Ω_t is the relevant information set.

There is an approximate version of UIP that is a bit more intuitive, and also easier to work with. The expected dollar return on pound deposits has two components, corresponding to the two terms on the righthand side of the exact version: the one-period pound interest rate and the expected appreciation of the pound. The approximate version of UIP expresses this in a linear form:[4]

$$i_{\$,t} = i_{£,t} + E[p_{t+1} - p_t \,|\, \Omega_t] \tag{6.4}$$

where p_t is the natural log of $P_{\$/£,t}$ ($\$/£$ subscript suppressed) and $E[p_{t+1} - p_t \,|\, \Omega_t]$ is the expected percent (log difference) appreciation in the pound between t and $t+1$. The intuition of UIP is clear: the expected dollar return on dollar deposits on the lefthand side equals the expected dollar return on pound deposits on the righthand side.

The UIP expression in equation (6.4) generates an intuitive, asset-market notion of fundamentals, one that will speak to those more familiar with equity and bond valuation. Start by rewriting equation (6.4) as

$$p_t = (i_{£,t} - i_{\$,t}) + E[p_{t+1} \,|\, \Omega_t].$$

Projecting this expression one period forward, and taking expectations, we can also write:

$$E[p_{t+1} \,|\, \Omega_t] = E[(i_{£,t+1} - i_{\$,t+1}) \,|\, \Omega_t] + E[p_{t+2} \,|\, \Omega_t].$$

Substituting this expression for $E[p_{t+1} \,|\, \Omega_t]$ into the previous equation yields:

$$p_t = (i_{£,t} - i_{\$,t}) + E[(i_{£,t+1} - i_{\$,t+1}) \,|\, \Omega_t] + E[p_{t+2} \,|\, \Omega_t]$$

Repeating this projection and substitution for dates beyond $t+1$ yields our asset-market version of fundamentals:

$$p_t = E\left[\sum_{\tau=0}^{T-t-1} (i_{£,t+\tau} - i_{\$,t+\tau}) \mid \Omega_t\right] + E[p_T \mid \Omega_t] \qquad (6.5)$$

Thus, in a manner similar to a dividend discount model, the exchange rate fundamental is a sum of expected future (one-period) interest differentials, plus a "long-run" value of the exchange rate.[5] These future interest differentials are the net cash flows that accrue to holding foreign currency deposits. The second term—the long-run value—is typically pinned down with PPP.

6.2 Macro Models: An Overview

Most readers familiar with microstructure finance are unfamiliar with models of exchange rate determination, so I review them here.[6] There are four major models, and macro fundamentals drive all four:

1. flexible-price monetary model
2. sticky-price monetary model
3. portfolio balance model
4. general equilibrium model

All four are squarely in the asset-market approach. The forward-looking nature of the asset approach implies that current values of macro variables are not the whole story—the market's expectation of these variables' future values is also important. For the purposes of this book, it is worthwhile to review the major models because they provide valuable perspective for the more "macro-level" analysis of later chapters.

Flexible-Price Monetary Model

Though simple and intuitive, the PPP relation described above has little structural content because it determines the exchange rate from two variables that are themselves endogenous. Naturally, these features make it a fine candidate as a building block: embedding the relation in a more fully articulated model both exploits its simplicity and provides structure. This is exactly the strategy of the monetary models. Note too that PPP does not provide a direct link to policy, in particular to monetary policy. By embedding PPP in a model that is articulated in the monetary dimension, the monetary models provide that direct link.

The first of the two monetary models, the flexible-price model, starts with the assumption that PPP always holds (key references include Mussa 1976 and Frenkel 1976). It is, in fact, a straightforward extension of the PPP relation: It uses the PPP expression for the exchange rate and substitutes alternative expressions for the two price levels P_{US} and P_{UK}. Recall that the PPP expression from equation (6.3) is

$$P_{\$/£} = P_{US}/P_{UK}.$$

Taking logarithms of both sides yields an equivalent expression that is a bit easier to work with:[7]

$$p_{\$/£} = p_{US} - p_{UK}.$$

The substitute expressions for p_{US} and p_{UK} come from the heart of macroeconomics—the equation describing equilibrium in the money market.[8] The money market is in equilibrium when the supply of money in real terms (i.e., price adjusted) equals the demand. Demand for money is modeled as a function of both real income (transactions demand) and the nominal interest rate (an opportunity cost of holding money). Equilibrium is typically expressed in log-linear form as

$$m_{US} - p_{US} = \alpha y_{US} - \beta i_{\$}, \tag{6.6}$$

where $m_{US} - p_{US}$ is the (log) real money supply and $\alpha y_{US} - \beta i_{US}$ is the (log) real money demand, with m_{US} as log nominal money supply, p_{US} as log price level, y_{US} as log real output, and i_{US} as the short-term nominal interest rate. Solving for the price level in separate U.S. and U.K. equations, we have:

$$p_{US} = m_{US} - \alpha y_{US} + \beta i_{\$}$$
$$p_{UK} = m_{UK} - \alpha y_{UK} + \beta i_{£} \tag{6.7}$$

Plugging our price-level expressions in equation (6.7) into the PPP relation gives us the flexible-price monetary model:

$$p_{\$/£} = (m_{US} - m_{UK}) - \alpha(y_{US} - y_{UK}) + \beta(i_{\$} - i_{£}). \tag{6.8}$$

This is the simplest version of the model. The link to money supplies —and therefore monetary policy—is clear. The link to the "flexible-price" title is less clear. Indeed, in a strict sense we have not used the assumption of perfectly flexible exchange rates and prices: It is not a necessary condition for PPP, nor is it required for the price-level expressions in equation (6.6). Instead, the name comes from the need to distinguish this model from its sticky-price cousin (which we return to below).

Another link that is not yet clear is the model's connection to expected future macro fundamentals, the hallmark of the asset approach. This link is introduced by adding the UIP relation described in equation (6.4) above, which pins down expected returns on short-term interest-bearing assets. Using the UIP relation that $(i_{US,t} - i_{UK,t})$ $= E[\Delta p_{\$/\pounds,t+1} | \Omega_t]$, and suppressing the $\$/\pounds$ subscript, we can write

$$p_t = f_t + \beta(E[\Delta p_{t+1} | \Omega_t]), \tag{6.9}$$

where we have defined f_t, the current fundamental, as

$$f_t = (m_{US} - m_{UK}) - \alpha(y_{US} - y_{UK}). \tag{6.10}$$

The rational expectations solution to equation (6.9) brings the link to future fundamentals into sharp focus:[9]

$$p_t = \sum_{i=0}^{\infty} \gamma_i E[f_{t+i} | \Omega_t], \tag{6.11}$$

where $\gamma_i \equiv [\beta/(1+\beta)]^i/(1+\beta)$. Today's spot rate therefore depends not only on the current state of monetary fundamentals, but also on the stream of expected future fundamentals. This asset-approach representation is analogous to the dividend-discount model used in finance for equity valuation. The "discount" rate here, γ_i, is wholly a function of β, the sensitivity of money demand to the interest rate (equation 6.6).[10]

Sticky-Price Monetary Model

The sticky-price monetary model, also called the overshooting model, has the same conceptual underpinnings as its flexible-price cousin (the key reference is Dornbusch 1976). The models share two essential ingredients. First, at their core is equilibrium in the money market, described above in equation (6.6). Second, the sticky-price model also assumes UIP, described above in equation (6.4); this is the ingredient that places the model, like the flexible-price model, squarely in the asset approach. Two of its ingredients, however, are substantial departures from the flexible-price model. First, prices are sticky over the short run, adjusting only gradually to the long-run flexible-price equilibrium. (The level of aggregate demand governs this adjustment.) Second, PPP does not hold in the short run, though it does hold in the long run, once the price level has fully adjusted to its flexible-price level.[11]

The equation summarizing the sticky-price model is similar to that for the flexible-price model in equation (6.9):

$$p_t = f_t + \beta(E[\Delta p_{t+1} \mid \Omega_t]) + w_t \tag{6.12}$$

The only difference is the additional term w_t, a wedge term that does not arise when prices are flexible (see, e.g., Flood and Taylor 1996). The wedge term captures the short-run departure from PPP caused by sticky prices. Consider for example a shock that shifts the money supply m, starting from a steady state in which $w_t = 0$. This shift can have an immediate and substantial impact on the exchange rate p_t because that variable is perfectly flexible. Because the price level p_{US} is not perfectly flexible, however, this results in a departure from PPP—w_t is no longer zero. This effect on w_t is transitory, though, because in the long run prices adjust fully. The difference between the flexible- and sticky-price models is therefore transitory as well.

The sticky-price model is appealing not only because it relaxes the flexible-price model's uncomfortable assumptions, but also because it can amplify the effect of a change in fundamentals, referred to as exchange rate overshooting. The appeal of this overshooting result is that it squares with empirical findings that exchange rates are excessively volatile when compared with the volatility of fundamentals as specified in, say, the flexible-price model. (Note that high volatility relative to flexible-price fundamentals should not be confused with high absolute volatility; indeed, changes in major spot rates have a standard deviation two-thirds that of equity returns: roughly 12 percent per annum, versus 18 percent for the S&P 500.)

The overshooting result is important enough in exchange rate economics that it deserves attention. A simple experiment provides some clear intuition. Consider the case of an unexpected, permanent increase in the money supply, m_{US}. First, in the flexible-price model, the effect is straightforward: a 10 percent increase in money induces

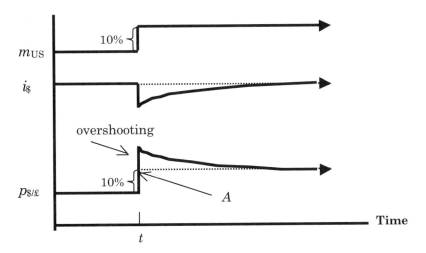

Figure 6.1
Illustration of overshooting.

an immediate 10 percent increase in the price level p_{US} (price flexi-
bility) and an immediate 10 percent depreciation of the dollar (to restore PPP, which holds at all times). Thus, there is no overshooting,
nor undershooting, because the exchange rate jumps to its long-run
10 percent-depreciated level.

In the sticky-price model, overshooting is best understood using
the UIP relation (equation 6.4). Suppose that before the increase in
money, the economy is in steady state, so $i_{\$,t} = i_{£,t}$, $E[\Delta p_{t+1} \mid \Omega_t] = 0$,
and the price level is not adjusting. Figure 6.1 shows this steady
state, before the time labeled t. Now, a key difference in the sticky-
price model is that by assumption the increase in money has no immediate effect on the price level. Therefore, from equation (6.6), the
increase in money supply requires an immediate fall in $i_\$$ to clear the
money market, so that now $i_\$ < i_£$; this is the usual liquidity effect of
an increase in the money supply (output y is fixed in simple versions
of the model). Consider the immediate effect of the fall in $i_\$$ on the
exchange rate: the dollar should depreciate (an increase in $p_{\$/£}$), but
by how much? Recall that the flexible-price model produces an immediate 10 percent dollar depreciation to its new long-run level—
neither overshooting nor undershooting. Suppose the sticky-price
model is the same—an immediate 10 percent dollar depreciation to
the same long-run level (pinned down by PPP), with $E[\Delta p_{t+1} \mid \Omega_t] = 0$
thereafter, labeled as point A in figure 6.1. But point A cannot be an

equilibrium: if $i_\$ < i_\pounds$, then UIP, which holds by assumption, is violated (i.e., $i_\$ < i_\pounds$ and $E[\Delta p_{t+1} \mid \Omega_t] = 0$ are incompatible). This rules out equilibrium at point A. Either overshooting or undershooting must occur.[12]

To see which is the right answer (overshooting or undershooting), we need to determine which is consistent with UIP. Note from equation (6.4) that with $i_\$ < i_\pounds$, it must be that $E[\Delta p_{t+1} \mid \Omega_t] < 0$, that is, the dollar must be expected to appreciate in the future (a lower dollar price of the pound—a negative Δp_{t+1}—is dollar appreciation). Intuitively, this future dollar appreciation is needed to compensate dollar depositors for a lower interest rate.[13] But the only way that the dollar can appreciate toward its long-run 10-percent-depreciated level in the future is if the dollar *depreciates* today by *more* than 10 percent, making room for the necessary trend appreciation. No other path is compatible with UIP. The dollar must overshoot.

An important reason I have included additional detail on this model is that it provides some intuition for the impact of a change in interest rates on the exchange rate. Understanding this interest rate/exchange rate link is important for the following two macro-oriented chapters. Note from figure 6.1 that the *drop* in $i_\$$ induces immediate dollar *depreciation* (an increase in the dollar price of a pound). This is consistent with most people's intuition: lower dollar interest rates make dollar deposits less attractive, other things equal, causing portfolios to shift out of the dollar.

Portfolio Balance Model

Though still squarely anchored in the asset approach, the portfolio balance model departs from the monetary models in two essential ways (key references include Kouri and Porter 1974 and the survey by Branson and Henderson 1985). First, of the four asset-approach models, this is the only one without PPP as an ingredient. This means the long-run exchange rate must be pinned down some other way. Second, this model does not impose UIP, and thus, expected dollar returns on different-currency deposits need not be equal. This leaves room for a currency risk premium, that is, an expected return bonus for holding particular currencies. The macro literature refers to this as imperfect substitutability between domestic and foreign assets (the same term introduced in the micro material in chapter 2).

The portfolio balance model is, as its name suggests, a model which balances demand for various asset classes against supply. The exchange rate brings them into balance. The exchange rate achieves this by affecting demand/supply in two ways. First, an expected *change* in the exchange rate affects foreign-asset demand because it has a direct effect on the expected dollar return on foreign assets (the right side of equation 6.4). Second, the *level* of the exchange rate affects foreign-asset supply. This works over time through a traditional macro channel, the trade balance: a lower value of the dollar pushes the trade balance toward surplus, which, through the balance of payments, increases foreign assets in domestic portfolios.[14]

A simple specification of this model includes three demand functions, one for each of three available asset classes: money (M), domestic bonds (B), and foreign bonds in foreign currency (B^*). Each of these demands depends on the same two variables: the domestic nominal interest rate i and the expected dollar return on foreign-currency bonds $i^* + E[\%\Delta P]$, where i^* is the foreign nominal interest rate and $E[\%\Delta P]$ is the expected percent depreciation of the dollar. (It is best to think of these as short-term bonds with no capital gains/losses from interest rate changes.)

Money Demand $= M^D(i, i^* + E[\%\Delta P])$ with

$$M^D_1 < 0, \quad M^D_2 < 0 \tag{6.13}$$

Bond Demand—Domestic $= B^D(i, i^* + E[\%\Delta P])$ with

$$B^D_1 > 0, \quad B^D_2 < 0 \tag{6.14}$$

Bond Demand—Foreign $= B^{D^*}(i, i^* + E[\%\Delta P])$ with

$$B^{D^*}_1 < 0, \quad B^{D^*}_2 > 0 \tag{6.15}$$

An asterisk denotes foreign variables, and subscripts denote partial derivatives. These equations embed the second exchange rate effect noted above—the effect of expected changes in the spot rate P. The signs of the partial derivatives that appear below each equation are sensible. Other things equal, an increase in the domestic interest rate i reduces money demand (higher opportunity cost), increases the demand for domestic bonds (higher return), and reduces the demand for foreign bonds (lower relative return). An increase in the expected dollar return on foreign-currency bonds reduces money demand (lower relative return), reduces the demand for domestic bonds (lower relative return), and increases the demand for foreign bonds (higher return). Note that wealth does not affect relative demands here: By assumption, changes in wealth induce equal percent changes in each of the three demands, so their portfolio shares are unaffected.

We need two additional equations to complete the model:

$$W = M^D + B^D + PB^{D^*} \tag{6.16}$$

$$\Delta B^{S^*} = T(P) + i^* B^{D^*} \qquad \text{with} \quad T_1 > 0. \tag{6.17}$$

Equation (6.16) is the wealth constraint: wealth must be allocated to these three asset classes. Equation (6.17) imposes a constraint on the *supply* of foreign-currency assets held by domestic residents: from balance of payments identities, changes in domestic holdings of foreign assets must equal the current account (per note 14); the current account in turn has two components, the trade balance $T(P)$ and net interest receipts on foreign bonds, $i^* B^{D^*}$. From the partial derivative $T_1 > 0$, we see that the trade balance depends positively on the level of the exchange rate P. That is, a depreciation (more dollars per pound) pushes the trade balance toward surplus, which must be matched with an increase in net foreign assets. This is the second of the two exchange rate effects noted above—the effect of the exchange rate's *level* on foreign asset supply.

What drives the exchange rate in this approach are changes in relative asset supplies. To see this, note that a market-clearing exchange rate can be derived for particular supply levels of M, B, and B^*. Subsequent changes in these supplies have both short-run effects on the exchange rate (allowing a non-zero ΔB^{S^*} in equation 6.17) and long-run effects (after steady state has been achieved with $\Delta B^{S^*} = 0$). Note, too, that there is nothing in the model that equates expected dollar returns on different currency deposits, that is, nothing that equates i with $i^* + E[\%\Delta P]$. Indeed, it is precisely these departures from UIP that are needed to clear markets. These departures are the currency risk premium introduced above—the expected return bonus for holding particular currencies.

For estimating this model from real-world data, more structure is added to both the demand and supply sides. On the demand side, one typically assumes Normally distributed returns and mean-variance optimization. On the supply side, determining which asset classes to measure is the main issue. Typically, instead of using bonds, one uses outstanding government debt. The rationale for focusing on government debt is that changes in supply necessarily imply changes in net private holdings. For many privately issued asset classes (such as bank deposits or corporate bonds), in contrast, changes in *net* supply are not possible because for every private issuer there is a private holder. Another difficult issue on the supply side is that, whatever asset classes one chooses, it is hard to measure their *levels* with any precision. Because measuring supply *changes* is easier, this model is typically tested for its ability to account for exchange rate changes, rather than its ability to account for exchange rate levels. Even as an account of changes, though, the model does not fare well empirically (see Branson and Henderson 1985; Lewis 1988).

An Analogy: Exchange Rate Models and Microstructure Models

I close this section with an analogy that links the microstructure models of chapter 4 with the exchange rate models of this chapter. The analogy is based on whether a model's focus is primarily on return, primarily on risk, or balanced between the two. As noted in the introduction to chapter 4, there are two traditional modeling approaches in microstructure, the information approach and the inventory approach. The information approach focuses more on return; risk plays no direct role in these models because players are risk neutral (as in the Kyle and sequential-trade models of chapter 4), so prices contain no risk premium. The inventory approach, in contrast, focuses more on risk. Under the inventory approach, imperfect risk sharing takes center stage and information effects on returns are not present. More recently, a hybrid approach has emerged within microstructure with a more balanced treatment of both risk and return (the simultaneous-trade model of chapter 4 being one example).

There is a similar pattern in the asset-approach models of this chapter. Like microstructure's information models, the two monetary models focus on how information affects returns; risk, on the other hand, has no effect on those returns. Like microstructure's inventory models, the portfolio balance model focuses on risk and the determination of equilibrium risk premia. In terms of information and returns, basic portfolio balance models are rather simplistic—they abstract from key categories of fundamentals such as output, relative goods demand, and to a great extent monetary policy. Finally, the analogue of microstructure's hybrid model is the general equilibrium model of exchange rates (the focus of the next section): in both cases there is considerable richness in both the impounding of information in price and the determination of risk premia.

6.3 Microfoundations: Tastes and Technology

The terms "microfoundations" and "tastes and technology" are common in macroeconomics, but less familiar outside. Microfoundations refers to the grounding of analysis in well-defined decision problems faced by individuals or groups. Grounding analysis this way is standard within microeconomics, hence the prefix micro. In microeconomic analysis, individuals have a clear sense of both their objectives and constraints, and they do their best to fulfill their objectives. These well-defined objectives are called "tastes" because they embody the preferences of individuals for various outcomes.[15] The constraints in macro models with microfoundations are called "technology." Technology encompasses the production side of the real economy (or the endowment process in a pure exchange economy) and defines the feasible choices—the size of the pie.

Though the three macro models reviewed in the previous section are not grounded in well-defined problems faced by individuals, the fourth of our macro models—the general equilibrium (GE) model—is. The microfoundations of the GE exchange rate model are the same as those adopted more generally in macroeconomics—the "two T's" of tastes and technology. As one might imagine, though, a grounding in tastes and technology can still accommodate many different specifications. Here I review the specification of the GE model only at a broad level. Though details are missing, a broad perspective is sufficient for clarifying how the GE model's microfoundations differ from the microfoundations of the microstructure approach.[16]

General Equilibrium Model

The GE model of exchange rate determination begins with maximization of a representative individual's utility.[17] Specification of utility as a function of various consumption opportunities has, naturally, important implications for equilibrium exchange rates. (The microstructure approach also includes utility maximization, but as we saw in chapter 4, utility is specified very simply, typically in terms of terminal nominal wealth.) The firm grounding in utility is the taste part of the model's microfoundations. The technology part of the model's microfoundations lies in the models' tightly specified production and transaction technologies. The production technology summarizes all input-output relationships in the production of real goods. The transaction technology summarizes the rules that apply to transactions. For example, early GE exchange rate models require individuals to hold domestic currency for purchasing domestic or foreign goods (in the literature this is called a "cash-in-advance" constraint). This requirement is important for exchange rate determination because it drives the demand for currencies. (Later GE models produce demand for money from the tastes side by putting money directly in the utility function.)

Unlike the three macro models above, however, the focus in GE models is on the real exchange rate, defined as

Real exchange rate $= P_{\$/\pounds}(P_{UK}/P_{US})$.

The real exchange rate is the nominal exchange rate $P_{\$/\pounds}$ adjusted by the relative price of goods. (Though I have not used it yet, the term nominal exchange rate is customarily used for $P_{\$/\pounds}$ when there is any possibility of confusion.) The real exchange rate is determined in this model as the relative price of foreign-to-domestic goods that matches the marginal rate of substitution in consumption among those goods (or, as in Obstfeld and Rogoff 1995, the marginal rate of substitution among inputs in final-good production). Given this real rate, to produce an expression for the nominal exchange rate $P_{\$/\pounds}$ one can then substitute for P_{US} and P_{UK} using the expressions for money demand in each country from equation 6.6. (Recall that this is the same procedure we followed for the flexible-price model, except that in that case the real exchange rate was assumed fixed at one, a direct implication of assuming PPP always holds.)

Early GE exchange rate models are generalizations of the flexible-price monetary model, allowing multiple goods and real shocks (such as shocks to demand or productivity). More recent GE models—sometimes called new open-economy macro models—are generalizations of the sticky-price monetary model (see Obstfeld and Rogoff 1995, 1996). These models allow for sticky nominal prices, which permits departures from PPP, in much the same spirit as the departures from PPP that arise in the original sticky-price model.

One major contribution of the GE models is their value for conducting welfare analysis. This comes from their well-specified microfoundations on both the demand (tastes) and on the supply (technology) sides of the economy. The recent GE models, for example, allow welfare analysis of fixed versus floating exchange rate regimes (see, e.g., Devereux and Engel 1999).

Another feature of GE models that warrants attention is their treatment of risk. The representative individual in this model is risk averse, so asset classes, including currency, can earn risk premia. The representative-individual framework, however, requires that risks be perfectly shared, so there are no unsystematic risks borne in equilibrium, only systematic risks. This is natural for a general equilibrium approach. But within microstructure, for example, there are risks that affect prices that are not systematic in this sense (e.g., the inventory risk covered in chapter 2).

Empirically, GE models—like the other three macro models—have not yet produced exchange rate equations that fit the data. They have been unable to overturn or explain the negative findings of Meese and Rogoff (1983a). Within the context of the macro-asset approach, why floating exchange rates behave as they do over horizons up to a couple years remains a puzzle.

6.4 Microfoundations: Information and Institutions

Unlike the micro-foundations in exchange rate economics, with its focus on well-defined tastes and technology, the microstructure approach is grounded in what I call the "two I's": information and institutions. This distinction is one of emphasis. General equilibrium exchange rate models certainly have an information dimension, but it is typically simple, incorporating only public information. Microstructure models certainly include tastes and utility maximization, but the specification of those tastes is simple, typically limited to *nominal* wealth levels rather than including factors that are, by their nature, *real* quantities, such as consumption and leisure.

Let me clarify the difference between technology and institutions. Recall from the GE macro model that "technology" refers primarily to the supply side of the real economy, whereas "tastes" refers to the demand side. In microstructure modeling, however, the supply side of the real economy plays no direct role.[18] Institutions, on the other hand, do play a central role in microstructure models. Institutions embody the "rules of the game" that govern the interaction between agents and, therefore, affect outcomes. (By rules of the game, I have in mind chapter 4's summaries of each model's key features, in particular the part labeled "institutions." These institutional features also influence the other two parts of the model summaries, i.e., which players participate and what information is available to each player.) Because there is a sense in which the GE model's technology "precedes" interaction, it is arguably deeper, more "primitive," than institutions. That is a theoretical plus. But the proof is in the empirical pudding.[19]

Continuing on this line of comparing/contrasting the macro- and microstructure approaches, figure 6.2 relates the models of this chapter to the microstructure approach. I introduced the first of the models shown, purchasing power parity (PPP), in section 6.1 as a goods market perspective on exchange rate fundamentals. It was not, however, grounded in microeconomic analysis of well-defined problems faced by individuals. The same is true of the first three of the four asset-approach models: the flexible-price monetary model (FPM), the sticky-price monetary model (SPM), and the portfolio balance model (PBM). In contrast, the fourth asset-approach model —the GE model—is grounded in well-defined problems faced by individuals, with an emphasis on tastes and technology. The microstructure models of chapter 4 emphasize information and institutions instead.

Let me close this section on the two "I's" of the microstructure approach by drawing attention to their interaction. Consider a simple example of how institutions can affect the processing of information, and ultimately whether that information is impounded in price. In chapters 1 and 5, I addressed the volume amplification effects of the FX hot potato, which results from the passing of unwanted inventories from dealer to dealer following an initial customer trade (i.e., it results from risk management in a multiple-dealer setting). Now, if (1) information is impounded in price via learning from order flow—as is common to all the microstructure models of chapter 4—and (2) order flow is noisier as a result of dealer risk management, then the institutional structure can produce less informative prices. This was one of the main insights of the simultaneous-trade model (section 4.4). Interaction between risk management and information processing is an exciting area of study within microstructure research.

6.5 A False Dichotomy: Micro Issues versus Macro Issues

Though the notion of microfoundations helps to organize thinking, the orientation can be misleading because issues in exchange rate economics—as elsewhere in financial economics—do not divide

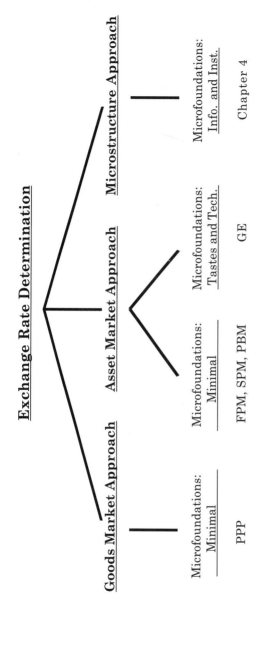

Figure 6.2
Three approaches to exchange rates and their models. PPP denotes purchasing power parity model. FPM denotes flexible-price monetary model. SPM denotes sticky-price monetary model. PBM denotes portfolio balance model. GE denotes general equilibrium model.

Micro Issues   Macro Issues

Figure 6.3
Issues spectrum.

neatly into "micro" issues and "macro" issues. Instead, issues fall along a spectrum, as figure 6.3 shows.

The more micro end of the spectrum includes issues such as optimal market design, efficient regulation, and the determination of transaction costs. These are bread and butter issues within microstructure research. The more macro end includes issues such as medium/long-run exchange rate determination, forward-discount bias, and home bias (the first two of which I address in detail in the next chapter). Between the extremes are issues such as volatility determination, central bank intervention, and transaction taxes (the first of which I address in chapter 7 and the second in chapter 8).[20]

It is important, in my judgment, to distinguish between tools and the issues to which they are applied. I introduce the issues spectrum not only to frame the later chapters, but also because it helps explain the gap between exchange rate economics on the one hand and microstructure finance on the other. Within microstructure finance, the tools have been applied to bread and butter microeconomic issues that, for the most part, do not interest macro-oriented exchange rate economists. Though one might suppose that because these tools were developed for micro issues they are not likely to help with macro issues, they are actually quite useful. The analysis in chapters 7 and 8 (on longer horizon exchange rate determination, central bank intervention, etc.) will demonstrate this.

An example may clarify why exchange rate economists view microstructure with skepticism. The example comes from the call for papers that initiated a market microstructure research group in the United States (the group is part of the National Bureau of Economic Research). The call for papers came with a list of topics —a list that was important for defining the scope and spirit of the group's agenda. Though all eleven topics are bread and butter microstructure, macroeconomists might quickly dismiss them. The topics include:

- minimum tick-size and competitiveness
- measurement and control of transaction costs
- regulation and the evolution of market design
- definition, measurement, and determinants of liquidity
- costs and benefits of alternate trading mechanisms
- cross-border listing and trading of securities
- trading technology and information systems
- implications of market design for risk management and financial engineering

These topics do not exactly make the macroeconomist's heart flutter. The remaining three topics were

- globalization of financial markets
- the role of information in price discovery
- domestic and international comparisons of trading costs

Of the eleven topics, only the first two of these last three would catch the eye of most macroeconomists, but these two are broad enough to catch most anybody's eye. It is not clear how microstructure tools could be relevant to these topics' macro aspects; the link between the last topic and macroeconomics is not obvious either, unless one is familiar with the literature linking trading costs to the home bias puzzle. That literature shows that foreign holdings are turned over more than domestic holdings, which is difficult reconcile with home bias being due to higher foreign trading costs (see Tesar and Werner 1995, and note 3 of chapter 1).

The upshot is that researchers working with microstructure tools tend not to apply them to issues on the macro end of the issues spectrum, and those who are working on the macro end have not felt it worthwhile to invest in apparently inappropriate microstructure tools. For these tools to be applied to more FX issues on the macro end, either macroeconomists need introduction to the tools or those with the tools need to extend their study rightward on the spectrum. Both, in fact, are occurring. As the process continues, the uneasy dichotomy between macro and micro approaches will fade.

7   Macro Puzzles: The Challenge for Microstructure

This chapter examines traditional exchange rate puzzles and shows how microstructure tools are used to address them. The chapter is not intended to put these puzzles to rest: they wouldn't be traditional if they weren't stubborn. My intent is to provide a sense for how to address "macro" puzzles by looking under the "micro lamppost." For those unfamiliar with the lamppost metaphor, it comes from a parable of a guy who drops his keys while getting into his car, in the middle of a dark parking lot. Another fellow sees him searching over in a corner of the lot—a well-lit corner—and asks,

"What are you doing?"

"Looking for my keys—I dropped them getting into my car."

"Then why are you looking way over here?"

"Because this is where the light is."

Is there any hope of finding the exchange rate keys under the microstructure lamppost? Chapter 1 provides some evidence that the microstructure lamppost is not so far removed. In this chapter, I extend that evidence and show that the lamppost has indeed cast light on the key puzzles. I also identify directions for future application of the microstructure approach.

The three puzzles I consider are the "big three" introduced in chapter 1:

• The determination puzzle: exchange rate movements are virtually unrelated to our best measures of fundamentals

• The excess volatility puzzle: exchange rates are excessively volatile relative to our best measures of fundamentals

• The forward bias puzzle: excess returns in foreign exchange are predictable and inexplicable

The first section addresses the determination puzzle by using order flows. It draws on recent empirical work by Evans and Lyons (1999). In the second section, I contrast order flow analysis with an older approach, the so-called flow approach to exchange rates, which uses balance of payments flows (e.g., current accounts and capital accounts), not order flows. Section three returns to the big three puzzles, in particular the excess volatility puzzle, drawing on empirical work by Killeen, Lyons, and Moore (2000a). The last section addresses the forward bias puzzle. The explanation I offer for this puzzle is new to the literature.

7.1 The Determination Puzzle

Exchange rate economics has been in crisis since Meese and Rogoff (1983a) showed that our models are empirical failures: the proportion of monthly exchange rate changes our textbook models can explain is essentially zero. In their survey, Frankel and Rose (1995, 1704, 1708) summarize as follows:

The Meese and Rogoff analysis at short horizons has never been convincingly overturned or explained. It continues to exert a pessimistic effect on the field of empirical exchange rate modeling in particular and international finance in general.... Such results indicate that no model based on such standard fundamentals like money supplies, real income, interest rates, inflation rates, and current account balances will ever succeed in explaining or predicting a high percentage of the variation in the exchange rate, at least at short- or medium-term frequencies.[1]

This is the determination puzzle. Immense effort has been expended to resolve it.[2]

If determinants are not macro fundamentals like interest rates, money supplies, and trade balances, then what are they? Two alternatives have attracted a lot of attention among macroeconomists. The first is that exchange rate determinants include extraneous variables, which are typically modeled as speculative bubbles. (A bubble is a component of an asset's price that is nonfundamental. A bubble can cause price to rise so fast that investors are induced to buy, even though the bubble may burst at any time. See, e.g., Meese 1986; Evans 1986.) On the whole, however, the empirical evidence on bubbles is not supportive: in their survey, Flood and Hodrick (1990) conclude that existing evidence is unconvincing. A second alternative to macro fundamentals is nonrational behavior. For example,

exchange rates may be determined, in part, from avoidable expectational errors (Dominguez 1986; Frankel and Froot 1987; Hau 1998).
On a priori grounds, many financial economists find this second alternative unappealing. Even if one is sympathetic, however, there is a
wide gulf between the presence of nonrational behavior and accounting for exchange rates empirically.[3]

This section addresses the determination puzzle using the microstructure approach, drawing heavily from work presented in Evans
and Lyons (1999). One advantage of the microstructure approach is
that it directs attention to variables that have escaped the attention of
macroeconomists. Meese (1990, 130) offers a telling quote along these
lines: "Omitted variables is another possible explanation for the lack
of explanatory power in asset market models. However, empirical
researchers have shown considerable imagination in their specification searches, so it is not easy to think of variables that have escaped
consideration in an exchange-rate equation." Among the variables
escaping consideration, order flow may be the most important. As
we saw in chapter 4, order flow is the proximate determinant of price
in microstructure models, regardless of institutional structure. This
ensures that the causal role played by order flow is robust to different market structures.

A Hybrid Model with Both Macro and Micro Determinants

To establish a link between the micro and macro approaches, chapter
1 introduces models with components from both. The hybrid model I
suggest in that first chapter takes the form:

$$\Delta P_t = f(i, m, z) + g(X, I, Z) + \varepsilon_t$$

where the function $f(i, m, z)$ is the macro component of the model
and $g(X, I, Z)$ is the microstructure component. Chapters 4, 5, and 6
provide explicit specifications for how interest rates i, money supplies m, order flows X, and inventories I might enter these two functions. (Recall that z and Z denote unspecified other determinants.)
An important take-away from those chapters is that $f(i, m, z)$ and
$g(X, I, Z)$ depend on more than just current and past values of
their determinants—they also depend, crucially, on expectations of
determinants' future values. This stands to reason: rational markets
are forward looking, so these expectations are important for setting
prices today.

Though I have split this stylized hybrid model into two parts, the two parts are not necessarily independent. This will depend on the main micro determinant—order flow X—and the type of information it conveys. Per chapters 1 and 2, order flow conveys two main information types: payoff information and discount rate information. In macro models, information about future payoffs translates to information about future (i, m, z). One way order flow can convey information about future (i, m, z) is by aggregating the information in individuals' expectations of (i, m, z). (Recall that as a measure of expectations, order flow reflects people's willingness to back their beliefs with money; and like actual expectations, this measure evolves rapidly, in contrast to measures derived from macro data.) When order flow conveys payoff information, macro and micro determinants are interdependent: order flow acts as a proximate determinant of price, but standard macro fundamentals are the underlying determinant.[4]

If order flow X conveys discount rate information only, then the two sets of determinants (i, m, z) and (X, I, Z) can indeed be independent. To understand why, suppose the discount rate information conveyed by order flow X is about portfolio balance effects (e.g., persistent changes in discount rates, due to changing risk preferences, changing hedging demands, or changing liquidity demands under imperfect substitutability—see chapter 2).[5] Now, consider the two monetary macro models (flexible and sticky-price). Portfolio balance effects from order flow X are unrelated to these models' specifications of $f(i, m, z)$. This is because the monetary models assume that different-currency assets are perfect substitutes (i.e., they assume that Uncovered Interest Parity holds: assets differing only in their currency denomination have the same expected return). Thus, effects from imperfect substitutability are necessarily independent of the $f(i, m, z)$ of these monetary models. In the case of the macro portfolio balance model, in contrast, portfolio balance effects from order flow X are quite likely to be related to the determining variables (i, m, z). Indeed, in that model, price effects from imperfect substitutability are the focus of $f(i, m, z)$.[6]

Consider the hybrid model from a different perspective—a graphical perspective. The top panel of figure 7.1 illustrates the connection between fundamentals and price under the traditional macro view (i.e., as reflected in the models of chapter 6). Information about fundamentals is publicly known, and so is the mapping from that

The Macro View

The Microstructure View

The Hybrid View

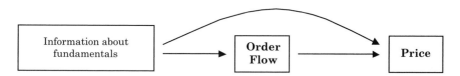

Figure 7.1
Spanning macro and microstructure graphically. The top panel illustrates the connection between fundamentals and price under the traditional macro view (i.e., as
reflected in the models of chapter 6): information about fundamentals is public, and so
is the mapping to price, so price adjustment is direct and immediate. The middle panel
shows the traditional microstructure view (as reflected in the models of chapter 4). The
focus in that case is fundamental information that is not publicly known. This type of
information is first transformed into order flow, which becomes a signal to the price
setter (e.g., dealer) that price needs to be adjusted. Actual markets include both, which
is illustrated in the bottom panel—the hybrid view.

information to price. Consequently, price adjustment is direct and immediate. The middle panel shows the traditional microstructure view (as reflected in the models of chapter 4). The focus in that case is on fundamental information that is not publicly known. In those models, information is first transformed into order flow, which becomes a signal to the price setter that price needs to be adjusted. The bottom panel presents the hybrid view. Here, the model accommodates both possibilities: information that affects price directly and information that affects price via order flow. Armed with models that allow for both, we can let the data determine their relative importance.

Before describing the hybrid model estimated by Evans and Lyons (1999), let me address some front-end considerations in modeling strategy. First, the determination puzzle concerns exchange rate behavior over months and years, not minutes. As we saw in chapter 5, most empirical work in microstructure is estimated at the transaction frequency. The first order of business is to design a trading model that makes sense at lower frequencies. Several features of the Evans-Lyons model contribute to this (as I will note specifically below, as I present the features). Second, because interdealer flow is more transparent, it is more immediately relevant to FX price determination than customer-dealer order flow. The hybrid model should reflect this important institutional feature. (Of the chapter 4 models, only the simultaneous-trade model has this feature.) Third, the model should provide a vehicle for understanding the behavior of order flow in figure 1.2. That figure presents cumulative interdealer order flow in the $/DM and $/yen markets over the four-month Evans (1997) data set, the same data set used by Evans and Lyons (1999). A puzzling feature is the persistence: there is no obvious evidence of mean reversion in cumulative order flow. How can this be consistent with the findings reviewed in chapter 5, where individual dealer inventories have a very short half-life (i.e., their positions revert to zero rapidly)? The Evans-Lyons model accounts for this seeming incongruity.

A Daily Frequency Model

The model of is a variant of the simultaneous-trade model. Because I reviewed that model in chapter 4, I will focus on substantive differences. For reference, note that I also summarize the Evans-Lyons

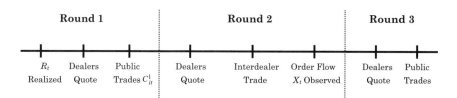

Figure 7.2
Daily timing in the Evans-Lyons model.

model in figure 7.3 (in the same manner that I use figures to summarize each of the models of chapter 4).

There are N dealers in the model, indexed by i, a continuum of nondealer customers (the public), and an infinite number of trading days. Dealers and customers all have negative exponential utility. Within each day, there are three rounds of trading:

Round 1: Dealers trade with the public

Round 2: Dealers trade among themselves to share risk

Round 3: Dealers trade with the public to share risk more broadly.

Figure 7.2 shows the timing within each day.

At the beginning of each day, the payoff to holding foreign exchange is R_t, which is composed of a series of increments ΔR_t, so that

$$R_t = \sum_{\tau=1}^{t} \Delta R_\tau. \tag{7.1}$$

The payoff increments ΔR_t are i.i.d. Normal$(0, \sigma_R^2)$ and are observed publicly at the beginning of each day. These realized increments represent the flow of public macroeconomic information—the macro component of the model $f(i, m, z)$. For concreteness, one can think of this abstract payoff increment ΔR_t as changes in interest rates.

Per figure 7.2, after observing the payoff R_t, each dealer sets a quote for his public customers. As in the simultaneous-trade model, quotes are scalar two-way prices, set simultaneously and independently.[7] Denote this dealer i quote in round 1 of day t as P_{it}^1. Evans and Lyons show that in equilibrium, all dealers choose to quote the same price, denoted P_t^1. Each dealer then receives a customer-order realization C_{it}^1 that is executed at his quoted price P_t^1, where $C_{it}^1 < 0$ denotes a customer sale (dealer i purchase). Each of these N customer-

Players:

- N dealers (risk-averse and strategic)
- a continuum of "customers" (risk-averse and nonstrategic), whose collective risk-bearing capacity is less than infinite

Information:

- daily payoff R_t on foreign exchange is the sum of daily increments ΔR_t, with each ΔR_t distributed Normal$(0,\sigma_R^2)$
- all participants observe R_t at the beginning of day t
- in round one of each day, each dealer i receives a customer order C_{it}^1, distributed Normal$(0,\sigma_C^2)$
- after round two of each day, all dealers observe that day's interdealer order flow X_t

Institutions:

- there are an infinite number of trading days
- each trading day, there are three rounds of trading: customer-dealer, then interdealer, then another customer-dealer
- dealers end each day with no net position (i.e., there are no daily frequency inventory effects)

<u>Quoting</u>

- dealer quoting is simultaneous, independent, and required
- quotes are available to all dealers
- a quote is a single price at which the dealer agrees to buy and sell any amount

<u>Trading</u>

- trading is simultaneous and independent
- trading with multiple partners is feasible

Figure 7.3
Summary of the Evans-Lyons (1999) model.

order realizations is distributed:

$$C_{it}^1 \sim \text{Normal}(0, \sigma_C^2),$$

and they are uncorrelated across dealers. Importantly, the C_{it}^1 realizations are not publicly observable. It will be useful to define the aggregate public demand in round 1 as

$$C_t^1 = \sum_{i=1}^{N} C_{it}^1.$$

One important choice in specifying the model is the correlation between customer orders C_{it}^1 and the stream of payoff increments ΔR_t. This choice determines whether the macro and micro components of the model—the $f(i, m, z)$ and $g(X, I, Z)$—are interdependent. If there is no correlation, it is not possible for order flow to convey payoff information. Because Evans and Lyons (1999) have only four months of order flow data, they are unable to determine empirically whether order flow conveys payoff information, discount rate information, or both. Because of this, they choose to model the customer orders C_{it}^1 as distributed independently of the payoff stream R_t—arguably, a less controversial choice. This means that, in their model, the only kind of information that order flow can convey is discount rate information. Because their model rules out inventory effects at the daily frequency (as we shall see below), the discount rate information in their model is necessarily about portfolio balance effects.

Round 2 is the interdealer trading round. Each dealer simultaneously and independently quotes a scalar two-way price to other dealers P_{it}^2. These interdealer quotes are observable and available to all dealers in the market. Evans and Lyons show that, like in round 1, all dealers choose to quote the same price, denoted P_t^2. Each dealer then simultaneously and independently trades on other dealers' quotes. (Orders at a given price are split evenly across any dealers quoting that price.) Let T_{it} denote the (net) interdealer trade initiated by dealer i in round 2 of day t.[8]

Importantly, at the close of round 2 all dealers observe the net interdealer order flow on that day:

$$X_t = \sum_{i=1}^{N} T_{it}. \tag{7.2}$$

This order flow information is important to the model because it conveys the size and sign of the public order flow in round 1. To understand why, consider the interdealer trading rule derived by Evans and Lyons:

$$T_{it} = \alpha C_{it}^1, \tag{7.3}$$

where α is a constant (positive) coefficient. Each dealer's trade in round 2 is proportional to the customer order he receives in round 1. This implies that when dealers observe the interdealer order flow $X_t = \Sigma_i T_{it} = \alpha C_t^1$, they can infer the aggregate public order flow C_t^1 in round 1.

In round 3, dealers share overnight risk with the non-dealer public. This feature is important in distinguishing this model from its high-frequency cousin, the simultaneous-trade model. (In the simultaneous-trade model the public does not re-enter, and therefore cannot share risk borne by dealers.) Unlike round 1, the public's trading in round 3 is nonstochastic. To start the round, each dealer simultaneously and independently quotes a scalar two-way price P_t^3 (also common across dealers). These quotes are observable and available to the public at large.

A crucial assumption made by Evans and Lyons is that dealers set prices in round 3 such that the public willingly absorbs all dealer inventory imbalances, so that each dealer ends the day with no net position.[9] As an empirical matter, it is common practice for FX dealers to end each day with no net position, which squares with the empirical findings in chapter 5. Note too that this assumption rules out inventory effects on price at the daily frequency (because dealers do not hold overnight positions that require compensation). The round-3 price that dealers actually quote to induce public absorption of these imbalances depends on the round-2 interdealer order flow X_t: this interdealer order flow informs dealers of the size of the total position that the public needs to absorb (as noted, $X_t = \alpha C_t^1$).

More precisely, to determine the round-3 price, dealers need to know two things: the total position that the public needs to absorb (which they learn from X_t), and the public's risk-bearing capacity. Regarding the latter, the public's capacity for bearing foreign-exchange risk is assumed less than infinite (i.e., Evans and Lyons assume that foreign- and domestic-currency assets are not perfect substitutes.) This is the key assumption: it makes room in the model for portfolio balance effects on price. Consistent with negative exponential utility, the public's total demand for foreign exchange in round 3, denoted C_t^3, is a linear function of its expected return conditional on public information:

$$C_t^3 = \gamma E[\Delta P_{t+1}^3 + R_{t+1} \mid \Omega_t^3]. \tag{7.4}$$

The positive coefficient γ captures the aggregate risk-bearing capacity of the public: A larger γ means the public is willing to absorb a larger foreign-exchange position for a given expected return. Ω_t^3 is the public information available at the time of trading in round 3 (which includes all past R_t and X_t).

The Pricing Relation

Evans and Lyons (1999) show that the price at the end of day t is:[10]

$$P_t = \beta_1 \sum_{\tau=1}^{t} \Delta R_\tau + \beta_2 \sum_{\tau=1}^{t} X_\tau. \tag{7.5}$$

The change in price from the end of day $t - 1$ to the end of day t can therefore be written as:

$$\Delta P_t = \beta_1 \Delta R_t + \beta_2 X_t. \tag{7.6}$$

where β_2 is a positive constant (that depends on γ and α).[11] It is not surprising that this price change includes the payoff increment ΔR_t: upon realization, the increment ΔR_t becomes a known (i.e., risk-free) component of the continuing daily payoff R_t, and its discounted value is impounded in price (β_1).

Let me provide some intuition for the portfolio balance effect—the $\beta_2 X_t$ term. This term is the required price adjustment that induces re-absorption of the random order flow C_t^1 that occurred at the beginning of the day. The value of the parameter β_2 insures that at the round-3 price:

$$C_t^1 + C_t^3 = 0,$$

that is, that the dealers have no net overnight position. To understand the link to order flow, recall that the round-3 price depends on two things: the public's risk-bearing capacity (summarized by γ), and the total position that the public needs to absorb. As noted, dealers learn about the total position the public needs to absorb from order flow X_t. This produces the relation between interdealer order flow and the subsequent price adjustment.

Let's walk through an example. Consider the price at the close of day t, as described by equation (7.5). The next day's increment to the daily payoff R, ΔR_{t+1}, is uncertain, but all previous realizations of the payoff increment ΔR are known and are impounded in price. (Expectations of future realizations do not enter equation 7.5 due to the simple specification of ΔR_t and C_t^1 as independently distributed across time with mean zero.) To understand the portfolio balance term, $\beta_2 \Sigma_\tau X_\tau$, recall that

$$X_t \equiv \sum_{i=1}^{N} T_{it} = \alpha C_t^1.$$

Therefore, we can write

$$\sum_{\tau=1}^{t} X_\tau \propto \sum_{\tau=1}^{t} C_\tau^1.$$

The sum of the portfolio shifts C_τ^1 represent changes in "effective" asset supply, in the sense that shifts out of FX are an increase in the net supply that the remainder of the public must absorb. (I couch this in terms of supply to connect with traditional portfolio balance intuition, as outlined in chapter 6.) The total increase in net supply is the sum of past portfolio shifts out of FX:

$$\text{Increase in net supply} = -\sum_{\tau=1}^{t} C_{\tau}^1.$$

As is standard in portfolio balance models, increases in supply lower price, whereas decreases in supply raise price. This is why a negative cumulative X_t in equation (7.5) lowers price: If cumulative X_t is negative, this implies that cumulative C_t^1 is also negative, which is an increase in net supply, requiring an decrease in price to clear the market. X_t is the variable conveying this information about the decrease in net supply (C_t^1 is unobservable). P_t depends on the sum of the X_i because each additional decrease in supply C_t^1 requires a *persistent* incremental increase in price.

Here is a simple diagram that illustrates the basic economics of the model. Figure 7.4 presents a one-period example, where the uncer-

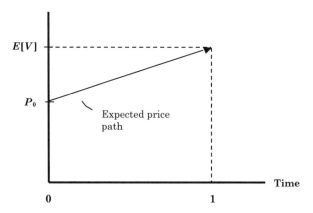

Figure 7.4
Portfolio balance effects: one-period example. The market-clearing gap $E[V] - P_0$ is a function of the risky asset's net supply. In traditional portfolio balance models, variation in gross supply is the driver. In the Evans-Lyons model, gross supply is fixed, but net supply is moving over time due to shifts in demand that are unrelated to $E[V] - P_0$. These demand shifts are the exogenous realizations of C_{it}^1. In contrast to the dissipation of the portfolio balance effect on price in the one-period example, the price effects do not dissipate in the Evans-Lyons model because payoff uncertainty is resolved smoothly over time.

tain payoff V is realized at time 1. The market-clearing gap $E[V] - P_0$
—the risk premium—will be a function of the risky asset's net supply. In traditional portfolio balance models (see chapter 6), demand
D is a function of relative returns, and supply S is time-varying. That
is, price P_0 is determined according to

$$D(E[V] - P_0) = \tilde{S},$$

where the tilde denotes random variation. In these traditional models,
changes in supply S are unrelated to $E[V]$; market-clearing price is
moving in a way similar to the way the price of a bond—with a
fixed, known payoff—has to adjust to alter its expected return.

The Evans-Lyons model looks different. In their model (gross)
supply is fixed. But what I am calling "net supply" is moving over
time, due to demand shifts that are unrelated to $E[V] - P_0$. These
demand shifts are the realizations of C_{it}^1.[12] Conceptually, their model
looks more like

$$D(E[V] - P_0, \tilde{C}) = \bar{S},$$

where $\bar{S}$ denotes fixed gross supply and $\tilde{C}$ denotes shifts in net supply, that is, shifts in demand unrelated to $E[V] - P_0$. In this one-
period example, the higher the $t = 0$ realization of $\tilde{C}$, the lower the
net supply to be absorbed by the rest of the public, and the higher
the market-clearing price P_0 (to achieve stock equilibrium). In a
sense, then, the multi-period model of Evans and Lyons is akin to a
single-period model in which net supply is "shocked" multiple times
before trading takes place. At the time of each "shock," price needs
to adjust a bit more.

Let me contrast this pricing relation in equation (7.5) with the
pricing relation in the simultaneous-trade model of chapter 4 (equation 4.20). The key difference, though not obvious from the equations, is that X_t is conveying a different type of information. In the
Evans-Lyons model, X_t conveys information about portfolio balance
effects only: Daily inventory effects are ruled out by the assumption
of no overnight dealer positions and payoff information is ruled out
by the assumption that there is no correlation between the C_{it}^1's and
the payoff increments ΔR_t. In the simultaneous-trade model, on the
other hand, it is the portfolio balance effects that are ruled out: The
public does not trade in period 2 of that model, so dealers must hold
the inventory imbalance among themselves when V is realized. Because there is no risk sharing with the public, risk premia at the

public level do not arise. This feature of the simultaneous-trade model is more appropriate for intraday analysis than it would be for lower frequency analysis. The simultaneous-trade model does, however, admit the two types of order flow information that the Evans-Lyons model rules out: payoff information and information about inventory effects. Both operate in the simultaneous-trade model through interdealer order flow X, which conveys payoff information in that model because interdealer trades incorporate the private payoff signals. X conveys information about inventory effects in the same way that order flow conveys information about portfolio effects in the Evans-Lyons model: A larger X implies a larger initial purchase by the public, and therefore a larger short position that dealers as a whole have to bear. It is the size of this position that drives the inventory effect on price.

Before moving to the Evans-Lyons results, I want to address another of their model's important features. Recall that one of their modeling objectives is to clarify the behavior of order flow in figure 1.2. Specifically, cumulative order flow is puzzlingly persistent: there is no obvious evidence of mean reversion in cumulative order flow, yet, empirically, individual dealer inventories have a short half-life. How can these two facts be consistent? The Evans-Lyons model provides an explanation. First, note that dealer inventories in the Evans-Lyons model are short-lived: no dealer carries an inventory longer than one day. At the same time, cumulative interdealer order flow in their model is persistent—in fact, it follows a random walk (i.e., there is no mean reversion whatsoever). Equations (7.2) and (7.3) hold the key to this random-walk result. Interdealer order flow each day is proportional to the public order flow that occurs at the beginning of that day. Because this public order flow is i.i.d. across dealers and time, cumulative interdealer order flow follows a random walk. In the end, these seemingly incongruous facts are consistent because, ultimately, dealers can only decumulate inventory by trading with the public, so aggregate decumulation is not reflected in interdealer flow.[13]

Evans-Lyons Results

The equation Evans and Lyons actually estimate is the following:

$$\Delta p_t = \beta_1 \Delta(i_t - i_t^*) + \beta_2 X_t + \eta_t, \tag{7.7}$$

where Δp_t is the change in the log spot rate (DM/\$ or yen/\$) from the end of day $t - 1$ to the end of day t, $\Delta(i_t - i_t^*)$ is the change in the overnight interest differential from day $t - 1$ to day t (* denotes DM or yen), and X_t is the interdealer order flow from the end of day $t - 1$ to the end of day t (negative denotes net dollar sales).

There are two changes in this equation relative to equation (7.6). First, the payoff increment ΔR_t in equation (7.6) represents the macro innovations in the model, or $f(i, m, z)$. For estimation, Evans and Lyons have to take a stand on what to include in the regression for ΔR_t. They choose to include changes in the nominal interest differential; that is, they define $\Delta R_t = \Delta(i_t - i_t^*)$, where i_t is the nominal dollar interest rate and i_t^* is the nominal non-dollar interest rate (DM or yen). As a measure of variation in macro fundamentals, the interest differential is obviously incomplete. The reason Evans and Lyons do not specify a full-blown macro model is because other macro variables (e.g., money supply, output, etc.) are not available at the daily frequency. Accordingly, one should not view their model as fully accommodating both the macro and micro approaches. At the same time, if one were to choose a single macro determinant that needs to be included, interest rates would be it: Innovations in interest differentials are the main engine of exchange rate variation in macro models (e.g., the sticky-price monetary model).[14] Moreover, using the change in the interest differential rather than the level is consistent with monetary macro models: in monetary models, shocks to price are driven by unanticipated changes in the differential.[15]

The second difference in equation (7.7) relative to (7.6) is the replacement of the change in the level of price ΔP_t with the change in the log price Δp_t. This difference makes their estimation more directly comparable to previous macro specifications, as those specifications use the log change (which is approximately equal to a percentage change). As an empirical matter, using Δp_t is inconsequential: the two different measures for the change in price produce nearly identical results.

Table 7.1 presents estimates of the Evans-Lyons model (equation 7.7) using daily data for the DM/\$ and yen/\$ exchange rates. The coefficient β_2 on order flow X_t is correctly signed and significant, with t-statistics above five in both equations. To see that the sign is correct, recall from the model that net purchases of dollars—a positive X_t—should lead to a higher DM price of dollars. The traditional

Table 7.1
Estimates of the Evans-Lyons Model

$$\Delta p_t = \beta_1 \Delta(i_t - i_t^*) + \beta_2 X_t + \eta_t$$

	β_1	β_2	R^2
DM	0.52	2.10	0.64
	(1.5)	(10.5)	
Yen	2.48	2.90	0.45
	(2.7)	(6.3)	

T-statistics are shown in parentheses. (In the case of the DM equation, the t-statistics are corrected for heteroskedasticity; there is no evidence of heteroskedasticity in the yen equation, and no evidence of serial correlation in either equation.) The dependent variable Δp_t is the change in the log spot exchange rate from 4 P.M. GMT on day $t-1$ to 4 P.M. GMT on day t (DM/\$ or yen/\$). The regressor $\Delta(i_t - i_t^*)$ is the change in the one-day interest differential from day $t-1$ to day t (* denotes DM or yen, annual basis). The regressor X_t is interdealer order flow between 4 P.M. GMT on day $t-1$ and 4 P.M. GMT on day t (negative for net dollar sales, in thousands of transactions). Estimated using OLS. The sample spans four months (May 1 to August 31, 1996), which is 89 trading days. (Saturday and Sunday order flow—of which there is little—is included in Monday.)

macrofundamental—the interest differential—is correctly signed, but is only significant in the yen equation. (The sign should be positive because, in the sticky-price monetary model for example, an increase in the dollar interest rate i_t induces an immediate dollar appreciation—increase in DM/\$—per chapter 6.)

The overall fit of the model is striking relative to traditional macro models, with R^2 statistics of 64 percent and 45 percent for the DM and yen equations, respectively. Moreover, the explanatory power of these regressions is almost wholly due to order flow X_t: regressing Δp_t on $\Delta(i_t - i_t^*)$ alone, plus a constant, produces an R^2 statistic less than 1 percent in both equations and coefficients on $\Delta(i_t - i_t^*)$ that are insignificant at the 5 percent level.[16] That the interest differential regains significance once order flow is included, at least in the yen equation, is consistent with omitted variable bias in the interest-rates-only specification.

The size of the order flow coefficient is consistent with estimates based on single-dealer data reviewed in chapter 5. The coefficient of 2.1 in the DM equation of table 7.1 implies that a day with one thousand more dollar purchases than sales induces an increase in the DM price by 2.1 percent.[17] Given an average trade size in the sample of \$3.9 million, this implies that

$1 billion of net dollar purchases increases the DM price of a dollar by 0.54 percent.

Equivalently, at a spot rate of 1.5 DM/$, $1 billion of net dollar purchases increases the DM price of a dollar by 0.8 pfennig. Turning now to the chapter 5 estimates, those results at the single-dealer level show that information asymmetry induces the dealer to increase price by one one-hundredth of a pfennig (0.0001 DM) for every incoming buy order of $10 million. That translates to 1 pfennig per $1 billion, versus the 0.8 pfennig per $1 billion found by Evans and Lyons. Though linearly extrapolating the single-dealer estimate (based on individual order sizes around $10 million) to $1 billion of order flow is certainly not an accurate description of single-dealer price elasticity, with multiple dealers it may be a good description of price elasticity marketwide.

Robustness Checks

To check robustness, Evans and Lyons examine several obvious variations on the model. For example, they include a constant in the regression, even though the model does not call for one; the constant is insignificant for both currencies and has no substantive effect on the other coefficients. Second, in the spirit of Uncovered Interest Parity, they include the level of the interest differential in lieu of its change; the level of the differential is insignificant in both cases. Third, they test for simple forms of nonlinearity, such as adding a squared order flow term, or testing for piece-wise linearity. Though the squared order flow term is insignificant in both equations and they find no evidence of piece-wise linearity in the DM equation, they do find some evidence of piece-wise linearity in the yen equation (there is a greater sensitivity of the yen/$ price to order flow in the downward direction, though estimates for both directions are positive and significant). Fourth, they test whether the order flow/ price relation depends on the gross level of activity. They find that it does: in the DM equation, the order flow coefficient is lowest on days when the number of transactions is at a middling level (i.e., the pattern is U-shaped); in the yen equation, they find that the order flow coefficient is lowest on days when the number of transactions are at a low level (i.e., the coefficient increases with activity level).[18] Their model is not rich enough to account for these coefficient variations structurally. Fifth, Evans and Lyons decompose contemporaneous order flow into expected and unexpected components (by projecting order flow on past flow). In their model, all order flow X_t is unexpected, but this need not be the case in the data (in fact, daily order flow is essentially unforecastable using past flow). They find, as one would expect, that order flow's explanatory power comes from its unexpected component.

Isn't This Just Demand Increases Driving Price Increases?

At first blush, it might appear that the Evans-Lyons results are right out of Economics 101: of course when demand goes up, price goes up. But this misses the most important lesson. A premise of textbook exchange rate models (chapter 6) is that we don't need order flow to push prices around. Rather, when public information arrives, rational markets adjust price instantaneously (i.e., excess demand from new information causes price to adjust without trading needing to take place). That order flow explains such a large percentage of price moves underscores the inadequacy of this public information framework. The information the FX market is aggregating is much subtler than textbook models assume. This we learn from our order flow regressions.

But What Drives Order Flow?

An important challenge for the microstructure approach is determining what drives order flow, that is, the first link in the fundamentals / order flow / price chain (figure 7.1). Here are three promising strategies for shedding light on this question. Strategy one is to disaggregate order flow. For example, interdealer order flow can be split into large banks versus small banks, or investment banks versus commercial banks. Data sets on customer order flow can be split into nonfinancial corporations, leveraged financial institutions (e.g., hedge funds), and unleveraged financial institutions (e.g., mutual and pension funds). Do all these trade types have the same price impact? Someone believing that order flow is just undifferentiated demand would predict that they do. In fact, they do not, as we shall see in chapter 9. Certain types of orders (e.g., those from financial institutions) convey more information, and therefore have more price impact. People who view order flow as undifferentiated demand overlook this level of analysis—they overlook the fact that order flow is a vehicle for conveying information. Understanding the information intensity of different trade types brings us closer to this market's underlying information structure.

Strategy two for determining what drives order flow focuses on public information intensity. Consider, for example, periods encompassing scheduled macro announcements. Does order flow account for a smaller share of price variation within these periods? Or is order flow an important driver of price even at these times, perhaps helping to reconcile differences in people's mapping from public information to price? Work along these lines, too, will shed light on the forces driving order flow.[19]

Strategy three for determining what drives order flow focuses on discriminating payoff information from discount rate information. If order flow conveys payoff information, then it should forecast important macro variables like interest rates, money supplies, and trade balances. New order flow data sets that cover many years of FX trading—such as the data set I examine in chapter 9—provide enough statistical power to test this. At a broad level, separating these two types of nonpublic information has implications for how we define the concept of "fundamentals." Order flow that reflects information about payoffs—like expectations of future interest rates—is in keeping with traditional definitions of exchange rate fundamentals. But order flow that reflects changing discount rates may encompass nontraditional exchange rate determinants (e.g., changing risk tolerance of financial institutions or changing hedging demands), calling perhaps for a broader notion of fundamentals.

Comments on Causality

Under the Evans-Lyons model's null hypothesis, causality runs strictly from order flow to price. Accordingly, under the null, their estimation is not subject to simultaneity bias. (Unlike the classic supply-demand identification problem, Evans and Lyons are not simply regressing price on quantity; quantity—i.e., volume—and order flow are fundamentally different concepts.) Within microstructure theory more broadly, this direction of causality is the norm: it holds in the models outlined in chapter 4 (i.e., the Kyle auction model, the sequential-trade model, and the simultaneous-trade model), despite the fact that price and order flow are determined simultaneously. In these models, price innovations are a function of order flow innovations, not the other way around. Put differently, order flow is indeed a cause of price changes, but only a proximate cause; the underlying cause is nonpublic information (about payoffs or about discount rates).

Although there is no simultaneity bias under the null hypothesis, alternative hypotheses do exist under which causality is reversed. The example that has received the most attention recently is specific to a particular period and market: October 1998, in the dollar/yen market (after collapse of the hedge fund Long Term Capital Management). In that case, there is evidence that feedback selling of dollars by distressed participants fueled the dollar's fall from about 130 yen/\$ to about 118 yen/\$ *in a single day*. As the story goes, speculators attempting to stop their already substantial losses felt they had to sell into a falling market, thereby making it fall further. In this case, causality appears to have been two-way. Using data on actual order flows over that period, I examine this special episode as a case study in chapter 9.

7.2 The Flow Approach

Chapter 6 surveys the modern approaches to exchange rates. One "premodern" approach not addressed in that chapter is the balance of payments flow approach (which macroeconomists call, simply, the flow approach; see also note 1, chapter 1). Given the microstructure approach's emphasis on order flow, is there a relation between the microstructure and flow approaches? Both focus squarely on the role of transactions in determining rates. In this sense, the antecedents of the microstructure approach were in that earlier literature (see, e.g., Robinson 1937 and Machlup 1939; Rosenberg 1996 provides recent perspective). However, despite their apparent similarity, the two approaches are distinct and differ in important ways.

First let me review the flow approach, which is a broadened version of the goods market approach (introduced in chapter 1). Under the goods market approach, demand for currencies comes primarily from purchases and sales of goods. For example, an increase in exports increases foreign demand for domestic currency to pay for those exported goods. In this simple form, the implication is rather intuitive: countries with trade surpluses experience appreciation (which comes from the currency demand created by the surplus).

Under the flow approach, currency demand comes not only from goods flows, but also from capital flows. (The former is captured in a country's balance of payments by the current account; the latter is captured by the capital account.) For example, an increase in the flow of investment abroad increases demand for foreign currency to pay for those investments.

This description embeds two of the three main differences between the flow and microstructure approaches. First, under the flow approach—like its goods market cousin—exchange rate determination is a kind of by-product, in the sense that the rate is not determined in its own speculative market. One consequence is that flow approach models typically do not conform to modern standards of financial market efficiency. (For example, publicly available information can be used in flow approach models to generate excess speculative returns.) The microstructure approach is different in that the exchange rate is indeed determined within its own speculative market. All stocks of currency are willingly held, and only individuals possessing superior information can earn excess speculative returns.[20]

The second main difference embedded in the description of the flow approach is its exclusive focus on balance of payments accounts. As an empirical matter, this was part of the flow approach's undoing because these particular flows have little explanatory power for exchange rates (Meese and Rogoff 1983a). The microstructure approach focuses instead on the flows the price setters (dealers) can actually see. These need not correspond to balance of payments transactions (see section 9.1).

The third main difference between the flow and microstructure approaches is their treatment of beliefs. To illustrate, consider an analogy from the material on rational expectations models in chapter 7. A key insight of the rational expectations model is that prices do not simply clear markets, they also convey information. Early attempts to analyze equilibrium with differentially informed traders ignored the effect of prices on beliefs. *This parallels an essential difference between the flow and microstructure approaches.* Under both approaches, the exchange rate is determined from order flow. Under the flow approach, however, the order flow—and subsequent price —communicates no incremental information to individuals regarding others' information. Under the microstructure approach, however, order flow does communicate information to individuals, and different types of order flow can communicate different amounts of information. This is the information the market needs to aggregate, and microstructure theory describes how that aggregation is achieved.[21]

Consider this point in the context of the Evans-Lyons model of the previous section. A key feature of their model is that order flow plays two roles. First, holding beliefs constant, order flow affects price through the traditional process of market clearing. Second, order flow also alters beliefs because it conveys information that is not yet common knowledge. That is,

$$\text{Price} = P(X, B(X, Z_1), Z_2).$$

Price P depends both directly and indirectly on order flow X. The indirect effect is through beliefs $B(X, Z_1)$, where Z_1 and Z_2 denote other determinants. This is the information role ignored in early attempts to analyze equilibrium with differentially informed traders. Since the advent of rational expectations, models that ignore this information effect from order flow are viewed as less compelling.

7.3   The Excess Volatility Puzzle

This section addresses the second of the big three puzzles: the excess volatility puzzle. By excess we mean that exchange rates are much more volatile than our best measures of fundamentals. Though other asset markets share this property (e.g., stock markets; see Shiller 1981), the puzzle in FX markets is in many ways distinctive.[22] Consider, for example, the fact that most exchange rates are not allowed to float freely; many are managed through intervention by central banks. This allows one to address the volatility puzzle in ways not possible in other markets. To understand why, note first that exchange rates are generally less volatile when managed. Given this, one can compare regimes with different management intensities to identify why volatility differs, thereby shedding light on the volatility's causes. This approach is common in the literature (e.g., Flood and Rose 1995; Killeen, Lyons, and Moore 2000a). The analysis I present here draws primarily on the empirical findings of Killeen, Lyons, and Moore (KLM).

Before reviewing the KLM findings, let me provide more perspective on the "cross-regime" approach to exchange rate volatility.[23] Why is it that similar macro environments produce more volatility when exchange rates float freely? There are two main approaches to this question, one theoretical and one empirical. The theoretical approach was pioneered by Dornbusch (1976) in his sticky-price monetary model (see chapter 6). Dornbusch shows that when goods prices are sticky but the exchange rate is free to jump, then economic shocks have a disproportionately large effect on the exchange rate— so-called overshooting. From the perspective of excess volatility, the sticky-price monetary model generates the kind of "amplification" that might explain why floating rates are more volatile than fundamentals. This theoretical explanation is not borne out empirically, however: the sticky-price model does not fit the data.

The second main approach to why floating rates are more volatile is empirical. A good example is Flood and Rose (1995, 5), who put the cross-regime logic as follows:

Intuitively, if exchange rate stability arises across regimes without corre-sponding variation in macroeconomic volatility, then macroeconomic vari-ables will be unable to explain much exchange rate volatility. Thus existing models, such as monetary models, do not pass our test; indeed, this is also true of any potential model that depends on standard macroeconomic vari-ables. We are driven to the conclusion that the most critical determinants of exchange rate volatility are not macroeconomic.

The central idea here starts with the Flood-Rose finding that manag-ing rates does not change the volatility of fundamentals (fundamen-tals as described by the models of chapter 6). So if the volatility reduction from managing rates is not coming from changed behavior of these fundamentals, then it is unlikely these are critical fundamen-tals. In a sense, then, the Flood-Rose conclusion deepens the puzzle.

KLM take a different tack—they exploit a natural experiment, using the switch from the European Monetary System (EMS) to European Monetary Union (EMU), which in terms of regimes is a switch from a target zone to a rigidly fixed rate.[24] Starting in January 1999, the euro country currencies have been rigidly fixed to one another. Before January 1999, however—particularly before May 1998—there was still uncertainty about which countries would par-ticipate in EMU. There was also uncertainty about the timing of in-terest rate harmonization (which had to occur among the countries adopting the euro).

KLM's analysis of this experiment leads them to the following punchline: exchange rates are more volatile under flexible rates be-cause of order flow. Order flow conveys more information under flexible rates, which increases volatility. Fixed exchange rates prevent order flow from conveying information—as a driver of returns, it is "turned off." The intuition for why this happens is tied to demand elasticity. Under floating, the elasticity of public demand is (endogenously) low, due to higher volatility and aversion to the risk this higher volatility entails. This makes room for the types of portfolio balance effects that arise in the Evans-Lyons model, and allows order flow to convey information about those effects. Under (perfectly credible) fixed rates, the elasticity of public demand is infinite: return volatility shrinks to zero, making the holding of foreign exchange effectively riskless. This eliminates portfolio balance effects and precludes order flow from conveying this type of information. Consequently, order flow as a return driver is shut down.[25]

Figure 7.5 provides an initial, suggestive illustration of the KLM results. It shows the relationship between the FF/DM exchange rate and cumulative order flow (interdealer order flow from EBS—see below). The vertical line is May 4, 1998, the first trading day after the announcement of the conversion rates of the euro-participating currencies. The relationship between the two series before May 4 is clearly positive: the correlation is 0.69. After May 4—indeed, even a bit before May 4—there is a sharp unwinding of long DM positions with no corresponding movement in the exchange rate. The effect of order flow on the exchange rate appears to have changed from one of clear impact to one of no impact. (Though total variation in the exchange rate is small, from a trading perspective the variation in the January to May period is significant.) The model KLM develop provides a more formal framework for addressing this issue (to which I now turn).

The Killeen-Lyons-Moore Model

The KLM model is a variation on the Evans-Lyons model of section 7.1. The intraday trading structures of the two models are identical. (Accordingly, my exposition is fullest where the two models depart.) The key difference is the interday structure: in the KLM model, trading days fall into one of two regimes, a flexible-rate regime followed by a fixed-rate regime. The shift from flexible to fixed rates is a random event that arrives with constant probability p at the end of each trading day (after all trading). Once the regime has shifted to fixed rates it remains there indefinitely. This formulation has two

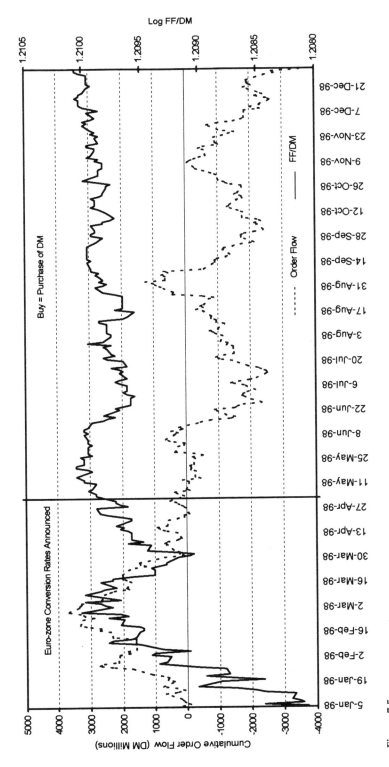

Figure 7.5
The level of the FF/DM exchange rate (solid) and cumulative interdealer order flow (dashed) over EBS in 1998.

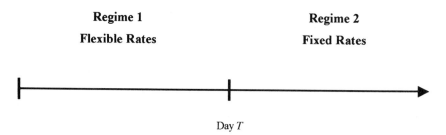

Figure 7.6
Two trading regimes. Under the flexible-rate regime, payoff increments ΔR_t are distributed Normally, with mean zero and variance Σ_R. The shift from flexible to fixed rates is a random event, the arrival of which is shown here at the end of day T. Once the regime has shifted to fixed rates it remains there indefinitely. On the first morning of the fixed-rate regime, the central bank (credibly) commits to pegging the exchange rate at the previous day's closing price and maintains $\Delta R_t = 0$ thereafter.

important advantages. First, the effective horizon over which foreign exchange is priced in the flexible-rate regime remains constant. Second, the parameter p provides a compact means of describing regime shifts as far or near.

Each day t, foreign exchange earns a payoffs R_t, which is composed of a series of increments:

$$R_t = \sum_{\tau=1}^{t} \Delta R_\tau. \tag{7.8}$$

The ΔR_t increments are observed publicly each day before all trading. As before, these increments represent innovations over time in public macroeconomic information (e.g., changes in interest rates). Under the flexible-rate regime, the ΔR_t increments are i.i.d. Normal $(0, \sigma_R^2)$. On the first morning of the fixed-rate regime, the central bank (credibly) commits to pegging the exchange rate at the previous day's closing price and maintains $\Delta R_t = 0$ thereafter. FX dealers and customers all have identical negative exponential utility, with coefficient of absolute risk aversion θ. The gross return on the risk free asset is equal to one.

Figures 7.2 and 7.6 describe the intraday and interday timing of the model, respectively. (Figure 7.2 appears above in my review of the Evans-Lyons model.) Within each day, there are three rounds of trading: first dealers trade with the public, then dealers trade among themselves (to share the resulting inventory risk), and finally dealers trade again with the public (to share inventory risk more broadly). Figure 7.6 describes the two trading regimes, using T to denote the last day of flexible-rate trading.

Each day begins with public observation of the payoff increment ΔR_t. Each dealer quotes a price to his customers, denoted P_{it}^1, and then receives a customer-order realization C_{it}^1 that is executed at his quoted price. ($C_{it}^1 < 0$ denotes net customer selling—dealer i buying.) The individual C_{it}^1's are distributed:

$$C_{it}^1 \sim \text{Normal}(0, \sigma_C^2).$$

They are uncorrelated across dealers and uncorrelated with the payoff increment ΔR_t. These orders represent exogenous portfolio shifts of the nondealer public. Their realizations are not publicly observable, and they arrive every day, regardless of regime. It will be useful for us to define the aggregate public demand in round 1 as

$$C_t^1 = \sum_{i=1}^N C_{it}^1.$$

In round 2—the interdealer round—each dealer quotes a price to other dealers. These interdealer quotes are observable and available to all dealers. Each dealer then trades on other dealers' quotes. (Orders at a given price are split evenly across dealers quoting that price.) Let T_{it} denote the (net) interdealer trade initiated by dealer i in round 2 (negative for dealer i selling). At the close of round 2, all dealers observe the interdealer order flow X_t from that period:

$$X_t = \sum_{i=1}^N T_{it}. \tag{7.9}$$

As in the Evans-Lyons model, in round 3 of each day dealers share overnight risk with the nondealer public. Unlike round 1, the public's motive for trading in round 3 is nonstochastic. Initially, each dealer quotes a scalar price P_{it}^3 at which he agrees to buy and sell any amount. These quotes are observable and available to the public. Public demand for the risky asset in round 3, denoted C_t^3, is less than infinitely elastic. With the earlier assumptions, this allows one to write public demand as a linear function of the expected return:

$$C_t^3 = \gamma E[\Delta P_{t+1}^3 + R_{t+1} \mid \Omega_t^3], \tag{7.10}$$

where

$\gamma \propto \text{Var}^{-1}[\Delta P_{t+1}^3 + R_{t+1}].$

As in section 7.1, the positive coefficient γ captures the elasticity of public demand—the public's aggregate risk-bearing capacity. The information in Ω_t^3 is that available to the public at the time of trading in round three of day t (which includes all past R_t and X_t).

Equilibrium

The focus in the KLM analysis is on the exchange rate's level. The level at the end of day t can be written as

$$
P_t = \begin{cases}
\beta_1 \displaystyle\sum_{\tau=1}^{t} \Delta R_\tau + \beta_2 \sum_{\tau=1}^{t} X_\tau & \text{under flexible rates } (t \leq T) \\[2ex]
\beta_1 \displaystyle\sum_{\tau=1}^{T} \Delta R_\tau + \beta_2 \sum_{\tau=1}^{T} X_\tau + \beta_3 \sum_{\tau=T+1}^{t} X_\tau & \text{under fixed rates } (t > T)
\end{cases}
$$

$$(7.11)$$

The parameters β_2 and β_3 are the price impact parameters—they govern the price impact of order flow. These β's depend inversely on γ (the return sensitivity of public demand); they also depend on the variances σ_R^2 and σ_C^2.

The message of equation (7.11) is important. It says that in the flexible regime, there should be a cointegrating relationship between the level of the exchange rate, cumulative macro fundamentals ΔR_t, and cumulative interdealer order flow X_t.[27] This prediction is striking: in textbook exchange rate models there is no relationship between order flow and exchange rates, much less a long-run relationship as implied by cointegration. An implication is that order flow's impact on exchange rates is permanent (which is also true in the Evans-Lyons model). This speaks directly to the theme in chapter 1 that microstructure variables can have long-lived effects. (Permanent impact does not imply that order flow cannot also have transitory effects, particularly intraday. In this model, though, inventory effects across days are ruled out, as explained in section 7.1.)

Differences across Exchange Rate Regimes

We want to understand how the role of order flow differs under different exchange rate regimes. To do so, consider equations (7.9) and

(7.10). Specifically, the parameter γ that represents the elasticity of public demand is regime dependent. This comes from the regime dependence of the return variance, $\mathrm{Var}[\Delta P_{t+1} + R_{t+1} \mid \Omega_t^3]$, in the definition of γ in equation (7.10). KLM show that

$$\gamma_{\text{fixed}} > \gamma_{\text{flexible}}. \tag{7.12}$$

Public demand is therefore more elastic in the fixed-rate regime than under the flexible-rate regime. The implication for the price impact parameter β in equation (7.11) is the following:

$$\beta_2 > \beta_3. \tag{7.13}$$

This says that exchange rates react more to order flow under flexible rates than they do under fixed rates. In the limit of fixed rates that are perfectly credible (i.e., for which $\mathrm{Var}[\Delta P_{t+1} + R_{t+1} \mid \Omega_t^3] = 0$), we have

$$\beta_3 = 0. \tag{7.14}$$

The exchange rate does not respond to order flow in this case. The intuition is simple enough: Under perfect credibility, the variance of exchange rate returns goes to zero because public demand is perfectly elastic, and vice versa. (If the fixed regime were less than 100 percent credible, then public demand would not be infinite—FX would still be a risky asset.)

Further Intuition for the Solution

Consider P_{T+1}, the price at the close of the first day of the fixed-rate regime. Forex is a riskless asset at this point, with return variance equal to zero. With a return variance equal to zero, the elasticity of public demand is infinite and the price impact parameter β_3 in equation (7.11) equals zero. This yields a price at the close of trading (round 3) on day $T + 1$ of

$$P_{T+1} = \beta_1 \sum_{t=1}^{T} \Delta R_t + \beta_2 \sum_{t=1}^{T} X_t.$$

The summation over the payoff increment ΔR_t does not include an increment for day $T + 1$ because the central bank maintains ΔR_t at zero in the fixed regime. Though X_{T+1} is not equal to zero, this has no effect on price because $\beta_3 = 0$, as noted. This logic holds throughout the fixed-rate regime.

To understand why order flow has price impact under floating, consider the price at the close of the final day of floating, day T. According to equation (7.11),

$$P_T = \beta_1 \sum_{t=1}^{T} \Delta R_t + \beta_2 \sum_{t=1}^{T} X_t.$$

At the close of day T, the payoff R_{T+1} is uncertain because ΔR_{t+1} is uncertain. (Expectations of future variables do not enter this expression due to the simple specification of ΔR_t and C_t^1 as independently distributed across time with mean zero.) The second term that depends on X_t is the portfolio balance term. The logic of this term under floating is exactly the same as the portfolio balance term in the Evans-Lyons model of section 7.1. That is, the sum of the portfolio shifts C_t^1 represent changes in "effective" asset supply, in the sense that they are a change in net supply that the remainder of the public must absorb. The total decrease in net supply is the sum of past portfolio shifts into foreign exchange:

$$\text{Decrease in net supply} = \sum_{t=1}^{T} C_t^1.$$

As is standard in portfolio balance models, increases in supply lower price and decreases in supply raise price. This is why a positive cumulative X_t in equation (7.11) raises price: if cumulative X_t is positive, this implies that cumulative C_t^1 is also positive, which is a decrease in net supply, requiring an increase in price to clear the market. X_t is the variable that conveys this information about net supply (C_t^1 is unobservable). P_T depends on the sum of the X_t because each additional decrease in supply C_t^1 requires an incremental increase in price. These portfolio balance effects disappear as payoff uncertainty shrinks to zero (as in the fixed-rate regime).

The KLM Data Set

The KLM data set includes daily order flow in the German mark–French franc market for one year, 1998. The data are from EBS, the electronic interdealer broking system described in chapter 5. (At the time, EBS accounted for nearly half of interdealer trading in the major currencies, which translates into about a third of total trading in these currencies; the Evans-Lyons data that are the basis of section

7.1 reflect the other half of interdealer trading—the direct portion.) By KLM's estimate, their sample accounts for about 18 percent of trading in the DM/FF market in 1998. Daily order flow includes all orders passing through the system over twenty-four hours, starting at midnight GMT (weekdays only).

The data set is rich enough to allow measurement of order flow X_t two ways: number of buys minus number of sells (as in Evans and Lyons 1999) and amount bought minus amount sold (in DM). KLM find that the two measures behave quite similarly: the correlation between the two X_t measures in the flexible-rate portion of the sample (the first four months) is 0.98. They also find that substituting one measure for the other in their analysis has no substantive effect on their findings.

Let me provide a bit more detail on EBS. As noted in chapter 3, EBS is an electronic broking system for trading spot foreign exchange among dealers. It is limit-order driven, screen-based, and ex ante anonymous (ex-post, counterparties settle directly with one another). The EBS screen displays the best bid and ask prices, together with information on the cash amounts available for trading at these prices. Amounts available at prices other than the best bid and offer are not displayed. Activity fields on this screen track a dealer's own recent trades, including price and amount, and also track the recent trades executed on EBS systemwide.

There are two ways that dealers can trade currency on EBS. Dealers can either post prices (submit "limit orders"), which does not insure execution, or dealers can "hit" prices (submit "market orders"), which does insure execution. To construct a measure of order flow, trades are signed according to the direction of the latter—the initiator of the transaction.

When a dealer submits a limit order, he or she is displaying to other dealers an intention to buy or sell a given cash amount at a specified price.[28] Bid prices (limit order buys) and offer prices (limit order sells) are submitted with the hope of being executed against the market order of another dealer—the "initiator" of the trade. To be a bit more precise, not all initiating orders arrive in the form of market orders. Sometimes, a dealer will submit a limit order buy that is equal to or higher than the current best offer (or will submit a limit order sell that is equal to or lower than the current best bid). When this happens, the incoming limit order is treated as if it were a market order and is executed against the best opposing limit order immediately. In these cases, the incoming limit order is the initiating side of the trade.

Results

Figure 7.5 illustrates the relationship between cumulative order flow and the exchange rate. We saw that the effect of order flow on the exchange rate appears to have changed from one of clear impact to one of no impact. The results that follow address this more formally, based on the KLM model's testable implications.

The analysis proceeds in two stages. First, KLM address whether there is evidence of a cointegrating relationship between interdealer order flow and price, as the model predicts. This first stage also examines the related issues of stationarity and long-run coefficient sizes. The second stage addresses the degree to which order flow is exogenous (as their model assumes). This stage includes a test for reverse Granger causality, that is, statistical causality running from the exchange rate to order flow.

Stage 1:   Cointegration and Related Issues

Let us begin by repeating equation (7.11) from the model, which establishes the relationship between the level of the exchange rate P_t, a variable summarizing public information ($\Sigma \Delta R_t$), and accumulated order flow (ΣX_t):

$$P_t = \begin{cases} \beta_1 \sum_{\tau=1}^{t} \Delta R_\tau + \beta_2 \sum_{\tau=1}^{t} X_\tau & \text{under flexible rates } (t \leq T) \\ \beta_1 \sum_{\tau=1}^{T} \Delta R_\tau + \beta_2 \sum_{\tau=1}^{T} X_\tau + \beta_3 \sum_{\tau=T+1}^{t} X_\tau & \text{under fixed rates } (t > T) \end{cases}$$

Like Evans and Lyons (1999), KLM use the interest differential as the public-information variable (the Paris interbank offer rate minus the Frankfurt interbank offer rate).

The KLM model predicts that before May 4, 1998, all these variables are nonstationary and are cointegrated. After May 4, the model predicts that the exchange rate converges to its conversion rate, and should be stationary. During this latter period (May to December), therefore, equation (7.11) only makes sense if the price-impact coefficient, β_3, goes to zero (as the model predicts), or if accumulated order flow becomes stationary. Otherwise, the regression is unbalanced, with some stationary variables, and some nonstationary variables.

Stationarity

The first step is to test whether the relevant variables are nonstationary. KLM find that, in the first four months of 1998, they were (inference based on Dickey-Fuller tests). In the remaining eight months, the exchange rate was stationary, as expected, but both cumulative order flow and the interest differential remained nonstationary. These results are consistent with a price impact parameter β_3 in the latter period of zero. It is important to determine, however, whether equation (7.11) actually holds for the flexible-rate period in January–April, that is, whether the variables are cointegrated as the model predicts.

Cointegration

KLM use the Johansen procedure to test for cointegration (Johansen 1992). The unrestricted vector autoregression (VAR) is assumed to consist of the three variables—the exchange rate, cumulative order flow, and the interest differential—as well as a constant and a trend. After testing various possible lag lengths, KLM find evidence that a lag length of four is appropriate.

The cointegration tests show that there is indeed one cointegrating vector. (They reject the null of no cointegrating vectors in favor of the alternative of at least one cointegrating vector, but they cannot reject the null of one cointegrating vector in favor of the alternative of at least two.) This implies that a linear combination of the three variables is stationary, as the KLM model predicts.

KLM go one step further and implement the test for cointegration without the interest differential. They find evidence of one cointegrating vector in that case, too, now between the exchange rate and cumulative order flow. The finding of one cointegrating vector in both the bivariate and trivariate systems suggests that the interest differential enters the trivariate cointegrating vector with a coefficient of zero. When KLM estimate the parameters of the cointegrating vector directly, this is exactly what they find: they cannot reject that the interest differential has a coefficient of zero. By contrast, the coefficient on cumulative order flow is highly significant and correctly signed. (The size of the coefficient implies that a 1 percent increase in cumulative order flow moves the spot rate by about 5 basis points.[29]) These findings of cointegration and an order flow coefficient that is correctly signed are supportive of their model's emphasis on order flow in the long run. At the same time, the lack of explanatory power in the interest differential suggests that this specialization of the payoff increment ΔR_t is deficient (in keeping with the negative results of the macro literature more generally).

Exogeneity of Order Flow

An important question facing the microstructure approach is the degree to which causality can be viewed as running strictly from order flow to the exchange rate, rather than running in both directions. The KLM framework provides a convenient way to address this question. In particular, if a system of variables is cointegrated, then it has an error-correction representation (see Engle and Granger 1987; also Hamilton 1994, 580–581). These error-correction representations provide clues about the direction of causality. Specifically, the error-correction representation allows one to determine whether the burden of adjustment to long-run equilibrium falls on the exchange rate, on cumulative order flow, or both. If adjustment falls at least in part on order flow, then order flow is responding to the rest of the system (i.e., it is not exogenous in the way specified by the Evans-Lyons and KLM models).

The KLM findings suggest that causality is indeed running strictly from order flow to price, and not the other way around. KLM test this by estimating the error-correction term in both the exchange rate and order flow equations (flexible-rate period, January–April). They find that the error-correction term is highly significant in the exchange rate equation, whereas the error-correction term in the order flow equation is insignificant. This implies that adjustment to long-run equilibrium is occurring via the exchange rate. More intuitively, *when a gap opens in the long-run relationship between cumulative order flow and the exchange rate, it is the exchange rate that adjusts to reduce the gap, not cumulative order flow.* In the parlance of the literature, the insignificance of the error-correction term in the order flow equation means that order flow is *weakly exogenous*. Further, KLM show that there is no evidence of Granger causality running from the exchange rate to order flow (i.e., there is no evidence of feedback trading). This combination of weak exogeneity and absence of Granger causality implies that cumulative order flow is *strongly exogenous*. Finally, the KLM error-correction estimates suggest that about one-third of departures from long-run equilibrium is dissipated each day.

Concluding Thoughts

To summarize, the KLM analysis addresses the excess volatility puzzle on two fronts, one theoretical and one empirical. On the theoretical front, they provide a new approach—based on order flow—for why volatility is high when exchange rates float freely. The punchline of their approach is that an important source of volatility is order flow, or, more precisely, the information order flow conveys. Under floating, the elasticity of public demand is (endogenously) low, due to higher volatility and aversion to the risk that higher volatility entails. This makes room for the portfolio balance effects that arise in the Evans-Lyons model and allows order flow to convey information about those effects. Under (perfectly credible) fixed rates, the elasticity of public demand is infinite: return volatility shrinks to zero, making the holding of foreign exchange effectively riskless. This eliminates portfolio balance effects and precludes order flow from conveying this type of information. Thus, under fixed rates, order flow as a return driver is shut down. Under managed rates (i.e., intermediate regimes), order flow as a return driver is muted.

A nice feature of the KLM approach to excess volatility, relative to other approaches, is that its implications can be brought to the data. There are many theoretical papers on excess exchange rate volatility (see, e.g., Hau 1998 and Jeanne and Rose 1999, and references to earlier work contained therein). But in general, little of the existing theoretical work is easily implemented empirically. The order flow focus of the KLM approach makes it readily implementable. That said, the specific results that KLM offer are only suggestively supportive of their particular story. Much more empirical analysis along these lines remains to be done.

Two of the KLM empirical findings are especially relevant for interpreting work on order flow more generally. First, they find that Granger causality runs from order flow to the exchange rate, but not vice versa. True, Granger causality is not the same as economic causality; nevertheless, the result does help assuage concern. Second, they find that gaps in the relationship between cumulative order flow and the level of the exchange rate engender an exchange rate response but not an order flow response. This result, too, helps assuage concern about the direction of causality between these two variables.

One might be tempted to conclude that four months of data is too little to produce reliable analysis of cointegration; however, an important aspect of the KLM results should assuage this concern. Recall that KLM find rapid adjustment back to the cointegrating relationship (their error-correction estimates suggest that about one-third of departures from long-run equilibrium is dissipated each day). The half-life of these departures is therefore only about two days. Four months of data is enough to cover about forty-five of these half lives, quite a lot in the context of estimating cointegrating relationships. For comparison, estimates of adjustment back to the cointegrating relationship of Purchasing Power Parity generate half-lives around five years. One would need over two hundred years of data to estimate PPP error correction with as many half-lives in the sample.

Finally, note that the KLM model provides a different perspective on exchange rate credibility. In their model, a credible fixed rate is one in which the private sector, not the central bank, willingly absorbs innovations in order flow.[30] The textbook treatment of fixed-rate regimes, in contrast, is centered on the willingness of the central bank to buy and sell domestic currency at a predetermined price; that is, the central bank absorbs the order flow. If the central bank needs to intervene, the fixed exchange rate regime is already in difficulty because the private sector's demand for order flow is no longer perfectly elastic. It may be useful to revisit currency crises and our analysis of them with this possibility in mind.

7.4   The Forward Bias Puzzle

The systematic bias in currency forward rates has attracted more attention than any other puzzle in international finance (surveys include Hodrick 1987; Froot and Thaler 1990; Lewis 1995; Engel 1996). The bias is such that when $F_{t,1} > P_t$—today's one-period forward rate is "predicting" that the spot rate will rise—the spot rate does not tend to rise as much as predicted (i.e., P_{t+1} typically ends up below $F_{t,1}$).[31] In fact, among the major floating currencies against the dollar, when the forward rate predicts the spot rate will rise, it usually falls! The forward rate systematically gets the direction wrong.

In this section, I consider the puzzle from three angles: the statistician's perspective, the economist's perspective, and the practitioner's perspective. My explanation for the bias draws heavily from the practitioner's perspective.

The Statistician's Perspective

Viewed as a regression, the test for bias in forward rates is based on the following equation:

$$p_{t+1} - p_t = a + b(f_{t,1} - p_t) + u_{t+1} \qquad (7.15)$$

where p_{t+1} denotes the spot rate realized at time $t+1$ (\$/other), $f_{t,1}$ denotes the time-t forward rate for transactions settled at $t+1$ (\$/other), and u_{t+1} is a purely random error term. (Lower case denotes natural logarithm, so the difference in natural logs $p_{t+1} - p_t$ is roughly equal to dollar depreciation in percent. Similarly, the gap between the forward and spot rates $f_{t,1} - p_t$ is roughly equal to a percent difference, and is typically referred to as the forward discount on the dollar.)[32] Under the null hypothesis of an unbiased forward rate, estimates of the coefficient b should be one: when the forward rate predicts the spot rate will rise by Y percent, then the spot rate does rise, on average, by Y percent, for any given Y.

Actual estimates of the coefficient b using monthly data are significantly different from one. In fact, they are typically negative—as suggested above—averaging about -0.9 (the average from some 75 studies surveyed by Froot and Thaler 1990). Consider the graphic depiction in figure 7.7. The two-standard-error band ($\pm 2\sigma$) around the null hypothesis, denoted H_0, is not even close to including the typical estimate of -0.9. Indeed, most studies even reject the hypothesis that $b = 0$. (The size of the band shown should not be taken too literally; it is drawn to be consistent with the fact that estimates often do not include zero within the band.)

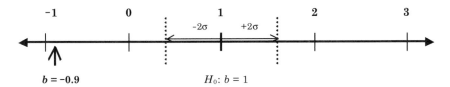

Figure 7.7
Statistician's perspective on forward bias. H_0 denotes the null hypothesis.

The Economist's Perspective

For economists, the statistical rejection of unbiasedness is all the more uncomfortable because the forward rate systematically predicts the wrong direction. This discomfort is partly due to the strikingly counterintuitive nature of the result. At a more substantive level, though, the result is economically uncomfortable because getting the direction wrong makes explaining the bias difficult.

To understand why, consider the fact that for any "anomaly" documented in financial markets, economics offers two standard explanations. One is *inefficiency*—markets are making systematic errors in neglecting profit opportunities. The second explanation is that the bias represents a *risk premium*—excess return that compensates for risk borne in taking advantage of the bias. If the bias simply compensates for risk, it is not a violation of market efficiency.[33] The trick—for those partial to this risk-premium explanation—is to show empirically that the bias is consistent with models of the degree to which bearing risk should be compensated. So large a bias makes this difficult.

Researchers' empirical attempts to link the bias to risk models have not been successful, despite hundreds of papers that, collectively, put all the standard models to the test. In his survey, Hodrick (1987) concludes that "we do not yet have a model of expected returns [i.e., a model of compensation for risk] that fits the data." In their survey, Froot and Thaler (1990) conclude that among the main approaches to evaluating the risk-premium explanation, "none offer the hypothesis much support." In a similar vein, Engel's (1996) survey concludes that "models of the risk premium have been unsuccessful at explaining the magnitude of this failure of unbiasedness." From the economist's perspective, the bias remains a puzzle.

It is noteworthy that standard economic models share the property that risk premiums arise due to covariance between returns and some other variable. What differentiates the models is what they define that other variable to be. There are three basic approaches: real economy models, asset market models, and portfolio balance models. In real economy models (e.g., Obstfeld and Rogoff 1996), the relevant covariance is with growth in aggregate consumption. In asset market models—like the capital asset pricing model—the key covariance is with returns on a market portfolio. In portfolio balance models (e.g., Branson and Henderson 1985), the key covariance is typically that across exchange rates (though covariance with other asset returns can be included). In the end, Engel's statement that "models of the risk premium have been unsuccessful" applies to all three of these covariance approaches.

Despite little evidence for the risk-premium hypothesis, the alternative hypothesis of inefficiency is uncomfortable. Part of this discomfort is philosophical: to most financial economists, inefficiency is—by its nature—uncomfortable. Further discomfort arises in this instance, however, because the forward bias was first documented some twenty years ago, at which time market participants might have been unaware of the bias. Twenty years and hundreds of studies later, it is no longer reasonable to consider the bias as anything but public information. Yet the bias continues. Why?

The Practitioner's Perspective: Limits to Speculation

This book addresses the bias puzzle by adopting a practitioner's perspective, which leads naturally to an explanation of bias based on what I call limits to speculation. This line of reasoning falls within the broader microstructure approach in two ways. First, the explanation relies on the microstructure approach's central link—the link between price adjustment and order flow. Second, the explanation relies on institutional realities assumed irrelevant within traditional approaches.

Before presenting the explanation, let me first introduce a question that a statistician or economist would not naturally ask, but practitioners would: *How large would the forward bias have to be before currency trading strategies yield a Sharpe ratio equal to, say, a buy-and-hold equity strategy?*[34] Financial institutions commonly use Sharpe ratios to measure the performance of their proprietary trading. The ratio is defined as:

$$\text{Sharpe ratio} = \frac{E[R_s] - R_{rf}}{\sigma_s}, \tag{7.16}$$

where $E[R_s]$ is the expected return on the strategy, R_{rf} is the risk-free interest rate, and σ_s is the standard deviation of the returns to the strategy.[35] Over the last fifty years, the Sharpe ratio for a buy-and-hold strategy in U.S. equities has been about 0.4 on an annual basis (the excess return in the numerator is about 7 percent and annualized return standard deviation in the denominator is about 17 percent).

Under the null hypothesis of no bias in the forward rate ($b = 1$ in equation 1), the Sharpe ratio of currency strategies is zero—there is no expected return differential (i.e., $f_{t,1}$ does not tend to over-predict subsequent spot rate changes). As b departs from 1, however, the numerator becomes positive. The larger the bias, the larger the numerator. The denominator, on the other hand, is not a function of the bias. Rather, it is determined by exchange rate variances and covariances. Another determinant of the denominator is the number of exchange rates included in the currency trading strategy—a greater number of currencies provides more diversification, other things equal.

Strikingly, it is only when b equals about −1 or 3 that the Sharpe ratio for currency strategies is about the same as that of equities, or 0.4. (This assumes a currency strategy that diversifies across the six largest markets; I provide further details below.) If b falls anywhere in the interval $(-1, 3)$, then a currency strategy designed to exploit bias has a lower return per unit risk than a simple equity investment.

From the practitioner's perspective, the two-standard-error band that the statistician draws around the null of $b = 1$ misses the point. If instead, I draw a band around the null of $b = 1$ that corresponds to speculative significance—as opposed to statistical significance—then the reality looks more like that shown in figure 7.8. If a Sharpe ratio of 0.4 is the practitioner's threshold for determining tradable opportunities, then the interval from $b = -1$ to $b = 3$ would not be attractive. These values for b define an inaction range—a range within which the forward rate bias does not attract speculative capital. Viewed this way, the puzzle of forward bias is not a glaring profit opportunity.

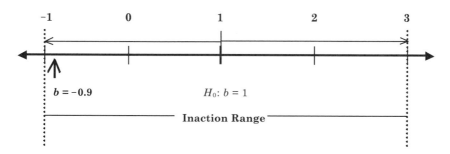

Figure 7.8
Practitioner's perspective on forward bias. H_0 denotes the null hypothesis.

An Explanation in Four Parts

My explanation for the persistence of the bias has four parts, which I sketch at the outset so the structure is clear. Then I address each of the parts in more detail, providing supporting evidence and theory. Finally, I offer thoughts on why the bias is in the direction of $b < 1$, an issue distinct from the question of why the bias persists.

Part 1:   Anomaly Persistence: If speculative capital is not allocated to exploiting the forward bias, then the forward bias will persist.

Part 2:   Institutional Allocation of Speculative Capital: Institutions with a comparative advantage in exploiting forward bias allocate their speculative capital based, in large part, on Sharpe ratios.

Part 3:   Sharpe Ratio of Currency Strategies: Sharpe ratios of reliable (i.e., non-data-snooped) currency strategies that exploit forward bias are roughly 0.4 on an annual basis, similar to that of a simple strategy of buying and holding an equity index.

Part 4:   Underallocation of Speculative Capital: Because a Sharpe ratio of 0.4 is well below most institutions' minimum threshold for inducing capital allocation, the anomaly persists.

Part 1:   Anomaly Persistence

Part one of the explanation may seem intuitively obvious: "If speculative capital is not allocated to exploiting the forward bias, then the forward bias will persist" But it deserves a closer look. A skeptic would rightly assert that order flow is not necessary to move price.

By this logic, if the current spot rate or the current forward rate (or both) are at an incorrect level, and this is common knowledge within the market, then these rates should adjust immediately to the correct level, without any role for order flow. This logic would seem to hold particularly well in the foreign exchange market. After all, goes the traditional view, all fundamental information in this market is public information. This is not a market that needs order flow to move price (as compared to, say, the market for a particular stock, where order flow can communicate inside information about earnings).

There is a big leap of faith, however, between the true statement that "order flow is not necessary to move price" and the belief that, in fact, "order flow plays little role in moving price."[36] Consider two points that clarify why this leap of faith is so big—one theoretical and the other empirical.

Theory clarifies the conditions under which order flow plays no role, conditions that do not hold in the FX market (see also chapter 2). Specifically, unless both of the following are true, order flow will play a role in moving price: (1) all information relevant for exchange rates is publicly known, and (2) the mapping from that information to prices is also publicly known. The second of these conditions is patently violated. Even the first is unlikely to hold (e.g., it does not hold in the Evans-Lyons model, which includes a rather natural information structure).

Empirical evidence also runs counter to the view that "order flow plays little role in moving price." Section 7.1 shows that the effects of order flow on price are quite strong. Moreover, the R^2 statistics reported in that section indicate that order flow accounts for the lion's share of exchange rate variation.

Part 2: Institutional Allocation of Speculative Capital

Part 2 of the explanation is the most contentious: Institutions with a comparative advantage in exploiting forward bias allocate their speculative capital based, in large part, on Sharpe ratios. Let me stress at the outset that this assertion is based on my discussions with proprietary traders at banks and hedge funds. The message from those discussions is clear: proprietary traders think in terms of Sharpe ratios, and as a result, they consider the forward bias trade relatively unattractive.[38] Irrespective of the theoretical questions this focus on Sharpe ratios raises, its empirical predominance is undeniable (so its impact on prices and returns cannot be ruled out on simple theoretical grounds).

This part of the explanation is the most contentious because, absent other frictions, capital should not be allocated based on "variance" risk. Rather, capital should be allocated based on covariance with some larger objective (e.g., covariance with the market return, as in the Capital Asset Pricing Model). Empirically, the covariance between returns on, say, the MSCI World Equity Index and returns on bias-exploiting currency strategies is small. This suggests that the risk of currency strategies is largely diversifiable. Thus, though their return-per-unit total risk may be low, their return-per-unit *systematic* risk is high—too high to be consistent with standard covariance models (i.e., too high for people who are concerned with covariance not to take advantage). Hence, from the covariance perspective, the puzzle endures.

For completeness, let me address why institutions might choose to behave this way, because it appears as though trading opportunities are not fully exploited. (I reiterate, however, that institutions *do* behave this way. It is this empirical fact that is most essential to my argument, not the theoretical rationale for why this behavior arises.)[39] The model I have in mind is in the spirit of Shleifer and Vishny's (1997) model, in which agency frictions in professional money management lead to less aggressive trading, or what they call limits to arbitrage. (I intentionally use the term "limits to speculation" in this section to establish a conceptual link to that earlier work.) Specifically, consider an agency-friction model—which I only sketch here—where the optimal contract between a firm and a proprietary trader is one that holds the trader responsible for own-variance, not covariance. Traders do not want their compensation tied to securities they do not trade; doing so with a covariance-based contract reduces profit incentives and opens the door to disruptive levels of idiosyncratic risk.[40] Given this "constrained-optimal" contract, limited speculative capital is allocated to trading opportunities with the highest Sharpe ratio.

One way around these agency frictions is to imagine a market with a very large number of individual speculators, each taking a small position against the forward bias. In this case, agency friction does not arise, and speculators' collective actions eliminate the bias in forward rates. The trouble with this approach is that, in reality, individual speculators do not have specialized knowledge, low transaction costs, low monitoring costs, and diversified portfolios (see, e.g., Goodhart and Taylor 1992, who argue that minimum positions in currency futures are too large for most individuals to maintain a diversified portfolio). Individuals are at a comparative disadvantage with respect to these factors, which more than offsets the benefit of the eliminated agency costs. When considering this tiny-speculator model and why it is not applicable, a reader might ask why it is that he/she is not trading the forward rate bias. The answer will surely include several factors noted here.

Part 3: Sharpe Ratio of Currency Strategies

Part 3 of the explanation contends that Sharpe ratios of strategies for exploiting forward bias are roughly 0.4 on an annual basis, similar to that of a simple strategy of buying and holding an equity index.[37] This part is straightforward. Table 7.2 presents Sharpe ratios (annual basis) for various simple strategies applied to the six most liquid currencies over the period from January 1980 to December 1998

Table 7.2
Sharpe Ratios (Annual Basis) from Pure Currency Strategy

	Strategy 1: Equal Weighted	Strategy 2: > Median Discount	Strategy 3: < Median Discount
Sharpe Ratio: No Costs	0.48	0.46	0.49
Sharpe Ratio: With Costs	0.37	0.39	0.41

Strategies for profiting from forward bias entail selling foreign currency forward when $f_{t,1} > p_t$ and buying foreign currency forward when $f_{t,1} < p_t$. The three strategies shown are implemented using the six largest currency markets: \$/DM, \$/yen, \$/£, \$/Swiss, \$/FF, and \$/C\$. The "Equal Weighted" strategy has an equal position weight each month in each of the six forward markets. The ">Median Discount" strategy only takes a position in a forward market in a given month if that month's forward discount is greater than the median forward discount for that currency over the sample (weights are equal across forward positions taken). The "<Median Discount" strategy only takes a position in a forward market in a given month if the month's forward discount is less than the median forward discount for that currency over the sample (weights are equal across forward positions taken). The Sharpe ratio estimate with costs assumes a cost of ten basis points per transaction (includes price impact of trade). The sample is monthly data, from January 1980 to December 1998 (1980 is about the time when forward bias was first documented in the literature).
Source: Datastream.

(monthly data). The second column presents Sharpe ratios before netting transaction costs. The third column presents Sharpe ratios after netting transaction costs. The transaction cost adjustment is based on the strategy's turnover and is set at ten basis points per transaction. (This is conservative: if this were a $1 billion currency fund, then the price impact of exchanging one-sixth of the portfolio could double or triple this cost; see section 7.1.) But do not be distracted by transaction costs; even without transaction costs, the Sharpe ratios do not rise above 0.5. Thus, part 3 of the explanation does not depend on transaction costs.

Naturally, by selecting more complicated strategies than those presented in table 7.2, we can raise in-sample Sharpe ratios. That is why my wording of part 3 includes the word "reliable," by which I mean not generated from data snooping. The equal-weighted strategy exploits most of the gains from currency diversification, without introducing unwarranted degrees of freedom. I consider it a sound, conservative benchmark.

Part 4: Underallocation of Speculative Capital—The Inaction Range

Part 4 of the explanation closes the loop with part 1. Because a Sharpe ratio of 0.4 is well below most institutions' minimum threshold for inducing capital allocation, the anomaly persists. As an empirical matter, most large financial institutions do not devote their proprietary capital to currency strategies that exploit forward bias (what I call "pure currency strategies"). Those that do, typically devote only a small share of their capital to this type of speculation.

But how far below the minimum Sharpe ratio threshold is "well below"? I have interviewed several proprietary traders and proprietary desk managers regarding the threshold Sharpe ratios they use for determining speculative capital allocation, and the most common response is a Sharpe ratio of 1 (annual basis). Healthy skepticism is warranted here, however: suggesting to others that one's own threshold is high is an obvious means of enhancing industry reputation. From my interviews, though, I feel safe in asserting that there is limited interest at these major institutions in allocating capital to strategies with Sharpe ratios below 0.5.

Empirical Support

Several empirical findings are consistent with my inaction band explanation based on Sharpe ratios.[41] One testable implication is the
following. If my explanation is true, then the coefficient b should be
closer to one in periods when forward discounts $(f_{t,1} - p_t)$ are further from zero, other things equal (see equation 7.15). To understand
why, note that the numerator of the Sharpe ratio is a function of two
variables: the size of the forward discount and the value of the coefficient b. Holding fixed both the value of b and the denominator of
the Sharpe ratio (equation 7.16), a forward discount further from
zero implies a larger Sharpe ratio. A larger Sharpe ratio, in turn,
attracts more speculative capital, which induces adjustment in prices
toward consistency with unbiasedness (i.e., toward the level consistent with no inaction range). The data bears out this prediction.
Huisman et al. (1998), for example, find that unbiasedness holds
much more tightly in periods when the forward discounts are further
from zero. Using time-averaged data, Flood and Taylor (1996) find
the same result.

Consider a second implication of my explanation: currencies with
lower variances should have a coefficient b closer to one, other things
equal. This implication works from the denominator of the Sharpe
ratio: for given level of b and a given forward discount size, a lower
variance implies a larger Sharpe ratio. As above, a larger Sharpe
ratio attracts more speculative capital, which induces adjustment in
prices toward consistency with unbiasedness.[42] The data bears out
this prediction, too. Flood and Rose (1996), for example, find that
estimates of b within the lower volatility European Monetary System
are about 0.6.

*Why Isn't the Coefficient **b** in the Middle of the Inaction Range?*

The four-part explanation above clarifies why the bias can persist,
without violating speculative efficiency. It does not explain why the
coefficient b (at -0.9) lies near one edge of the inaction range $(-1, 3)$.
For this, one needs a meta-model—a model that determines the exchange rate when pure currency speculation does not occur. The
meta-model must confront the fact that inaction in terms of pure
currency speculation does not imply an absence of FX order flow.

Sources of order flow that remain include customers in the FX market that do not engage in pure currency speculation, which includes the great majority of mutual funds, pension funds, and nonfinancial corporations.

To begin our formulation of a meta-model, let us divide the customer portion of the order flow pie (see section 3.1) into three slices. The three slices are

1. Leveraged investors

2. Unleveraged investors

3. Nonfinancial corporations

The first slice is what practitioners call leveraged investors. These are the proprietary bank traders and hedge funds that are the focus of the previous paragraphs. As noted, this is the slice that has a comparative advantage in implementing pure currency strategies to exploit forward bias. Despite their comparative advantage, however, on average they devote little of their capital to this type of speculation. The second slice is what practitioners call unleveraged investors. These are institutions like mutual funds, pension funds, and insurance companies. The last slice is nonfinancial corporations. With this breakdown, we can write aggregate customer order flow as

$$C_t = C_t^L + C_t^U + C_t^N, \tag{7.17}$$

where the superscripts L, U, and N denote leveraged investors, unleveraged investors, and nonfinancial corporations, respectively.

Turning now to exchange rate determination, previous chapters provide a basis for writing

$$p_{t+1} - p_t = f(C_t, Z_t), \tag{7.18}$$

where Z_t denotes other determinants. Let us specialize this by writing:[43]

$$p_{t+1} - p_t = g(C_t^L, C_t^U, C_t^N, Z_t). \tag{7.19}$$

This provides a vehicle for explaining exchange rate behavior when the pure currency strategy no longer drives the aggregate order flow C_t (through the C_t^L channel).[44] This is a departure from standard macro models because those models' assumption of Uncovered Interest Parity (UIP) is tantamount to assuming that aggregate order flow *is* driven primarily by pure currency strategies.

Chapter 7

The meta-model relies instead on the portfolio shifts of the latter two slices—the unleveraged investors and nonfinancial corporations. These two institution types have a comparative *dis*advantage in implementing pure currency strategies. They are better characterized by limited participation in currency markets, as they do not monitor and trade in currency markets continuously. Their trades are incidental to, or bundled with, activities directed primarily at other objectives (e.g., a nonfinancial corporation that times its repatriation of overseas earnings for tax reasons, or an international mutual fund that shifts its country allocations based on a changing view of local-currency equity returns). Suppose that each period a subset of these institutions—a different subset each period—considers trading in the FX market. (This description of periodic adjustment draws from a large literature on "limited participation," which started with Grossman and Weiss 1983. They assume that agents adjust their cash balances periodically, with a different subset of agents returning to the bank to replenish each period. Periodic adjustment is typically interpreted as shorthand for unmodeled adjustment costs, e.g., monitoring costs.[45]) Limited participation in FX markets by unleveraged investors and nonfinancial corporations implies that their portfolio shifts across currencies are gradual.

Consider in this setting the effect of an increase in the foreign interest rate.[46] Given limited participation, portfolios adjust toward the higher expected returns only gradually. This contrasts sharply with standard asset market models, such as the sticky-price monetary model, in which a (real) foreign rate increase causes instantaneous appreciation of the foreign currency (as we saw in chapter 6). In the limited participation model, the instantaneous effect is spread over time, producing a period through which the foreign interest rate is higher, and the foreign currency continues to appreciate due to the order flow from gradual portfolio adjustment toward the foreign currency. This yields a coefficient b in equation (7.15) at the negative end of the inaction range (which is what we set out to explain).[47]

This model qualifies as a meta-model in the sense that the order flow driving the exchange rate—C_t^U and C_t^N—is not from pure currency strategies, as is implicit in UIP. It comes instead from other motivations (per the examples above). If the width of the inaction band from pure currency strategies were zero, order flow from gradual portfolio shifts would not affect exchange rates because it would be swamped by order flow from pure strategies in C_t^L. In the absence of the flow from pure currency strategies, the flow from gradual adjustment becomes an important determinant.

This raises a fascinating question: How much order flow is required to "enforce" forward rate unbiasedness? Section 7.1 suggests the amount is quite large. Specifically, the estimated impact of inter-dealer order flow on price is 50 basis points per $1 billion; this translates into an impact of customer order flow of 100 basis points per $1 billion (assuming customer order flow is multiplied by two in interdealer trading—not unreasonable given the hot potato amplification of volume examined in chapter 5; see also chapter 9). An exchange rate that is 20 percent away from a level consistent with unbiased forward rates would require $20 billion of order flow to correct.[48] That may not seem like a lot, but remember that to maintain the exchange rate at the new level, the $20 billion order flow cannot be reversed. An indefinite commitment of $20 billion of capital is large relative to what financial institutions—even collectively—are willing to commit to this particular trade. In a sense, then, this market's immense depth may actually impede correction of misalignments by making Milton Friedman's celebrated "stabilizing speculators" an institutional impracticality.

New Notion of the "Risk Premium"

I close this section with some comments that bring us back to the beginning of the forward bias discussion and the two traditional explanations of inefficiency versus risk premium. As noted above, the explanation provided here for the bias' persistence does not violate market efficiency in the speculative sense of that term: there are no supernormal profit opportunities going unexploited (given that the Sharpe ratio criterion is the solution to a constrained optimization problem). Does this mean that the explanation falls in the risk premium category? In a sense, yes; risk aversion is preventing market participants from exploiting the return differentials implied by the bias. That said, participants are not responding to risk as they would in a frictionless environment. That is why traditional risk premium models—based on covariance—are unable to account for return differentials empirically.

If my Sharpe ratio driven, inaction-band explanation is correct, it suggests that there is far more "room" in financial market equilibrium than frictionless models predict. Other empirical evidence supports this view. An oft-cited example is the pricing of shares in "Siamese twin" companies, such as Royal Dutch and Shell (see, e.g., Froot and Dabora 1999). Royal Dutch and Shell are a controlled experiment in relative valuation. The companies are linked to one another by corporate charter, which mandates that cash flows to the equity holders of each company should be distributed in a strict 60/40 ratio. One would expect that equivalent share classes should trade at prices in fixed 60/40 proportions, but this is not the case: deviations from the 60/40 ratio have ranged from −30 percent to +15 percent over the last twenty years (the 60/40 dividend split is applicable throughout). This is not a case of establishing a relative valuation between, say, IBM and Intel. The relative value of Royal Dutch and Shell should be determined much more precisely, yet large disparities persist because, in the end, the trade is not appealing enough to attract sufficient order flow.[49] If there is this much room in pricing in so controlled a setting, what does this say about asset pricing more generally?

8   Microstructure and Central Bank Intervention

Exchange rates directly affect international competitiveness and the performance of national economies. Indeed, they are arguably the world economy's most important prices. Add to this importance the fact that exchange rate volatility appears excessive, and it is not surprising that government intervention is more common than in other capital markets.

This chapter applies microstructure tools to central bank intervention. Within exchange rate economics, intervention is a classic topic. It is also a natural topic for micro analysis. I begin by describing traditional methods of intervention analysis, which use the tools of macroeconomics. This provides perspective on how and where a micro approach can add value. Section 8.2 reviews theoretical work on intervention that lies within the microstructure approach. Section 8.3 presents recent empirical work whose goal is to measure the price impact of central bank trades. The focus in that section is recent work by Evans and Lyons (2000), which builds on the model presented in chapter 7 (making it especially accessible with that earlier material in hand).[1]

Before I begin, I want to address an issue that runs throughout this chapter: the issue of whether different-currency assets are imperfect substitutes. Imperfect substitutability is important because it governs whether portfolio balance effects are driven by order flow (irrespective of whether those orders are from the central bank or the private sector). If—for a given expected return—investors are completely indifferent to holding dollar- or yen-denominated assets (perfect substitutability), then portfolio shifts like those in the Evans-Lyons model (C_{it}^1) will have no effect. If investors care about currency denomination, then risk premiums and portfolio balance effects should arise (see also the portfolio balance model described in chapter 6).

As an empirical matter, we have not yet reached consensus on the relevance of FX portfolio balance effects.[2] Views about their presence have shifted over the last twenty years from negative to moderately positive. The earlier negative view was based on early empirical work that finds no evidence of portfolio balance effects (e.g., Dooley and Isard 1982; Frankel 1982; Frankel and Engel 1984; Lewis 1988; for an overview see Dominguez and Frankel 1993b, 105). These studies examine FX markets at a broad level and address whether different-currency returns are driven by changing asset supplies. In general, these studies suffer from lack of statistical power because changing asset supplies are notoriously difficult to measure. Studies that focus narrowly on the effects of central bank intervention—a kind of "event study" on changing asset supplies—are more successful in finding effects from portfolio balance (e.g., Loopesko 1984; Dominguez 1990; Dominguez and Frankel 1993a). But even with this narrow focus on intervention events, results are not exclusively positive (e.g., Rogoff 1984).

The Evans and Lyons (2000) analysis of portfolio balance effects—reviewed in section three—is a new approach, one that measures portfolio balance effects directly from the order flow of private market participants (i.e., not central banks). Though this new approach is not without drawbacks, it does avoid several of the drawbacks of the earlier literature. For example, the Evans-Lyons approach is arguably more powerful (statistically) than the approach of the early broad-level studies because it does not rely on measuring changing assets supplies, making it less vulnerable to measurement error. It may also be more powerful than the event-study intervention approach because it does not rely on the relatively small number of intervention events available for that type of analysis. (Moreover, the average size of interventions is small: For the United States, average size reported by Dominguez and Frankel 1993b is only $200 million; U.S. intervention since then has been larger, typically in the $300 million to $1.5 billion range, though less frequent—see Edison 1998).

Let me try to make this point about statistical power more vivid. Envision the FX market as a "choke point" where portfolios are actually being balanced (which includes the portfolios of central banks). Measures of order flow provide precise measures of this rebalancing and the price effects that arise as a result. As a choke point, the FX market is the venue where market participants (effectively) say to one another, "Here, hold this," where "this" might be

Assets	Liabilities
FXR: ↓ $100 million **DGB:** no change	**MS:** ↓ $100 million

Figure 8.1
Fed balance sheet: Unsterilized purchase of $100 million with yen. FXR is foreign exchange reserves, DGB is domestic government bonds, and MS is money supply—that is, money in circulation (currency plus monetary base).

10 billion euros. If we are to detect portfolio effects anywhere, this may be the right place to look.

8.1   Macro Motivation for a Micro Approach

Exchange rate regimes—for example, floating, managed floating, and fixed—are defined by the degree and type of central bank intervention used. There are two basic types:[3]

1. Unsterilized intervention

2. Sterilized intervention

As we shall see, unsterilized intervention affects the domestic money supply and, as a result, the interest rate. Sterilized intervention, on the other hand, has no effect on the money supply and therefore no effect on the (short-term) nominal interest rate.

Consider the following example, which clarifies how sterilization neutralizes the effect of an intervention on the money supply. Figure 8.1 presents a stylized version of a central bank balance sheet. It has three basic categories, two on the asset side and one on the liability side. Central bank assets include foreign exchange reserves (FXR) and domestic government bonds (DGB). The main central bank liability is money in circulation—the money supply (MS).[4]

First, consider the effect of an unsterilized intervention. The unsterilized intervention in figure 8.1 is a purchase of $100 million by the U.S. Federal Reserve Bank (Fed) using Japanese yen. The Fed would do this if it wanted to support the value of the dollar: it adds to the market demand for dollars.

To carry out intervention, the Fed could contact a dealing bank, say Citibank, and buy the $100 million at Citibank's offer quote.[5]

Settling this trade involves a transfer of $100 million worth of yen to Citibank. This reduces Fed foreign exchange reserves, FXR, and money in circulation, MS, by the same amount.[6] The reduction in the money supply is Citibank's payment of $100 million to the Fed. (In reality, this payment by Citibank takes the form of reducing by $100 million Citibank's account at the Fed, rather than an actual transfer of cash. Private banks maintain such accounts to fulfill regulatory requirements.) The contraction of the dollar money supply pushes up short-term dollar interest rates, other things equal.

Note that this interest rate increase from the intervention reinforces the dollar-strengthening effect of the Fed's order flow (the order to buy dollars in the FX market). To understand why, recall from chapter 6 that asset approach models (such as the sticky-price monetary model) predict that an *increase* in the dollar interest rate should cause the dollar to immediately *appreciate*. (The intuition for this effect is that, other things equal, a higher interest rate—nominal and real—on dollars makes dollar-denominated assets more attractive.) Interest rates are an important part of fundamental value in these models. Indeed, from the perspective of chapter 6's monetary models, it is the interest rate that causes dollar appreciation when intervention is sterilized, not the order flow.

Consider now what happens when the intervention is sterilized. In this case, the intervention trade in the FX market is offset by another trade designed to nullify the effect of the first on the money supply and interest rate. This offsetting transaction is called an open-market operation—a Fed purchase of domestic government bonds, DGB. In this case, the offsetting transaction is a purchase of $100 million worth of domestic government bonds, which re-injects 100 million dollars back into the economy. This sterilized intervention is shown on the central bank's balance sheet in figure 8.2.

To keep them straight, I have labeled the two transactions in figure 8.2 with (1)s and (2)s. The first transaction is the same as the unsterilized intervention in figure 8.1: foreign exchange reserves fall and money supply falls. The second transaction—the purchase of $100 million worth of domestic government bonds—increases the money supply by $100 million. The net effect on the money supply (and therefore the interest rate) after both transactions is zero.

Let's walk through the transactions in more detail. Suppose that this offsetting sterilization trade in domestic bonds is transacted with Bank of America (B of A). Settling this trade involves a transfer of $100 million worth of domestic government bonds to the Fed—the

Assets	Liabilities
FXR: ↓ $100 million (1)	**MS:** ↓ $100 million (1)
DGB: ↑ $100 million (2)	**MS:** ↑ $100 million (2)

Figure 8.2
Fed balance sheet: Sterilized purchase of $100 million with yen. FXR is foreign exchange reserves, DGB is domestic government bonds, and MS is money supply—that is, money in circulation (currency plus monetary base). Transaction (1) is the unsterilized intervention; transaction (2) is the offsetting sterilization.

increase in the asset category DGB—and credit of $100 million to B of A's account with the Fed. This credit is an increase in Fed liabilities—the increase in MS shown in the T-account. Taken together, these two transactions leave the liability side of the Fed's balance sheet unchanged: The reduction in Citibank's deposits at the Fed are offset by the increase in B of A's deposits at the Fed, leaving Fed deposits from the banking system as a whole unchanged. Even though an FX transaction has taken place, the key fundamentals of money supply and interest rate remain unaltered.

How Can Sterilized Intervention Work?

How can sterilized intervention influence the exchange rate if it does not alter the money supply and interest rate? Viewed from the macro models presented in chapter 6 (e.g., the flexible-price monetary model and the sticky-price monetary model), the answer is not clear. With no changes in money supply or interest rates, there is no change in fundamentals (as defined by these models), so there is no change in the exchange rate.

There are, however, two channels identified in the macro literature through which sterilized intervention might still work:

1. The signaling channel: Sterilized intervention may signal *future* money supply and interest rate changes, thereby affecting the exchange rate today.

2. The portfolio-balance channel: Sterilized intervention may affect the exchange rate because it changes the currency denomination of the supplies of assets held by the public.

The signaling channel is easy to understand within the macro models of chapter 6: if the central bank is signaling future money supply changes, then it is indeed changing fundamentals, so forward-looking markets will move the exchange rate today. (The future change in interest rates need not involve another FX transaction, i.e., it need not be the result of future unsterilized intervention.)[7] Though easy to understand theoretically, empirically the signaling channel is not well supported: subsequent changes in money supply tend not to be consistent with the changes "predicted" by interventions (see, e.g., Kaminsky and Lewis 1996).

The portfolio balance channel is a bit subtler. To understand this channel we need to move among the models of chapter 6 from the monetary models to the portfolio balance model. Unlike the signaling channel, portfolio balance effects of sterilized intervention do not operate through expected future payoffs (using the terminology introduced in chapter 2); they operate through discount rates. To understand why, note that when central bank intervention is sterilized, something has changed (though not the interest rate). From the balance sheet example above, we see that the sterilized intervention increases the Fed's holdings of dollar bonds and decreases the Fed's holdings of yen bonds (foreign exchange reserves, FXR, are held in interest-bearing bonds rather than currency). Thus, the intervention reduces the public's total holding of dollar bonds and increases the public's total holding of yen bonds. If dollar bonds and yen bonds were perfect substitutes, then the public would be happy to make this change and no adjustment in expected returns would be necessary (i.e., no adjustment in risk premia would be necessary). If these bonds are imperfect substitutes, then changes in expected returns are necessary to induce the public to make the change. These expected return changes must occur from changes in the current level of the exchange rate because payoff expectations—for example, interest rates—are not moving when intervention is sterilized.[8]

Though similar in spirit, there is a difference between this macro portrayal of imperfect substitutability and the micro portrayal I introduced in the chapter 2 when discussing order flow information. The difference is how the market learns about the size of the needed exchange rate change. Under the macro story, the size of the portfolio shift forced on the public is known publicly (or, if not, it is estimated using public information). All agents then agree on the proper market-clearing exchange rate. Under the microstructure story, in contrast, the market learns about the market-clearing exchange rate from the engendered order flow itself. Non-zero order flows imply that more adjustment is required.

Announced, Unannounced, and Secret Intervention

The previous paragraph made a distinction between intervention that is publicly known and intervention that needs to be estimated. In the intervention literature, the terms used are announced intervention and unannounced intervention. Announced interventions are released by the central bank or other officials over major news wires simultaneously with the intervention trade. (These official news releases do not typically provide full information: they often specify only that a central bank is trading without divulging the size of the order.) Unannounced intervention is executed with a private bank dealer or dealers without any official news release. From an information perspective, unannounced intervention comes in two varieties. When the central bank itself places unannounced orders, the counterparty dealer(s) know that the central bank is on the other side. Consequently, though there is no official news release, the market does learn over the day that there has been intervention, and subsequent reports by newswires typically convey what the market has learned. Alternatively, central banks sometimes place orders through agents who do not reveal that a central bank is the source of the order—so-called secret intervention. One reason a central bank might want to do this is to mimic the trades of private players. (This mimicking strategy was described to me by former Fed official Scott Pardee).

Let me summarize the above discussion of intervention types. There are nine types embedded in the discussion, illustrated by the 3×3 diagram in figure 8.3.

Intervention in Practice

In practice, intervention in major FX markets these days is typically (1) sterilized, (2) unannounced, (3) effected through brokers, and (4) infrequent. (That said, practices do differ across central banks, and even across time at the same central bank.) As a consequence of features (1) and (2), most of the literature on intervention is focused on

	Sterilized: no signal	Sterilized: signal	Unsterilized
Announced			
Unannounced, but partially revealed			
Secret			

Figure 8.3
Types of intervention.

the lower left 2 × 2 block of figure 8.3.[9] Let me address each of these four features in more detail.

Intervention is typically sterilized in managed float systems. This is certainly the case for the managed float systems that govern the two largest spot markets: $/euro and $/yen. (These two systems are in fact much closer to the pure float model than to the pure fixed model.) The Fed, for example, sterilizes all its intervention as a matter of standard operating procedure (per Dominguez and Frankel 1993b: "The stated U.S. policy is to sterilize its foreign exchange intervention operations always and immediately"). The Bank of Japan and the Bundesbank also typically sterilize, though not always (Edison 1993). In pure fixed-rate systems, on the other hand, interventions are frequently unsterilized; to be credible, central banks need to adjust their monetary policies to defend the peg.

Most interventions are also not officially announced over major news wires simultaneously with the trade (Dominguez and Frankel 1993b), although there is a trend toward more announcements. Even without official announcement, varying degrees of information gets revealed. Consider the following description by officials at the Fed (Smith and Madigan 1988):

Depending upon the degree of intervention visibility that is desired, we will either call banks and deal directly or operate through an agent in the broker's market. Most operations are conducted in the brokers' market, though at the beginning of a major intervention episode we have sometimes chosen to deal directly with several banks simultaneously to achieve maximum visibility. Within the brokers' market we can be more or less aggressive, hitting existing quotes or leaving trailing quotes.

When the central bank operates through an agent, the intervention can be kept completely secret: the counterparty dealer trades and settles with the agent, so the central bank source can remain unknown. Hung (1997) reports that about 40 percent of U.S. intervention between 1985 and 1989 was conducted secretly (secret by Hung's definition means never reported in newspapers/newswires). Klein's (1993) findings are similar; moreover, he finds that many of the interventions reported in newspapers never actually occurred, casting some doubt on the accuracy of information in these reports. To summarize, though we do not know the exact breakdown between secret intervention and partially revealed intervention, both types are well represented in the major market data.

The last of the four empirical features is that central bank intervention in major currency markets is infrequent. One has to be careful on this score, however, because intervention tends to be episodic. For example, from September 1995 to the end of 1997, the United States never intervened, and it has intervened on only a handful of days since then. The Bank of Japan, in contrast, has intervened more frequently over the same period (though official data are not available). The United States also completely refrained from intervention from 1981–1984 (during the first Reagan administration, which followed a laissez faire approach to currency markets). U.S. intervention was much more active from 1985–1992, however: over this period the United States intervened thirty-six days per year, on average.

The Importance of Intervention: Fixed versus Floating Rates

One can frame the importance of intervention by considering what is perhaps the most central issue in exchange rate economics: the choice between fixed and floating exchange rates (see also section 7.3). As with most policy alternatives, policymakers are not limited to choosing one or the other. Rather, most exchange rate systems are hybrids, including the systems governing $/euro and $/yen. Nevertheless, understanding the polar extremes of pure fixed and pure floating helps to clarify the tensions inherent in hybrid systems. It is precisely these tensions, and policymakers' attempts to relax them, that generate the interesting open issues regarding intervention.

Consider first a pure float, which is defined by the absence of intervention: the central bank leaves the determination of rates wholly to the markets. The central bank therefore never trades in the FX market and never adjusts exchange rate fundamentals (e.g., interest rates) in order to influence the exchange rate. Monetary policy is free to tackle other policy objectives, such as stimulating growth or reducing inflation.[10]

The mechanics of maintaining a fixed exchange rate are more involved. With open, unfettered capital markets, maintaining a fixed exchange rate requires that fundamentals (interest rates, money supplies, etc.) are kept at levels consistent with the peg. When fundamentals are inconsistent, financial markets react rapidly by, for example, selling overvalued domestic currency to the central bank, thereby draining the central bank's FX reserves.

This simple description of what happens under fixed rates when fundamentals are inconsistent with the peg begs two important questions:

1. What exactly are these "fundamentals" that may be inconsistent with the peg?

2. How does the central bank know when these fundamentals and the peg are consistent?

The macro models in chapter 6 provide (theoretical) answers to both of these questions: the fundamentals are the driving variables in the macro models' exchange rate equations, and the equations themselves provide the combinations consistent with a given peg. But empirically, these equations are a poor description of actual exchange rate behavior. If not from macro models, then, how in the real world does a central bank know when consistency between the peg and fundamentals has been achieved? The answer is disarmingly simple: the central bank learns whether consistency has been achieved from order flow. That is,

Fundamentals (broadly defined) are consistent with the peg when there is no longer a significant imbalance between buyer-initiated and seller-initiated orders—that is, private order flow is not significantly different from zero.

This is not a trivial point; it is an indication that even central banks have always done real-time monitoring of movements in fundamentals at the microstructural level—by monitoring order flow.[11] Indeed, one can view changes in central bank reserves during crisis episodes as a summary measure of private order flow (because the central bank is typically the only buyer of the local currency during crises).

Order Flow and the Macro Approach

Though the term "order flow" as used in microstructure finance was not used in the macro literature on intervention before the mid-1990s, the idea that trades are important for pushing prices around was certainly present. Consider, for example, the following paragraph from Dominguez and Frankel (1993b):

> The next question is how much of intervention policy's influence on the exchange rate is the "news" effect and how much is the effect of actual official purchases and sales of foreign currency occurring at the same time? It is clear that news has an effect to the extent that it causes investors to revise their expectations of future rates of return. They buy or sell foreign currency in response to the change in expected returns and thereby drive up or down the current price of foreign exchange.

Perhaps most interesting about this passage is that even when the channel is the news effect on expectations, the proximate cause of the price change is still order flow—through the induced orders of private sector investors. For both effects then—the news effect and the direct effect of official transactions—the authors have order flow in mind as the proximate driver.[12] In 1993, when the Dominguez-Frankel book was published, we had little empirical sense of the per-dollar price impact of orders. This is precisely what the microstructure approach is now providing.

8.2   Microstructure Models of Intervention

This section reviews recent theoretical work that applies microstructure models to central bank intervention. Two themes that distinguish this theoretical work are that it (1) recognizes asymmetric information of different types, and (2) it addresses transparency (secrecy) head on.

Addressing the asymmetric information theme first, there are in fact two basic types that are relevant for intervention (see also Evans and Lyons 2000). The first type is well recognized in the macro literature: asymmetric information between the central bank and the public. The mere fact that the central bank controls several exchange rate fundamentals (e.g., interest rates and inflation) gives it superior information about the paths of those fundamentals. Another example of central bank information advantage is its access to privileged information (e.g., data that are not yet public). This "type 1" information asymmetry between the central bank and public is at the center of traditional intervention theory.

The second type of asymmetric information is the type that exists between private agents. Traditional models of intervention based on asymmetric information of the first type do not include this second type; all private agents in those earlier models learn about changes in fundamentals simultaneously, and the mapping from these changed fundamentals to price is common knowledge.

This "type 2" asymmetric information between private agents is arguably more general than the first—at least as it relates to intervention—because it plays a role in determining the effectiveness of intervention irrespective of the channel through which the intervention effects operate. Consider, for example, the signaling channel: irrespective of whether an intervention is sterilized, some agents observe the central bank's trade before others, and the market's understanding of this will affect the price response.[13] This is also true for portfolio balance channel: the portfolio shift that the intervention trade is forcing on the public is not publicly observed, so price adjustment occurs via learning from the trading process.

Theoretical work within microstructure focuses more on asymmetric information of type 2. This is the case for two recent papers on intervention: Montgomery and Popper (1998) and Bhattacharya and Weller (1997). Montgomery and Popper use a variation of the rational expectations model to address whether, by using intervention, the central bank can contribute to the efficiency of the market's aggregation of type-2 information. In effect, intervention in their model helps to achieve efficient sharing of information that would otherwise not occur. The focus of the Bhattacharya and Weller paper is a bit different. They use a hybrid Kyle/rational expectations model to show why, in the presence of type-2 asymmetric information, a central bank may prefer not to reveal its exchange rate target, nor the size of its intervention. Their analysis provides a micro-based perspective on secrecy, with information elements that are missing from earlier work.

Let me turn to the secrecy theme more directly by providing a brief review of the literature on central bank secrecy that preceded Bhattacharya and Weller's microstructure approach. Dominguez and Frankel (1993b, 60) provide insight on that earlier literature when they write:

[Many] reasons have been offered to explain why central banks may want to keep their intervention operations secret. We recount them here, without regard to how convincing they may be. These explanations of central bank secrecy can, in turn, be grouped into three broad categories: reasons based on a central bank's convictions regarding the efficacy of intervention at a point in time, reasons based on the perceived depth or underlying volatility of the foreign exchange market at a point in time, and reasons based on [central bank] portfolio adjustment.

The first of these broad categories is based on the fact that, at times, central banks may act secretly because they actually prefer intervention to be *ineffective*. For example, the decision to intervene may be coming from another branch of government, over the central bank's objections. The second category of reasons for secret intervention is based on the idea that the central bank may want, for example, to calm so-called "disorderly" markets by providing a sense of a two-way market. The notion here is that if intervention were observable, this would signal that private participants are not willing to provide liquidity on one side of the current market (presumably leading to greater disorder). The third category of reasons for intervention secrecy—which Dominguez and Frankel consider more persuasive—is based on the fact that central banks frequently adjust their portfolio holdings without any intent to move the exchange rate; they don't want the market to confuse these transactions with purposeful intervention, so they intervene secretly.

Note that for both the first and third of these categories, the central bank is choosing secrecy so that its price impact is *minimized*, whereas "effective" intervention is typically associated with maximized price impact. For the second category, too, the central bank is not choosing secrecy to maximize price impact, but to prevent undesirable movements that might otherwise occur. In sum, none of the three categories provides a rationale for increasing the efficacy of intervention in the usual sense.

Like Bhattacharya and Weller, Vitale (1999) addresses why central banks prefer secrecy using a variation of the Kyle model. To provide a deeper view on this new line of intervention theory, let me describe the Vitale model and his analysis in a bit more detail. (It is quite accessible on the basis of the Kyle model material presented in chapter

4.) The added perspective on secrecy is helpful background for the empirical analysis I present in section 8.3.

The Vitale (1999) Model

Vitale's model uses a one-period Kyle framework. At first blush, it may seem that a Kyle model of major FX markets is inappropriate: It posits a trading structure that is centralized and batched, whereas the major markets trade in a decentralized dealer structure. Vitale offers a clever and compelling motivation for this modeling choice: the batch market serves as a metaphor for lack of transparency. When actual central bank orders are routed through an individual dealer, the subsequent trades of that dealer are interpreted as noisy signals of the intervention (noisy due to low transparency). Kyle's batch framework captures this aspect of intervention because the Kyle marketmaker cannot observe the identity of his or her clients and therefore cannot distinguish between informed and uninformed traders. Nevertheless, the orders the Kyle marketmaker receives still convey information about fundamental value.

The Vitale model's single risky asset is foreign exchange, whose random payoff V is Normally distributed, with mean P_0 and variance σ_V^2. (Vitale refers to the payoff V as the fundamental, and I adopt this same terminology in describing his model.[14]) There is a single, risk-neutral dealer who transacts foreign exchange with a group of liquidity traders and a central bank. The central bank is informed, in the sense that it knows the realization of V. All orders from the liquidity traders and the central bank are grouped together—batched—so it is not possible for the dealer to observe the source of orders. The dealer sees only the total order flow, which he uses to extract information about the fundamental V and to set the market-clearing price P (according to a zero-profit condition, as in Kyle). In the Vitale model, then, the central bank is the informed insider, replacing the private informed trader of the Kyle model. As was the case for the Kyle insider, the central bank can influence the exchange rate only by altering the dealer's expectations about V.

The model has three other key ingredients:

1. Intervention does not affect the value of V (i.e., it is sterilized).
2. Intervention targets the exchange rate P to some level $\bar{P}$.

3. The central bank minimizes a loss function that depends on the gap between P and its target $\bar{P}$, and on the cost of intervention.

The loss L takes the form:

$$L = X(P - V) + b(P - \bar{P})^2, \tag{8.1}$$

where X is the central bank's (market) order. The parameter b indicates the degree of commitment to the predetermined target $\bar{P}$ (b is nonnegative and is common knowledge). The first term in the loss function reflects the capital commitment or cost of intervention: if the central bank is buying foreign currency at a local-currency price above V, this is costly—a loss.

This loss function makes it clear that if the central bank were to reveal both its intervention trade X and its target $\bar{P}$, then the dealer could back out the fundamental value V (because V would be the only unknown). With the dealer knowing V, no attempt to target the exchange rate would be effective—only the dealer's expectation of V matters. Suppose instead that the central bank attempts to fool the dealer by announcing false intervention trades. Vitale shows that these announcements would not be credible (implying that the central bank would derive no benefit).

The essence of the model is contained in the loss function, particularly in the fact that the target $\bar{P}$ and the fundamental V are not in general equal. This creates the central tension. It is exactly when the target is not consistent with the fundamental and announcements are not credible that sterilized intervention is useful. Vitale shows that, in effect, the central bank can buy credibility via costly trading, which allows it to push the exchange rate toward its target.

Vitale's main result is that the central bank always prefers to conceal its target. When the target is secret, the realized exchange rate is distributed more tightly around the target, which minimizes the expected loss. (That the exchange rate has a distribution comes from the realization of uncertain liquidity trader demands.) The basic intuition is the following: If the marketmaker knew anything about the target, he could adjust the signals derived from order flow to make them more informative about the fundamental V (in much the same way that signals were adjusted in chapter 4 to form new, more informative signals—typically denoted with Z). The more informative the order flow, the more tightly the price P is distributed about V, which is not what the central bank wants. A secret target gives the central bank the greatest possible room to manipulate the beliefs of the marketmaker.

8.3   Measuring the Price Impact of Intervention Trades

An important difference between private trades and central bank trades is that private traders typically want to minimize price impact, whereas central banks want to maximize price impact. Central bank trading desks do their best to "time" their intervention trades to increase their price impact. In the past, this has been more a matter of feel than anything else: data were just not available to determine rigorously which market states are the high-impact states.[15]

With the advent of electronic trading and the data that electronic trading provides, research on this topic is at a turning point. Central bankers enjoy detailed data on their own trades (timing, size, execution method, etc.). This allows them to generate a real-time picture of exactly how intervention trades are absorbed in the markets, including changes in liquidity provision (e.g., limit orders at brokers), the path of induced private order flow, and so on. From the perspective of central bank research, this type of direct microstructure analysis is an exciting prospect. Outside central banks, however, direct analysis of individual intervention trades is generally not possible because detailed intervention data are not released. (The Swiss National Bank data analyzed by Payne and Vitale 2000 is a notable exception.)

A recent paper by Evans and Lyons (2000) circumvents these data constraints by measuring intervention's price impact using an indirect approach. They address the following question: What does the price impact of *private* trades teach us about the likely impact of intervention trades?[16] Private trade data include comprehensive coverage of trade characteristics like time of day and state of the market, which is not the case of intervention data—even data available to central banks (interventions are relatively infrequent and are clumped in terms of time of day). Another important feature of the Evans-Lyons paper is that their data are not limited to high-frequency prices, but also include, crucially, order flow. Measuring order flow is essential for determining trades' impact on prices. Evans and Lyons's indirect approach is based on the fact that central bank trades of a certain type—sterilized, secret, and conveying no signal—and private trades are indistinguishable.[17] This allows them to analyze rather precisely the likely price impact of this intervention-trade type.

Secret   Announced

Figure 8.4
Intervention transparency spectrum.

The Evans-Lyons analysis shifts attention toward a type of inter-vention that has received little attention of late. Since the publication of Dominguez and Frankel (1993b), something of a consensus has arisen that for intervention to be effective, it should be announced and coordinated across multiple central banks. The Evans-Lyons analysis does not dispute the effectiveness of this type of interven-tion; indeed, because their analysis is based on private trades only, it has nothing to say about this type of intervention. Rather, the Evans-Lyons analysis highlights the effectiveness of intervention that lies on the other end of the transparency spectrum (see figure 8.4). Private trades are—by their very nature—"sterilized," so why not learn all we can from the price impact of this type of trade?

Why Price Impact Might Be State Dependent

To understand why a given sized trade may have different price impact in different market states, let us revisit the concept of event uncertainty (introduced in chapter 5). The term refers to uncertainty about whether or not private information is present (in contrast to most trading models, where it is known with certainty that it is present).[18] Under event uncertainty, the information content of trades varies depending on the market's state. In the Easley and O'Hara (1992) model, *trades are more informative—that is, have more price impact—when trading intensity is high.* To understand why, con-sider an environment in which new private information may exist, but does not necessarily exist. For example, suppose that with prob-ability p no new information exists and with probability $(1 - p)$ some traders have observed some new information (either good or bad, with known probabilities). Easley and O'Hara demonstrate that rational dealers in this context will view a lack of trading as evidence that new private information is not present. The upshot is that if trading intensity is low, then an incoming trade induces a smaller update in beliefs because it is more likely to be purely liquidity motivated. On the flip side, trades occurring when trading intensity is high are more likely to be signaling private information. Though

Evans and Lyons (2000) do not analyze state-dependent price impact explicitly, they do allow for it in their empirical specification.

A Model with Central Bank Trades

The intervention model that Evans and Lyons (2000) employ is a variation on the Evans-Lyons model introduced in chapter 7. Accordingly, I focus here on the salient differences. The model is designed to show how the trading process reveals information conveyed by different types of intervention.[19] It accommodates the main intervention types (figure 8.3) and the main channels through which intervention can be effective.

Though the model can accommodate all nine intervention types, the empirical implementation in Evans and Lyons (2000) focuses on the lower left cell of the matrix in figure 8.3: sterilized intervention that is secret and conveys no signal about future central bank policy. Evans and Lyons do not address the issue of coordinated intervention, though the model can be extended in this direction. (When extending the model to address coordination, one should recognize that coordination per se is more likely to operate through the signaling channel than the portfolio balance channel.)

Intervention Trades

Each day, one FX dealer among N is selected at random to receive an order from the central bank. Let I_t denote the intervention on day t, where $I_t < 0$ denotes a central bank sale (dealer purchase). The central bank order arrives with the public orders at the end of round 1, and like the public orders, it is observable only to the dealer receiving the order. (Recall that in the model there are three trading rounds each day: customer-dealer trade, interdealer trade, and another round of customer-dealer trade.) The central bank trade is distributed Normally:[20]

$$I_t \sim \text{Normal}(0, \sigma_I^2).$$

In the case of sterilized intervention with no signaling, the central bank trade I_t and the daily payoff increments ΔR_τ are uncorrelated:

$$\text{Corr}(I_t, \Delta R_\tau) = 0,$$

for all t and τ.

Model Solution

The model's solution is quite similar to that in the model of chapter 7. Specifically, the equilibrium trading rules for round 2 interdealer trading take the form

$$T_{jt} = \alpha C_{jt}^1 \tag{8.2}$$

$$T_{it} = \alpha(C_{jt}^1 + I_t), \tag{8.3}$$

where I use the subscript j to denote all dealers not receiving the central bank order, and subscript i for the one dealer who does receive the central bank order. With these trading rules, the change in price from the beginning of day t to the beginning of day $t+1$ takes the familiar form:

$$P_{t+1} - P_t = \beta_1 \Delta R_t + \beta_2 X_t, \tag{8.4}$$

where X_t is—as before—the interdealer order flow observed at the end of each day's round 2 interdealer trading.

As in the Evans-Lyons model of chapter 7, the price impact of order flow X_t arises here purely for portfolio balance reasons. It reflects the price adjustment required to induce the public (in round 3) to absorb the total portfolio shift from the day's round 1 trading. The only difference here is that the central bank's portfolio shift—in the form of I_t—must be absorbed by the public as well.

The punchline is as powerful as it is unsurprising: when sterilized intervention is secret and conveys no signal of future payoffs R_t, the market treats it like it would any other private trade. Put differently, private trades in this model are equivalent to secret, sterilized interventions that have no impact on future monetary policy. Central banks—by choosing to intervene in this manner—can expect their intervention to be as effective in moving price as the representative private trade.

Summary of Key Intervention Results

Evans and Lyons (2000) present several results. First, using *hourly* data from the $/DM and $/yen markets, they find that private orders (interdealer) have an immediate effect of about 1 percent per $2 billion.[21] This is similar in magnitude to the impact measured from daily order flow in chapter 7. All of this immediate effect does not persist, however. (Persistent effects are surely more important to officials who consider the current exchange rate misaligned.) Intervention strategy needs to be adjusted to maximize persistent effects: the maximum occurs when trading intensity is about one standard deviation above its mean. When intervention strategy is adjusted accordingly, Evans and Lyons find that buy orders have a persistent effect of about 1 percent per $3 billion. These results suggest, for example, that if European officials want a 10 percent more valuable euro, and they want that adjustment to persist, they would have to sell about $30 billion of their foreign exchange reserves, and do so in a way that mimics private transactions (subject to the caveat noted in note 21).

The Evans-Lyons analysis also provides explicit guidance for intervention in the form of both time-dependent rules and state-dependent rules. Their time-dependent rules indicate that dollar for dollar, order flow has the largest positive price impact during the London afternoon (12–6 P.M., British Summer Time—BST). During their sample, New York begins significant trading at about 3 P.M. BST (8 A.M. EST), so this interval includes the first three hours of the New York trading day (which is, incidentally, the interval within which most Fed intervention occurs). The state-dependent rules indicate that order flow has the largest positive price impact (1) when trading volume is high—consistent with event uncertainty—and (2) when markets are not especially turbulent or calm.[22] These results are consistent with those of Dominguez (1999), who also finds larger intervention effects during periods of heavy trading (and also around macro events).

Evans and Lyons interpret their findings as evidence of imperfect substitutability, a necessary condition for the efficacy of the portfolio channel. There is something of a consensus among financial economists that portfolio balance effects from intervention are nonexistent, or at least too small to be readily detectable. This has led some people to dismiss portfolio balance theory as irrelevant. Evans and Lyons's approach harnesses additional statistical power that allows them to detect the effects. The upshot: portfolio balance theory may be more relevant than was thought.

Let me close this chapter by considering where the microstructure approach to intervention is headed. The type of market data that are now coming available allow very precise tracking of how the market absorbs actual central bank trades and any information in them.

Central bank's with precise knowledge of their own trades—for example, timing, announcements, stealth level, and so on—will be able to estimate the impact of these various "parameter" settings. Armed with appropriate data, a central bank could learn exactly how trading is affected in all three market segments (direct interdealer, brokered interdealer, and customer-dealer). This would include learning about liquidity provision (on both sides of the market), transaction activity, and the process of price adjustment. It is something like a doctor who has a patient ingest blue dye to determine how it passes through the digestive system—the whole process becomes transparent. Such is the future of empirical work on this topic.

9   Customers: Underlying Demand in the Economy

.

This chapter is an introduction to the trading of FX customers. Understanding the demands of customers—the investors, the importers, the exporters, the corporate treasurers, and so on—is an important frontier for the microstructure approach. My goal is to present some first findings along this frontier. I refer to these findings as "first" because the data necessary for this analysis have become available only very recently. Much work remains to be done.

In section 9.1, I provide background on the available customer trade data. Though my empirical focus thus far has been on order flow between dealers, section one should help to bring customer-dealer trading into perspective. Section 9.2 describes the data in detail, including descriptive statistics. Because data such as these do not appear elsewhere in the literature, description beyond what is provided in chapter 5 is useful. Section 9.3 turns to regression analysis. It presents results from regressing price changes on customer order flow and tests some hypotheses introduced in section one. Because the sample is sufficiently long (6.5 years), these regressions use monthly data, in contrast to the regressions of the previous chapter that used daily data. (Recall that macroeconomic exchange rate models are also typically estimated using monthly data.) The final section, section 9.4, presents a case study on the remarkable drop in the yen/$ rate that occurred in October 1998 (around the time of the Long Term Capital Management collapse). In a single day, the yen/$ rate fell from about 130 to about 118, a change of roughly 10 percent.

9.1 Background on Customers

The role of customer order flow is central to microstructure theory. This is borne out by the models presented in earlier chapters: customer

flow is the essence of each, in that it is the customer orders that cat-
alyze a market response. By extension, it is not unreasonable to view
microstructure models in this respect as similar: their broad implications for the relation between exchange rates and customer flow
are the same (though the path of price adjustment may differ across
models).[1]

The importance of customer orders is obvious to practitioners
as well. Any FX trader or trading-desk manager would agree. One
trader I spoke with put it rather colorfully when he said that customer trades are the market's "crack cocaine," by which he meant
that the customer orders are the market's catalyst, and that catalyst is
quite powerful.[2] In keeping with this notion of customer flow as the
market's catalyst, proprietary information on those flows is a prime
driver of proprietary trading at the largest banks. (Smaller banks see
too little of the marketwide customer flow to make this information
useful.) Embedded in this behavior is the fact that banks find customer flow information valuable for *predicting* exchange rate movements. Thus far, this book has concerned itself only with *explaining*
movements, that is, accounting for movements using concurrent
flow. That customer flow has predictive power as well (i.e., today's
flow predicts future movements) adds a new dimension. It is this
predictive dimension that most interests the practitioner audience of
the microstructure approach.[3]

So why in previous chapters have I focused so much on order flow
between dealers? There are two reasons. The first is the simple fact
that until the dataset described below became available, researchers
had no alternative but to work with order flow between dealers.
The second reason is that despite the constraint on data availability,
there is justification for focusing on flow between dealers, due to the
differential transparency of customer-dealer and interdealer flow
(introduced in chapter 3). The reality of this market is that dealers
can observe some order flow from interdealer trades in which they
are not involved (e.g., from brokered trades). Customer-dealer trades,
on the other hand, are not observable except by the bank that receives them. Dealers therefore learn about other dealers' customer
orders as best they can by observing other dealers' interdealer trades,
and they set market prices accordingly. Although this learning from
interdealer orders is consistent with earlier chapters' empirical models, the ultimate driver of that interdealer flow is customer flow.

Let me provide a bird's eye view of how the customer flow data of
this chapter relates to the order flow data analyzed in earlier chap-

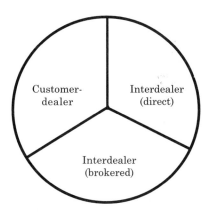

Figure 9.1
Trading volume pie.

ters. As noted in chapter 3, for the data sets of the 1990s volume in the major spot FX markets splits into three roughly equal categories: customer-dealer trades, direct interdealer trades, and brokered interdealer trades. Figure 9.1 provides an illustration. Chapter 7's analysis is based on data from the two interdealer categories. The work of Evans and Lyons (2000), for example, uses data wholly from the direct interdealer category. The work of Payne (1999) and Killeen, Lyons, and Moore (2000a) uses data wholly from the brokered interdealer category.

As noted in chapter 5, data on customer orders in the major spot markets are difficult to obtain. The only possible source given the market's current structure is private banks themselves, but in general these banks consider these data to be highly proprietary. Recently, however, Fan and Lyons (2000) obtained customer trade data from Citibank, a leading FX trading bank. (Citibank is among the top three worldwide, with a market share in major-currency customer business in the 10–15 percent range.) Citibank made these data available only on a time-aggregated basis—all the customer orders received by this bank worldwide are aggregated into daily order flows (executed trades only). The data set therefore does not include individual trades. Consequently, transaction-level analysis along the lines of that introduced in chapter 5 is not possible.

Against this drawback, this data set has many advantages:

1. The data span more that five years, so analysis at longer horizons (e.g., monthly) is possible.

2. The data cover the two largest markets: \$/euro and \$/yen. (Before the launch of the euro—January 1999—order flow data for the "euro" are constructed from flows in the constituent currencies against the dollar.)

3. The data include both spot and forward trades, but are netted of any trades in FX swaps (because FX swaps do not have net order flow implications; see chapter 3).

4. The data are split into three customer-type categories, corresponding to the three categories introduced in section 7.4: nonfinancial institutions (e.g., corporations), unleveraged financial institutions (e.g., mutual funds), and leveraged financial institutions (e.g., hedge funds).

Advantage (4) provides considerable statistical power for uncovering the underlying causes of order flow's impact on price. Do all orders have the same price impact? Or might some order types—say the orders of hedge funds—convey more information than others? Our ability to disaggregate order flow to answer these questions brings us closer to a specification of the underlying information sources.

Order Flows versus Capital Flows

When macroeconomists hear the word "flows," they think of balance of payments flows: real trade flows in the current account and capital flows in the capital account.[4] This book, in contrast, has hammered (mercilessly?) on the concept of order flow. This is an appropriate point to loop back on the relation between the two because we have left the world of interdealer trading and are now considering the currency demands of customers, which represent the underlying demands in the economy. They are the players whose demand shifts matter for persistent price movements. (As an empirical matter, dealers' net demands are too short-lived to matter over longer horizons, beyond the information they convey about underlying customer demands.[5]) Because balance of payments flows are familiar territory for macroeconomists, this becomes a natural contact point for readers from that background.

Now that we are examining underlying demands in the economy, are we closer to macroeconomic notions of balance of payments flows? At first blush, it might appear that we are not much closer.

Consider, for example, the goods market approach introduced in chapter 1 and revisited in section 7.2. True, that approach provides a link to the balance of payments because—under that approach—demand for currencies depends on two balance of payments categories, imports and exports (e.g., imports increase the demand for foreign currency to pay for those imports, and that increase in demand causes the foreign currency to appreciate). But we also learned in chapter 1 that less than 5 percent of spot transactions comes from imports and exports. The goods market approach is but a small piece of the total order flow picture.

Another reason why our examination of underlying demands in the economy may not bring us much closer to balance of payments notions is because balance of payments transactions and FX transactions are not the same; a one-to-one relationship between the two does not exist. To understand why, consider an import of $100 million of Japanese goods into the United States by a U.S. multinational. (One could also use a capital account transaction for this example.) Suppose the transaction is invoiced in yen, but the U.S. multinational pays the invoice from yen it already holds at its Japanese subsidiary. An import is logged, but there is no corresponding order in the FX market; the link is not one-to-one. In time, one might expect some rebalancing of the multinational's "portfolio," but that need not occur immediately, and it need not involve order flow in the FX market (e.g., suppose the Japanese subsidiary responds by increasing its working capital borrowing in yen).[6] The bottom line is that balance of payments flows do not necessarily generate corresponding order flow in the FX market. If learning from order flow is how dealers determine price, then portfolio shifts in the form of balance of payments flows will not be counted unless and until they generate order flow.

Though the preceding paragraphs suggest that the links between customer flows and the balance of payments is loose, there are indeed links. At the very least, we are certainly closer conceptually to the balance of payments in this chapter than in any of the previous chapters. The empirical analysis of this chapter helps tighten the link by separating order flow components according to "current account intensity" and "capital account intensity." For example, our customer data allow us to separate the orders of nonfinancial corporations—which includes the demands from current account transactions—from the orders of financial institutions, who in relative terms are far more involved in capital account transactions. (Foreign direct investments by nonfinancial corporations, which enter the capital account, are an important exception.) In section 9.3, we test whether these two different order flow types have similar price impact. The results shed light on which trader types tend to move price.[7]

Predictions about Customer Flow from Earlier Models

One of the conceptual contributions of the Evans-Lyons model was its explanation for why the cumulative interdealer flow in figure 1.2 can follow a random walk, whereas at the same time the positions of individual dealers return to zero at the close of each trading day. The essential feature of the model that produces this return-to-zero result is that the aggregate position of dealers is fully absorbed by the public each day. This market-clearing mechanism has strong implications for total customer flow. For example, it implies that:

HYPOTHESIS 1:   Marketwide, customer order flow each day should net to zero.

This follows from the model's result that dealers finish each day with no net position, which was itself a consequence of the assumption that dealers' risk-bearing capacity is small relative to the whole market, that is, relative to all nondealers together.

The data presented below on customer order flow data represent the orders received by one bank, not the customer flow received by all banks. One would not therefore expect it to net exactly to zero each day, even if the portfolio shifts model were literally true. With these limited data, then, hypothesis 1 is untestable. Suppose, however, that the single-bank data represent a random sample, say 10 percent, of the marketwide customer order flow on any given day. In this case, the Evans-Lyons model predicts that

HYPOTHESIS 2:   For a single bank, customer order flow each day should differ from zero due only to random sampling error.

HYPOTHESIS 3:   For a single bank, customer order flow each day should be uncorrelated with changes in the exchange rate.

Hypothesis 3 follows from the fact that the customer-order sample is assumed here to be random. (It should therefore contain on average as many realizations of the model's beginning of day "shock" orders as it does end of day "absorption" orders—the model's C_1's and C_3's, respectively.)

It is also possible, however, that all customer orders are not equally informative of subsequent market movements. Suppose, for example, that customer order flows are not alike in terms of their market impact. One might imagine two categories of customers: high-impact customers and low-impact customers. If this were the right description of the world, then a bank's customer orders might not be representative of the customer-order population because the bank could have a disproportionate share of high-impact customers.

9.2 A First Look at Customer Order Flow

Table 9.1 presents summary statistics for the three main customer categories: nonfinancial corporations, leveraged financial institutions (e.g., hedge funds), and unleveraged financial institutions (e.g., mutual funds).[8] The sample covers January 1993 to June 1999. For the euro, the total trading volume across the three customer categories is roughly balanced. For the yen, this is not the case: nonfinancial cor-

Table 9.1
Customer Trades: Volumes and Order Flow

	Euro			Yen		
	Total Trading Volume	Cumul. Order Flow	Daily Standard Deviation	Total Trading Volume	Cumul. Order Flow	Daily Standard Deviation
Nonfinancial Corporations	539	−25.7	0.09	259	3.3	0.07
Leveraged Financial	667	2.5	0.16	681	16.1	0.16
Unleveraged Financial	507	11.8	0.13	604	−1.8	0.15
Total	1,713	−11.4	0.23	1,544	17.6	0.23

Billions of euros for Euro and billions of dollars for Yen. Euro denotes the $/euro market. Yen denotes the $/yen market. The sample for both currencies is January 1993 to June 1999. (Before the launch of the euro in January 1999, volume and order flow are constructed from trading in the euro's constituent currencies.) Positive order flow in the case of the euro denotes net demand for euros (following the convention in that market of quoting prices in dollars per euro). Positive order flow in the case of the yen denotes net demand for dollars (following the convention in that market of quoting prices in yen per dollar). Daily standard deviation measures the standard deviation of daily order flow.

porate trading is less than half that for the other two categories (these breakdowns may be bank specific, however). For both markets, the daily order flow of the nonfinancial corporations is the least volatile. Cumulative order flow displays quite different characteristics across the three customer categories. For the euro, unleveraged financial institutions are the largest net buyers and nonfinancial corporations are the largest net sellers. In the yen market, leveraged financial institutions are the largest net buyers (of dollars) and unleveraged financial institutions are the largest net sellers (though slight).

I turn now to plots of the customer flows, which provide a first glimpse of the possible link to exchange rate movements. Figure 9.2 shows cumulative customer order flows and the level of the exchange rate in both the $/euro and $/yen markets.[9] Positive correlation is evident. Comparing these plots to figure 1.2—which uses the four months of daily interdealer data from Evans 1997—one sees that the correlation in figure 9.2 is not as tight at higher frequencies. At lower frequencies, say monthly, the relation is manifested clearly. The next section addresses this lower frequency relation more formally using regression analysis.

These plots also have implications for the three hypotheses introduced in section 9.1. Hypothesis 1 stated that marketwide customer flow each day should net to zero. Because these plots show only one bank's customer flow, not the whole market's, one is not able to reject this hypothesis based on these data alone. Hypotheses 2 and 3, on the other hand, are directly testable. Hypotheses 2 and 3 stated that this bank's daily customer flow should differ from zero due only to random sampling error, and should therefore be uncorrelated with exchange rate movements. These hypotheses appear to be rejected: cumulative order flow received by this bank is correlated with exchange rate movements.

What could explain this positive correlation? One possibility is that it is not really there—the correlation is not statistically significant. But I show in the next section that the relation *is* statistically significant. Another possibility is that hypothesis 1—from which hypotheses 2 and 3 are derived—may not hold (i.e., marketwide customer flow each day does not net to zero). For example, collectively, dealers may be maintaining nonzero positions. Though this would not be surprising from day to day, it would indeed be surprising at weekly frequencies and lower (and these lower frequencies are more relevant for the correlation in figure 9.2). Accordingly, I do

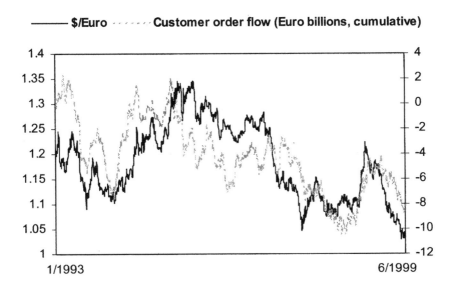

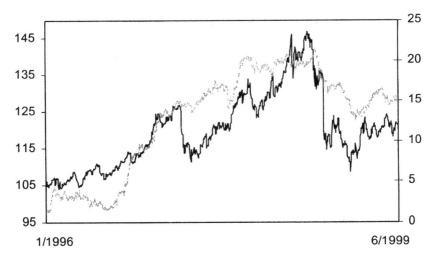

Figure 9.2
Cumulative customer flow and exchange rates. The plots show the spot exchange rate
and cumulative customer order flow received by the source bank. The sample for the
$/euro plot is January 1993 to June 1999. The sample for the yen/$ plot is January 1996
to June 1999 (the January 1993 to December 1995 period is not included due to the lack
of Tokyo office data). The spot exchange rate is expressed on the lefthand scale. The
cumulative customer order flow is expressed on the righthand scale (in billions of
euros for the $/euro plot and in billions of dollars for the yen/$ plot).

not consider this a compelling reason to believe that the positive correlation is due to a rejection of hypothesis 1. Another reason that hypothesis 1 may not (appear to) hold is that dealers *are* achieving their collective zero position, but do so by hedging with instruments that do not enter our sample (e.g., currency futures or options). Per chapters 3 and 5, however, the evidence suggests that FX dealers use these methods of risk management rarely, if at all (cf. Naik and Yadav 2000 for dealer hedging in other financial markets).

Without any convincing reason to reject hypothesis 1, there remain at least two other possibilities consistent with that hypothesis that can explain the correlation in figure 9.2. (I offer these as suggestions for future work; I cannot settle the issue based on analysis presented here.) First, it is possible that the customers of this bank are on average better informed. For example, Citibank is one of the very top FX trading banks in the world, so it may attract a disproportionate share of the most informative customer business. (More concretely, suppose the orders of hedge funds are the most informative and this bank receives more than its share of hedge fund orders.) A second possibility consistent with hypothesis 1 that can explain the correlation relies instead on this bank's sheer size. Suppose this bank's customers are the same as customers marketwide, but because the bank has such a large slice of total customer flow, its trades in the interdealer market generate disproportionate price impact. (A model along these lines could include a cost of "monitoring" the trading activity of various banks; in this setting it may be cost efficient to place disproportionate weight on the interdealer trades of the largest banks, despite their customers being no better informed than the average customer; see, e.g., Calvo 1999.) Further theoretical work will undoubtedly produce additional explanations. As additional customer flow data become available, empiricists will be able to distinguish among them.

The Evans-Lyons Sample: May–August 1996

Before turning to regression analysis, let me provide an additional plot that focuses on the $/euro over the same four-month period analyzed by Evans and Lyons (1999). Recall that the Evans-Lyons data reflect order flow in the direct interdealer segment over a four-month period, May through August 1996. Those data, and their re-

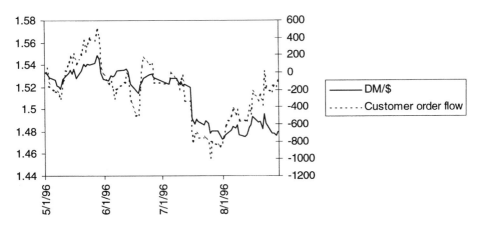

Figure 9.3
Cumulative customer flow and exchange rates over the Evans-Lyons sample. The plot shows the cumulative customer order flow in the $/euro market received by the source bank from May 1 to August 31, 1996, and the spot exchange rate over the same period. The spot rate is expressed in DM/$ on the lefthand scale. The cumulative customer order flow is expressed in millions of euros on the righthand scale (positive for net dollar purchases).

lation to the exchange rate, appear in figure 1.2. Figure 9.3 presents the May to August slice from the longer order flow series shown in figure 9.2. They are plotted against the DM/$ rate for comparison purposes because the DM/$ rate is the rate plotted in figure 1.2. Despite these data being the composite order flow for all the euro's constituent currencies (against the dollar), the flow series tracks the DM/$ rate quite closely. (Most of the constituent flow against the dollar is in the DM market.) It is heartening that the customer-dealer and interdealer flows tell a similar story. Integrated analysis of series from these different segments is an important area for future research.

9.3   Institution Types, Price Impact, and Information Structure

I turn now to regression analysis of the price impact of customer order flow. These results draw from the analysis presented in Fan and Lyons (2000). Table 9.2 presents results for the following model:

$$\Delta p_t = \beta_0 + \beta_1(\text{Aggregate Customer Flow})_t + \varepsilon_t, \tag{9.1}$$

where Δp_t is the monthly change in the log spot exchange rate. Esti-

Table 9.2
Price Impact of Aggregate Customer Orders

$\Delta p_t = \beta_0 + \beta_1(\text{Aggregate Customer Flow})_t + \varepsilon_t$

	β_1	R^2
Monthly Data		
Euro	0.8	0.16
	(3.8)	
Yen	1.2	0.15
	(3.0)	

T-statistics are shown in parentheses. The dependent variable Δp_t is the monthly change in the log spot exchange rate (the $/euro rate and the yen/$ rate, respectively). The order flow regressors are measured over the concurrent month (in billions of euros for the euro equation and billions of dollars in the yen equation). Estimated using OLS (standard errors corrected for heteroskedasticity). The sample is January 1993 to June 1999. Constants (not reported) are insignificant in both equations.

mates of this model provide a more rigorous measure of the correlations displayed in figure 9.2. Fan and Lyons estimate the model at the monthly frequency, which is the most common frequency for estimating macro exchange rate models.[10]

Order flow is significant in both regressions, with t-statistics well above three. The R^2 statistics are respectable when compared to those typically found for empirical macro models (typically in the 0–10 percent range), but remain far below those produced at the daily frequency by Evans and Lyons (1999) using direct interdealer order flow.

In the euro equation, the coefficient estimate of 0.8 implies that a net purchase of one billion euros increases the dollar price of a euro by about 0.8 percent. Similarly, in the yen equation, the estimate of 1.2 implies that a net purchase of $1 billion increases the yen price of a dollar by about 1.2 percent. These price-impact coefficients are roughly twice the size of those estimated by Evans and Lyons (1999), who found that a net purchase of $1 billion increases the DM price of a dollar by about 0.5 percent. (In fact Evans and Lyons find that some of the price impact at the daily frequency dissipates, suggesting that a comparable monthly frequency impact would be less than 0.5 percent.)

One might expect the customer flow to have a larger coefficient for two reasons. First, the source bank's customer flow may be correlated with other banks' customer flow, and because those other

Table 9.3
Price Impact of Disaggregated Customer Orders

$\Delta p_t = \beta_0 + \beta_1(\text{Unlev. Fin. Flow})_t + \beta_2(\text{Lev. Fin. Flow})_t + \beta_3(\text{Non-fin. Corp. Flow})_t + \varepsilon_t$

	β_1	β_2	β_3	R^2
Monthly Data				
Euro	1.5	0.6	−0.2	0.27
	(4.6)	(1.6)	(−0.5)	
Yen	1.1	1.8	−2.3	0.34
	(1.9)	(4.9)	(−3.5)	

T-statistics are shown in parentheses. The dependent variable Δp_t is the monthly change in the log spot exchange rate. The three order flow regressors are the order flows from unleveraged financial institutions, leveraged financial institutions, and nonfinancial corporations. Order flows are measured over the concurrent month (in billions of euros for the euro equation and billions of dollars in the yen equation). Estimated using OLS (standard errors corrected for heteroskedasticity). The sample is January 1993 to June 1999. Constants (not reported) are insignificant in both equations.

banks' flow is not included in the regression, the source bank's flow is getting "credit" for the impact. Second, if customer flow generates rounds of knock-on interdealer flow via hot potato trading, then this should induce an offsetting reduction in the interdealer flow's price impact (because each dollar of interdealer flow corresponds to less customer flow).

For the future agenda of the microstructure approach, a more important model is the following:

$$\Delta p_t = \beta_0 + \beta_1(\text{UF Flow})_t + \beta_2(\text{LF Flow})_t + \beta_3(\text{NF Flow})_t + \varepsilon_t, \qquad (9.2)$$

where Δp_t is the monthly change in the log spot rate, as before, and the three regressors are the three customer flow categories introduced above: UF denotes unleveraged financial institutions, LF denotes leveraged financial institutions, and NF denotes nonfinancial corporations. As Fan and Lyons point out, this regression is important because it addresses whether orders of some participants are more informative than those of others (as opposed order flow simply being undifferentiated demand). Analyzing order flow's parts illuminates the information structure that underlies trading in this market.

The results in table 9.3 indicate that these three different types of order flow do indeed have different price impact. The orders of nonfinancial corporations have no price impact in the $/euro market and, strikingly, appear to be negatively correlated with price changes in the $/yen market. The orders of financial institutions, on the other hand, have uniformly positive price impact. In the $/euro market, the key players (at least over this period) appear to be the unleveraged investors, or what practitioners call the "real money" accounts. (The "real money" nickname for these players—e.g., mutual funds, pension funds, life insurance companies, etc.—is based on their having real money to invest, as opposed to borrowed money.) Though the unleveraged investors are important in the $/yen market as well, they are not as important as the leveraged investors. The flows of leveraged investors in the $/yen market show the largest price impact in the table, as well as the greatest level of statistical significance. Note, too, that the R^2 statistics are roughly double those produced in the univariate model presented in table 9.2.

These results suggest that order flow is not simply undifferentiated demand. Rather, the source of the order flow matters quite a lot. Put differently, if some banker were to subscribe to the undifferentiated demand view of the world, then I know other banks that would be delighted to exchange certain types of order flow information for other types, dollar for dollar. Looking forward, an interesting avenue for further research is whether the three parts of order flow have different properties. For example, does cumulative order flow from unleveraged investors follow something close to a random walk, as their real money nickname suggests? In contrast, might the cumulative order flow of leveraged investors like hedge funds mean revert over horizons of a couple months, as they unwind their temporary speculative positions? Might the orders of non-financial corporations show the opposite tendency, that is that positive flow this period means likely positive flow next period? These are important questions, the answers to which may help uncover not only the deeper concurrent relationships between order flow and price changes, but also the forecasting relationships that many banks appear to have identified.[11]

9.4   Case Study: The Collapse of the Yen/$ Rate, October 1998

One of the most remarkable events in the post–Bretton Woods era of floating exchange rates is undoubtedly the remarkable drop in the yen/$ rate that occurred in October 1998. In a single day, the rate fell from about 130 to about 118, a change of roughly 10 percent. On that day, bid-offer spreads were said to have topped one yen, that is, one percent or more in a market that usually trades with a spread of 1–2 basis points (and is arguably the second most liquid market in the world, behind the $/euro market). There was no identifiable macroeconomic news, at least not news that is usually associated with exchange rate fundamentals. The financial news at the time was concentrated on the collapse of Long Term Capital Management (LTCM), a hedge fund whose positions around the world had become so illiquid that unwinding them became impossible without driving the fund's capital below zero.

Major banks attribute the yen/$ rate's drop to "the unwinding of positions by hedge funds that had borrowed in cheap yen to finance purchases of higher-yielding dollar assets"—the so-called yen carry trade (*The Economist*, 10/10/98).[12] This portfolio shift—and the selling of dollars that came with it—was forced by the scaling back of speculative leverage following the LTCM crisis. Though received wisdom suggests that this particular mechanism was at work, we still have little direct evidence. One paper, Cai et al. (1999), provides a first cut on the issue. Its authors model volatility around the event using an aggregate order flow measure and a comprehensive list of macro announcements. (Their aggregate order flow measure is the same weekly data from the U.S. Treasury used by Wei and Kim 1997.) They do find that there is an independent role for order flow, even after accounting for an extensive list of public news. But their volatility model and aggregate flow measures cannot determine which players were pushing prices in which direction.

Here I adopt a case study approach. I examine the behavior of order flows by different players around the time of the event. Which institution types were doing the dollar selling? Identifying the sellers' types gives us insight into why the selling occurred (e.g., were they institutions that may have been "distressed," in the sense of being compelled to sell due to institutional constraints like loss limits?).

In figure 9.4, panel a, I plot the daily yen/$ exchange rate and the total customer order flow, which includes all three of the customer categories. The vertical line marks the beginning of the yen/$ rate's fall. An order flow "trigger" for the collapse is not present, at least from the aggregate data. There is a small, downward blip in total order flow at the very beginning of the rate's collapse, but it quickly reverses itself. If anything, the aggregated flow received by this bank suggests that the dollar selling began well before the actual collapse,

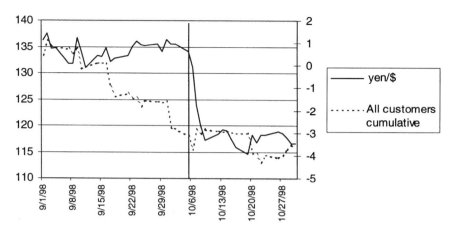

Figure 9.4. Panel a
Cumulative total customer flow and the yen/$ rate around the October 1998 collapse.

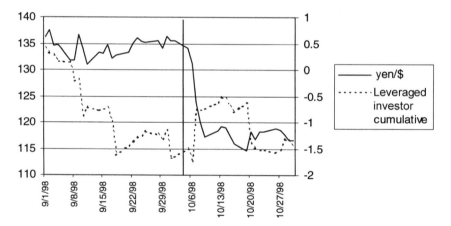

Figure 9.4. Panel b
Cumulative flow of leveraged financial institutions and the yen/$ rate around the
October 1998 collapse.

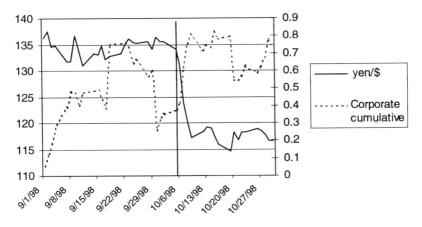

Figure 9.4. Panel c
Cumulative flow of nonfinancial corporations and the yen/$ rate around the October 1998 collapse.

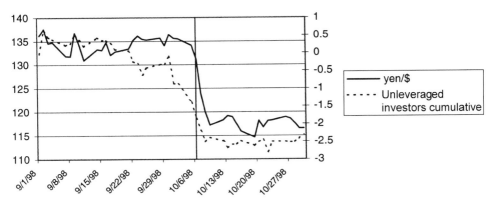

Figure 9.4. Panel d
Cumulative flow of unleveraged financial institutions and the yen/$ rate around the October 1998 collapse.

around September 15. From September 15 to October 6, about $3 billion were sold by the source bank's customers.

The story becomes much richer as we disaggregate the customer categories. Figure 9.4, panel b, shows that much of the advance selling of dollars in September was due to leveraged investors such as hedge funds. These leveraged investors did not, however, account for any abrupt selling at the time of the collapse (contrary to received wisdom). Rather, they appeared to have *provided* liquidity, buying about $1 billion at the time the dollar's price was collapsing. Panel c shows that nonfinancial corporations were also buying dollars at the time of the price collapse; their total buying was about half the size of the buying by leveraged financial institutions, or $0.4 billion. The story takes shape in panel d, which shows the powerful selling by unleveraged financial institutions at the time of the collapse. Not only do these institutions appear to have been the trigger, they also added fuel to the fire, selling about $2.5 billion over the days preceding and including the collapse.

It will be interesting in the future to identify which of these unleveraged financial institutions were the most important. Were they U.S. institutions or Japanese? Did they become distressed in some way precipitated by the LTCM collapse, or is the "distressed players" view of the event misguided? Some practitioners believe, for example, that the apparent heading among real-money institutions comes instead from increasing emphasis on benchmarks (and the correlated retreats toward benchmark weights that sharp market moves can engender). Perhaps the unleveraged financial institutions' portfolio shift was not uncommonly large, but it happened to be coupled with a particularly distressed set of leveraged financial institutions who could not provide the liquidity they would normally provide. There is much room for future work to address these possibilities.

What are some of the larger implications of this yen/$ case study? So abrupt a shift to a new exchange rate level (without macro news, and persistent) leads one to consider the possibility of path dependence, which means that the actual path followed by a variable plays a role in determining its ultimate resting point. (For example, a large exchange rate swing can alter the structure of industries within a country—foreign suppliers versus domestic—which can change the long-run equilibrium exchange rate.) The type of path dependence I have in mind in this case comes from the sequencing of trades by various customer types and how that sequencing may have mattered for the ultimate exchange rate. For example, keeping the path of total customer flow the same, if it had been the unleveraged financial institutions that had gradually fled dollars in early September, rather than the leveraged institutions, might the new level of the yen/$ rate in late October have been different? Though path dependence of this kind is not a property of the earlier chapters' models, it is an interesting possibility for future work to consider.

Another larger implication of the case study is that liquidity in FX markets varies over time, sometimes quite substantially. (In chapter 4, I provided a working definition of liquidity as an order's price impact.) The order flow coefficients in tables 9.2 and 9.3 imply that the relatively small portfolio shifts in figure 9.4 should have had price impact that was much smaller, perhaps a few percent, rather than the roughly 10 percent change that occurred. Though time-varying liquidity is also not a property of the earlier chapters' models, it is an issue that future work must consider. What triggers liquidity changes? Might what appears on the surface to be changing liquidity be due instead to changing order flow composition (given the differential impact shown in the previous section)?

10   Looking Forward

This final chapter is prospective. It addresses four topics: (1) what we have learned, (2) what we still need to learn, (3) policy implications, and (4) the FX market's future. Section 10.1 summarizes what we have learned, focusing on the larger lessons. These larger lessons can be divided into two broad groups, those that are more macro-oriented and those that are more micro-oriented. In section 10.2, I turn to what we don't yet know. What, for example, are the major open questions? These questions are important directions for future research. Beyond the major open questions, I also summarize other topics that warrant additional work.

My review of what we've learned and what we have yet to learn provides a nice segue to policy implications, section 10.3. Though policy implications are implicit in the earlier chapters, they are easily overlooked. Issues to which these implications apply include data collection by official institutions (for measuring and monitoring market liquidity), central bank intervention, transaction taxes, capital controls, and trading institution design. My main goal is to clarify where additional work on the policy front is likely to be fruitful.

Section 10.4 closes the chapter with a discussion of how the institutions of the FX market are evolving. As noted in chapter 3, over the last ten years these institutions have changed considerably (e.g., the major role now played by electronic brokers), and the pace has not slowed. To what extent might these near-term changes render the microstructure approach obsolete? In fact, the approach can be successfully applied even if the structure does change. A goal of section 10.4 will be to explain why.

10.1 What We Have Learned

Application of microstructure tools to FX markets has generated insights that are new even to the broader microstructure literature. For example, almost none of the work within microstructure finance addresses macro asset pricing puzzles, in the spirit of the three big puzzles I address in chapter 7. The microstructure approach to FX, on the other hand, has been oriented toward macro-level puzzles from the beginning, largely because people working in the area are trained as macroeconomists.

Another example of cross-fertilization between FX microstructure and the broader microstructure field relates to information. The information structure of traditional models is relevant primarily for equity markets. In the case of single stock, for example, earnings announcements are a critical information event. Insiders with private information about earnings would try to trade in advance of the announcement (unless prohibited from doing so), hence the role for order flow as an intermediate link between information and price. But inside information of this kind in major FX markets is unlikely—market participants do not in general have inside information about macroeconomic changes (e.g., interest rates, public announcements, etc.). Despite this, order flow in FX markets does move prices, and does so persistently. The search for precisely what this nonpublic information might be is enlarging perspective within microstructure regarding the nature and role of information.

The lessons learned thus far from work on order flow in FX markets can be divided into two broad groups: those that are more macro-oriented and those that are more micro-oriented.[1] The field is still young, so more work is required before these lessons can be considered definitive. As data sets covering longer time periods become available, these lessons surely will be refined.

Let me begin with the more macro-oriented lessons. Though they appear in earlier chapters, it is useful to collect them here. Six lessons in particular seem especially important as we move forward.

Macro-Oriented Lessons

Order Flow Drives Long Horizon Prices
Order flow is the proximate cause of a large share of longer horizon exchange rate movements. Even when based on order flow data sets

that include only a fraction of marketwide flow, the concurrent impact of these flows accounts for 40–70 percent of the persistent movements in prices (i.e., at monthly horizons and longer, see, e.g., Payne 1999; Evans and Lyons 1999; Evans 2000; Rime 2000). As richer order flow data sets become available (e.g., as they span a larger share of the market and sign the flows more precisely), that percentage may rise still higher.

Even Macro Announcements Affect Price via Order Flow
The flipside of the first lesson is that concurrent macro announcements and other readily identifiable macro changes do not *directly* explain a large share of longer horizon price movements. Direct mapping from concurrent macro changes to prices appears to be limited (Evans 2000; Evans and Lyons 1999). Rather, order flow appears to mediate most price movements (Evans and Lyons 2001). (Recall the "hybrid model" in figure 7.1 that allowed information to affect prices either directly, or indirectly via the order flow link.) Though in some sense this result is a rediscovery of the well-known empirical failure of macro models, work in FX microstructure is clarifying the factors that supplement concurrent macro changes as a driver of prices.

Price Elasticity with Respect to Order Flow Is High
The elasticity of the exchange rate with respect to customer order flow is roughly 0.8 percent per $1 billion (e.g., in the $/euro market, per table 9.2; elasticity with respect to interdealer order flow is roughly half that size). With world financial wealth measured in trillions of dollars, this is puzzlingly high. The result is consistent with a common view that Milton Friedman's "stabilizing speculators" are not bold enough. Why this boldness might be lacking remains an open question. From an information-theoretic perspective, however, high elasticity may not be so puzzling: small net flows may be conveying significant amounts of information.

Order Flow Is a Factor in Floating Rate Volatility
We now have substantial evidence that order flow is an important proximate factor driving volatility and may account for apparently excessive volatility under floating regimes (see, e.g., Evans and Lyons 1999; Killeen, Lyons, and Moore 2000a). Though work on order flow as a driver of price is focused on the *sign* of the relation-

ship, there are also implications for volatility: a good model of return first moments is a good model of return second moments (but not vice versa). Also relevant for this lesson is recent work by Osler (2001). She finds that stop-loss orders on the buy (sell) side tend to cluster at prices just above (below) round numbers, which can cause trends to gain momentum once support and resistance levels are crossed.

Acceleration of Information in Price

Empirical results in FX markets are not consistent with the "accelerationist view" that order flow simply accelerates the impounding of information in price by, say, a few minutes (figure 3.4). As noted above, our best measures of signed public-information flow are virtually uncorrelated with the direction of exchange rate movements (at horizons of one year or less). This is incompatible with the accelerated-by-a-few-minutes view.

At the same time, a fascinating possibility is that an accelerationist story is indeed operating, but over much longer horizons. Suppose order flow conveys individuals' expectations about macro fundamentals that are more distant (i.e., beyond the next month, quarter, or even year). In that case, order flow serves to telescope this forward-looking information into today's spot rate. Note too that this possibility is consistent with findings that over longer horizons (e.g., three to five years), macro variables do begin to account for a substantial share of exchange rate variation (despite concurrent macro-fundamentals being virtually uncorrelated with exchange rates; see, e.g., Mark 1995; Flood and Taylor 1996).

Order Flow Does Not Have to Sum to Zero

The Evans and Lyons (1999) model shows why order flow between dealers does not have to sum to zero. This is important conceptually because many people are under the mistaken impression that order flow must sum to zero (and therefore that any flow measure that correlates positively with price must be unrepresentative in some way). This is not always the case.

Let me turn now to more micro-oriented lessons. By micro-oriented, I mean that they are based on intraday analysis of individual dealers. As such, they parallel more closely the bread and butter work within microstructure finance.

Micro-Oriented Lessons

Order Flow Is Private Information
The behavior of individual dealers shows that they consider FX
order flow to be informative and that they set prices accordingly
(Lyons 1995, and other references in chapter 2). This empirical result
at the micro level accords well with the importance of order flow at
lower frequencies mentioned earlier. Moreover, all orders are not
alike in terms of their information content. Identifying which orders
are the most informative and who is behind them is illuminating
the market's underlying information structure. This type of analysis
goes well beyond the question of whether or not institutions affect
prices; it uses microstructure models to uncover new facets of financial information.

Dealer Inventories Affect Price
Inventory control among spot FX dealers is strong relative to that
found for other markets. Most spot FX dealers prefer to end their day
flat—that is, with no net position. Accordingly, the half-life of the
typical dealer's inventory is significantly less than one day, and has
been estimated to be as low as ten minutes (e.g., Lyons 1998). These
half-lives are much shorter than those found in equity and futures
markets, where half-lives longer than one week are common.[2] Not
only do FX dealers control their inventories intensively, some also
adjust their prices to induce inventory-decumulating order flow.
(Lyons 1995 finds these inventory effects on price, but Yao 1998 does
not find them for the dealer he track; see also Bjonnes and Rime 2000
and Romeu 2001.) This finding of inventory effects on price is important: they are the linchpin of the whole inventory branch of
microstructure theory, despite the fact that empiricists working on
markets other than FX have not found them.[3]

Hot Potato Trading Contributes to Trading Volume
Dealers describe hot potato trading as an important source of the FX
market's enormous trading volumes. The large share of trading between dealers that we find in FX relative to other markets is consistent with a significant role for hot potato trading. On the theoretical
front, our models show that hot potato trading is consistent with
optimizing behavior (e.g., Lyons 1997a). On the empirical front, we

also find direct evidence that hot potato trading is present (e.g., Lyons 1996b).

Central Banks in Microstructure Analysis
As a result of work on FX markets, analysis is being applied to types of institutions not traditionally studied in microstructure, most notably central banks (see, e.g., Dominguez 1999; Vitale 1999; Kirilenko 1997). Central banks are not profit motivated, which introduces an interesting (and policy relevant) dimension to modeling.

10.2   Directions for Research

Let me begin with what are, in my judgment, the four most important open issues in FX microstructure research.

Open Issue 1:   Does the Information in FX Order Flow Reflect Payoff Information, Portfolio Balance Information, or Both?

Chapter 2 covered the economics of order flow information. In that chapter, we saw that order flow can have persistent effects on price through two basic channels: payoffs and discount rates. Evans and Lyons (1999, 2000) model the persistent effects wholly as discount rate effects, which macroeconomists typically call portfolio balance effects.[4] This feature of the Evans-Lyons model comes from their assumption that customer order flow C_t is uncorrelated with current and future payoffs R_t. We cannot rule out, however, the possibility that order flow conveys information about future payoffs. Consider a simple variation on the Evans-Lyons model that clarifies how this might work. Suppose customer orders are correlated with future payoffs R_{t+k}, where k is, say, one to five years. This could occur if payoff expectations held by individual customers are changing, based on a constant flow of dispersed bits of information relevant to forming those expectations (bits that not all customers share). Dealers wishing to aggregate the information in those changing expectations would respond to order flow the same way as in the original Evans-Lyons model. If this variation on the model were correct, then one would expect order flow to forecast future macroeconomic variables (as suggested by the long horizon accelerationist view mentioned earlier). With the longer order flow series now available (e.g., the seven years of \$/euro data described in chapter

9), we are just now getting enough statistical power to test this. Work along these lines will help close the current gap between order flow analysis and macro analysis.[5]

Open Issue 2:   To What Extent Is Reverse Causality Present—from Prices to Order Flow—and Under What Circumstances (e.g., Distressed Institutions) Is It More Acute?

The full body of microstructure theory treats causality as running from order flow to price. To rationalize the reverse causality, one would have to develop an optimizing model in which investors at the price-determining margin trade with positive feedback. This is not an easy task, particularly since there is no compelling evidence of ongoing positive momentum in exchange rate returns. Moreover, as an empirical matter, work such as that of Killeen, Lyons, and Moore (2000a) finds that in statistical terms, (Granger) causality does indeed run from order flow to price, and not vice versa. The above theoretical and empirical arguments notwithstanding, causality almost surely runs both directions, at least part of the time. Chapter nine's analysis of the October 1998 plummeting of the dollar's value against the yen provides some suggestive evidence of falling prices inducing additional selling. If this selling was indeed "distressed" selling brought about by loss limits or other institutional constraints, it will be important to model these types of institutional constraints, and to determine empirically to what extent they aggravate extreme market movements.

Open Issue 3:   Why Doesn't Customer Order Flow Sum to Zero?

In the last of the five macro-oriented lessons in section 10.1, I noted that the Evans-Lyons model shows why total order flow *between dealers* does not need to sum to zero. At the same time, that model does predict at the daily frequency (and lower) that the sum of customer orders should be zero. Yet the private bank customer data analyzed by Fan and Lyons (2000)—and in chapter 9—does not sum to zero. Rather, it is positively correlated with exchange rate movements, in much the same way that order flow between dealers is correlated with exchange rate movements. What accounts for this? The answer is not clear, but the question is vitally important. Empirical work on the links between customer flow and exchange rates is the next frontier for the microstructure approach. Customers do, after all, represent the underlying demand in the economy. Might it be the case that Citibank, as a clear market leader, attracts a disproportionate share of informative customer flow, leading to the positive correlation? This is a possibility, but is as yet unsubstantiated. Another possibility is that Citibank is just like other commercial banks in terms of order flow composition, but because it is so large, other banks tend to put additional weight on each dollar of its trading. As additional bank data sets with customer flows become available, researchers should be able to discriminate among the various hypotheses.

Open Issue 4: Why Is the Price Impact of Trades From Different Customer Types So Different?

This question, distinct from open issue 3, is at the heart of the research strategy that aspires to illuminate the underlying information structure by disaggregating order flow. Do some types of order flow convey more information about future macro paths? Do some types convey more information about their own future flow or the future flow of others? Answers to these questions will soon be in our grasp.

Other Directions for Future Work

The following list summarizes several issues that in my judgment warrant attention in future work.

Data Integration
It will be valuable to integrate order flow data from all three trade types (direct interdealer, brokered interdealer, and customer-dealer). Two issues come immediately to mind that integrated data sets would allow us to address.[6] First, integrated data across the two interdealer trade types would allow us to examine when and why dealers prefer one trading mechanism to the other. Does the share of trading executed in the direct interdealer market increase in times of market turbulence because dealers are reluctant to expose limit orders on broker screens at these times? This is an important question for institution design: if liquidity in the broker market tends to dry up when the market is turbulent, then increasing reliance on brokered trading may mean that the market is becoming less resilient

(i.e., more vulnerable to liquidity breakdowns at times of extreme price movements). Unlike work on equity markets (Goldstein and Kavajecz 2000; Reiss and Werner 1999), work on FX microstructure has not yet made progress on this issue.

A second issue that integrated data sets would allow us to address is how customer trades feed into trades between dealers. To date, much of the empirical work on trades' price impact is focused on trades between dealers. But from a policy perspective (e.g., central bank intervention), this is less important than measuring the price impact of trades by customers. Perhaps more important, integrated data sets would clarify the process by which the information in customer flow is impounded in prices. The impounding occurs at the interdealer stage (e.g., the Evans-Lyons model), but interdealer orders are only noisy signals of the underlying customer demands. It is unclear how much noise this two-stage process introduces into prices.

Time Necessary to Achieve Strong-Form Efficiency

Related to that last point is the issue of strong-form efficiency. A strong-form efficient market is one in which price impounds all information, public and private. An important source of private information to banks is the order flow they receive from their own customers. How long does it take the FX market to impound the information in customer flows in price? One day? A week? Banks that rely on these customer flows to forecast exchange rates contend that these flows have forecasting power at the one-month horizon. If true, it will be a challenge to model where that longer horizon forecasting power is coming from.

When Is Technical Analysis Rational?

Technical analysis is typically defined as valuation analysis that relies wholly on past prices. Conceptually, this type of analysis asserts that patterns embedded in past prices may help to forecast future prices. In the FX market, it is well documented that some participants rely on technical analysis, at least some of the time (see, e.g., Taylor and Allen 1992). Is this a rational strategy? Perhaps. The interesting question here is akin to that asked by Muth (1960) in his seminal article on rational expectations, "When are adaptive expectations rational?" Muth solved for the class of time-series processes for which adaptive expectations are efficient in an information sense.

In our context, we might ask, "Under what information structures (and processes by which agents learn from trading) might specific technical rules be rational?" For work that is moving in this direction, see Osler (2000, 2001).

This issue of rational feedback trading—a type of technical analysis—certainly has implications for the direction of causality issue. Future work might draw from existing microstructure analysis of crashes and portfolio insurance because these are models in which feedback trading is rational.

Why Is the Conventional Quote Size $10 Million?
In direct interdealer trading, the convention is for two-way quotes to be good for up to $10 million (or 10 million euros in the $/euro market). This size has important consequences for market liquidity, but we know virtually nothing about how the convention came about. It could simply be that FX dealers' cost functions are U-shaped as a function of trade size, with the $10 million point being the cost minimizing size (see O'Hara 1995, 28). No work to date has addressed this question.

Credit Risk and Market Structure
It is common for FX market participants to suggest that we have the current, commercial bank driven dealer structure because commercial banks are ideally suited to manage credit risk. It is true that the counterparty credit risk in FX transactions is enormous, but if this really is what is supporting the dealer-market structure, it would be a radical departure from the way the field of microstructure has traditionally thought about "equilibrium" institutions. The traditional focus of work on equilibrium institutions is on the management of asymmetric information and price risk, not default risk.[7]

10.3   Policy Implications

There are five broad areas where I envision microstructure analysis of FX markets having impact on policy. The first of these, central bank intervention, was addressed in chapter 8, so I will not include it here. I introduce the remaining four areas with an eye toward future work that is likely to be useful. Though in some areas I make specific recommendations, in other areas recommendations will have to wait for further analysis of these policy questions.

Policy Area 1:   The Price Impact of Order Flow

It would be useful for official institutions to begin collecting data on FX order flows. This will be particularly valuable for policymaking in developing countries. Specifically, order flow data allow one to quantify the price impact of currency trades (both transitory and persistent), as demonstrated repeatedly in earlier chapters. This has a direct bearing on market liquidity. Indeed, price impact is what liquidity is all about: the lower the price impact, the higher the liquidity, other things equal. It would be interesting to get a sense for how price impact in developing-country markets changes as a function of the state of the market (devaluation likelihood, etc.). Also, one could determine whether customer forward trades have the same price impact as customer spot trades of similar size. If not, one could quantify the difference. (Many developing countries restrict or even forbid forward trading on the belief that such trading is more "speculative" in nature than spot trading and is therefore more destabilizing.) One might also compare price impact across countries, to determine which institutional structures are better at promoting liquidity.[8]

The question of price impact is related to the issue of stability. Policymakers in some developing countries believe that additional liquidity is destabilizing. In theory, it is less liquidity that is destabilizing, not more liquidity: the less the liquidity, the larger the price impact and the more prices move, other things equal. To make the case that other things are not equal, in a way that might reverse the relationship between liquidity and stability, one might use the discipline of microstructure trading models to identify the countervailing forces at work.

Another issue that is particularly relevant in the developing-country context is the stability of pegged rates (though this issue extends to pegged rates in the industrialized world as well). Microstructure-style trading models help us to understand how and why particular types of orders have price impact when exchange rates are pegged (see, e.g., Calvo 1999; Corsetti, Morris, and Shin 1999). As an empirical matter, we have a lot to learn about the types of order flow that cause pegs to collapse (see Carrera 1999). A better understanding of these issues will aid in the design of more resilient pegged regimes.

Policy Area 2: Emerging Market Design

A bread and butter policy issue in microstructure finance is how best
to design markets. This issue is relevant to FX as well, though treatment of it is limited by the fact that major currencies are traded in
a truly worldwide market, which makes it difficult for any single
regulatory authority to impose structural changes. Any country
attempting to alter or constrain the structure of trading within its
own borders would find order flow migrating rapidly to other trading venues. As a practical matter, worldwide harmonization of this
type of policy change is infeasible at present.

The place where design of currency markets remains a hot topic
is in emerging markets. Most of these currencies are not traded on
a worldwide basis, due to lack of convertibility of one form or another. Because trading in these currencies is largely within-country,
it is feasible to legislate market design in a way that is not possible
in major markets. Microstructure analysis is well-suited to address
questions concerning whether fledgling FX markets should be
organized as auction markets, as dealer markets, or both (for analysis along these lines, see Kirilenko 1997), as well as the level of
transparency that should be required. Institutions like the International Monetary Fund confront this type of policy question regularly.
The microstructure approach can provide valuable guidance.

Policy Area 3: International Currencies

What role should specific currencies play in the international monetary and financial system? Recent introduction of the euro has
brought this question to a level of policy relevance not seen since the
early 1970s (when the Bretton Woods fixed-rate system collapsed).
Discussion of the role for an international currency—that is, a single
currency that acts as a universal means of exchange—centers on
three key aspects: (1) use as a reserve currency by central banks, (2)
use as an invoicing currency for international transactions, and (3)
use as a vehicle currency for currency transactions (vehicle currencies are used when the transaction cost of trading two currencies
directly is higher than the cost of trading them indirectly, via two
transactions through the vehicle currency). In aspects (2) and (3),
a single currency's success as an international currency is heavily
dependent on the level of transaction costs. Therefore, to predict

whether the euro will be successful as an international currency, one needs to model the transaction costs that will arise once it is fully adopted. Though not an easy task, it is one that microstructure analysis is well suited to address. This type of analysis can also identify which institutional features of the new euro will help reduce those transaction costs. In this analysis, a central issue is the degree to which a reduction in transaction costs stimulates trading, both directly, and indirectly through adoption as a vehicle currency. These volume and liquidity responses to various policy alternatives are the focus of recent work by Hartmann (1998a, b, 1999), Portes and Rey (1998), and Hau, Killeen, and Moore (2000).

Policy Area 4: Transaction Taxes

The issue of transaction taxes has attracted much attention among exchange rate economists. Proponents of levying transaction taxes tend to associate high volume with excessive speculation. As the literature has shown, however, much of this volume reflects dealer risk management (hot potato trading), rather than speculation. Imposing a transaction tax would therefore impede risk management. Though unintentional, this misunderstanding of the causes of high volume could lead to bad policy. I emphasize the word "could" here because microstructure analysis only adds a new dimension to this important policy question, it does not invalidate the arguments of transaction tax supporters. Looking forward, I expect that the microstructure approach has a good deal more to contribute to this policy issue. (For recent treatments using microstructure tools, see Hau and Chevallier 2000; Habermeier and Kirilenko 2000.)

10.4   Where FX Is Going—Implications for This Book

The major FX markets have undergone important changes over the last ten years. Perhaps the most important change is the shift from voice-based interdealer brokers to electronic interdealer brokers. This trend away from human-intermediated transactions is evident in many securities markets throughout the world.[9] It shows no sign of abating.

The shift from voice-based interdealer brokers to electronic brokers is important in itself because, as described in chapter 3, electronic brokers provide a different (mostly higher) level of order flow transparency than was provided by the voice-based brokers. This alters dealers' information sets, which affects their trading strategies.

A larger implication of the shift to electronic brokers, however, is that it suggests a future for spot FX trading that is more centralized, electronic, and—this is the crucial part—open to customers. Major markets are likely to shift toward a structure with open, electronic limit order books that are accessible to a large number of market participants.[10] Under this scenario, institutions we have been calling "customers" would be able to provide liquidity to one another, rather than having to depend on dealers. At that point, they would cease being customers—in the sense of always demanding liquidity—transformed instead into both liquidity demander and supplier.

Why might one believe that the market is going in this direction? Three pieces of evidence support the view. First, in June 2000, three investment banks (Goldman Sachs, Merrill Lynch, and Morgan Stanley Dean Witter) announced that they will be launching an electronic system of this kind for the U.S. bond markets (government and corporate bonds). The U.S. bond market is currently organized as a dealer market with characteristics similar to those in FX. Though other security markets—for example, equity and derivatives markets —have already shifted to a centralized electronic structure, those other markets do not share the same FX market characteristics that the bond markets share, and are therefore not as appropriate as models. Second, in the last couple years, many new companies have introduced forms of centralized trading for customers (e.g., FXall, Atriax, FXchange, FXconnect, FXtrade, Gain.com, MatchbookFX.com, among others). These new companies typically promote themselves as operating at the fringes of the dealer-market structure. But there is nothing obvious that prevents one of them from growing to a scale that captures the network externalities inherent in concentrating liquidity into a single pool.[11]

The third piece of evidence that, in my judgment, points to more centralized FX trading in the future is that systems like EBS can be opened up to larger customer-companies quite easily. The customer relationships are there: the banks that own EBS are the same banks that have customer relationships via their dealing services. The technology is not a major hurdle. The switch could be flipped in much the same way as it promises to be flipped in the U.S. bond markets. What might the catalyst be? A natural catalyst would be significant growth in market share by one of the new electronic entrants. If EBS decided to open its system to customers, it would be difficult for any competitor to beat it. From the EBS perspective, it is essential to maintain the threshold effects of network externalities in its favor—if the market is going in the direction of centralized customer trading, EBS cannot afford to wait.

Does immanent market structure change threaten the relevance of the microstructure approach? This is an important question—crucial, really, for the future relevance of this book. My answer will not surprise anyone who has read the previous nine chapters. The microstructure approach is concerned with much more than whether the market is organized with a single dealer, multiple dealers, or a limit order book. The role of order flow in conveying information transcends market structure, and the types of information that order flow conveys—particularly the types with persistent price effects—are unlikely to change radically when (if) the FX market changes in the future. Put another way, the underlying information structure of this market has more to do with the properties of the asset being traded—foreign exchange—than it does with the market structure per se. Order flow will continue to tell us something about people's views on how public information should be mapped into price. It will continue to tell us something about current risk tolerances and expectations about the future. In short, it will continue to convey dispersed information that needs to be aggregated. And that is what this book is all about.

Notes

Chapter 1. Overview of the Microstructure Approach

1. Another approach in exchange rate economics—the "flow" approach—is a variant of the goods market approach, so I do not include it separately in my three-approach taxonomy. In addition to currency demand from goods flows, the flow approach includes currency demand from the other main category of a country's balance of payments—the capital account. Like its goods market cousin, the flow approach does not typically model the exchange rate in a way consistent with financial market efficiency. I return to the parallels between the flow and microstructure approaches in chapter 7.

2. The field of macroeconomics is also moving in the direction of relaxing these three assumptions. See, for example, the literatures on asymmetric information (e.g., Gordon and Bovenberg 1996; Morris and Shin 2000), non-representative-agent macro (e.g., Caballero, Engel, and Haltiwanger 1997), microfoundations of monetary policy (e.g., Rotemberg and Woodford 1997), and new open-economy macro (Obstfeld and Rogoff 1996).

3. I continue with this three-point characterization in chapter 4 (which reviews microstructure theory) by providing model summaries in three parts: Information, Players, and Institutions.

4. Markets with limit order books include the Paris and Hong Kong stock exchanges, both of which are operated electronically. Chapter 3 provides more detail along these lines.

5. That dealers learn only from order flow is too extreme. It arises in standard microstructure models because these models assume that all information is private. Macro models go to the other extreme, assuming all information is public. I return to this in chapter 7, where I present an empirical model that admits both public and private information.

6. My own view is that this central question—How does altering the trading mechanism alter price?—has unwittingly narrowed the scope of questions to which microstructure tools have been applied. I return to this issue in section 3.4, after laying more groundwork.

7. Regarding spreads, let me communicate an experience that may speak to the reader. I recall years ago presenting a paper on exchange rates that was firmly embedded in

the macro-orientation of the asset approach. Someone in the audience asked me a question about bid-ask spreads. What went through my mind—though not my lips—was "I couldn't care less about bid-ask spreads." To me, at the time, bid-ask spreads were simply a nuisance parameter, bad manners next to an otherwise elegant approach. At the time, spreads meant microstructure to me, and microstructure meant spreads. I no longer subscribe to this view.

8. Walrasian-style mechanisms do exist in real-world financial markets; they are often used to open trading (see, e.g., work on the pre-opening of the Paris Bourse by Biais, Hillion, and Spatt 1999). Indicative orders are collected for a period before actual trading begins, and these orders are used to determine the opening price (the orders become executable at the opening, but typically can be retracted before the opening).

9. Actual orders come in different types, which I cover in chapter 3.

10. Andersen and Bollerslev (1997) establish another link between microstructure and lower frequency relevance. They show that forecasts of low-frequency volatility are more precise when based on high-frequency data.

11. Within international finance more broadly, there are four main puzzles, the three listed above plus the "home bias" puzzle, which is that investors under-invest internationally. I do not include the home bias puzzle above because it is not clear it stems from the exchange rate, whereas the other three puzzles directly involve the exchange rate. Nevertheless, microstructure tools have already proven valuable for addressing home bias (e.g., the trading model of Brennan and Cao 1997 and the empirical results of Kang and Stulz 1997, among others).
    These three exchange rate puzzles have analogs in other markets. For equities, papers recognizing the three puzzles include Roll 1988, Shiller 1981, and Mehra and Prescott 1985, respectively. (However, the equity-market version of the forward bias puzzle—the so-called equity premium puzzle—is a much looser analog than the other two: the large risk premium on equity is rather stable over time and remains positive, whereas the large risk premium in FX changes over time, including frequent changes in sign.) Microstructure tools are just beginning to be applied to those major equity puzzles (see, for example, Easley, Hvidkjaer, and O'Hara 1999).

12. Examples of information that needs to be aggregated by the FX market include information about differential interpretation of news, about changing institutional risk tolerance, and about changing hedging demands, among others (reviewed in chapter 2).

13. Of course, the microstructure approach also has its drawbacks (e.g., lack of publicly available data over long periods). I consider those drawbacks in later chapters.

14. The precise list of determinants depends on which model within the larger asset approach is selected. Here our interest is simply a broad-brush contrast between the asset and microstructure approaches. I return to precise specifications of the asset approach in chapters 6 and 7.

15. Work using structural models includes Glosten and Harris (1988), Madhavan and Smidt (1991), and Foster and Viswanathan (1993), all of which address the NYSE; structural models in a multiple-dealer setting include Snell and Tonks (1995) for stocks, Lyons (1995) for currencies, and Vitale (1998) for bonds.

16. I use the notation "DM/$" here because I am referring specifically to the value of an exchange rate, which is quoted in the marketplace as the deutschemark price per

dollar. When referring in general terms to an FX market, practitioners typically list the dollar first: orally, they refer to this market as "dollar-mark," typically written as the "$/DM market," or simply as "$/DM" (the Bank for International Settlements also follows this dollar-first convention in its FX market surveys; see section 3.2). In this book, I remain true to these differing conventions. When describing an actual *rate*, precision requires me to write it as it is traded (e.g., DM/$, yen/$, and $/£). When referring in general terms to a particular *market*, I always list the dollar first ($/DM, $/yen, and $/£). Finally, when I use the symbol P in equations to denote the exchange rate as a price, P always denotes the dollar price of the other currency ($/other).

17. Because the Evans (1997) data set does not include the size of every trade, this measure of order flow is in fact the *number* of buys minus sells. That is, if a dealer initiates a trade against another dealer's DM/$ quote, and that trade is a dollar purchase (sale), then order flow is +1 (−1). These are cumulated across dealers over each 24-hour trading day (weekend trading—which is minimal—is included in Monday).

18. Readers familiar with the concept of co-integration will recognize that it offers a natural means of testing for a long-run relationship. In chapter 7, I present evidence that cumulative order flow and the level of the exchange rate are indeed cointegrated (i.e., the relationship between order flow and price is not limited to high frequencies). I also present models in chapter 7 that show why a long-run relationship of this kind is what one should expect.

Chapter 2. The Economics of Order Flow Information

1. A related, less extreme view is that order flow may convey some non-public information but the information it conveys is likely to become public soon. In this case, order flow advances the impounding of information in price by only, say, a few minutes. This less extreme view is not consistent with the data, however. To a first approximation, our best measures of public information flow are uncorrelated with the direction of exchange rate movements (at annual or higher frequencies), whereas order flow *is* correlated with exchange rate movements. I return to this issue in chapter 3.

2. I have in mind here the major FX markets. This kind of private information is more reasonable in emerging markets. For example, the IMF (1995) reports that Mexican investors were the first to flee Mexico in the period immediately prior to the December 1994 devaluation. It is not unreasonable to believe that certain people close to the devaluation decision had inside information and were able to act on it.

3. This section emphasizes empirical work that uses order flow data, as opposed to empirical work that uses price data only.

4. A third method for testing whether order flow effects are persistent—related to the first two—is testing for cointegration between cumulative order flow and the level of the exchange rate (see Killeen, Lyons, and Moore 2000a; Bjonnes and Rime 2000).

5. Hartmann (1999) finds that FX spreads widen with unexpected volume, which is consistent with an adverse selection component.

6. In the case of FX, volatility over the lunch period can still be calculated because trading continues in other trading locations, such as Singapore and Hong Kong. Andersen, Bollerslev, and Das (2000) verify the significance of this volatility increase over lunch. They do find, however, that some other results in the Ito et al. paper are

sensitive to an outlier in the data set. Covrig and Melvin's analysis (1998) of the same Tokyo experiment excludes the outlier observation, but still finds evidence that Japanese banks are relatively well informed, corroborating the Ito et al. interpretation. The Covrig-Melvin evidence is based on price leadership by Japanese banks. For related evidence on volatilities during the London—New York trading overlap, see Hsieh and Kleidon (1996).

7. By "better" I mean lower conditional variance.

8. Empirical evidence of inventory effects on FX prices is in Lyons (1995).

9. To understand why the change in the risk premium—i.e., the expected return—changes price, think of a pure discount bond: when the market interest rate—the expected return—changes, the price of the bond must change, even though the cash flow at maturity does not change.

10. This logic is also behind my choice of V in this book to denote payoffs, rather than the more customary F; the symbol F is too easily interpreted as the whole of fundamentals, an interpretation that is too narrow in my judgment.

11. This expectations story is also applicable to information about discount rates, in which case it would fall into type (2) or type (3).

12. Other proxies for expectations—such as time-series measures like ARIMA or VAR models—do not share this backed-by-money, information-encompassing property. A quote by Frankel and Rose (1995, 1701) provides some perspective on these time-series measures. In their words, "To use an ARIMA or VAR process as a measure of what agents expect, is to ascribe to them simultaneously not enough information, and too much. It does not ascribe to them enough information, because it leaves out all the thousands of bits of information that market investors use.... It ascribes to them too much information ... because it assumes that they know the parameters of the statistical process from the beginning of the sample period." Also relevant is the discussion in Engel (1996), where he describes "peso problems" in exchange rates as a case where the market had more information than empiricists, and "learning" as a case where the market had less information than empiricists (ex-post).

13. Within the literature on asset pricing more broadly (e.g., the pricing kernel approach), work on time-varying discount rates is sometimes referred to as addressing "stochastic discount factors." As is mine, the focus of this literature is on variation in the risk-premium component of discount rates, not the risk-free-rate component.

14. Though this discount rate effect on price emerges in most models as a risk premium, for technical convenience sometimes models are specified with risk-neutral dealers who face some generic "inventory holding cost," which produces similar results.

15. Readers familiar with microstructure theory will recognize that this figure assumes that there is no fixed component to the spread—i.e., the effective spread shrinks to zero as the size of the incoming order shrinks to zero. This is a detail that need not concern the more macro-oriented reader.

16. For evidence of imperfect substitutability across stocks, see Scholes (1972); Shleifer (1986); Bagwell (1992); and Kaul et al. (2000), among others. For at least two reasons, imperfect substitutability may be more applicable to currency markets than to markets in individual stocks. First, note that the size of the order flows that the \$/euro market needs to absorb are on average more than 10,000 times those absorbed in a

representative U.S. stock (e.g., the average daily volume on individual NYSE stocks in 1998 was about $9 million, whereas the average daily volume in $/DM spot was about $150 billion). Second, there are far more individual stocks that can substitute for one another in portfolios than there are individual currencies (particularly major currencies).

Chapter 3.   The Institutional Setting

1. This statistic is from the Bank for International Settlements, BIS (1999a). I examine BIS survey data in more detail in section 3.2.

2. BIS (1999a), 17.

3. Briefly, covered interest parity is a no-arbitrage condition that implies that $F_{\$/£}/P_{\$/£} = (1 + i_\$)/(1 + i_£)$, where $F_{\$/£}$ is today's one-period forward rate ($\$/£$), $P_{\$/£}$ is today's spot rate, $i_\$$ is today's one-period nominal interest rate in dollars, and $i_£$ is today's one-period nominal interest rate in pound sterling. In economic (and order flow) terms, taking offsetting positions on the lefthand side of this equation is equivalent to taking offsetting positions on the righthand side (in markets free of capital controls).

4. One fascinating branch of related work on derivatives involves derivative and spot market interaction (as opposed to analysis of a derivatives market in isolation). The question is whether introducing a derivatives market can rectify specific market failures. See, for example, Brennan and Cao (1996) and Cao (1999), among many others.

5. There is a large literature on limit-order auction markets. See, for example, Glosten (1994); Biais, Hillion, and Spat (1995); Chakravarty and Holden (1995); Harris and Hasbrouck (1996); Handa and Schwartz (1996); Seppi (1996).

6. The terms "dealer" and "marketmaker" are typically interchangeable in the academic literature. When there is a distinction, the term dealer is used for dealership-market settings (like the FX market) and marketmaker is used for hybrid auction-dealership settings (like the New York Stock Exchange). My use of these terms will be consistent with this distinction throughout the book. I should also note that FX practitioners typically use the term "trader" to describe a dealer. Because the term trader is rather general, I opt for more specific terms when possible.

7. There is a screen called Reuters FXFX that displays dealer quotes, but these quotes are not firm. (I provide more detail on the FXFX screen in chapter 5.) Though quotes on the electronic brokerage screens that I describe later in this section are firm, these brokerage quotes reflect only a subset of firm quotes in the market at any given time. For currency options, though some trading occurs on exchanges, most occurs in a decentralized, multiple-dealer setting. For currency futures, trading around the world tends to be centralized in various futures exchanges.

8. Though the spot FX market and the U.S. government bond market currently share a similar structure, the way the bond market trades is evolving toward a more centralized auction structure (like the Paris Bourse and Hong Kong Stock Exchange, as described above). See section 10.4 for more detail. Other countries' bond markets have already moved to a centralized auction format (e.g., the Italian government bond market). Recent work in the burgeoning literature on bond market microstructure includes Fleming and Remolona (1999) and Vitale (1998).

9. See BIS (1999a). The interdealer share of volume for NASDAQ and SEAQ (London's Stock Exchange Automated Quotations System) is less than 40 percent (see Reiss and Werner 1995).

10. One of the big changes in the FX market over the last few years is the shift away from voice-based brokers, where prices are advertised over intercoms at dealers' desks, and toward electronic brokers, where prices are advertised over a screen. Indeed, there is evidence that the electronic brokers have also taken market share away from direct interdealer trading (BIS 2001). Currently, the dominant electronic broker in $/euro and $/yen is EBS. The other major electronic broker is Reuters 2000-2. For more on this shift to electronic brokerage, see the *Financial Times* "Survey: Foreign Exchange," 5 June 1998. Interdealer brokers are also quite important in U.S. bond markets.

11. I should mention two important variations on this story. First, banks do their best to "internalize" as much customer order flow as possible. That is, they want to match the incoming customer buy orders with incoming customer sell orders. When successful, any net flows that get passed on to the interdealer market are much reduced. Second, the order flow lifecycle does not really "end" once nondealers reabsorb net balances. Rather, that reabsorption moves through a "chain" of liquidity providers, the first nondealer link being hedge funds and banks' proprietary trading desks, and the last link being so-called "real money accounts." The real money accounts, such as mutual funds and pension funds, are institutions that absorb positions over longer horizons. Chapter 9 on customer trading provides more perspective.

12. One important source of noise comes from the fact that brokered trading systems do not indicate the size of all individual transactions in real time, so it is not possible from information about transactions' signs to construct an exact order flow measure. For example, on the D2000-2 system, dealers only see an r on both the bid side and the offer side if the quantity available at the best price is $10 million or more; otherwise, they see the quantity available. If, after a trade, the screen is still showing r on both the bid and offer sides, then one cannot infer the size. Often, though, a trade causes the size to drop below $10 million, or the quantity on one side is exhausted, in which case dealers have received information about size. EBS, the other major electronic broker, is similar. Both systems also provide a high-frequency (but not complete) listing of deals as either "paid" or "given," where paid indicates buyer-initiated and given indicates seller-initiated.

Research data sets are a bit different. (In chapter 5 I review the data sets that cover brokered interdealer trading.) These data sets, constructed from records well after actual trading, provide exact measures of order flow, but these measures were not in the dealers' information sets while trading.

13. For comparison, a stock selling at $50 per share with a spread of only 10 cents would still translate into a spread of 20 basis points—10 times that in $/euro.

14. There is a common misconception that dealers within a given bank pass their positions from Tokyo to London to New York during each trading day. This is not true in general—individual dealers are responsible for managing their own positions. What *is* true is that the bank's book of customer limit orders is passed from Tokyo to London to New York. These unexecuted orders are not the same as dealer positions.

15. There are two nice multimedia resources that bring still more perspective on the life of an FX dealer: (1) Goodhart and Payne 1999, and (2) Citibank's "Bourse Course." The former provides a visual account of trading in an electronic interdealer broker

system (Reuters Dealing 2000-2). The latter is a simulated trading game designed to replicate the FX market; it includes trading of all three types depicted in figure 3.1. (Contact Citibank directly for more information.)

16. Chapter 5 describes the Reuters Dealing 2000-1 system in detail, including the rich data it generates for empirical work.

17. For the equity dealer comparison, I use the numbers from Hansch et al. 1999 for the London Stock Exchange because, unlike the NYSE, the LSE was a pure dealership market and therefore more comparable to FX. The authors find that dealers make a profit of roughly 10 basis points on the average transaction. Though the authors do not provide an average turnover by dealer, they do provide data that allow a rough estimate. The average daily turnover for FTSE-100 stocks is about $10 million (£6.9 million). This total turnover is divided among dealers (active dealers make markets in many stocks). Given the market shares the authors report for the more active dealers, and given the number of stocks in which each makes markets, the estimated average turnover of $10 million per dealer is about right.

18. The median quoted spread in the sample of 0.0003 DM/$ is the mode as well: that spread size accounts for about three-quarters of all the dealer's bilateral interdealer quotes.

19. The story is a bit subtler here, though, because this dealer does not have much customer business. In my judgment, the right way to think about this dealer is that he was supplying liquidity and inventory management services to other dealers that have more customer business. So, in effect, there is a kind of "tiering" in the interdealer market—FX dealers are not a homogeneous lot. My understanding is that dealers of this type are much less profitable now that electronic interdealer brokers play such an important role (table 3.2 corresponds to a trading week in 1992).

20. An important determinant of whether $100,000 per day is "large" is the amount of bank capital this dealer ties up when trading. If the capital required were $1 billion per day—equal to his total volume—then $100,000 would be rather small. In reality, the capital required to support a dealing operation like this one, which involves only intraday positions, is far smaller than $1 billion. For more on whether banks' FX profits come from positioning versus intermediation, see Ammer and Brunner (1997).

21. Beyond the BIS, there are several institutions that serve as semi-official coordinators in establishing FX trading practices and serving as forums for debate. In the United States, that institution is the Foreign Exchange Committee of the Federal Reserve Bank of New York. For more information, see their Web site at ⟨www.ny. frb.org/fxc⟩.

22. The role of derivatives in determining market resilience and efficiency was a topic of increasing public policy concern in the 1990s. The considerable emphasis afforded derivatives in the BIS survey is in keeping with this policy concern. One should not lose sight, however, of the fact that in FX it is the spot markets that generate most of the order flow (per my point in the text about the largest of the FX derivative markets—that for forex swaps—generating lots of turnover, but no order flow).

23. The statistic of 10 percent for 1989–1992 is $(390/356) - 1$, with 390 being the corrected spot turnover for 1992 of $400(800/820)$ and 356 being the corrected spot turnover for 1989 of $350(600/590)$. Corrected spot turnovers for the other years are calculated similarly. Note that this correction should be viewed as approximate for the spot turnover because the mix of currencies that are traded spot does not match exactly the mix of currencies in total turnover.

24. Part of this large amount of dollar trading (but only part) is due to use of the dollar as a vehicle currency. When the dollar is used as a vehicle, then when trading two non-dollar currencies one does so indirectly, by going through the dollar first. With the launch of the euro, the dollar's role as an international currency has received much attention recently. See, for example, Hartmann 1998a and Portes, and Rey 1998. Much of the analysis in this area turns on microstructural matters; it is a natural application of microstructure tools to what has traditionally been a macro topic.

25. Of the major central banks, only the Bank of Japan was intervening much in the major markets at this time. See chapter 8 for more on intervention.

26. Do not be misled by the expression "transacted by brokers" that appears in the first sentence of section 7 (BIS 1999a): brokers do not themselves transact; they merely facilitate the transactions of dealers (for a fee).

27. The U.K. market is the biggest in terms of spot trading, accounting for about 28 percent of the worldwide spot total (table E-9).

28. There is a second major policy issue in equity-market transparency that is more relevant to pre-trade information: Is the public entitled to see all the price quotes that the dealers observe? As for pre-trade transparency in FX, an issue that warrants greater policy attention is whether customer limit orders at individual banks should be exposed to the market at large (as was recently imposed on the U.S. NASDAQ market; see Weston 2000). Aggregation of these limit orders represents, in some sense, the wider market's latent demand.

29. I should add, though, that transparency in centralized exchange markets (stock and futures exchanges) was historically imposed by the members on themselves, prior to government regulation. For work on transparency in equity markets see, for example, Naik, Neuberger, and Viswanathan (1999) and Pagano and Roell (1996).

30. In June 2000, three investment banks (Goldman Sachs, Merrill Lynch, and Morgan Stanley Dean Witter) announced that they were launching a centralized electronic system for the U.S. bond markets (government and corporate bonds). This system, if successful, represents a fundamental transformation of that market, not just in terms of increased transparency, but also in terms of access and cost of liquidity.

31. As an aside, there is an interesting argument why increasing transparency of the trading process might *reduce* the information in prices: increased transparency might reduce incentives to invest in information production. This effect does not arise in standard trading models because the amount of private and public information is assumed fixed.

32. I consider this possibility further in chapter 10.

Chapter 4.   Theoretical Frameworks

1. For a broader treatment of theoretical microstructure, see O'Hara (1995). For a recent survey, see Madhavan (2000). For historical perspective on trading models, see Keynes (1936); Hicks (1939); Working (1953); and Houthakker (1957). For early reviews of microstructure theory's relevance for the FX market, see Flood (1991) and Suvanto (1993).

2. Even in quote-driven markets, though, order flow still drives price, not the other way around (as we shall see in the models of this chapter).

3. See chapter 1 for a discussion of this hypothetical Walrasian auctioneer.

4. Regarding the role of order flow in inventory models, O'Hara (1995, 16) puts it this way: "What is required here is that order flow be stochastic without being informative about future market or price movements. This is the general view taken in virtually all inventory-based microstructure models."

5. I do not mean to suggest that inventory models are trivial or unimportant. Quite the contrary—inventory models gave microstructure finance its start (see, e.g., Garman 1976; Stoll 1978; Amihud and Mendelson 1980; Ho and Stoll 1983), and they are vital for understanding certain issues. For understanding the issues I address in this book, however, they need to be coupled with information models. See O'Hara (1995) for an in-depth treatment of inventory models.

6. Price P is a sufficient statistic for the value V if the conditional density of V, given P and a private signal S_i, is independent of S_i. Note that this does not imply that P reveals V (i.e., it does not imply that the variance of V conditional on P is zero). It means only that signal S_i contributes no additional information.

7. Varian (1985) analyzes equilibria of this kind. He uses the term "opinion" to denote uninformative differences in belief. One implication of being uninformative is that when others learn opinions, via price or otherwise, this does not induce them to alter their beliefs. See also Harris and Raviv (1993).

8. In all the models of this chapter there is also a riskless asset, but its economic role is trivial, so I omit it from exposition. See the appendix for a discussion.

9. For expositional clarity, I use zero-mean payoff values for all the models of this chapter. A positive mean adds nothing to the economics of the problem and can, in fact, obscure the economics. In the appendix I include non-zero means when presenting the basic inference tools. For those concerned about the possibility that prices can be negative, one can set the mean of fundamentals arbitrarily high, making the probability of negative prices in equilibrium arbitrarily small. For empirical work on the distribution of (floating) exchange rate returns, see Hsieh (1988).

10. Like the process for fundamentals, it is more natural to think of the endowment process as having a positive mean. I choose the zero-mean formulation in this case too for expositional clarity—the underlying economics is unchanged.

11. When applied in an international context, this specification implies that agents from different countries are maximizing the utility of wealth measured in the same numeraire, namely dollars. If instead investors in different countries care about returns measured in their own currency, then (small) expected return differentials arise as a result of Jensen's Inequality (sometimes referred to as Siegel's Paradox; see Siegel 1972). As an empirical matter, though, there is wide agreement within the international finance literature that these Jensen's Inequality effects play a negligible role in exchange rate determination. Given this, I do not introduce them in this book. For more detail, see the nice discussion in Obstfeld and Rogoff (1996), 586–588.

12. Though trading is simultaneous with price determination, the uninformed trader can calculate his demand in advance as a function of every possible price. Think of the order he submits as being conditonal on the market-clearing price.

13. Transforming signals this way—so they are distributed about a variable of interest, in this case the signal S—is a technique I will use repeatedly in this chapter.

14. The Grossman and Stiglitz (1980) version of the model has a finite number of traders $i = i, \ldots, n$, so the assumption of perfectly competitive behavior is less of a stretch than in the two-trader case here (but still problematic). One technique commonly used to address the issue is to assume that the informed and uninformed represent separate continuums of traders, so that no one trader has a measurable impact on price.

15. The literature on rational expectations models of trading is vast. Papers on how prices aggregate information include Grossman (1977); Grossman and Stiglitz (1980); Hellwig (1980); and Diamond and Verrecchia (1981). For papers on the existence of equilibria and their degree of revelation, see the overview in Jordan and Radner (1982). Papers that address connections between rational expectations models and microstructure models include Hellwig (1982); Kyle (1989); and Rochet and Vila (1995). For a multiple-period rational expectations model and its application to the home-bias puzzle in international finance, see Brennan and Cao (1997). For applications to FX markets, see Bhattacharya and Weller (1997) and Montgomery and Popper (1998).

16. Though much macro information satisfies the first of these two criteria, very little macro information satisfies the second. See chapter 2 for more detail on specific types of nonpublic information.

17. In general, opportunities for profitable manipulation require situations where markets are more liquid when investors are unwinding their trades than when the original trades are made. For models that do permit some manipulation in equilibrium, see, e.g., Allen and Gorton (1992); Lyons (1997a); and Vitale (2000).

18. For expositional clarity, I continue to use this zero-mean specification—it has no impact on the underlying economics.

19. The original Kyle paper (1985) has this same direct observation of V, rather than a signal of V, as in the rational expectations auction model earlier in this chapter. Changing the Kyle specification so that the informed trader observes a signal of V is straightforward. Note that changing the specification of the rational expectations model so that the informed trader observes V directly would result in full revelation: the demand of the informed trader in equation (4.3) would be either positive or negative infinity at any price other than the fully revealing price.

20. Note that the demand function introduced earlier in equation (4.3) does not appear here. That demand function is inappropriate because the informed trader does not take price as given (i.e., he is strategic).

21. See Subrahmanyam (1991); Admati and Pfleiderer (1988); and Holden and Subrahmanyam (1992), respectively. For a recent application of the Kyle (1985) model in FX, see Vitale (1999). References to other variations on the Kyle model are available in O'Hara (1995).

22. Recall from the introduction to this chapter that the traditional focus of inventory models is transitory variation in price around fixed expected payoffs, caused by some inventory cost (the cost typically arises from risk aversion). The focus of information models, in contrast, is permanent price adjustment toward changing future payoffs.

23. Most of the "single-dealer" models in the theoretical literature actually admit multiple dealers, but Bertrand (price) competition suffices to restrict the problem to one dealer.

24. For expositional clarity I am associating these insights with the sequential-trade model. Given the sequencing of models in this chapter this is certainly the place that they enter. These ideas have a history, however, that predates Glosten and Milgrom (1985), the paper that develops the sequential-trade model. See, for example, Bagehot (1971) and Copeland and Galai (1983).

25. More formally, price follows a Martingale with respect to an information set Ω_t if $E[P_{t+1} \mid \Omega_t] = P_t$.

26. See Easley and O'Hara (1987, 1992); and Easley et al. (1996), respectively.

27. This is especially true when considering multiple-dealer models that capture important features of the foreign exchange market. Work on multiple-dealer theory more generally includes Ho and Stoll (1983); Leach and Madhavan (1993); Biais (1993); Perraudin and Vitale (1996); Vogler (1997); Werner (1997); Hau (1998); and Viswanathan and Wang (1998). Most of these papers model a centralized interdealer market rather than a decentralized market like that in FX. Also, unlike the simultaneous-trade model, most of these models include either fundamental private information or risk aversion, but not both.

28. Think of the common signal S as, say, a public macro announcement. The private signal S_i allows for information advantage beyond that which will arise from observing order flow. An example often cited by dealers is that S_i could capture knowledge of customers' identity and trading motives—hedge fund trades may have more price impact than corporate trades. I choose to model this more metaphorically with S_i, rather than introducing identity explicitly. Evidence that customer identities do indeed matter is provided in chapter 9.

29. It is a simple matter to add spreads to the quotes that apply to the trading between customers and dealers (e.g., to determine the number of participating dealers endogenously). Adding spreads to the interdealer quotes is more complex.

30. An unknown m becomes intractable, however, because it generates a non-Normal position disturbance.

31. Other features are captured in various extensions of the model, including variable order flow transparency (Lyons 1996a) and interday trading (Evans and Lyons 2000).

32. That utility is negative under the negative exponential is not problematic: utility functions capture the ordinal ranking of outcomes, not the absolute utility attached to any given outcome. Adding a large positive constant to all these utility values would not change individuals' decisions.

33. This is not to suggest that wealth redistribution is irrelevant in financial markets. One needs to use judgment about whether the question being addressed is one for which redistribution is likely to matter.

Chapter 5. Empirical Frameworks

1. See Goodhart and Figliuoli (1991) and Bollerslev and Domowitz (1993), among many others. At the daily frequency, early work includes Glassman (1987); Bossaerts and Hillion (1991); and Wei (1994).

2. See Lyons (1995); Goodhart et al. (1996); Yao (1998a); and Evans (1997). For an emerging experimental literature on markets organized like FX, see Flood et al. (1999). For a simulation methodology, see Flood (1994). For work on information networks embedded in FX trading technologies, see Zaheer and Zaheer (1995). For work on emerging-market currencies, see Goldberg (1993), Goldberg and Tenorio (1997), Carrera (1998); Galati (2000); and Becker, Chadha, and Sy (2000).

3. Two Web sites are valuable for obtaining more information on the systems that produce the data. The first covers the Reuters dealing systems, D2000-1 and D2000-2: ⟨www.reuters.com/transactions/tran00m.htm⟩. The second covers the EBS system used for brokered interdealer trading: ⟨www.ebsp.com⟩.

4. Though in number, fewer than 90 percent of the world's dealers in major spot markets use the Dealing 2000-1 system, a higher percentage of the dollar value goes through the system because the most active dealers use the system quite intensively.

5. Speaking of "electronic trading systems" without first separating direct and brokered trading can be quite misleading in terms of the information available to dealers while trading. The D2000-2 system, like EBS, competed with traditional voice-based brokerage, and now these systems dominate the FX brokerage business (the voice-based brokers have been driven out). Dealing 2000-1 is the electronic means for direct trading. In terms of information dissemination, though, electronic trading in these two different segments is very different: a communication over D2000-1 is strictly bilateral, whereas brokered trading communicates much more information to other dealers.

6. A data set of customer orders that hit the literature just as this book was going to print is that in Osler (2001). Her data include roughly 10,000 customer limit orders (including stop loss orders) from a "large" bank from September 1999 to April 2000 (mostly $/yen and $/euro).

7. There is a large and important body of empirical work that is based on these FXFX data. My focus in this book, however, is order flow and its effects on price. Accordingly, work based on FXFX data does not figure as prominently here as it does in the literature. For a survey that includes much of this FXFX work, see Goodhart and O'Hara (1997).

8. A recently introduced data set—not summarized above—that makes progress in integrating data from multiple market segments is that in Bjonnes and Rime (2000).

9. A more recent approach that is not on my list is the structural sequential-trade approach pioneered by Easley et al. (1996). This approach has not yet been applied to FX markets.

10. The cited papers provide a good deal more detail on the approach for interested readers. For an application to the Tokyo Stock Exchange, see Hamao and Hasbrouck (1995).

11. When this approach is applied in a limit order auction setting, order flow is measured as described in chapter 1: trades are signed according to the direction of market orders, with limit orders being the passive side of each trade. This is tantamount to assuming that information is conveyed by market orders, whereas liquidity-providing limit orders convey no information. In general, in models where informed traders can choose between market and limit orders, they choose market orders, in part because they do not want to advertise superior information in advance of execution (see, e.g., Harris and Hasbrouck 1996).

12. The variable x_t takes different definitions in different applications, and can even be defined more generally as a vector of characteristics. One common variation on the use of signed order flow for x_t is the use of a signed trade indicator, which takes the value of one for an incoming buy and minus one for an incoming sell. Use of this trade indicator parallels closely the second of the two empirical approaches presented here— the Trade-Indicator approach.

13. In chapter 2, I defined private information as information that (1) is not known by all people, and (2) produces a more precise price forecast than public information alone. By this definition, superior information about FX dealer inventories that allows one to more accurately forecast inventory effects is private information. However, this type of private information may not help forecast price in the long run, which precludes it from being counted as information by the definition employed in the VAR approach (equation 5.6).

14. The estimate by Payne (1999) may in fact be an underestimate because he uses order flow from brokered interdealer trading (versus direct interdealer flow, such as that used by Evans and Lyons 1999). Bjonnes and Rime (2000) find that brokered interdealer order flow conveys less information than direct flow. Reiss and Werner (1999) find a similar result for trading among dealers on the London Stock Exchange. See also Saporta (1997).

15. To be fair, Huang and Stoll (1997) do estimate their TI model for three different categories of trade size. This amounts to modeling size via splitting one's sample, rather than modeling size explicitly.

16. Price can of course be moving over time for other reasons. I have chosen to hold these other reasons constant in the figure to highlight this specific source of transaction-price variation.

17. In this case, too, prices can be moving over time for other reasons. Also, the figure assumes that the width of the spread does not change. This is the simplest case, and it holds in some inventory models; however, it is not a general property of inventory models. See O'Hara (1995) for more detail along these lines.

18. In implementing the model for NYSE stocks, the indicator Q_t typically takes on values $\{-1, 0, 1\}$, where 0 is assigned if the trade is executed at the posted bid-ask midpoint. Execution at the midpoint does not occur in pure dealer markers. But the NYSE is not a pure dealer market (see chapter 3). It is possible on the NYSE for incoming orders to be executed at the midpoint (e.g., if two limit orders—one buy and one sell—arrive simultaneously with limit prices at the posted midpoint).

19. Let me provide an example of the type of question that spread decomposition can address (one that is relevant to FX, given increasing concentration of the market among the largest dealing banks). The example comes from a recent paper by Weston (2000). He asks whether competition-increasing reforms on the Nasdaq reduced the order-processing component of the spread. (Recall that the order-processing component also includes "rents.") He finds that they did, suggesting that the pre-reform spreads were less than perfectly competitive.

20. Other work using structural models includes Foster and Viswanathan (1993), which, like Madhavan and Smidt (1991), addresses the NYSE; structural models in a multiple-dealer setting include Snell and Tonks (1995) for stocks and Vitale (1998) for bonds.

21. The model in Lyons (1995) also makes another change to accommodate FX institutions: it incorporates the fact that FX dealers use inventory control methods that are not available to a specialist (e.g., laying off inventory at another dealer's price). To keep things simple, I omit this second change from the version of the model presented here.

22. Estimation of the model can also accommodate variation in desired inventory. See Lyons (1995).

23. The moving-average error term here comes from the inference problem embedded in the model; see Madhavan and Smidt (1991) for details. I should also add that one might be tempted to believe that estimation of this equation using OLS would be biased because of correlation between X_{jt} and ε_{it} due to correlation between S_t and ε_{it} (from equation 5.21). This is not true, however: because dealer i knows both S_t and ε_{it} at the time of quoting, correlation between X_{jt} and ε_{it} is inconsistent with quotes being regret free (i.e., it is inconsistent with rational expectations).

24. Recent work on markets other than FX may provide an explanation why the inventory effects on the dealer's own prices are so weak: non-FX dealers appear to hedge a lot of their inventory risk using derivatives rather than winding down the inventory itself (Reiss and Werner 1998; Naik and Yadav 2000). FX dealers, on the other hand, do not use derivatives much; they find it less expensive to control inventory with actual spot trades (see Lyons 1995).

25. The work on transaction volume in financial markets is vast. See, for example, Karpoff (1986, 1987) and Wang (1994).

26. We do not yet know, for example, what share of interdealer trading is due to hot potato trading.

Chapter 6.   Exchange Rate Models

1. When I use the symbol P in equations to denote the exchange rate, it will always represent the dollar price of other currencies (i.e., \$/other).

2. See the survey by Froot and Rogoff (1995) in the *Handbook for International Economics*.

3. Note that, though I motivated the model with the law of one price, it is not necessary that the law of one price hold for every good. PPP might still hold if, for example, policymakers are successfully intervening in the FX market to maintain PPP. That said, there are many reasons why PPP does not hold in the short run (such as nontradable goods, trade barriers, and many others).

4. The approximation is close over shorter periods of time as long as interest rates and rates of currency appreciation are not too large. Over periods of years or over periods of hyperinflation the approximation can be quite imprecise.

5. This formulation is intended to speak to readers from the field of finance who are more familiar with valuation based on discounted cash flows. Readers from international economics will see their more familiar formulation based on discounted monetary and real variables in the following subsection.

6. For more detail, see the surveys by Taylor (1995) and Isard (1995). In particular, these surveys provide ample evidence of these models' lack of empirical success (which I revisit in chapter 7).

7. Readers familiar with exchange rates will recognize this version of PPP as the absolute version. The relative version is expressed in first differences in logs, or $\Delta p_{\$/£} = \Delta p_{US} - \Delta p_{UK}$, where the difference operator Δ denotes the change from time $t - 1$ to time t.

8. This is the equation for the "LM" curve in the familiar IS-LM model. Note that here the "money market" is used in the narrow, macroeconomic sense of the market for actual money, not in the broader practitioner sense of the market for fixed-income securities with maturity of one year or less.

9. I present here only the solution that excludes rational bubbles. As is standard, equation (6.9) has an infinite number of rational expectations solutions, but the others include a bubble component in the price path. For more on solution techniques in rational expectations models, see Blanchard and Fischer (1989), 261–266.

10. The poor empirical performance of this and other macro models of this chapter is documented in Meese and Rogoff (1983a, b), and surveyed more recently in Frankel and Rose (1995).

11. Strictly speaking, PPP holds in the long run only in simpler versions of this model. It does not hold in versions with real shocks, or other shocks requiring adjustment in the long-run real exchange rate.

12. Overshooting does not necessarily occur in versions of the model that allow output y to vary.

13. In fact, $i_{US} < i_{UK}$ throughout the adjustment period in the standard model, which means that the dollar is expected to appreciate monotonically toward its long-run level.

14. More precisely, as a matter of balance of payments accounting, a current account surplus must be offset in the capital account with a net increase in domestic claims against the foreign economy (assuming no reserve transactions on the part of central banks).

15. Another dimension of "tastes" in these models is the preferences of policymakers, e.g., over various monetary policy rules.

16. For an extensive, nontechnical overview see Stockman (1987). For more recent GE models, which include sticky prices, see Obstfeld and Rogoff (1996).

17. The word "general" in the name of this model stresses that the model includes a wide array of different markets, all of which must clear simultaneously in equilibrium (e.g., individual goods markets, labor markets, bond markets, FX markets, etc.).

18. Whether this statement is strictly true depends on the breadth of one's definition of microstructure. One literature that links to the real economy using microstructure models is that on insider trading. In Leland (1992), for example, insider trading can affect a firm's real investment.

19. Recall from the previous section that I referred to the GE model's cash-in-advance constraint as "technology." In contrast to production technology, it might be more precise to refer to the cash-in-advance constraint as an institution, albeit a rather simple one.

20. Volatility determination has traditionally attracted a lot of attention from the macro end of the spectrum. More recently, though, the literature has begun to address

FX volatility from the micro end of the spectrum, which is why I list this issue in the middle group. Recent contributions from the micro end include Wei (1994); Andersen (1996); Andersen and Bollerslev (1998); Hau (1998); Jeanne and Rose (1999); and Cai et al. (1999).

Chapter 7. Macro Puzzles

1. Per earlier chapters, the relevant literature is vast. At longer horizons, e.g., longer than two years, macro models begin to dominate the random walk (e.g., Chinn 1991; Mark 1995). But exchange rate determination remains a puzzle at horizons less than two years (except in cases of hyperinflation, in which case the inflation differential asserts itself as a driving factor, in the spirit of PPP—see chapter 6).

2. The determination puzzle exists in equity markets as well—see Roll (1988). Roll can account for only 20 percent of daily stock returns using traditional equity fundamentals, a result he describes as a "significant challenge to our science." The microstructure approach had not been applied directly to the determination puzzle in equity markets when Evans and Lyons (1999) applied it in the FX market.

3. Another alternative to traditional macro modeling is the recent "new open-economy macro" approach (e.g., Obstfeld and Rogoff 1995—see chapter 6). I do not address this alternative here because, as yet, the approach has not produced empirical exchange rate equations that alter the Meese-Rogoff (1983a) conclusions.

4. If order flow is an informative measure of macro expectations, then it should forecast surprises in important variables (like interest rates). New order flow data sets that cover up to six years of FX trading—such as the data set I examine in chapter 9—provide enough statistical power to test this. The Evans (1997) data set used by Evans and Lyons (1999) is only four months, so they are not able to push in this direction.

5. Chapter 2 introduces two subcategories of discount rate information: information about inventory effects and information about portfolio balance effects. I do not consider information about inventory effects in this chapter because inventory effects are transitory, and are therefore unlikely to be relevant for longer horizon macro puzzles.

6. As a practical matter, however, the underlying causes of order flow X may not captured by traditional specifications of (i, m, z) in empirical portfolio balance models. Note, too, that I do not consider the general equilibrium (GE) macro model in this discussion. For the GE model, it is difficult to make meaningful statements about whether X and (i, m, z) are independent when X is conveying information about portfolio balance effects: it depends on the GE model's specific features. (To clarify terms, when X is conveying this type of information in GE models, it is conveying information about "pricing kernels"—the general-equilibrium analogue of discount rates.)

7. As in the simultaneous-trade model, introducing a bid-offer spread (or price schedule) in round one to endogenize the number of dealers is a straightforward extension.

8. Recall from chapter 4 that simultaneous and independent interdealer trades T_{it} implies that dealers cannot condition on one another's trades in a given round.

9. This is tantamount to assuming that—when it comes to bearing overnight risk—the dealers' capacity is small relative to the capacity of the whole public.

10. Note that this equation describes a cointegrating (i.e., long-run) relationship that includes the level of price and cumulative interdealer order flow, which we revisit in section 7.3.

11. This model can also be used to generate multiple equilibria. Introducing multiple equilibria obscures the essential portfolio balance logic, however, so I do not pursue this direction here.

12. In the Evans-Lyons model, these are exogenous. If one were to model them explicitly, they could arise from any number of motives, including hedging demand, liquidity demand, and changing risk preferences.

13. Consider an example. Starting from $X_t = 0$, an initial customer sale to a dealer does not move X_t from zero because X_t measures interdealer order flow only. After the customer sale (say of one unit), then when dealer i unloads the position by selling to another dealer, dealer j, X_t drops to -1. A subsequent sale by dealer j to another dealer, dealer k, reduces X_t further to -2. If a customer happens to buy dealer k's position from him, then the process comes to rest with X_t at -2. In this simple scenario, order flow measured only from trades between customers and dealers would have reverted to zero: the concluding customer trade offsets the initiating customer trade, putting a stop to the hot potato. The interdealer order flow, however, does not revert to zero.

14. Cheung and Chinn (1999b) corroborate this empirically: their surveys of foreign exchange traders show that the importance of individual macroeconomic variables shifts over time, but "interest rates always appear to be important."

15. As a diagnostic, though, Evans and Lyons also estimate the model using the *level* of the differential, in the manner of Uncovered Interest Parity, and find similar results.

16. There is a vast empirical literature that attempts to increase the explanatory power of interest rates in exchange rate equations (by introducing individual interest rates as separate regressors, by introducing nonlinearities, etc.). Because these efforts have not been successful, it is very unlikely that variations on the interest rate specification could alter the relative importance of order flow.

17. Recall from chapter 5 that one of the shortcomings of the Evans (1997) data set is that it does not include the size of each trade, so that order flow is measured as the number of buys minus the number of sells. (However, the data set does include the total volume over the sample, so that an average trade size can be calculated.) This shortcoming must be kept in perspective, however: if the Evans-Lyons results were negative, then data concerns would be serious indeed—the negative results could easily be due to noisy data. But their results are quite positive, which noise alone could not produce. Indeed, that there is noise in the data only underscores the apparent strength of the order flow/price relation.

18. These higher coefficients at higher activity levels are consistent with the "event uncertainty" model described in chapter 5 (see Easley and O'Hara 1992). It should be noted, though, that the daily frequency of the Evans-Lyons analysis is lower than the typical transaction frequency tests of event uncertainty. Results from intraday analysis of the Evans (1997) data paint a different picture—see chapter 8.

19. A direct role for macro announcements in determining order flow warrants exploring as well. Another possible use of macro announcements is to introduce them directly into an Evans-Lyons-type regression. However, this tack is not likely to be

fruitful: there is a long literature showing that macro announcements are unable to account for exchange rate first moments (though they do help to account for second moments—see Andersen and Bollerslev 1998).

20. See Osler (1998) and Carlson and Osler (2000) for models in which current account flows are central to exchange rate determination. Unlike traditional flow approach models, the exchange rate in these models is determined in its own speculative market.

21. I would add that this analogy also sheds light on the asset approach. In the asset approach, too, there is no inference effect of order flow on price because all information is public, by assumption (i.e., public information is a sufficient statistic for price).

22. Contrary to popular belief, in an absolute sense, exchange rates are less volatile than stock prices: the annual standard deviation of exchange rate returns is in the 10–12 percent range for major currencies against the dollar, whereas the annual standard deviation of equity market returns is in the 15–20 percent range (and for individual stocks it is higher still).

23. Exchange rate regimes are not limited to floating and fixed. They fall along a spectrum. Ordered in terms of increasing commitment to the exchange rate target, these regimes include: (1) free float, (2) dirty float, (3) target zone, (4) peg—fixed or crawling, (5) currency board, and (6) monetary union. A dirty float involves some limited intervention. A currency board is an institutional commitment to dedicate monetary policy to the exchange rate target. For more on the differences between these regimes, see, for example, Krugman and Obstfeld (2000).

24. The transition from EMS to EMU was indisputably a transition toward exchange rate fixity. KLM assume that EMU was perfectly credible after the weekend of May 2–3, 1998—the date the eleven "in" countries were selected and the date the internal conversion rates for the euro-zone were determined. Extending their model to environments of imperfectly credible fixed rates is a natural direction for further research.

25. The logic of this example—based on the polar extreme of perfectly fixed rates—also holds for intermediate regimes under which some volatility remains.

26. Nonstationary variables are cointegrated if there exists a linear combination of them that is stationary. Cointegration means that although many developments can cause permanent changes in these three series, there is an equilibrium relation that ties them together in the long run. A good reference on cointegration is Hamilton (1994), chapter 19.

27. EBS has a prescreened credit facility whereby dealers can only see prices for trades that would not violate their counterparty credit limits, thereby eliminating the potential for failed deals due to these limits.

28. In their sample, the mean value of cumulative order flow is DM1.38 billion.

29. This is a theoretical point. Empirically, it appears that there was little intervention by the national central banks or the ECB in the period from May to December 1998 (verification is difficult because these banks are not terribly forthcoming with intervention data over this period).

30. This type of bias is often referred to as "conditional bias" to distinguish it from "unconditional bias." Conditional bias refers to the fact that to predict whether P_{t+1} will be lower than $F_{t,1}$, one needs to "condition" (i.e., base the prediction) on whether $F_{t,1} > P_t$. Forward rates would be unconditionally biased if the average of $F_{t,1} - P_{t+1}$ is

statistically different from zero (there is no conditioning in this case on time t information). Unconditionally, major-currency forward rates tend to be unbiased (see, for example, Perold and Schulman 1988).

31. A no-arbitrage relation called covered interest parity (introduced in an early footnote in chapter 3) requires that the forward discount equal the interest differential (as long as there are no capital market controls that prevent arbitrage trades). This yields a regression that is equivalent to equation (7.15) with the one-period interest differential on the righthand side ($i_\$ - i_{\text{other}}$) in lieu of the forward discount ($f_{t,1} - p_t$). Many authors in this literature estimate equation (7.15) in this interest-differential form (in effect, a test of uncovered interest parity—introduced in chapter 6).

32. Though I have introduced the two main economic explanations for bias—inefficiency versus risk premium—there is a third explanation that any anomaly must confront, namely measurement error (broadly defined), i.e., that the anomaly doesn't really exist. In the forward bias literature, the measurement error explanation is typically referred to as the "peso problem." The name comes from a period through which the Mexican peso was consistently selling at a forward discount because the market felt devaluation was possible. When, over many years, the devaluation didn't occur, it appeared in-sample as though the forward rate was biased, consistently over-predicting the exchange rate change. Estimates of the coefficient b are biased in this case because the measured changes in exchange rates do not match what the market expected (a small sample problem). Engel (1996) provides several arguments that make the peso problem explanation difficult—but not impossible—to defend in the context of the major exchange rates. (See Lewis 1995 for a thorough survey in which she rightly points out that alternative hypotheses to the bias anomaly are not mutually exclusive.)

33. The currency trading strategy here would entail selling foreign currency forward when $f_{t,1} > p_t$ and buying foreign currency forward when $f_{t,1} < p_t$. To understand why, recall that when $f_{t,1} > p_t$, then on average p_{t+1} ends up below $f_{t,1}$. One can expect to profit from locking in a sale of foreign currency at a dollar price of $f_{t,1}$ when the expected market price (value) at $t+1$ is below $f_{t,1}$. Similarly for the case when $f_{t,1} < p_t$: one can expect to profit from having locked in a purchase of foreign currency at a dollar price of $f_{t,1}$ when the expected market price (cost) at $t+1$ is above $f_{t,1}$. (One could trade this in an equivalent way by borrowing in the low interest rate currency and investing in the deposit of the high interest rate currency.) Finally, by "buy-and-hold equity strategy" I mean a simple strategy of buying and holding an equity index fund (e.g., a fund that tracks the S&P 500 index).

34. The Sharpe ratio, named after Nobel prize winner William Sharpe, has a natural interpretation in the standard diagram used to illustrate the Capital Asset Pricing Model (CAPM): with expected return on the vertical axis and return standard deviation on the horizontal axis, every security (or portfolio) that lies on a ray originating from the vertical axis at the risk-free rate has the same Sharpe ratio. For example, in a CAPM with lending and borrowing, every point on the ray from the risk-free rate through the tangency point on the efficient frontier has the same Sharpe ratio. In a frictionless environment, using a Sharpe ratio criterion to select among investments is optimal only if the investments are mutually exclusive.

35. Remember that order flow and volume are quite different: order flow is signed volume (i.e., sell orders have a negative sign).

36. It is true that the high historical returns on U.S. equities are themselves a puzzle (the so-called equity premium puzzle). Given those high risk-adjusted equity returns,

underallocation of speculative capital to forward bias is unsurprising. See also the Sharpe ratio discussion in Backus, Gregory, and Telmer (1993), based on an earlier sample.

37. There is scope for additional research here. One could design a survey in the spirit of Cheung and Chinn (1999a) and Cheung and Yuk-Pang (2000) that asks decision-makers at these institutions why they commit so little capital to trading against forward bias.

38. For more empirical evidence of the central role played by Sharpe ratios at hedge funds and proprietary trading desks, see the leading practitioner publication from Managed Account Reports, Inc., e.g., MAR/Hedge 2000. MAR/Hedge uses the Sharpe ratio to rank hedge funds' performance. The ranking is provided each month.

39. Corporate finance provides many reasons why idiosyncratic risk can be value destroying (e.g., damage to relationships with employees, customers, and suppliers, costs of financial distress, and so on; see the accessible survey by Bishop 1996). Formalization of my sketch of why Sharpe ratio–based contracts can be optimal need not rely, however, on this particular agency friction. Other frictions commonly employed in finance that produce interesting constrained-optimal decision rules include borrowing constraints, solvency constraints, and short-sale constraints. (See, for example, He and Modest 1995.) My view from discussions with practitioners is that Sharpe ratio–driven allocation of capital is optimal, given the institutional constraints they face, and not an example of near-rationality, or suboptimal rules of thumb.

40. Baldwin (1990) presents what is to my knowledge the first inaction-range model for the forward bias. In his model, transaction costs alone generate the inaction range. His mechanism is therefore quite different from that proposed here, in that my inaction range is based on the evaluation of risk, whereas his is purely a function of expected return. For a recent model of inaction ranges in international goods markets, see Obstfeld and Taylor (1997).

41. This idea provides a direct link to the two other major puzzles addressed in this chapter: the determination puzzle (section 7.1) and the excess volatility puzzle (section 7.3). The connecting link is the elasticity of public demand. A lower conditional return volatility means a higher elasticity of public demand, other things equal (and vice versa). In this section, I focus on Sharpe ratios; those previous sections focus on the broader, more abstract notion of imperfect substitutability.

42. A big advantage of carving up public order flow this way (as opposed to, say, chartists versus fundamentalists—see Frankel and Froot 1990) is that one can readily identify these trade categories in empirical work. Indeed, I present estimates of models along the lines of equation (7.19) in chapter 9.

43. As an empirical matter, just because leveraged investors do not implement pure currency strategies does not mean they do not trade in FX markets. The FX trading of leveraged investors is, for the most part, focused in areas where they enjoy informational advantage. Take, for example, the proprietary trading desks at major banks. These banks have order flow information that is private, which they use to determine speculative positions. This type of position taking need bear no particular relation to the trades that would result from pure currency strategies.

44. See Moore and Roche (1999) for a general-equilibrium application of limited participation to the forward bias puzzle. Their model also includes habit persistence and consumption externalities.

45. This particular thought experiment is essentially the same as that of Froot and Thaler (1990, 188). Missing from their story, however, is a reason why the seemingly large profit opportunity can persist (indeed, they describe this missing feature as an "apparently serious flaw" in their story). My explanation does provide persistence: it comes from institutions' Sharpe ratio based evaluation of risk. In the last sentence of their article, Froot and Thaler point in the general direction of my approach when they write, "Although much of the risk in these strategies may be diversifiable in principle, more complex diversified strategies may be much more costly, unreliable, or difficult to execute." See also Carlson (1998) for a gamblers' ruin model of why institutions put tight limits on FX position taking. For a microstructure analysis of interest rate increases at times of fixed-rate crisis, see Lyons and Rose (1995).

46. As an empirical matter, this story of gradual adjustment to monetary policy changes is borne out in the data—see Eichenbaum and Evans (1995).

47. One might wonder whether the bias from a coefficient b of -0.9 is large enough to be consistent with an exchange rate that is misaligned by 20 percent. To understand why it can be consistent, note that the 20 percent misalignment is in the current exchange rate *level*, which impounds the whole stream of future one-month bias realizations; 20 percent is not an indicator of bias over short horizons (otherwise it truly would be an extraordinary trading opportunity).

48. Though order flow is clearly insufficient, I do not mean to suggest that the disparity is not being traded. Long Term Capital Management, for example, was one of several institutions that selectively opened positions based on this disparity.

Chapter 8.   Microstructure and Central Bank Intervention

1. Readers interested in surveys of the macro literature on intervention should see Dominguez and Frankel (1993b); Edison (1993); and Sarno and Taylor (2000b). Beyond surveying the literature, Dominguez and Frankel (1993b) also contains considerable analysis of its own, much of it based on survey expectations of exchange rate movements. As noted in chapter 1, one can think of order flow as another way to proxy for the same expectations.

2. For evidence of imperfect substitutability across stocks, see Scholes (1972); Shleifer (1986); Bagwell (1992); and Kaul, Mehrotra, and Morck (2000), among others. For at least two reasons, imperfect substitutability may be more applicable to individual currency markets than to markets in individual stocks. First, the size of the order flows that major currency markets need to absorb are on average more than 10,000 times those absorbed in a representative U.S. stock (the average daily volume on individual NYSE stocks in 1998 was about $9 million, whereas the average daily volume in $/DM spot was about $150 billion). Second, there are far more individual stocks that can substitute for one another in portfolios than there are individual currencies (particularly major currencies).

3. I use the term "intervention" here to mean any trade by a central bank in the FX market with the objective of influencing the exchange rate.

4. Referring to the liability side of the central bank balance sheet as "money supply" is a bit loose, but is valuable for expositional clarity. A more precise breakdown would distinguish between currency in circulation and monetary base. The latter gives rise to the money multiplier familiar from macroeconomics.

5. Central banks now also trade via interdealer brokers like EBS. Because broker-market counterparties are dealing banks, the balance sheet effects are the same. One difference that arises from trading via brokers that is not reflected in balance sheets is the degree of transparency: central bank trades done directly with a single dealer are less transparent than central bank trades done via brokers (more on this below, including the use of agents to protect central bank secrecy).

6. Though not essential to the story, it should be noted that foreign exchange reserves held by central banks are not held in the form of currency, which earns no interest, but mostly in the form of foreign government bonds. Foreign bonds have to be liquidated to generate the yen used for payment by the Fed. Making this point explicit helps one understand why there is not also an effect on the yen money supply from the Fed "injecting" $100 million worth of yen: the net effect of these transactions on the Fed's holding of yen currency is zero.

7. Harder to understand is why the central bank would want to intervene in an unannounced way if it intends to send a signal to the market. (I describe unannounced intervention below.) There is no obvious rationale for this. See Dominguez and Frankel (1993b) for a discussion.

8. Equations (6.14) and (6.15)—which describe the macro portfolio balance model—provide a sense for how the two bond demands would have to adjust to accommodate a change in supply: with fixed interest rates, expected dollar depreciation, $E[\%\Delta P]$, must change. Holding the long-run nominal value of the dollar fixed, an increase in the current value of the dollar will increase the expected rate of dollar depreciation. This effect is akin to changing the price of a bond—which has a fixed terminal payoff—in order to change its expected return (yield).

9. I do not address the distinction between coordinated and uncoordinated central bank intervention (i.e., coordination across central banks). For more on this topic, see the surveys cited at the outset of this chapter.

10. Or, as is common more recently, monetary policy can be dedicated to achieving explicit inflation targets.

11. It is important to remember that order flow being near zero does not imply that trading volume must be near zero.

12. Less clear from the context of the quoted paragraph is whether Dominguez and Frankel consider the news effect—which "causes investors to revise their expectations of future rates of return"—to include only the signaling channel (i.e., payoff information), or whether it includes the portfolio balance channel (which also changes expectations of future returns). If the latter, then their direct effect on price is probably best thought of as representing the third information category of chapter 2: information about inventory effects.

13. This is true even in the case where intervention is announced. For announced intervention to eliminate information asymmetry, it would have to: (1) be fully credible; (2) be fully informative regarding the size, direction, and timing of the trade; and (3) occur in advance of, or simultaneously with, the trade. There are no "announced" interventions in the existing empirical literature that fulfill these conditions. Moreover, even these conditions—as strong as they are—are not sufficient to eliminate an order flow role: it would also have to be true that market participants agree on intervention's implications.

14. Recall from the discussion of the Kyle model in section 4.2 that the risk neutrality of the dealer precludes portfolio balance effects on price. Because of this narrow context, use of the term "fundamental" is appropriate. Regarding broader notions of fundamentals, see the discussion in section 2.3.

15. It is worth noting that, at times, the objective of central banks is to *minimize* the price impact of their trades. This is the case, for example, when they are trying to rebalance their portfolio of foreign exchange reserves, without any intention of moving exchange rates. The intervention rules from the Evans and Lyons (2000) analysis are useful for this objective as well.

16. For other empirical papers on intervention that use microstructure-style approaches, see Bossaerts and Hillion (1991); Goodhart and Hesse (1993); Peiers (1997); Naranjo and Nimalendran (2000); Chang and Taylor (1998); Fischer and Zurlinden (1999); Dominguez (1999); De Jong et al. (1999); Payne and Vitale (2000) and Chaboud and LeBaron (2001).

17. Though indistinguishable, this is not to say that trades of these two types come from the same distribution. Indeed, an interesting issue for future work is the extent to which the market would adjust the mean of expected central bank orders (in the spirit of the Lucas critique) if the central bank began to intervene secretly in a more aggressive way.

18. Recall from chapter 2 that my definition of private information is broad: information qualifies as private as long as it is not known by all people and produces a better forecast of price than public information alone. Private information does not have to be inside information about the Fed's next interest rate move.

19. The model also clarifies why this learning is based on trades between dealers. Interdealer flow is, in reality, the variable that price setters (dealers) are reacting to when intervention is secret.

20. The model treats the central bank trade as exogenous, with expected value zero. This might be viewed as a normalization around an "expected" intervention trade. Note too that the central bank here is initiating all its trades. This is reasonable because central banks are like other customers in this sense. In a fixed rate regime, however, where a central bank is obligated to absorb flow, the central bank will often be on the *passive* side: dealers and customers initiate trades with the central bank to lay off unwanted positions.

21. Evans and Lyons present this estimate as a "lower bound." In their model, interdealer flow is equal to customer flow times a constant, $\alpha \geq 1$. Thus, by measuring the price impact of interdealer order flow they are underestimating the price impact of customer trades—including the trades of the central bank—by a factor of α. Be that as it may, this 1-percent-per-\$2-billion estimate provides some sense for why portfolio balance effects from sterilized intervention have been so hard to detect empirically: the average intervention trade of \$200 million (Dominguez and Frankel 1993b) would have a price impact of only about 10 basis points.

22. Because I am referring to secret intervention here, there is no way for the public to respond to a change in central bank strategy and fully undo it. That said, one would expect the public's trading strategies—and dealer's pricing rules—to be affected by a changed intervention strategy. This is an interesting avenue for future theoretical work within the microstructure approach.

Chapter 9. Customers

1. By analogy, it is not unreasonable to view firms that trade on the NYSE as fundamentally the same as firms that trade on the NASDAQ, other things equal (i.e., similar cost of capital, similar relative valuation, etc.). The distinction between them boils down to what I called in chapter 3 the "microstructure effects" question. Per earlier chapters, the microstructure effects question is not the focus of this book.

2. Recall, too, the discussion and quotations in chapter 3 regarding customer order flows.

3. For practitioner-oriented research on order flow effects on exchange rates, see, e.g., Citibank's *Citiflows Global Flow and Volume Analysis* (various issues); Deutschebank's *Flowmetrics Monthly* (various issues); and Lehman Brothers' *Global Economic Research Series*, particularly the issue on "FX Impact of Cross-Border M&A." For evidence from practitioner surveys on the use of flow analysis, see Gehrig and Menkhoff (2000).

4. Balance of payments accounts are based on the concept of residency. They are a statistical record of the economic transactions taking place between a nation's residents and the rest of the world.

5. Recall that the Evans-Lyons model of chapter 8 was designed (in part) to show that even with short-lived dealer positions, interdealer order flow still has persistent effects on price because it conveys information about the persistent portfolio shifts of underlying customers.

6. One could argue that in frictionless general equilibrium, starting from pareto-optimal allocations, it is not clear why firms' ex ante "portfolios" are not instantaneously restored. As an empirical matter, this objection to my example is not so compelling. For many institution types, there are substantial (labor intensive) costs of adjusting their net positions in the market. This may produce path dependence in portfolio allocation, even if the relation between realized order flow and price is unique.

7. A future direction for research in this area is to isolate categories of trades that fit neatly into a particular balance of payments category. For example, one could isolate equity mutual funds. In this case, one could be confident that their FX trades fit neatly into the category called international portfolio investment.

8. A natural question is where the trades of central banks appear. The source of these data is reluctant to disclose the specifics. Though not reported in the table, the source bank does maintain a small fourth category of customer, called "miscellaneous." Though the trades within this category are quite small relative to the trades in the three main categories, the category is likely to include any central bank trades for which the source bank was the counterparty. (Recall from chapter 8 that central bank trades tend to be small relative to private trades.)

9. The yen plot begins in January 1996 because the source bank did not include customer flow data from its Tokyo office in its database until late 1995. (The Tokyo office is especially important for this bank's $/yen customer flow.) Note that this may account for the seemingly small share of non-financial corporate trading in total customer trading in $/yen shown in table 9.1: If nonfinancial corporations tend to trade via their regional office, whereas financial institutions tend to trade on a 24-hour basis worldwide, then the customer trades in the database before 1996 would be tilted toward the financial institutions.

10. Integrating macro variables into this monthly regression is an important topic for future work.

11. Because these customer flow data are not available publicly, forecasting power is not ruled out on the basis of market efficiency (e.g., on the basis of semi-strong form efficiency, under which price impounds all publicly available information). Note too that differential price impact leaves room for the (theoretical) possibility of market manipulation by customers who can disguise the source of trades. For a nice treatment of traditional forecasting techniques for FX markets, see Rosenberg (1996).

12. There is a comprehensive description of events in BIS (1999b).

Chapter 10.   Looking Forward

1. Recall from chapter 1 that my focus in this book is on analysis based on order flow. There is a lot of fine work on high-frequency exchange rates that does not integrate order flow. For more on this branch of the literature, see the survey by Goodhart and O'Hara (1997).

2. Resolving these differences may lie in the fact that non-FX marketmakers hedge inventory risk with instruments other than those in which they make the market (e.g., with related derivatives), whereas spot FX dealers find that inventory control using spot currencies alone is least expensive. See Reiss and Werner (1998) and Naik and Yadav (2000) for evidence that non-FX marketmakers do indeed use derivatives for inventory control.

3. For the NYSE, a possible resolution of these differences lies in the obligation of the NYSE specialist to smooth prices, a task that existing inventory may facilitate.

4. If, in the end, the portfolio balance view of order flow's price effects wins out, a subsidiary question remains: what is driving the portfolio shifts? Possibilities (mentioned in earlier chapters) include changing risk preferences, changing hedging demands, changing liquidity demands, and changing (payoff unrelated) opinions.

5. Part of closing the gap with macro analysis will come from theoretical advances. A natural direction along these lines is models of market incompleteness (of various types), which fit naturally with current empirical results on order flow. For a contact point with recent work on dynamic open-economy models, see Duarte and Stockman (2001).

6. A precondition for integrating data is availability. At present, much of the data used in this literature is not publicly available. (As noted in chapter 5, my Web site provides links to data sets that are publicly available.) Moving forward, one hopes that sources of these data will recognize the value of making them available to researchers generally.

7. Interested readers should see the material on FXNet—a system for managing settlement risk—on the EBS Web site (⟨www.ebsp.com⟩).

8. One paper that addresses speculative attacks in Mexico using a microstructure approach is Carrera (1999).

9. For an interesting article on the advent of electronic trading in FX, see *Euromoney* (2000). For equity markets, *Institutional Investor* (2000) is a nice treatment of the electronic trading threat to more traditional trading methods.

10. Frankel (1996, 62) was perhaps the first to write about such a scenario in FX, though he was considering a Tobin tax as the possible trigger. He wrote: "It is possible that the imposition of a Tobin tax ... would alter the structure of the market in a fundamental way. It might become more like other major financial markets, in which a sale or purchase by a customer generates only one or two transactions, rather than five or eight. This would be the case particularly if such a tax triggered a transition to a new trading structure equilibrium, with the decentralized dealer network ... replaced by a system in which foreign currency was traded on a centralized exchange in the manner of the NYSE." For more on the legal history relating to openness of broker systems to nondealers, see Levich (2001, 100).

11. For a theoretical treatment of whether centralized limit order structures are likely to capture liquidity and thereby dominate trading, see Glosten (1994). An issue not addressed in that paper that is important for FX is credit risk. I noted in the previous section that bank dealers may have a comparative advantage in managing the credit risk arising from large transactions with customers. New entrants who want to centralize this market around an electronic trading platform need to solve this problem because non-financial corporations do not want to take the counterparty credit risk that banks are comfortable taking. The standard approach is to establish a clearing house system with margin accounts (akin to those used in futures markets).

References

Admati, A., and P. Pfleiderer. 1988. A theory of intraday patterns: Volume and price variability. *Review of Financial Studies* 1: 3–40.

Allen, F., and G. Gorton. 1992. Stock price manipulation, market microstructure and asymmetric information. *European Economic Review* 36: 624–630.

Amihud, Y., and H. Mendelson. 1980. Dealership markets: Marketmaking with inventory. *Journal of Financial Economics* 8: 31–53.

Ammer, J., and Brunner, A. 1997. Are banks market timers or market makers? Explaining foreign exchange trading profits. *Journal of International Financial Markets, Institutions & Money* 7: 43–60.

Andersen, T. 1996. Return volatility and trading volume: An information flow interpretation of stochastic volatility. *Journal of Finance* 51: 169–204.

Andersen, T., and T. Bollerslev. 1997. Heterogeneous information arrivals and return volatility dynamics: Uncovering the long-run in high frequency returns. *Journal of Finance* 52: 975–1006.

Andersen, T., and T. Bollerslev. 1998. Deutsche mark-dollar volatility: Intraday activity patterns, macroeconomic announcements, and longer run dependencies. *Journal of Finance* 53: 219–266.

Andersen, T., T. Bollerslev, and A. Das. 2001. Variance-ratio statistics and high-frequency data: Testing for changes in intraday volatility patterns. *Journal of Finance* 56: 305–328.

Backus, D., A. Gregory, and C. Telmer. 1993. Accounting for forward rates in markets for foreign currency. *Journal of Finance* 48: 1887–1908.

Bagehot, W. 1971. The only game in town. *Financial Analysts Journal* 27: 12–22.

Bagwell, L. 1992. Dutch auction repurchases: An analysis of shareholder heterogeneity. *Journal of Finance* 47: 71–105.

Baillie, R., and T. Bollerslev. 1991. Intra-day and inter-market volatility in foreign exchange rates. *Review of Economic Studies* 58: 565–585.

Baldwin, R. 1990. Reinterpreting the failure of foreign exchange market efficiency tests: Small transactions costs, large hysteresis bands. NBER Working Paper 3319.

Bank for International Settlements. 1996. Central bank survey of foreign exchange market activity in April 1995. Publication of the Monetary and Economics Department, BIS, March.

Bank for International Settlements. 1999a. Central bank survey of foreign exchange market activity in April 1998. Publication of the Monetary and Economics Department, BIS, May (available at www.bis.org).

Bank for International Settlements. 1999b. A review of financial market events in autumn 1998. Publication of the Committee on the Global Financial System, October.

Bank for International Settlements. 2001. BIS 71st Annual Report, June (available at www.bis.org).

Bank for International Settlements. 2002. Central bank survey of foreign exchange market activity in April 2001. Publication of the Monetary and Economics Department, BIS, forthcoming (available at www.bis.org).

Bank of England. 1998. The UK foreign exchange and over-the-counter derivatives markets in April 1998, September (available at www.bankofengland.co.uk).

Becker, T., B. Chadha, and A. Sy. 2000. Foreign exchange bid-ask spreads in the Asian crisis. Typescript, International Monetary Fund, April.

Bessembinder, H. 1994. Bid-ask spreads in the interbank foreign exchange market. *Journal of Financial Economics* 35: 317–348.

Bhattacharya, U., and P. Weller. 1997. The advantage of hiding one's hand: Speculation and central bank intervention in the foreign exchange market. *Journal of Monetary Economics* 39: 251–277.

Biais, B. 1993. Price formation and equilibrium liquidity in fragmented and centralized markets. *Journal of Finance* 48: 157–184.

Biais, B., P. Hillion, and C. Spatt. 1995. An empirical analysis of the limit order book and the order flow in the Paris bourse. *Journal of Finance* 50: 1655–1689.

Biais, B., P. Hillion, and C. Spatt. 1999. Price discovery and learning during the pre-opening period in the Paris Bourse. *Journal of Political Economy* 107: 1218–1248.

Bishop, M. 1996. Corporate risk management. *The Economist*, survey October 2, 1996.

Bjonnes, G., and D. Rime. 2000. FX trading ... live: Dealer behavior and trading systems in foreign exchange markets. Typescript, Norwegian School of Management, August.

Blanchard, O., and S. Fischer. 1989. *Lectures on Macroeconomics*. Cambridge, MA: MIT Press.

Blume, L., D. Easley, and M. O'Hara. 1994. Market statistics and technical analysis: The role of volume. *Journal of Finance* 49: 153–182.

Board, J., and C. Sutcliffe. 1995. The effects of trade transparency in the London stock exchange. Report commissioned by the London Stock Exchange, January.

Bollerslev, T., and I. Domowitz. 1993. Trading patterns and prices in the interbank foreign exchange market. *Journal of Finance* 48: 1421–1443.

Bollerslev, T., and M. Melvin. 1994. Bid-ask spreads and volatility in the foreign exchange market: An empirical analysis. *Journal of International Economics* 36: 355–372.

Bossaerts, P., and P. Hillion. 1991. Market microstructure effects of government intervention in the foreign exchange market. *Review of Financial Studies* 4: 513–541.

Branson, W., and D. Henderson. 1985. The specification and influence of asset markets. In *Handbook of International Economics*, vol. 2, edited by R. Jones and P. Kenen. Amsterdam: North-Holland.

Brennan, M., and H. Cao. 1996. Information, trade, and derivative securities. *Review of Financial Studies* 9: 163–208.

Brennan, M., and H. Cao. 1997. International portfolio investment flows. *Journal of Finance* 52: 1851–1880.

Brock, W., and A. Kleidon. 1992. Periodic market closure and trading volume: A model of intraday bids and asks. *Journal of Economic Dynamics and Control* 16: 451–489.

Burnham, J. 1991. Current structure and recent developments in foreign exchange markets. In *Recent Developments in International Banking and Finance*, edited by S. Khoury. Amsterdam: Elsevier North Holland.

Caballero, R., E. Engel, and J. Haltiwanger. 1997. Aggregate employment dynamics: Building from microeconomics. *American Economic Review* 87: 115–137.

Cai, J., Y. Cheung, R. Lee, and M. Melvin. 1999. "Once in a generation" yen volatility in 1998: Fundamentals, intervention, or order flow? Typescript, Arizona State University, July.

Calvo, G. 1999. Contagion in emerging markets: When *Wall Street* is a carrier. Working paper, University of Maryland.

Cao, H. 1999. The effect of derivative assets on information acquisition and price behavior in a rational expectations equilibrium. *Review of Financial Studies* 12: 131–164.

Cao, H., and R. Lyons. 1998. Inventory information. Working paper, Haas School of Business, U.C. Berkeley, August.

Carlson, J., 1998. Risk aversion, foreign exchange speculation and gambler's ruin. *Economica* 65: 441–453.

Carlson, J., and C. Osler. 1999. Determinants of currency risk premiums. Typescript, New York Federal Reserve Bank, February.

Carlson, J., and C. Osler. 2000. Rational speculators and exchange rate volatility. *European Economic Review* 44: 231–253.

Carrera, J. 1999. Speculative attacks to currency target zones: A market microstructure approach. *Journal of Empirical Finance* 6: 555–582.

Chaboud, A., and B. LeBaron. 2001. Foreign exchange trading volume and Federal Reserve intervention. *Journal of Futures Markets*, forthcoming.

Chakrabarti, R. 2000. Just another day in the interbank foreign exchange market. *Journal of Financial Economics* 56: 29–64.

Chakravarty, S., and C. Holden. 1995. An integrated model of market and limit orders. *Journal of Financial Intermediation* 4: 213–241.

Chang, Y., and S. Taylor. 1998. Intraday effects of foreign exchange intervention by the Bank of Japan. *Journal of International Money and Finance* 18: 191–210.

Chen, Z. 1997. Speculative market structure and the collapse of an exchange rate mechanism. Working paper, London School of Economics.

Cheung, Y., and M. Chinn. 1999a. Traders, market microstructure, and exchange rate dynamics. NBER Working paper 7416, November. *Journal of International Money and Finance*.

Cheung, Y., and M. Chinn. 1999b. Macroeconomic implications of the beliefs and behavior of foreign exchange traders. NBER Working paper 7417, November.

Cheung, Y., M. Chinn, and I. Marsh. 1999. How do UK-based foreign exchange dealers think their market operates? CEPR Discussion Paper 2230, September.

Cheung, Y., and C. Yuk-Pang. 1999. Foreign exchange traders in Hong Kong, Tokyo, and Singapore: A survey study. U.C. Santa Cruz Department of Economics Working Paper #425, January.

Cheung, Y., and C. Yuk-Pang. 2000. A survey of market practitioners' views on exchange rate dynamics. *Journal of International Economics* 51: 401–423.

Chinn, M. 1991. Some linear and non-linear thoughts on exchange rates. *Journal of International Money and Finance* 10: 214–230.

Chinn, M., and R. Meese. 1994. Banking on currency forecasts. *Journal of International Economics* 38: 161–178.

Citibank. 2001. *Citiflows Global Flow and Volume Analysis* (various issues). London: Citibank, NA (email: citiflows@citicorp.com).

Clyde, W. 1993. Intraday foreign exchange market anomalies and microstructure. Working paper, Quinnipiac College, August.

Copeland, T., and D. Galai. 1983. Information effects and the bid-ask spread. *Journal of Finance* 38: 1457–1469.

Corsetti, G., S. Morris, and H. Shin. 1999. Does one Soros make a difference? The role of a large trader in currency crises. Typescript, Yale University, March.

Covrig, V., and M. Melvin. 1998. Asymmetric information and price discovery in the FX market: Does Tokyo know more about the yen? Typescript, Arizona State University.

Dacorogna, M., U. Muller, R. Nagler, R. Olsen, and O. Pictet. 1993. A geographical model for the daily and weekly seasonal volatility in the FX market. *Journal of International Money and Finance* 12: 413–438.

Danielsson, J., and R. Payne. 1999. Real trading patterns and prices in spot foreign exchange markets. Typescript, London School of Economics, February.

Degennaro, R., and R. Shrieves. 1997. Public information releases, private information arrival, and volatility in the foreign exchange market. *Journal of Empirical Finance* 4: 295–315.

De Jong, F., R. Mahieu, P. Schotman, and I. van Leeuwen. 1999. Price discovery on foreign exchange markets with differentially informed traders. CEPR Discussion Paper No. 2296, November.

De Jong, F., T. Nijman, and A. Roell. 1996. Price effects of trading and components of the bid-ask spread on the Paris bourse. *Journal of Empirical Finance* 3: 193–213.

Demsetz, H. 1968. The cost of transacting. *Quarterly Journal of Economics* 82: 33–53.

Deutschebank. 2001. *Flowmetrics Monthly* (various issues). London: Deutschebank AG London (email: robin.lumsdaine@db.com).

Devereux, M., and C. Engel. 1999. The optimal choice of exchange-rate regime: Price-setting rules and internationalized production. NBER Working Paper 6992.

Diamond, D., and R. Verrecchia. 1981. Information Aggregation in a Noisy Rational Expectations Economy. *Journal of Financial Economics* 9: 221–235.

Dominguez, K. 1986. Are foreign exchange forecasts rational? New evidence from survey data. *Economic Letters* 21: 277–281.

Dominguez, K. 1990. Market responses to coordinated central bank intervention. *Carnegie-Rochester Series on Public Policy*, vol. 32.

Dominguez, K. 1999. The market microstructure of central bank intervention. NBER Working Paper 7337, September.

Dominguez, K., and J. Frankel. 1993a. Does foreign exchange intervention matter? The portfolio effect. *American Economic Review* 83: 1356–1369.

Dominguez, K., and J. Frankel. 1993b. *Does Foreign-exchange Intervention Work?* Washington, D.C.: Institute for International Economics.

Domowitz, I. 1990. The mechanics of automated trade execution. *Journal of Financial Intermediation* 1: 167–194.

Dooley, M., and P. Isard. 1982. A portfolio-balance rational-expectations model of the dollar-mark rate. *Journal of International Economics* 12: 257–276.

Dornbusch, R. 1976. Expectations and exchange rate dynamics. *Journal of Political Economy* 84: 1161–1176.

Duarte, M., and A. Stockman. 2001. Rational speculation and exchange rates. Typescript, University of Rochester, March.

Dumas, B. 1996. Comment on Jorion. In *The Microstructure of Foreign Exchange Markets*, edited by J. Frankel et al. Chicago: University of Chicago Press.

Easley, D., S. Hvidkjaer, and M. O'Hara. 1999. Is information risk a determinant of asset returns? Typescript, Cornell University, November.

Easley, D., and M. O'Hara. 1987. Price, trade size, and information in securities markets. *Journal of Financial Economics* 19: 69–90.

Easley, D., and M. O'Hara. 1992. Time and the process of security price adjustment. *Journal of Finance* 47: 577–606.

Easley, D., N. Kiefer, M. O'Hara, and J. Paperman. 1996. Liquidity, information, and infrequently traded stocks. *Journal of Finance* 51: 1405–1436.

Edison, H. 1993. The effectiveness of central-bank intervention: A survey of the literature after 1982. *Special Papers in International Economics*, no. 18, Princeton University.

Eichenbaum, M., and C. Evans. 1995. Some empirical evidence on the effects of shocks to monetary policy on exchange rates. *Quarterly Journal of Economics* 110: 975–1009.

Engel, C. 1996. The forward discount anomaly and the risk premium: A survey of recent evidence. *Journal of Empirical Finance* 3: 123–192.

Engle, R., and C. Granger. 1987. Cointegration and error correction: Representation, estimation and testing. *Econometrica* 55: 251–276.

Engle, R., and J. Russell. 1998. Autoregressive conditional duration: A new model for irregularly spaced transaction data. *Econometrica* 66: 1127–1162.

Euromoney. 2000. A true exchange for forex. July.

Evans, G. 1986. A test for speculative bubbles in the sterling-dollar exchange rate. *American Economic Review* 76: 621–636.

Evans, M. 1997. The microstructure of foreign exchange dynamics. Typescript, Georgetown University, November.

Evans, M. 2001. FX Trading and Exchange Rate Dynamics. NBER Working Paper 8116, February.

Evans, M., and R. Lyons. 1999. Order flow and exchange rate dynamics. Typescript, U.C. Berkeley (available at www.haas.berkeley.edu/~lyons). Forthcoming in *Journal of Political Economy*.

Evans, M., and R. Lyons. 2000. The price impact of currency trades: Implications for Secret Intervention. Typescript, U.C. Berkeley, June, presented at the NBER Summer Institute, July.

Evans, M., and R. Lyons. 2001. Why order flow explains exchange rates. Typescript, U.C. Berkeley, March.

Fan, M., and R. Lyons. 2000. Customer-dealer trading in the foreign exchange market. Typescript, U.C. Berkeley, July.

Federal Reserve Bank of New York. 1998. Foreign exchange and interest rate derivatives markets survey: Turnover in the United States (available at www.ny.frb.org).

Fieleke, N. 1981. Foreign-currency positioning by U.S. firms: Some new evidence. *Review of Economics and Statistics* 63: 35–43.

Financial Times. 1998. Survey: Foreign exchange, June 5.

Fischer, J., and M. Zurlinden. 1999. Exchange rate effects of central bank interventions: An analysis of transaction prices. *Economic Journal* 109: 662–676.

Fleming, M., and E. Remolona. 1999. Price formation and liquidity in the U.S. treasury market: The response to public information. *Journal of Finance* 54: 1901–1916.

Flood, M. 1991. Microstructure theory and the foreign exchange market. *Review*, Federal Reserve Bank of St. Louis, 73 (November/December): 52–70.

Flood, M. 1994. Market structure and inefficiency in the foreign exchange market. *Journal of International Money and Finance* 13: 131–158.

Flood, M., R. Huisman, K. Koedijk, and R. Mahieu. 1999. Quote disclosure and price discovery in multiple-dealer financial markets. *Review of Financial Studies* 12: 37–60.

Flood, R., and R. Hodrick. 1990. On testing for speculative bubbles. *Journal of Economic Perspectives* 4: 85–101.

Flood, R., and A. Rose. 1995. Fixing exchange rates: A virtual quest for fundamentals. *Journal of Monetary Economics* 36: 3–37.

Flood, R., and A. Rose. 1996. Fixes: Of the forward discount puzzle. *Review of Economics and Statistics* 78: 748–752.

Flood, R., and M. Taylor. 1996. Exchange rate economics: What's wrong with the conventional macro approach? In *The Microstructure of Foreign Exchange Markets*, edited by J. Frankel, G. Galli, and A. Giovannini. Chicago: University of Chicago Press.

Foster, D., and S. Viswanathan. 1990. A theory of interday variations in volumes, variances, and trading costs in securities markets. *Review of Financial Studies* 3: 593–624.

Foster, D., and S. Viswanathan. 1993. Variations in trading volume, return volatility, and trading costs: Evidence on recent price formation models. *Journal of Finance* 48: 187–211.

Frankel, J. 1982. A test of perfect substitutability in the foreign exchange market. *Southern Economic Journal* 46: 406–416.

Frankel, J. 1996. How well do markets work: Might a Tobin tax help? In *The Tobin Tax: Coping with Financial Volatility*, edited by M. ul Haq et al. New York: Oxford University Press.

Frankel, J., and C. Engel. 1984. Do asset demand functions optimize over the mean and variance of real returns? A six-currency test. *Journal of International Economics* 17: 309–323.

Frankel, J., and K. Froot. 1987. Using survey data to test standard propositions regarding exchange rate expectations. *American Economic Review* 77: 133–153.

Frankel, J., and K. Froot. 1990. Chartists, fundamentalists, and trading in the foreign exchange market. *American Economic Review* 80: 181–185.

Frankel, J., G. Galli, and A. Giovannini, eds. 1996. *The Microstructure of Foreign Exchange Markets*. Chicago: University of Chicago Press.

Frankel, J., G. Galli, and A. Giovannini. 1996. Introduction. In *The Microstructure of Foreign Exchange Markets*, edited by J. Frankel, G. Galli, and A. Giovannini. Chicago: University of Chicago Press.

Frankel, J., and A. Rose. 1995. Empirical research on nominal exchange rates. In *Handbook of International Economics*, edited by G. Grossman and K. Rogoff. Amsterdam: Elsevier Science.

French, K., and R. Roll. 1986. Stock return variance: The arrival of information and the reaction of traders. *Journal of Financial Economics* 17: 99–117.

Frenkel, J. 1976. A monetary approach to the exchange rate: Doctrinal aspects and empirical evidence. *Scandinavian Journal of Economics* 78: 200–224.

Froot, K., and E. Dabora. 1999. How are stock prices affected by the location of trade? *Journal of Financial Economics* 53: 189–216.

Froot, K., and K. Rogoff. 1995. Perspectives on PPP and long-run real exchange rates. In *Handbook of International Economics*, edited by G. Grossman and K. Rogoff. Amsterdam: Elsevier Science.

Froot, K., and R. Thaler. 1990. Anomalies: Foreign exchange. *Journal of Economic Perspectives* 4: 179–192.

Galati, G. 2000. Trading volumes, volatility, and spreads in FX markets: Evidence from emerging market countries. Typescript, Bank for International Settlements, July.

Garman, M. 1976. Market microstructure. *Journal of Financial Economics* 3: 257–275.

Gehrig, T., and L. Menkhoff. 2000. The use of flow analysis in foreign exchange: Exploratory evidence. Typescript, University of Freiburg, Germany, August.

Gennotte, G., and H. Leland. 1990. Market liquidity, hedges, and crashes. *American Economic Review* 80: 999–1021.

Gersbach, H., and K. Vogler. 1998. Learning from informed and uninformed traders and the role of interdealer trading. Typescript, University of Heidelberg, March.

Glassman, D. 1987. Exchange rate risk and transactions costs: Evidence from bid-ask spreads. *Journal of International Money and Finance* 6: 479–490.

Glosten, L. 1989. Insider trading, liquidity, and the role of the monopolist specialist. *Journal of Business* 62: 211–236.

Glosten, L. 1994. Is the electronic open limit order book inevitable? *Journal of Finance* 49: 1127–1162.

Glosten, L., and L. Harris. 1988. Estimating the components of the bid-ask spread. *Journal of Financial Economics* 21: 123–142.

Glosten, L., and P. Milgrom. 1985. Bid, ask, and transaction prices in a specialist market with heterogeneously informed agents. *Journal of Financial Economics* 14: 71–100.

Goldberg, L. 1993. Foreign exchange markets in Russia: Understanding the reforms. *International Monetary Fund Staff Papers* 40: 852–864.

Goldberg, L., and R. Tenorio. 1997. Strategic trading in a two-sided foreign exchange auction. *Journal of International Economics* 42: 299–326.

Goldstein, M., and K. Kavajecz. 2000. Liquidity provision during circuit breakers and extreme market movements. Typescript, Babson College, November.

Goodhart, C. 1988. The foreign exchange market: A random walk with a dragging anchor. *Economica* 55: 437–460.

Goodhart, C., and L. Figliuoli. 1991. Every minute counts in financial markets. *Journal of International Money and Finance* 10: 23–52.

Goodhart, C., and T. Hesse. 1993. Central bank forex intervention assessed in continuous time. *Journal of International Money and Finance* 12: 368–389.

Goodhart, C., and M. O'Hara. 1997. High frequency data in financial markets: Issues and applications. *Journal of Empirical Finance* 4: 73–114.

Goodhart, C., and R. Payne. 1996. Micro structural dynamics in a foreign exchange electronic broking system. *Journal of International Money and Finance* 15: 829–852.

Goodhart, C., and R. Payne. 1999. The foreign exchange market: A multimedia representation, compact disk, distributed by Enterprise LSE Ltd. (www.enterprise-lse.co.uk).

Goodhart, C., and R. Payne, eds. 2000. *The Foreign Exchange Market: Empirical Studies with High-Frequency Data*. New York: St. Martin's Press.

Goodhart, C., and M. Taylor. 1992. Why don't individuals speculate in the forward foreign exchange market? *Scottish Journal of Political Economy* 39: 1–13.

Goodhart, C., T. Ito, and R. Payne. 1996. One day in June 1993: A study of the working of the Reuters 2000-2 electronic foreign exchange trading system. In *The Microstructure of Foreign Exchange Markets*, edited by J. Frankel, G. Galli, and A. Giovannini. Chicago: University of Chicago Press.

Gordon, R., and L. Bovenberg. 1996. Why is capital so immobile internationally? Possible explanations and implications for capital income taxation. *American Economic Review* 86: 1057–1075.

Grammatikos, T., and A. Saunders. 1986. Futures price variability: A test of maturity and volume effects. *Journal of Business* 59: 319–330.

Grossman, S. 1977. The existence of futures markets, noisy rational expectations and informational externalities. *Review of Economic Studies* 44: 431–449.

Grossman, S. 1988. An analysis of the implications for stock and futures price volatility of program trading and dynamic hedging strategies. *Journal of Business* 61: 275–298.

Grossman, S., and M. Miller. 1988. Liquidity and market structure. *Journal of Finance* 43: 617–633.

Grossman. S., and J. Stiglitz. 1980. On the impossibility of informationally efficient markets. *American Economic Review* 70: 393–408.

Grossman, S., and L. Weiss. 1983. A transactions-based model of the monetary transmission mechanism. *American Economic Review* 73: 871–880.

Grundy, B., and M. McNichols. 1989. Trade and the revelation of information through prices and direct disclosure. *Review of Financial Studies* 2: 495–526.

Guillaume, D., M. Dacorogna, R. Dave, U. Muller, R. Olsen, and O. Pictet. 1995. From the bird's eye to the microscope: A survey of new stylized facts of the intradaily foreign exchange markets. *Finance and Stochastics* 1: 95–129.

Habermeier, K., and A. Kirilenko. 2000. Securities transaction taxes and financial markets. Typescript, International Monetary Fund, June.

Hamao, Y., and J. Hasbrouck. 1995. Securities trading in the absence of dealers: Trades and quotes on the Tokyo stock exchange. *Review of Financial Studies* 8: 849–878.

Hamilton, J. 1994. *Time Series Analysis*. Princeton, N.J.: Princeton University Press.

Handa, P., and R. Schwartz. 1996. Limit order trading. *Journal of Finance* 51: 1835–1861.

Hansch, O., N. Naik, and S. Viswanathan. 1998. Do inventories matter in dealership markets? Evidence from the London Stock Exchange. *Journal of Finance* 53: 1623–1656.

Hansch, O., N. Naik, and S. Viswanathan. 1999. Preferencing, internalization, best execution, and dealer profits. *Journal of Finance* 54: 1799–1828.

Harris, L. 1986. A transaction data study of weekly and intradaily patterns in stock returns. *Journal of Financial Economics* 16: 99–117.

Harris, L., and J. Hasbrouck. 1996. Market versus limit orders: The SuperDOT evidence on order submission strategy. *Journal of Financial & Quantitative Analysis* 31: 213–231.

Harris, M., and A. Raviv. 1993. Differences of opinion make a horse race. *Review of Financial Studies* 6: 473–506.

Hartmann, P. 1998a. *Currency Competition and Foreign Exchange Markets: The dollar, the Yen, and the Euro.* Cambridge: Cambridge University Press.

Hartmann, P. 1998b. Do Reuters spreads reflect currencies' differences in global trading activity? *Journal of International Money and Finance* 17: 757–784.

Hartmann, P. 1999. Trading volumes and transaction costs in the foreign exchange market: Evidence from daily dollar-yen spot data. *Journal of Banking and Finance* 23: 801–824.

Hasbrouck, J. 1988. Trades, quotes, inventories, and information. *Journal of Financial Economics* 22: 229–252.

Hasbrouck, J. 1991a. Measuring the information content of stock trades. *Journal of Finance* 46: 179–207.

Hasbrouck, J. 1991b. The summary informativeness of stock trades: An econometric analysis. *Review of Financial Studies* 4: 571–595.

Hasbrouck, J. 1992. Using the TORQ database. Typescript, New York University (available at jhasbrouck.stern.nyu.edu/main).

Hasbrouck, J. 1997. One security, many markets. Typescript, New York Univeristy.

Hasbrouck, J., and G. Sofianos. 1993. The trades of market makers: An empirical analysis of NYSE specialists. *Journal of Finance* 48: 1565–1593.

Hau, H. 1998. Competitive entry and endogenous risk in the foreign exchange market. *Review of Financial Studies* 11: 757–788.

Hau, H. 2000. Information and geography: Evidence from the German stock market. Typescript, Insead, March.

Hau, H., and A. Chevallier. 2000. Evidence on the volatility effect of a Tobin tax. Typescript, Insead, April.

Hau, H., W. Killeen, and M. Moore. 2000. The euro as an international currency: Explaining the first evidence. Typescript, Insead, April.

Hausman, J., A. Lo, and C. MacKinlay. 1992. An ordered probit analysis of transaction stock prices. *Journal of Financial Economics* 31: 319–379.

Hayek, F. 1945. The use of knowledge in society. *American Economic Review* 35: 519–530.

He, H., and D. Modest. 1995. Market frictions and consumption-based asset pricing. *Journal of Political Economy* 103: 94–117.

Heere, E. 1999. Microstructure theory applied to the foreign exchange market. Ph.D. dissertation, Maastricht University, Faculty of Economics and Business Administration.

Hellwig, M. 1980. On the aggregation of information in competitive markets. *Journal of Economic Theory* 22: 447–498.

Hellwig, M. 1982. Rational expectations equilibrium with conditioning on past prices: A mean variance example. *Journal of Economic Theory* 26: 279–312.

Hicks, J. 1939. *Value and Capital*. Oxford: Clarendon Press.

Ho, T., and H. Stoll. 1983. The dynamics of dealer markets under competition. *Journal of Finance* 38: 1053–1074.

Hodrick, R. 1987. *The Empirical Evidence on the Efficiency of Forward and Futures Foreign Exchange Markets*. New York: Harwood Academic Publishers.

Holden, C., and A. Subrahmanyam. 1992. Long-lived private information and imperfect competition. *Journal of Finance* 47: 247–270.

Hong, H., and J. Wang. 1995. Trading and Returns Under Periodic Market Closures. Working paper, MIT, July.

Houthakker, H. 1957. Can speculators forecast prices? *Review of Economic Studies* 39: 143–151.

Hsieh, D. 1988. The statistical properties of daily foreign exchange rates: 1974–1983. *Journal of International Economics* 24: 129–145.

Hsieh, D., and A. Kleidon. 1996. Bid-ask spreads in foreign exchange markets: Implications for models of asymmetric information. In *The Microstructure of Foreign Exchange Markets*, edited by J. Frankel et al. Chicago: University of Chicago Press.

Huang, R., and R. Masulis. 1999. FX spreads and dealer competition across the 24 hour trading day. *Review of Financial Studies* 12: 61–94.

Huang, R., and H. Stoll. 1997. The components of the bid-ask spread: A general approach. *Review of Financial Studies* 10: 995–1034.

Huisman, R., K. Koedijk, C. Kool, and F. Nissen. 1998. Extreme support for uncovered interest parity. *Journal of International Money and Finance* 17: 211–228.

Hung, J. 1997. Intervention strategies and exchange rate volatility: A noise trading perspective. *Journal of International Money and Finance* 16: 779–793.

Institutional Investor. 2000. Trading meets the millennium. January.

International Monetary Fund. 1995. *International capital markets: Developments, prospects, and policy issues*, edited by D. Folkerts-Landau and T. Ito. Washington, DC: International Monetary Fund.

Isard, P. 1995. *Exchange Rate Economics*. Cambridge: Cambridge University Press.

Ito, T., R. Lyons, and M. Melvin. 1998. Is there private information in the FX market? The Tokyo experiment. *Journal of Finance* 53: 1111–1130.

Ito, T., and V. Roley. 1990. Intraday yen/dollar exchange rate movements: News or noise? *Journal of International Financial Markets, Institutions and Money* 1: 1–31.

Jacklin, C., A. Kleidon, and P. Pfleiderer. 1992. Underestimation of portfolio insurance and the crash of October 1987. *Review of Financial Studies* 5: 35–63.

Jeanne, O., and A. Rose. 1999. Noise trading and exchange rate regimes, NBER Working Paper #7104, April. Forthcoming in the *Quarterly Journal of Economics*.

Johansen, S. 1992. Cointegration in partial systems and the efficiency of single equation analysis. *Journal of Econometrics* 52: 389–402.

Jones, C., G. Kaul, and M. Lipson. 1994. Transactions, volume, and volatility. *Review of Financial Studies* 7: 631–651.

Jordan, J., and R. Radner. 1982. Rational expectations in microeconomic models: An overview. *Journal of Economic Theory* 26: 201–223.

Jorion, P. 1996. Risk and turnover in the foreign exchange market. In *The Microstructure of Foreign Exchange Markets*, edited by J. Frankel et al. Chicago: University of Chicago Press.

Kaminsky, G., and K. Lewis. 1996. Does foreign exchange intervention signal future monetary policy? *Journal of Monetary Economics* 37: 285–312.

Kandel, E., and N. Pearson. 1995. Differential interpretation of public signals and trade in speculative markets. *Journal of Political Economy* 103: 831–872.

Kang, J., and R. Stulz. 1997. Why is there a home bias? An analysis of foreign portfolio equity ownership in Japan. *Journal of Financial Economics* 46: 3–28.

Karpoff, J. 1986. A theory of trading volume. *Journal of Finance* 41: 1069–1087.

Karpoff, J. 1987. The relation between price changes and volume: A survey. *Journal of Financial and Quantitative Analysis* 22: 109–126.

Kaul, A., V. Mehrotra, and R. Morck. 2000. Demand curves for stock do slope down: New evidence from an index weights adjustment. *Journal of Finance* 55: 893–912.

Keynes, J. 1936. *The General Theory of Employment, Interest, and Money*. New York: Harcourt Brace (see especially chapter 12).

Killeen, W., R. Lyons, and M. Moore. 2000a. Fixed versus floating exchange rates: Lessons from order flow. Typescript, U.C. Berkeley, July.

Killeen, W., R. Lyons, and M. Moore. 2000b. The puzzle of the euro. Typescript, U.C. Berkeley, July.

Kim, O., and R. Verrecchia. 1991. Trading volume and price reactions to public announcements. *Journal of Accounting Research* 29: 302–321.

Kirilenko, A. 1997. Endogenous trading arrangements in emerging foreign exchange markets. Working paper, University of Pennsylvania (Wharton).

Klein, M. 1993. The accuracy of reports of foreign exchange intervention. *Journal of International Money and Finance* 12: 644–653.

Kouri, P., and M. Porter. 1974. International capital flows and portfolio equilibrium. *Journal of Political Economy* 82: 443–467.

Krugman, P., and M. Miller. 1993. Why have a target zone? *Carnegie-Rochester Conference Series on Public Policy* 38: 279–314.

Krugman, P., and M. Obstfeld. 2000. *International Economics*, 5th ed. Reading, Mass.: Addison-Wesley.

Kurz, M. 1997. Foreign exchange rates under alternative expectational paradigms: A resolution of the excess volatility puzzle. Working paper, Stanford University.

Kyle, A. 1985. Continuous auctions and insider trading. *Econometrica* 53: 1315–1335.

Kyle, A. 1989. Informed speculation with imperfect competition. *Review of Economic Studies* 56: 317–356.

Leach, J., and A. Madhavan. 1993. Price experimentation and security market structure. *Review of Financial Studies* 6: 375–404.

Lee, C., and M. Ready. 1991. Inferring trade direction from intradaily data. *Journal of Finance* 46: 733–746.

Lehman Brothers. 2000. *Global Economic Research Series: FX Impact of Cross-Border MA*. London: Lehman Brothers International (20 April).

Leland, H. 1992. Insider trading: Should it be prohibited? *Journal of Political Economy* 100: 859–887.

Levich, R. 2001. International Financial Markets: Prices and Policies, 2nd ed. New York: McGraw-Hill Irwin.

Lewis, K. 1988. Testing the portfolio balance model: A multilateral approach. *Journal of International Economics* 24: 109–127.

Lewis, K. 1995. Puzzles in international financial markets. In *Handbook of International Economics*, edited by G. Grossman and K. Rogoff. Amsterdam: Elsevier Science.

Loopesko, B. 1984. Relationships among exchange rates, intervention, and interest rates: An empirical investigation. *Journal of International Money and Finance* 3: 257–277.

Luca, C. 2000. *Trading in the Global Currency Markets*, 2nd ed. New York: Prentice Hall.

Lui, Y., and D. Mole. 1998. The use of fundamental and technical analyses by foreign exchange dealers: Hong Kong evidence. *Journal of International Money and Finance* 17: 535–545.

Lyons, R. 1995. Tests of microstructural hypotheses in the foreign exchange market. *Journal of Financial Economics* 39: 321–351.

Lyons, R. 1996a. Optimal transparency in a dealer market with an application to foreign exchange. *Journal of Financial Intermediation* 5: 225–254.

Lyons, R. 1996b. Foreign exchange volume: Sound and fury signifying nothing? In *The Microstructure of Foreign Exchange Markets*, edited by J. Frankel et al. Chicago: University of Chicago Press.

Lyons, R. 1997a. A simultaneous trade model of the foreign exchange hot potato. *Journal of International Economics* 42: 275–298.

Lyons, R. 1998. Profits and position control: A week of FX dealing. *Journal of International Money and Finance* 17: 97–115.

Lyons, R., and A. Rose. 1995. Explaining forward exchange bias . . . intraday. *Journal of Finance* 50: 1321–1329.

Machlup, F. 1939. The theory of foreign exchanges. Economica. Reprinted in *Readings in the Theory of International Trade*, edited by H. Ellis and L. Metzler. Philadelphia: Blakiston, 1949.

Madhavan, A. 1992. Trading mechanisms in securities markets. *Journal of Finance* 47: 607–642.

Madhavan, A. 1996. Security prices and market transparency. *Journal of Financial Intermediation* 5: 255–283.

Madhavan, A. 2000. Market microstructure: A survey. *Journal of Financial Markets* 3: 205–258.

Madhavan, A., and S. Smidt. 1991. A bayesian model of intraday specialist pricing. *Journal of Financial Economics* 30: 99–134.

Madhavan, A., and S. Smidt. 1993. An analysis of changes in specialist inventories and quotations. *Journal of Finance* 48: 1595–1628.

Madrigal, V. 1996. Non-fundamental speculation. *Journal of Finance* 51: 553–578.

MAR/Hedge. 2000. Monthly issues, Managed Account Reports, Inc., New York (available at www.marhedge.com).

Mark, N. 1995. Exchange rates and fundamentals: Evidence on long-horizon predictability. *American Economic Review* 85: 201–218.

Meese, R. 1986. Testing for bubbles in exchange markets. *Journal of Political Economy* 94: 345–373.

Meese, R. 1990. Currency fluctuations in the post–Bretton Woods era. *Journal of Economic Perspectives* 4: 117–134.

Meese, R., and K. Rogoff. 1983a. Empirical exchange rate models of the seventies. *Journal of International Economics* 14: 3–24.

Meese, R., and K. Rogoff. 1983b. The out-of-sample failure of empirical exchange rate models. In *Exchange Rate and International Macroeconomics*, edited by J. Frenkel. Chicago: University of Chicago Press.

Mehra, R., and E. Prescott. 1985. The equity premium: A puzzle. *Journal of Monetary Economics* 15: 145–161.

Melvin, M., and B. Peiers. 1997. The global transmission of volatility in the foreign exchange market. Working paper, Arizona State University.

Melvin, M., and X. Yin. 2000. Public information arrival, exchange rate volatility, and quote frequency. *Economic Journal* 110: 644–651.

Mendelson, H. 1987. Consolidation, fragmentation, and market performance. *Journal of Financial and Quantitative Analysis* 22: 189–208.

Menkhoff, L. 1998. The noise trading approach—Questionnaire evidence from foreign exchange. *Journal of International Money and Finance* 17: 547–564.

Montgomery, J., and H. Popper. 1998. Information sharing and central bank intervention in the foreign exchange market. Typescript, Santa Clara University, December.

Moore, M., and M. Roche. 1999. Less of a puzzle: A new look at the forward forex market. Typescript, Queen's University of Belfast, June.

Morris, S., and H. Shin. 2000. Rethinking multiple equilibria in macroeconomic modeling. *NBER Macroeconomics Annual 2000*.

Mussa, M. 1976. The exchange rate, the balance of payments, and monetary and fiscal policy under a regime of controlled floating. *Scandinavian Journal of Economics* 78: 229–248.

Muth, J. 1960. Optimal properties of exponentially weighted forecasts. *Journal of the American Statistical Association* 55: 290–306.

Naik, N., A. Neuberger, and S. Viswanathan. 1999. Trade disclosure regulation in markets with negotiated trades. *Review of Financial Studies* 12: 873–900.

Naik, N., and P. Yadav. 2000. Do market intermediaries hedge their risk exposure with derivatives? Typescript, London Business School, February.

Naranjo, A., and M. Nimalendran. 2000. Government intervention and adverse selection costs in foreign exchange markets. *Review of Financial Studies* 13: 453–477.

New York Federal Reserve Bank. 1995. *The Foreign Exchange Committee Annual Report, 1995*. New York: Federal Reserve Bank.

Obstfeld, M., and K. Rogoff. 1995. Exchange rate dynamics Redux. *Journal of Political Economy* 103: 624–660.

Obstfeld, M., and K. Rogoff. 1996. *Foundations of International Macroeconomics*. Cambridge, MA: MIT Press.

Obstfeld, M., and A. Taylor. 1997. Non-linear aspects of goods-market arbitrage and adjustment: Heckscher's commodity points revisited. *Journal of the Japanese and International Economies* 11: 441–479.

O'Hara, M. 1995. *Market Microstructure Theory*. Cambridge, MA: Blackwell Business.

O'Hara, M. 1999. Making market microstructure matter. *Financial Management* 28: 83–90.

O'Hara, M., and G. Oldfield. 1986. The microeconomics of market making. *Journal of Financial and Quantitative Analysis* 21: 361–376.

Osler, C. 1995. Exchange rate dynamics and speculator horizons. *Journal of International Money & Finance* 14: 695–720.

Osler, C. 1998. Short-term speculators and the puzzling behavior of exchange rates. *Journal of International Economics* 45: 37–57.

Osler, C. 2000. Support for resistance: Technical analysis and intraday exchange rates. *Economic Policy Review* 6: 53–68.

Osler, C. 2001. Currency orders and exchange-rate dynamics: Explaining the success of technical analysis. Typescript, Federal Reserve Bank of New York, March.

Pagano, M. 1989. Trading volume and asset liquidity. *Quarterly Journal of Economics* 104: 255–274.

Pagano, M., and A. Roell. 1996. Transparency and liquidity: A comparison of auction and dealer markets. *Journal of Finance* 51: 579–612.

Payne, R. 1999. Informed trade in spot foreign exchange markets: An empirical investigation. Typescript, London School of Economics, January.

Payne, R., and P. Vitale. 2000. A transaction level study of the effects of central bank intervention on exchange rates. Typescript, London School of Economics, July.

Peiers, B. 1997. Informed traders, intervention, and price leadership: A deeper view of the microstructure of the foreign exchange market. *Journal of Finance* 52: 1589–1614.

Perold, A., and E. Schulman. 1988. The free lunch in currency hedging: Implications for investment policy and performance standards. *Financial Analysts Journal* May–June, 45–50.

Perraudin, W., and P. Vitale. 1996. Interdealer trade and information flows in a decentralized foreign exchange market. In *The Microstructure of Foreign Exchange Markets*, edited by J. Frankel et al. Chicago: University of Chicago Press.

Portes, R., and H. Rey. 1998. The emergence of the euro as an international currency. *Economic Policy* 26: 307–343.

Reiss, P., and I. Werner. 1995. Transaction costs in dealer markets: Evidence from the London Stock Exchange. In *Industrial Organization and Regulation of the Securities Industry*, edited by A. Lo. Chicago: University of Chicago Press.

Reiss, P., and I. Werner. 1997. Interdealer trading: Evidence from London. Stanford Business School Research Paper No. 1430, February.

Reiss, P., and I. Werner. 1998. Does risk sharing motivate interdealer trading? *Journal of Finance* 53: 1657–1704.

Reiss, P., and I. Werner. 1999. Adverse selection in dealers' choice of interdealer trading system. Dice Working Paper no. 99-7, Ohio State University, June.

Rey, H. 2001. International trade and currency exchange. *Review of Economic Studies* 68: 443–464.

Rime, D. 2000. Private or public information in foreign exchange markets? An empirical analysis. Typescript, University of Oslo, March (available at www.uio.no/~dagfinri).

Robinson, J. 1937. The foreign exchanges. Reprinted in *Readings in the Theory of International Trade*, edited by H. Ellis and L. Metzler. Philadelphia: Blakiston, 1949.

Rochet, J., and J. Vila. 1995. Insider trading without normality. *Review of Economic Studies* 61: 131–152.

Rogoff, K. 1984. On the effects of sterilized intervention: An analysis of weekly data. *Journal of Monetary Economics* 14: 133–150.

Roll, R. 1988. R^2. *Journal of Finance* 43: 541–566.

Romer, D. 1993. Rational asset-price movements without news. *American Economic Review* 83: 1112–1130.

Romeu, R. 2001. Parameter stability in foreign exchange market microstructure. Typescript, University of Maryland, February.

Rosenberg, M. 1996. *Currency Forecasting: A Guide to Fundamental and Technical Models of Exchange Rate Determination*. Chicago: Irwin Professional Publishing.

Rotemberg, J., and M. Woodford. 1997. An optimization-based econometric framework for the evaluation of monetary policy. In *NBER Macroeconomics Annual*, edited by B. Bernanke and J. Rotemberg. Cambridge, MA: MIT Press.

Rubinstein, M. 2000. Rational markets: Yes or no? The affirmative case. U.C. Berkeley Research Program in Finance Working Paper RPF-294, June (available at www.haas.berkeley.edu/finance/WP/rfplist.html). Forthcoming in *Financial Analysts Journal*.

Saar, G. 1999. Demand uncertainty and the information content of the order flow. Typescript, Cornell University, July.

Saporta, V. 1997. Which interdealer market prevails? An analysis of interdealer trading in opaque markets. Bank of England, working paper 59.

Sarno, L, and M. Taylor. 2000a. The microstructure of the foreign exchange market. *Special Papers on International Economics*, Princeton University (available at http://www.princeton.edu/~ies).

Sarno, L., and M. Taylor. 2000b. Official intervention in foreign exchange markets. Typescript, University of Oxford, April.

Scholes, M. 1972. The market for securities: Substitution versus price pressure and the effect of information on sharp price. *Journal of Business* 45: 179–211.

Seasholes, M. 2000. Smart foreign traders in emerging markets. Typescript, Harvard University, January.

Seppi, D. 1996. Liquidity provision with limit orders and a strategic specialist. *Review of Financial Studies* 10: 103–150.

Shiller, R. 1981. Do stock prices move too much to be justified by subsequent changes in dividends? *American Economic Review* 71: 421–436.

Shleifer, A. 1986. Do demand curves for stocks slope down? *Journal of Finance* 41: 579–590.

Shleifer, A., and R. Vishny. 1997. The limits to arbitrage. *Journal of Finance* 52: 35–56.

Siegel, J. 1972. Risk, interest rates, and the forward exchange. *Quarterly Journal of Economics* 86: 303–309.

Slezak, S. 1994. A theory of the dynamics of security returns around market closures. *Journal of Finance* 49: 1163–1211.

Smith, R., and B. Madigan. 1988. Exchange market management and monetary policy in the United States. In *Exchange Market Intervention and Monetary Policy*, edited by Bank for International Settlements. Basel: BIS.

Snell, A., and I. Tonks. 1995. Determinants of price quote revisions on the London stock exchange. *Economic Journal* 105: 55–73.

Spiegel, M. 1998. Stock price volatility in a multiple security overlapping generations model. *Review of Financial Studies* 11: 419–447.

Spiegel, M., and A. Subrahmanyam. 1995. On intraday risk premia. *Journal of Finance* 50: 319–339.

Stockman, A. 1987. The equilibrium approach to exchange rates. *Federal Reserve Bank of Richmond Economic Review* 73, 2: 12–31.

Stoll, H. 1978. The supply of dealer services in securities markets. *Journal of Finance* 33: 1133–1151.

Subrahmanyam, A. 1991. Risk aversion, market liquidity, and price efficiency. *Review of Financial Studies* 4: 417–441.

Suvanto, A. 1993. Foreign exchange dealing: Essays on the microstructure of the foreign exchange market. ETLA—The Research Institute of the Finnish Economy. Helsinki: Taloustieto Oy.

Taylor, M. 1995. The economics of exchange rates. *Journal of Economic Literature* 83: 13–47.

Taylor, M., and H. Allen. 1992. The use of technical analysis in the foreign exchange market. *Journal of International Money and Finance* 11: 304–314.

Tesar, L., and I. Werner. 1995. Home bias and high turnover. *Journal of International Money and Finance* 14: 467–493.

Varian, H. 1985. Divergence of opinion in complete markets. *Journal of Finance* 40: 309–317.

Viswanathan, S., and J. Wang. 1998. Why is inter-dealer trading so pervasive in financial markets? Working paper, Duke University, February.

Vitale, P. 1998. Two months in the life of several gilt-edged market makers on the London Stock Exchange. *Journal of International Financial Markets, Institutions & Money* 8: 301–326.

Vitale, P. 1999. Sterilized central bank intervention in the foreign exchange market. *Journal of International Economics* 49: 245–267.

Vitale, P. 2000. Speculative noise trading and manipulation in the foreign exchange market. *Journal of International Money and Finance* 19: 689–712.

Vogler, K. 1997. Risk allocation and inter-dealer trading. *European Economic Review* 41: 417–441.

Wang, J. 1994. A model of competitive stock trading volume. *Journal of Political Economy* 102: 127–168.

Wei, S. 1994. Anticipations of foreign exchange volatility and bid-ask spreads. NBER Working Paper 4737.

Wei, S., and J. Kim. 1997. The big players in the foreign exchange market: Do they trade on information or noise? NBER Working Paper 6256, November.

Werner, I. 1997. A double auction model of interdealer trading. Stanford Business School Research Paper, no. 1454.

Weston, J. 2000. Competition on the Nasdaq and the impact of recent market reforms, *Journal of Finance* 55: 2565–2598.

Wolinsky, A. 1990. Information revelation in a market with pairwise meetings. *Econometrica* 58: 1–23.

Working, H. 1953. Futures trading and hedging. *American Economic Review* 43: 314–343.

Yao, J. 1998a. Market making in the interbank foreign exchange market. New York University Salomon Center Working Paper #S-98-3.

Yao, J. 1998b. Spread components and dealer profits in the interbank foreign exchange market. New York University Salomon Center Working Paper #S-98-4.

Zaheer, A., and Zaheer, S. 1995. Catching the wave: Alertness, responsiveness, and market influence in global electronic networks. Typescript, University of Minnesota, December.

Zhou, B. 1996. High frequency data and volatility in foreign exchange rates. *Journal of Business and Economic Statistics* 14: 45–52.

Index

and the microstructure approach, 4, 57–59

and the rational expectations auction model, 70

types, price impact, and information structure, 253–256

International currencies, 274–275

Intervention. *See* Central bank intervention

Inventory models, 46, 66, 141, 291n17, 292nn21, 24, 294n5, 303n2

Jensen's inequality, 287n11

Killeen, Lyons, and Moore model
and asset payoff, 194–198
and cointegration, 202–205
data set, 123–124, 200–202
equilibrium, 198
and excess volatility, 205–206

Kyle auction model
asset payoff, 79–82
and central bank intervention, 234–236
description of, 64–65, 76–77
details, 79–82
equilibrium, 82–84
and individual trades, 86
and information, 80–81
insights, 77–79
and institutions, 80–81
and liquidity and market efficiency, 77–79
marketmakers, 77–79, 79–82
and order flow, 78
players, 80–81
and risk-aversion, 85
and spread, 85

Lamppost metaphor, 171
Limit orders, 6–7, 290nn6, 11, 304n11
Liquidity, 77–79, 84, 260–261, 273, 284n11
London Stock Exchange, 56
Lyons data set, 117–118, 176–190

Macroeconomics
and asset approach to exchange rates, 15, 153–155
assumptions, 4, 279n2
and central bank intervention, 223–227
determination puzzle, 172–190
excess volatility model, 192–206

and exchange rate models, 155–163
flexible-price monetary model, 155–157
forward bias model, 207–220
and goods market approach to exchange rates, 2, 152–153
hybrid micro-macro models, 15–18, 173–176
and microfoundations, 164–170, 294n3, 303n5
and microstructure approach to exchange rates, 12, 14, 15–18, 264–268
and micro versus macro issues, 167–170
and purchasing power parity, 152–153, 155–157
sticky-price monetary model, 157–160
and tastes and technology, 164–170
trends in, 279n2
and uncovered interest parity, 153–155

Markets, auction and dealer, 40, 63–65, 274
Martingale, 289n25
Meta models, 217–218
Microfoundations, 164–170, 294n3, 303n5
Microstructure effects, 60–62, 302n1
Microstructure models
and analysis of crashes and collapses, 12, 59
and CARA-normal framework, 69, 105–112
of central bank intervention, 231–236
dealer-problem, 134–139
definitions in, 5–9
and the determination puzzle, 172–190
directions for research, 268–272
and discount-rate information, 30–31
effects versus tools, 59–62, 301n1
and exchange rate determination, 2–5, 13–14, 15–16
versus exchange rate economics, 1–2
and the flow approach to exchange rates, 190–192
and foreign exchange markets, 2, 4–5, 113–117, 125–126, 264–268, 267–268
hallmarks, 5–9
hybrid micro-macro, 16–18, 173–176
and imperfect substitutability, 221
and information economics, 4, 12–13
and institution design, 57–59
institutions, 4
inventory models, 46, 66, 141, 291n17, 292nn21, 24, 294n5, 303n2
and the Kyle auction model, 77–86